OLIVER FRANKS AND THE TRUMAN ADMINISTRATION

CASS SERIES: DIPLOMATS AND DIPLOMACY
ISSN: 1478-7237
Series Editor: Peter Catterall and Erik Goldstein

This series aims to provide a primarily biographical approach to the study of diplomacy and international relations in the twentieth century. How have diplomats and foreign ministers tackled not only the traditional business of managing relations between states, but also the rise of multilteral negotiations, the proliferation of international organisations and the increasing significance of economic diplomacy? This series seeks to contribute to an understanding of how diplomacy and international relations developed in the twentieth century.

Michael F. Hopkins, *Oliver Franks and the Truman Administration: Anglo-American Relations, 1948–1952*

Maurice East and Justin Robertson (eds), *Diplomacy in Developing Countries: The Post-Cold War Foreign Ministry*

Gerald J. Protheroe, *Biography of Sir George Russell Clark: Nation-Building and The Limitations of Personal Diplomacy*

OLIVER FRANKS
and the
TRUMAN ADMINISTRATION

Anglo-American Relations
1948–1952

Michael F. Hopkins

Liverpool Hope University College

FRANK CASS

LONDON • PORTLAND, OR

First published in 2003 in Great Britain by
FRANK CASS PUBLISHERS
Crown House, 47 Chase Side
London N14 5BP

and in the United States of America by
FRANK CASS PUBLISHERS
c/o ISBS, 5824 N.E. Hassalo Street
Portland, Oregon, 97213-3644

Website: www.frankcass.com

British Library Cataloguing in Publication Data

Hopkins, Michael F. (Michael Francis), 1953–
Oliver Franks and the Truman administration:
Anglo-American relations, 1948–1952. – (Cass series.
Diplomats and diplomacy)
1. Franks, Oliver Shewell Franks, Baron, 1905– – Career in diplomacy 2.
Ambassadors – Great Britain 3. Great Britain – Foreign relations – United States
4. United States – Foreign relations – 1945–1964 6. United States – Foreign
relations 1945–1953
I. Title
327.4'1073'09044

ISBN 0-7146-5303-9 (cloth)
ISSN 1478-7237

Library of Congress Cataloging-in-Publication Data

Hopkins, Michael F. (Michael Francis), 1953–
Oliver Franks and the Truman administration: Anglo-American relations,
1948–1952/Michael F. Hopkins.
p. cm. – (Cass series–diplomats and diplomacy)
Includes bibliographical references and index.
ISBN 0-7146-5303-9
1. Franks, Oliver, Baron, 1905– –Views on the United States. 2. Great
Britain–Foreign relations–United States. 3. United States–Foreign relations–Great
Britain. 4. United States–Foreign relations–1945–1953. 5. Great Britain–Foreign
relations–1945–1964. I. Title. II. Series.

DA585.F7 H67 2003
327.41073'092–dc21 2002031499

Typeset in 10.5/12.5pt Palatino by *FiSH* Books, London
Printed in Great Britain by MPG Books Ltd, Bodmin, Cornwall

To my mother and to the memory of my father

Contents

List of Illustrations ix

Series Editor's Preface xi

Preface xiii

Introduction xv

List of Abbreviations xviii

PART I: THE AMBASSADOR, THE EMBASSY AND THE ANGLO-AMERICAN RELATIONSHIP 1

1. Individuals and Institutions 3
2. Postwar Relations 27
3. New Ambassador 50

PART II: ESTABLISHING A REPUTATION 63

4. First Impressions 65
5. Cold War Allies 81

PART III: ACHIEVEMENTS 103

6. Dean Acheson 105
7. Devaluation of the Pound 119
8. Part of the European Queue or Special Partners? 139
9. The Korean War 158

PART IV: DIFFICULTIES 175

10. Anglo-American Tensions 177
11. A New Foreign Secretary 198

PART V: THE RETURN OF THE CONSERVATIVES 225
12. Working with Churchill and Eden 227

Epilogue: End of a Mission 246

Conclusion 251

Bibliography 259

Index 276

Illustrations

Between pages 142 and 143

1. Franks at the White House, 13 January 1949.
2. Sir Gordon Munro of the British Embassy, Oliver Franks, President Truman and Sir Stafford Cripps in the rose garden of the White House, 2 October 1948.
3. Sir Stafford Cripps, Lady Cripps, Lady Franks and Oliver Franks on the terrace of the British Embassy, 26 August 1948.
4. Ernest Bevin, the Foreign Secretary, on the podium at the signing ceremony for the North Atlantic Treaty, 4 April 1949.
5. Franks presenting the UK's instrument of ratification of the North Atlantic Treaty to acting Secretary of State, James E. Webb, 7 June 1949.
6. President Truman greets the arrival in Washington of Clement Attlee, the Prime Minister, December 1950.
7. Prime Minister Clement Attlee speaking to the press, Washington, December 1950.
8. British Commonwealth Ambassadors in Washington on visit to USA of Princess Elizabeth, 1 November 1951.
9. President Truman greeting Winston Churchill, the Prime Minister, on his arrival in Washington, January 1952.
10. British and American officials, 5 January 1952.

Series Editor's Preface

Sir Oliver Franks served as the British Ambassador to Washington for four critical years, 1948–52, in one of the most notable diplomatic missions of the century. It fell to Franks to establish a new relationship with the United States as it emerged as one of the world's superpowers while Britain was still seriously weakened by the effects of the Second World War. His Washington Embassy would witness, among many crises great and small, the burgeoning of the Cold War, the Berlin Blockade, the creation of NATO, the Korean War, the Anglo-Iranian crisis, and the devaluation of the pound. Franks, as this book demonstrates, handled the mission superbly.

Franks was not a career diplomat and Britain has traditionally appointed very few non-career ambassadors. It is worth observing that most of the non-career diplomats have been sent to Washington. There is something about the conduct of diplomacy in Washington which has often caused immense frustration to career ambassadors. Franks understood that Washington operated differently from the capitals of the Old World and it is worth noting that one of his first appointments was of an advisor on public relations.

An academic before the war, he had enjoyed a brief stint at the University of Chicago. As a wartime civil servant he had worked on supply and atomic issues with the United States, and subsequently was responsible for organising the British response to the proposed Marshall Plan. As a result he was familiar with many of the issues of importance to Britain in its dealings with America.

Franks's predecessor, Lord Inverchapel (Archibald Clark-Kerr) was deeply unhappy and leapt at the chance of leaving early. A brilliant ambassador in dangerous, war-torn postings, he was bored by the largely economic issues which predominated the diplomatic agenda. Franks on the other hand had already mastered these issues. The change of representative could not have been more marked, the flamboyant and eccentric Inverchapel, who would only write with a quill pen and had a penchant for risqué stories was replaced by the scholarly son of a Congregationalist minister who had taught philosophy before becoming a senior civil servant. Franks's personality fitted well in a city coping with the early stages of the Cold War and the unexpected burdens of world power that had so suddenly descended upon the United States. Franks also benefited from an extraordinary relationship with the American Secretary of State, Dean Acheson. It is telling that Acheson saw Franks more frequently than all the other ambassadors combined. Franks's ability to build working relationships with a wide spectrum of people, to work constructively to find solutions to problems, his ability to communicate clearly and effectively were all hallmarks of his approach to conducting his mission.

This is a study not just of Franks's role in Anglo-American relations but is an examination of the role of the British Embassy to Washington under Franks's ambassadorship. The British Embassy was (and still is) the largest diplomatic mission in Washington and any understanding of the conduct of diplomacy must extend beyond the head of mission to an understanding of embassy as a whole. It is only recently that the study of diplomacy as a discreet subject area has become widely established. In this study Michael Hopkins provides a valuable service through his thorough examination of the role that the British Embassy at Washington played during the critical years 1948–52 in the evolution and implementation of British foreign policy.

Erik Goldstein
Boston University

Preface

OLIVER FRANKS was acknowledged throughout his lifetime as one of Britain's greatest civil servants since 1945, all the more remarkable an achievement for someone who was not a career official. It was when he served as British Ambassador to the United States that he enjoyed the greatest opportunity for his talents. Yet no one has written a detailed account of these years. Franks's life and personality were astutely explored by Alex Danchev but he did not offer a systematic analysis of the ambassadorship. Nor did Robin Edmonds, in the most extensive of the many studies of this period in Anglo-American relations; moreover, he concentrated on the period 1945–50. This book aims to chart what Franks said and did during his embassy and to evaluate his influence. The role of an individual, however elevated, cannot be entirely separated from the activities of other figures and of various institutions. My aim is to try to disentangle these distinct elements so as to distinguish Franks's contribution, while giving credit to the contribution of others. The focus of this study is on Franks and the Embassy and its relations with the Truman administration, and Dean Acheson in particular, over the range of international issues that confronted the two countries in this seminal era. It does not aim to scrutinise domestic developments in the United States.

I would like to thank the staffs of the following libraries and archives for their assistance and permission to use their materials: the Public Record Office, Kew; the Brotherton Library, Leeds; the Bodleian Library, Oxford; the British Library of Political and Economic Science, London School of Economics; Birmingham University Library; Churchill College, Cambridge; Trinity College, Cambridge; the Liddell Hart Centre for Military Archives, King's College, London; the National Archives, Washington DC; Seeley G. Mudd Library, Princeton University, Princeton NJ; Harry S. Truman Library, Independence, Missouri; Sterling Memorial Library, Yale University; Manuscripts Division, Library of Congress, Washington D.C. I acknowledge the permission of Lady Younger, courtesy of Professor Geoffrey Warner, to quote from the Kenneth Younger Diary. Much of the research in these archives was facilitated by generous financial assistance from the Liverpool Hope research fund.

I owe a number of debts, intellectual and personal, to teachers, colleagues and friends. At school John Canning fired my historical imagination and encouraged my critical curiosity about the past. Professor David Dilks was a remarkable undergraduate teacher. I am grateful to him for the help that he has given me over many years. This book is the development of my PhD thesis begun under his supervision. It was completed under the guidance of Professor Edward M. Spiers, who brought to the task his characteristic good humour, consideration and efficiency. He also read through the whole of the draft of this book, as did both Professor Michael Dockrill and Dr Peter Lowe. I am grateful to each of them for the time and care they took over this, as well as the many other occasions of their generosity. Professor John Young has been over many years an equally kind and helpful friend and advisor. Professor Richard Aldrich took the trouble to read a number of chapters and offer his comments. Dr Peter Boyle was very generous with help when I embarked on this study and has retained his interest in its progress. Dr Pascal Venier has been a good friend and intellectual foil on many projects. I am also indebted to Dr Saki Dockrill; and to Dr Peter Catterall, the Series Editor, Andrew Humphrys at Frank Cass, and my copy-editor, Sheila Kane, for smoothing the path to publication.

Many people helped me during the research and writing: my aunt, Anne Dunleavy; Joan and Hugh Pryce; Vanessa Pryce; my brother Kevin and his wife Lynne. A long-promised thank you to Patricia O'Driscoll. I dedicate this book with affection and gratitude, to my mother and my late father.

Michael F. Hopkins

Introduction

Sir Oliver Franks served as British Ambassador to the United States from May 1948 to November 1952. His mission coincided with a formative period in the postwar world. It saw the emergence of the cold war, the implementation of the Marshall Plan, the creation of the North Atlantic Treaty, the alliance in the Korean War, the first steps towards European integration and the return to better relations with the former enemies, Japan and Germany, as they became assimilated into the international system.

Britain was at the centre of these events, just as it had been during the Second World War. A central facet of British involvement in the war had been the special relationship with the United States. Pursuit of common political and strategic goals had led to extensive military, intelligence, diplomatic and economic co-operation. Victory in 1945 meant an end to the wartime alliance but collaboration between the military and on intelligence was continued and the habit of consultation was sustained among middle and lower-ranking officials from both countries. It was only with the growing rift with the Soviet Union, from 1947 onwards, that the wartime intimacy of co-operation at the highest political level was restored. Britain's assets as an ally were recognised once more.

But for the British this involved a difficult balancing act between claiming great-power status and needing American assistance. An assessment of July 1945 recognised that the country was 'numerically the weakest and geographically the smallest of the Great Powers'. Moreover, 'in the minds of our big partners, especially in the United States, there is a feeling that Great Britain is now a secondary power and can be treated as such'.[1] A report of 29 June 1945 accepted that Britain would be overrun by its most probable potential enemy, the Soviet Union, unless it secured powerful allies. It was 'vital to ensure the full and early support in the war of the USA'.[2] Nor were the worries only strategic. J. M. Keynes's Cabinet Paper of 14 August drew a picture of great economic difficulties. American aid alone could prevent withdrawal from Empire and the abandonment of the Labour government's reforms.[3] British governments wanted to work with the United States not just because they needed its economic and military aid but also because they felt they shared the same goals.

No doubt the frequent claims of their superior wisdom and experience in international affairs made the British feel that they were bringing something of substance to the relationship. At times this outlook veered towards a condescending attitude towards the United States, typified by a Foreign Office minute of March 1944:

> It must be our purpose not to balance our power against that of America, but to make use of American power for the purposes which we regard as good . . . If we go about our business in the right way we can help steer this great unwieldy barge, the United States of America, into the right harbour. If we don't it is likely to wallow in the ocean, an isolated menace to navigation.[4]

If Franks became Ambassador at the time when the relationship enjoyed greater importance once more, then the British Embassy in Washington had an enhanced status, for the US capital was now the centre of power in the world, a process begun during the war. This meant that the Washington Embassy had the potential to be very important. So too did the Ambassador. This was not automatic. During the Second World War, the Embassy was a vitally important administrative centre but the Ambassador played a minor role. With the end of hostilities there was a return to normal diplomacy and the opportunity for the Ambassador to perform more important tasks.

What increased the likelihood that the Embassy would be able to take advantage of its new prominence was the appointment of an exceptional public servant as Ambassador. Previous accounts of Anglo-American relations in this era have given insufficient attention to the role of the Embassy and the Ambassador. Robin Edmonds's splendid study stresses Franks's importance but does not subject his term as envoy to systematic scrutiny, nor could he be expected to do so in a general work.[5] Yet such an analysis offers the possibility of revealing a great deal about the condition of relations between Britain and the United States, the mechanics of co-operation and the impact of a singular individual.

Assessment of his ambassadorship can only touch part of the rich tapestry of activities pursued by members of the mission. Franks said that he was preoccupied with what was essential to the relationship. He had the traditional ambassadorial responsibility of representing British policy and reporting American policy and opinion on the key issues of the day; and of ensuring there was mutual understanding and that difficulties did not result in a breakdown in relations. Much went on without Franks's direct involvement. Diplomats pursued their regular activities following his general guidelines and occasional interventions. Even on issues in which he took an active interest, a great deal was done by Embassy staff. Franks became involved when his authority or talents were particularly needed. The multifarious activities of the Embassy will emerge in the course of explaining Franks's handling of these central issues. The aim, therefore, is to analyse and evaluate the state of the relationship, the institutional involvement of the Embassy and the contribution of the individual, principally through the prism of the Ambassador's performance.

The prospects for making an impact, for being able to influence the shape of policy on both sides of the Atlantic, to have his ideas about both strategy and tactics adopted, depended partly upon his personal talents and how well he utilised them. It depended further upon the extent to which the institutional framework of the Embassy was suited to its new opportunities; and upon how well British and American politicians worked together in their burgeoning cold war alliance.

NOTES

1. *Documents on British Policy Overseas* (*DBPO*), 1st Series, Vol. I (London: HMSO, 1984), No. 102, p. 182, Sir Orme Sargent, 'Stocktaking after VE Day', 11 July 1945.
2. Quoted in G. Warner, 'The Anglo-American Special Relationship', *Diplomatic History*, Vol. 13, No. 4, Fall 1989, p. 479.
3. CP(45) 112, 14 August 1945 in *DBPO*, 1st Series, Vol. III (London: HMSO, 1984) No. 6, pp. 27–37.
4. Public Record Office (PRO), FO 371/38523, AN1538/16/45; cited in T. H. Anderson, *The United States, Great Britain and the Cold War 1944–1947* (Columbia, MI: University of Missouri Press, 1981), pp. 12–13.
5. Robin Edmonds, *Setting the Mould: The United States and Britain 1945–1950* (Oxford: Clarendon Press, 1986).

Abbreviations

AIOC	Anglo-Iranian Oil Company
AFEA	American Foreign Economic Administration
BIS	British Information Services
BJSM	British Joint Staff/Services Mission
CEEC	Committee of European Economic Co-operation
CIA	Central Intelligence Agency
CFM	Council of Foreign Ministers
COS	Chiefs of Staff
CPC	Combined Policy Committee
ECA	Economic Co-operation Administration
EDC	European Defence Community
ERP	European Recovery Plan
FBI	Federal Bureau of Investigation
FEC	Far Eastern Commission
FRUS	*Foreign Relations of the United States*
GATT	General Agreement on Tariffs and Trade
GCHQ	Government Communications Headquarters
HSTL	Harry S. Truman Library
ILO	International Labour Organisation
IMF	International Monetary Fund
JIC	Joint Intelligence Committee
MFN	most favoured nation
NSA	National Security Agency
OEEC	Organisation of European Economic Co-operation
PUSC	Permanent Under-Secretary's Committee
SCAP	Supreme Commander Allied Powers
UNRRA	United Nations Relief and Rehabilitation Administration

PART I:

THE AMBASSADOR, THE EMBASSY AND THE ANGLO-AMERICAN RELATIONSHIP

'In the unglamorous trenches of the bureaucracy, personal relations are usually undisturbed as the politicians at the top come and go.'

Raymond Seitz, 1998

'There are not so many powers that share our fundamental objectives so completely that we can afford to dispense with a crucial power that does – especially a crucial power that can enlist so much skill in the pursuit of our common diplomatic objectives. In sheer professionalism and skill, British diplomats have few if any equals throughout the world of diplomacy.'

Philip Zelikow, former Director of European Security Affairs of the National Security Council, 1996

— 1 —

Individuals and Institutions

ACCOUNTS OF ANGLO-AMERICAN relations, whether enthusiastic or critical, invariably concentrate on the main political figures – Franklin D. Roosevelt and Churchill, Kennedy and Macmillan, Reagan and Thatcher. Rarely do they mention ambassadors. Yet, if the British and US governments and, in particular, their Foreign Ministers initiated and directed policy, the centres for the conduct of relations lay in their embassies in Washington and London. Since by 1945 the balance of strength in the relationship had shifted so heavily in favour of the United States, Washington was the more important of the two missions. Although there were regular meetings between the US Secretary of State and the British Foreign Secretary and other ministers, though hardly at all between the President and the Prime Minister, the overwhelming bulk of relations was handled by the two embassies and, more particularly, by the British Embassy. An understanding of how that institution functioned is therefore central to any evaluation of Anglo-American relations. Its operations emerged from the interplay of: the influence of the wartime relationship; the nature of the US system, which inevitably shaped the character of the Embassy's work; the organisation of the Embassy and its nationwide network of offices and its links with other British government bodies in the United States; how the Embassy functioned; and, finally, the contribution of key personnel.

THE WARTIME RELATIONSHIP

The Second World War saw unprecedented closeness in relations between two sovereign states. It began in 1940 even before the United States' entry into the war. At the very top there was the Churchill–Roosevelt personal relationship. They met at the Arcadia Conference of December 1941 to January 1942, which ended with the US President urging the Prime Minister to 'Trust me to the bitter end.'[1]

Between 1939 and 1945 they corresponded 1,700 times and, after the United States entered the war, they had nine meetings, comprising about 120 days of personal contact.[2] Other personal relationships deepened ties. Harry Hopkins and Averell Harriman acted as US emissaries with London. In the US capital General George C. Marshall, Chief of Staff of the US Army, was an intimate of Field Marshal Sir John Dill, head of the British Joint Staff Mission (BJSM).[3]

Personal contact reached well beyond senior figures. It embraced thousands of British and US officials, producing a spirit of co-operation and openness. At the political level the main instruments for this were their two embassies, both of which grew rapidly in manpower and functions. The British Embassy of 1939 had fewer than 20 diplomats, much the same as in 1920.[4] During the war it reached 9,000. The US Embassy in London witnessed a very similar expansion.[5] There was close co-operation between the Foreign Office and the State Department. W. J. Gallman, minister and occasional Chargé d'Affaires at the US Embassy in London, remembered Whitehall officials as being very free in sharing information. The Foreign Office opened its files to him. A sense of the relations between the officials is conveyed in the remark of J. C. Donnelly of the North American Department that even occasional outbursts of American hatred for Britain amounted to family quarrels.[6] This left a legacy of mutual affection and a desire to continue working together. It would take the unifying role of another conflict, the cold war, to resurrect it. Yet the Ambassador's role was not so prominent. As Reynolds says, 'The Ambassador was reduced to the role of an overseer, keeping sight of the general issues of high policy, eliminating friction, acting as a spokesman and figure head for his country.'[7] This was because so many government departments had offices attached to the Embassy and specialist missions dealing directly with their American counterparts; and because Churchill and Roosevelt increasingly operated over the heads of the diplomats, both directly and through trusted intermediaries.

There was also close collaboration between the military. In the First World War the United States had remained an 'Associated Power', unwilling to countenance joint military command structures with the British and the French. However, in early 1941 military missions were established in Washington and London. At the Arcadia Conference General Marshall, a First World War veteran, managed to secure a unified command for all British and US forces on sea, land and in the air. A Combined Chiefs of Staff Committee, meeting in Washington, would handle strategy and logistics subject to the guidance of the President and the Prime Minister. This unified structure extended also to the operational level. Besides the Combined Chiefs of Staff Committee there was a whole series of combined boards assigned to deal with the allocation of war materials : the Combined Food Board, Combined Production Board, Combined Production and Resource Board, Combined Raw Materials Board, Combined Shipping Adjustment Board.[8]

What Churchill called the 'mixing up' of Britain and the United States covered two other vital areas, scientific information and intelligence. In 1940, Sir Henry Tizard went to the United States with details about radar, jet engines, chemical weapons, ship protection and anti-submarine devices, indeed 'everything that Britain was doing in the scientific field'.[9] His companion, Professor Cockroft, brought the most important information, for uranium research was then further advanced in Britain than in the United States. In spring 1941 the British Central Scientific Office was set up in Washington with a counterpart in London to co-ordinate the exchange of scientific information. The British and Americans then worked on the Manhattan Project to develop the atomic bomb. But by 1943 difficulties had arisen. They were resolved by discussions between Churchill and Roosevelt which produced the Quebec Agreement of 19 August 1943. It set up the Combined Policy Committee (CPC) whose members, Britain, Canada and the United States, would oversee the project. It was agreed that joint consent was needed before the bomb could be used. British scientists moved to Los Alamos and raw materials like heavy water and designs for machinery were supplied by Britain. On 13 June 1944 the Declaration of Trust established the Combined Development Trust to control uranium and thorium supplies. The 19 September 1944 Hyde Park *aide-mémoire* declared that atomic collaboration in both the military and commercial fields 'should continue after the defeat of Japan unless and until terminated by joint agreement'.[10]

Full co-operation in intelligence matters was also established. In May 1940 Colonel William Stephenson was sent to New York where he set up British Security Co-ordination to liaise with US intelligence agencies. Roosevelt sent Colonel Donovan to London in July, partly to determine whether Britain would continue the war and partly to estimate whether closer co-operation could be secured between the US Navy and the Admiralty. It was only after Pearl Harbor, in December 1941, that co-operation became fully effective and it principally covered the area of cryptography. The British had broken the seemingly unbreakable German machine code, Enigma. As the war progressed information from decyphered messages, codenamed Ultra, was made increasingly available to British and US commanders in the field. In 1943 Britain began supplying the United States with intelligence estimates prepared by the Joint Intelligence Committee (JIC); 1943 also saw the BRUSA agreement aimed at a co-ordinated interception of communications.[11] The high level of co-operation on military strategy and operations, on control and supply of resources and on the exchange of scientific information and intelligence led General Marshall to call it 'the most complete unification of military effort ever achieved by two Allied nations'.[12]

It was clear, however, that Washington had become the headquarters of the alliance. The major struggles over strategy and tactics were being fought from spring 1942 'largely on America's turf and reflected Washington's internal rivalries and organizational priorities'.[13] This was recognised by one British representative on various shipping missions to the United States as early as 1942:

> It must be accepted that policy will increasingly be decided in Washington. To proceed as if it can be made in London and 'put over' in Washington, or as if British policy can in the main develop independently and be only co-ordinated with American, is merely to kick against the pricks. Policy will thus be increasingly Washington-made policy. But it need not therefore be American. It may be Anglo-American.[14]

The dominance of the United States was confirmed in what was perhaps the most vital element for the British – American financial help. As the result of constant pleading from Churchill, Roosevelt launched the idea of Lend-Lease in December 1940. Britain would be provided with materials which it needed and repayment or their return would be arranged later. To deal with domestic opposition Roosevelt required certain British gestures in return; $50 million of gold held in South Africa was collected by a US destroyer, and American Viscose, a subsidiary of Courtaulds, had to be sold. Lend-Lease passed Congress in March 1941. A total of $20 billion (£5 billion) was borrowed, but Britain spent about £1.2 billion on 'Reverse Lend-Lease' to the United States. After the war, Britain was asked to repay only £162 million of the balance of £3.8 billion.[15]

The wartime experience, however, was not solely a story of smooth collaboration. The 'Churchill–Roosevelt connection was never as close as Churchill claimed, and President Roosevelt was not the thoroughgoing Anglophile Churchill made him out to be'.[16] There arose differences about the strategy to fight Hitler and over China in the Far Eastern campaign. Differences also arose over the British Empire which the Americans viewed critically. In general, relations between US and British troops were good. There were difficulties in 1941 and 1942 over the development of the atomic bomb, but these were resolved. Intelligence co-operation was only occasionally marred by irritations. A member of the American Foreign Economic Administration (AFEA) explained to his chief why China and the Soviet Union gained better Lend-Lease terms than Britain by pointing out that neither was 'a great traditional competitor of ours in international trade'.[17] Recent studies have drawn attention to the ambiguities of the relationship. Reference has been made to 'Allies of a Kind', 'Competitive Co-operation', and the 'Ambiguous Relationship'.[18]

The relationship in war had, therefore, contained two main elements. First, financial, economic and military aid to Britain. Secondly, co-operation with Britain as an equal partner (for most of the time at least). British governments after 1945 wanted both of these things to continue. This was not just because this would be the best means of preserving British great-power status, but because it was thought that this would be best for international affairs, since British experience could be allied to the power of the American novice. The prospects for achieving these goals were mixed. Some elements of the wartime relationship were ended, others were continued. How well the British could do would be influenced by the opportunities that the American political system gave them to pursue their policy.

THE US POLITICAL SYSTEM

The Embassy was charged with representing British interests and reporting US affairs in the context of a political system and a level of public involvement unique among the nations of the world. Moreover, its government was new to the idea of organising itself to operate as that of a great power. Even up to 1940 Washington, DC was a fairly small town.[19] Pearl Harbor changed all that.

At the heart of the system is the President, who can employ the machinery of state according to his preferred style of governance.The presidencies of Roosevelt and Truman epitomise differing practices. FDR kept the threads of policy firmly in his own hands and gave no one his complete confidence. Instead, he liked to encourage bureaucratic and individual competitiveness. While the Tennessee Democrat, Cordell Hull, was Secretary of State, the patrician WASP, Sumner Welles, was Under-Secretary of State, and acted as FDR's eyes and ears. The resultant tensions were designed partly to maintain control and partly because he hated making decisions. Truman was altogether different. He prided himself on his ability to delegate and support those he trusted. It was only in crises such as those over the Berlin Blockade and over Korea that the White House became the centre of policy-making – the exception being the Palestine/Israel question. Truman appointed strong secretaries of state and accepted guidance from them.[20] Clearly, any British ambassador who was able to establish close ties with Marshall or Acheson had an opportunity to influence US policy unavailable during the presidency of Roosevelt.

Yet even with a President like Truman, who delegated, policy-making was fragmented. There was no single source of authority in Washington for the conduct of foreign affairs.[21] The diplomats and the State Department had limited control and co-ordination of US external relations. This was shared between the White House, Congress and its committees, the State Department and other departments such as, after 1947, the Department of Defense and agencies such as the Central Intelligence Agency (CIA). US ministries had to answer to Congressional committees and sub-committees. There was no cohesive cabinet to formulate a common policy and there was a lack of a presidential secretariat to implement it. All this impeded decision-making. John Maynard Keynes captured it in his own inimitable way:

> To the outsider it looks almost incredibly inefficient. One wonders how decisions are ever reached at all. There is no clear hierarchy of authority. The different departments of the Government criticise one another in public and produce rival programmes. There is perpetual internecine warfare between prominent personalities ... There is just endless debate and sitting around ... Suddenly some drastic, clear-cut decision is reached, by what process one cannot understand, and all talk seems to have gone for nothing.[22]

An additional element was the division between what May calls the 'politicians' and the 'officials'. The 'politicians' included not only elected Presidents and members of Congress but also would-be presidents and their advisers and many others professionally or semi-professionally concerned with elections or the public side of government. The 'officials' could be civil servants but they were more likely to be lawyers, bankers or others enlisted, often for brief spells, to run departments, agencies or act as advisers. 'Politicians' were inclined to view policy in terms of public approval. This did not mean being swayed by every opinion poll or election result, but it involved judging a decision or action, in the long term at least, by the extent to which it enjoyed popular support. 'Officials' tended to be sceptical about the wishes of the people, whether in the short term or the long term. They felt there were national interests which experts like themselves could identify and that policy should be tested by the yardstick of whether it protected or advanced those interests. 'Officials' consequently derided 'politicians' for sacrificing national interests for votes or popular acclaim.[23]

This leads to a further ingredient – public opinion. Bryce said that in no country was public opinion so important. This meant that it was necessary to establish a consensus for policies. On many issues, however, the great mass of the population took little interest. What counted was the attitude of the foreign policy public, that is media, intellectuals and pressure groups, the 10–15 per cent of the people who regularly followed foreign policy.[24] What made public opinion so potent an element was the power of the media. Policy had to be made under scrutiny of the press, the radio and, increasingly after 1945, the television. In the face of this, American leaders were often forced to have a 'public' and a 'private' foreign policy. For example, over Greece in December 1944 the Americans publicly criticised while diplomats privately agreed with the British stance. US officials, however, were not above citing domestic pressures as justification for the policies they supported.[25] Secretaries of State have estimated that they and their principal advisers spend 50 per cent of their working hours preparing for or delivering testimony to Congress, and a further 25 per cent thinking about what to say to the press.[26]

A final component of the US system was its extraordinary openness to foreign influence. Americans were eager to hear what one thought about their politicians and their policies. They did not take offence if you entered into discussion and even argument about what was strictly their business.[27] The US federal system had no barriers to citizens of one state meddling in the affairs of another. After the Second World War, these traditions combined with the newness of high politics and the overlap and rivalry of branches that so fragmented decision-making, 'opened for interested non-citizens extraordinary opportunities for effectively inserting their opinions and recommendations'.[28]

THE WASHINGTON EMBASSY

The principal vehicle for inserting opinions and recommendations in pursuit of the government's two goals of continued partnership as an equal and of material assistance, was the Washington Embassy – together with its network of offices around the country. British expectations of success were high because of the achievements of wartime. In consequence, the Embassy, though reduced at the war's end, remained large. By 1949 it had a staff of about 1,000 with approximately 50 diplomats.[29] This made it the biggest in Washington, which is still true today. The scale of its operations was huge. Its 12 code clerks in 1949 handled 13,100 telegrams, letters and despatches. It had a daily average of 2,600 telephone calls. Three photostat machines were producing in the region of 10,000 pages of documents a month.[30]

The Embassy was at the centre of a countrywide system. There were ten Consuls-General in Boston, New York, Chicago, Philadelphia, New Orleans, Houston, Los Angeles, San Francisco, Detroit and Washington, DC; and there were a further 11 Consuls and 5 Vice-Consuls. In addition there were the offices of the British Information Services (BIS) in Washington, DC, Los Angeles and New York where it had its headquarters – though the Director-General was based in Washington, DC. BIS monitored American opinion, cultivated contacts and disseminated British publicity. Its officials, consequently, worked closely with the Embassy, sending it reports from tours of the country and advising about the publicity angles to particular issues.[31] If the Embassy handled political and economic questions, there was the Joint Staff Mission, established in 1941 and continued after the war, to maintain military contacts between Britain and the United States. It encompassed the Combined Chiefs of Staff Committee which survived in 1945 and was eventually merged into the NATO military machinery. The BJSM also co-ordinated lower-level contacts. For example, there were visits of officers and of ships and aeroplanes, many of which were agreed by the military commanders of the two nations without reference to the politicians.[32]

Another centre of British government representation was the United Nations Organization whose Charter was signed at the San Francisco Conference in June 1945. It comprised a General Assembly representing all its members and a Security Council of 11, of whom five were permanent members – Britain, France, Nationalist China, the Soviet Union and the United States – and six were elected for two-year terms. In February 1946, Sir Alexander Cadogan retired as Permanent Under-Secretary at the Foreign Office to become the first British Permanent Representative to the Security Council. He was succeeded by Sir Gladwyn Jebb in 1950. In times of crisis, such as the Korean War, it meant that the burdens of the Embassy were shared by the Permanent Representative who was based at Lake Success, New York. Jebb, in particular, proved to be adept in dealing with the US media.[33]

Each Whitehall department concerned with international activities had a representative at the Embassy.[34] This produced what has been called a 'mini Whitehall on Massachusetts Avenue'.[35] The Embassy had five main branches; first, the service attachés who had relations with the British Joint Staff Mission; secondly, the Commercial section; thirdly, the Chancery, which dealt with general political, Commonwealth and specialist areas, as well as the activities of the labour attaché and the scientific attaché; fourthly, the Treasury and Supply section originally separate departments but amalgamated in January 1949,[36] while British Security Co-ordination was absorbed by the Treasury Delegation in May 1945,[37] to deal with finance and, for part of our period, the European Recovery Programme; fifthly, Administration which covered the library, buildings, accounts and so on.

HOW THE EMBASSY FUNCTIONED

The Embassy's activities were a product partly of its place in the British bureaucracy and partly of American circumstances. Cabinet decisions were handled by the various departments of state. In relations with the United States this meant, for the most part, the Foreign Office; to a lesser degree the Treasury and military departments,[38] and, intermittently, other departments. Within the Foreign Office the American Department co-ordinated American affairs.[39] But, since many Anglo-American issues concerned larger matters, other branches of the Foreign Office were involved, such as the Western Organisations Department which covered NATO, or the Far Eastern Department which dealt with China, Japan and other oriental topics. Each department corresponded with the area specialists in the Embassy. The level of importance or secrecy of the issue determined the level of contact between London and Washington. So the Foreign Secretary and departmental ministers, the Permanent Under-Secretary and Deputy Under-Secretaries of the Foreign Office only had direct contact with the Embassy's three senior figures, the Ambassador, the Minister and the Counsellor, on the more serious matters.[40]

There was a daily routine at the Embassy. Communications came in, were registered and put to the area officers to handle, who dealt with them as required. This might mean answering a question or taking action which would be minuted and circulated to colleagues and to the Foreign Office. A second activity was to report interesting talks or action not taken on instruction. A third was to pass on details of an incident or a trend. There were, of course, obstacles to the efficient pursuit of these tasks. The area specialist needed might be sick or on leave. Interviews with the Secretary of State and assistants took time and could be inconclusive. Files could be needed simultaneously by different officials. Indeed, they could be mislaid.[41] Many of the cables could not be dealt with immediately. They required consideration. So each morning the Ambassador held meetings first with the Minister and then with the Counsellor to determine how best to achieve what London needed. Tactics were given careful attention. The Embassy's success depended greatly upon shrewdness in the pacing and direction of action.[42]

In essence the Embassy had two main roles. First, it had to ensure that the British government's policy was understood and that British interests were fully recognised. Secondly, it had to make certain that the true state of opinion in the United States was reported. This meant principally the views of the government, but it also meant discovering the outlook of government critics and the country at large.

The execution of these tasks was influenced by the circumstances of the US political system. Officials from the Embassy, as did their American counterparts in London, established processes of diplomatic and bureaucratic consultation with their opposite numbers. This was done in part through various Anglo-American committees, for example, the Combined Policy Committee which handled atomic issues and whose joint secretary 1947–48 was Donald Maclean.[43] However, a great deal of it was informal, based on a matrix of personal contacts, for Washington was more personal and less institutional than Whitehall.[44] The purpose of this, as one historian says, 'was to keep abreast of what one's opposite numbers in London or Washington were thinking – to have a sense not just of official policy but of the background debates and the alternative options'.[45] Given the diffusion of power in Washington, it was necessary to maintain links with a variety of government departments and agencies and with key members of Congress. Moreover, these contacts, at the State Department in particular, were at all levels, especially just below the top where decisions so often originate. There were considerable benefits from this. The British were able to influence State Department and other officials who were advising the politicians. Indeed, these officials often gave their views and their estimate of what policy was likely to be adopted even before the Secretary of State had formally decided.[46] In other words, the British could put their views and make proposals before the inter-departmental and Congressional trade-offs of the US system had solidified policy. When such solidified policy was presented for talks with allies it was often too late to achieve significant changes. The

Americans also benefited. In effect, they had a 'natural ally whose support could generally be assumed because of the similarity of interests and values and the habit of advance consultation'.[47]

Embassy contacts extended beyond the directly political world. They included what May called the 'officials' – lawyers, bankers and others brought in from private life to advise or work in government. Journalists, writers and labour leaders were also involved. These people spoke very freely to the British.[48] The hope was to reach what has been called the 'foreign policy public'. BIS provided journalists with non-secret Embassy guidance papers. W. P. N. Edwards of BIS said, 'We'd tell them, "After you have read that don't tell anybody you have, but that will tell you what the official British view is".'[49] This was achieved partly by private meetings and partly by social gatherings; for example, in his first year as Ambassador, Sir Oliver Franks accepted 260 invitations to all sorts of Washington parties, while he entertained some 5,000 people at the Embassy.[50] On these occasions British diplomats would also meet foreign envoys who might have a clearer view of a confusing topic or information not available to the British Embassy. In addition, there were regular meetings of the Commonwealth ambassadors at the British Embassy during the ambassadorship of Sir Oliver Franks.[51] The Canadians were especially helpful.[52] For the British the purpose was to discover not just what influential Americans thought, but how they thought – what were their mental processes in general and hence how any one group of them was likely to behave in a given situation.[53] Certain trends of opinion were of particular interest to the Embassy, such as US isolationism and the US view of the British Empire.[54] Moreover, the US government often used these contacts for an unofficial approach to the British.

Opinion beyond official Washington was also surveyed. Consular officials, members of BIS and Embassy officials made tours. The Foreign Office preferred to concentrate on highbrow contacts such as the Council on Foreign Relations, the Foreign Policy Association and the various financial and industrial bodies. The Embassy, however, pressed for and achieved contact with citizen groups like the Lions, Kiwanis and Rotarians.[55] Indeed, the Ambassadors aimed to visit most of the states during their time in the United States. BIS, in addition, helped to compile surveys of the US press. The Second World War forced the British to recognise the importance of the Middle West and so led to coverage of its press as well as that of the East Coast.[56] The results of these activities were presented in a Weekly Political Summary and in a Weekly Survey of the US Press and Radio that the Embassy sent to the Foreign Office. In all these contacts the British sought not only to gauge US opinion, but to present British ideas in the hope that these might have an influence.

Such a general background of understanding helped in the conduct of regular diplomatic relations. These included issues of varying importance – from the response to a parliamentary speech to the unfolding of relations with the Soviet Union, from arrangements about the itinerary of a ministerial visit to negotiations about financial aid. The sense of accord between the two nations was also most useful in coping with sudden crisis – from an urgent shortage of dollars to the Berlin Blockade, from a predicament over the European Defence Community to the North Korean invasion of South Korea. Times of exigency, to be sure, most revealed the intimacy and harmony of Anglo-American relations. In 1949 there arose for Britain a chronic shortage of dollars. The Washington Embassy was asked in an urgent message to press for US aid. The Ambassador, Sir Oliver Franks, called his leading aides: the Minister, the Treasury expert and the liaison officer with the European Co-operation Administration. Within an hour the task force had its programme. Franks telephoned the US Secretary of State, Acheson, for an early appointment. Each aide scheduled a meeting with his American opposite number fully prepared on what he was going to tell him. The next day Embassy officials went to key parts of US officialdom and briefed them. Said one State Department figure: 'When I was called to Acheson's office, I had already had one hour to look at the documents. I was ready with answers. Naturally I lean over backwards to do something for an Embassy like that.'[57]

Certain skills were called for on the part of the diplomats to maintain harmony in their three roles: the general habit of consultation and exchange of confidences; regular diplomatic relations; and the sudden crisis. A number of general talents were needed: the ability to inspire confidence; political judgement; discretion and a sense of responsibility; coolheadedness, that is not getting carried away in enthusiasm or indignation; reliability; adaptability.[58] In particular, a diplomat, and perhaps more especially the Ambassador, if he was to make the most of his job, must make friends and create a relationship in which intimate knowledge of the other party leads to tolerance and understanding. Friendship cannot be simulated for long. So the Ambassador must have an indefinable capacity for liking and being liked, as well as the power of objective analysis.[59] Furthermore, a diplomat must not appear as quickwitted as he actually is, for people seldom open up in conversation when confronted with profound knowledge and intellectual pre-eminence.[60] As Denis Healey said of the 1960s, the US system is very open to outside advice by individuals whose integrity is trusted and whose knowledge and intelligence are respected. Lord Harlech was practically a member of the Kennedy cabinet. Healey added that he had known quite junior Embassy officials make an important input to US strategic thinking and so he made a point of seeing such junior officials on his visits to Washington.[61] Quite clearly, then, the personal qualities of the major British diplomats in Washington – the Ambassador, Minister and Counsellor – were central to the degree of success that could be achieved in relations with the United States.

KEY PERSONNEL

The social background of the holders of these three senior offices in the 1940s and early 1950s largely conformed to the traditional image of British diplomats. Of the five figures who were either Political Minister or senior Counsellor, two had attended Eton, two had gone to Wellington College and one had gone to school in New Zealand, while four were educated at Oxford and one at Cambridge. If we include the Ambassadors since 1945, two (including Franks) went to Oxford and one was privately educated.[62]

William Denis Allen, born in New Zealand on 24 December 1910, was Counsellor from November 1946 to December 1949 when he returned to the Foreign Office to become head of the German Political Department. He was the only one of these officials to be educated at Cambridge (Pembroke College). In his memoirs, Eden wrote that Allen had 'a perfect command of his facts on all occasions and was immensely resourceful'.[63] He was succeeded by Bernard Alexander Brocas Burrows who served from January 1950 to July 1953. Born in July 1910, he was educated at Eton and Trinity College, Oxford. He was to leave Washington to become Political Resident in the Persian Gulf, and was to complete his career by serving as Permanent British representative on the North Atlantic Council. Although he possessed the demeanour of a 'gentle proconsul', some flavour of the exuberant spirits he brought to the Washington scene is recorded in the Shuckburgh diaries.[64]

All three of the Political Ministers established for themselves quite considerable reputations. None was more impressive than that of Sir John Balfour, usually known by colleagues and American counterparts alike as Jock. He was born in May 1894 and educated at Eton and New College, Oxford. He had considerable experience of working with the Americans. He had served as a Second, then a First Secretary in Washington in 1924 to 1928. In 1955 he was to have a third period in the United States as a member of the United Kingdom Delegation to the United Nations in New York.[65] He was Minister from April 1945 to July 1948. By the time of his departure, Charles Bohlen of the US State Department could speak of 'the extraordinary place in the confidence of the State Department and of Congress that Jock Balfour has enjoyed.'[66] It was clear that he would be sorely missed. Fortunately his successor, Frederick Robert Hoyer Millar, though not of the same stature in American eyes, was an able individual with considerable experience of the United States. He had served in Washington from January 1939 to June 1944. A profile of him by the US Embassy in London said he was always very co-operative with them, that he approached discussions with 'extreme frankness and never hesitated to state clearly both UK views and Brit. [*sic*] objectives to or criticism of Amer. [*sic*] proposals. He always, however, sought to find common ground.' The assessment concluded by saying that his place in the Foreign Office would be hard to fill.[67] Hoyer Millar was born in June 1900 and educated at Wellington College and New College, Oxford. He served as Minister from March 1948 until October 1950 – first as an additional Minister and then, from July onwards, as Balfour's replacement. His early arrival seems to have been designed to try and improve American views of Britain which were regarded as poor in the spring of 1948. It was hoped that a man of weight could lend force to the claim that Britain was a good long-term investment.[68] When he left Washington he became Deputy to the United Kingdom Representative at the North Atlantic Council. He subsequently became Permanent Under-Secretary in the Foreign Office in succession to Sir Ivone Kirkpatrick. A colleague later wrote of 'a person of great good sense and sound judgment who did so much to restore the slightly shaken morale of the office'.[69]

The new Political Minister was Christopher Eden Steel who held the position from November 1950 to August 1953. Born in February 1903, he was educated at Wellington College and Hertford College, Oxford. His arrival in Washington was particularly opportune, for it coincided with the emergence of the question of German rearmament. Having served as chief Foreign Office representative to the British authorities in West Germany, he brought first-hand knowledge and grasp of the issues to Anglo-American and NATO talks on the matter.[70]

Two figures fulfilled the role of ambassador in the years 1945–48. Lord Halifax served from January 1941 until May 1946. He was born in April 1881 and educated at Eton and Christ Church, Oxford, becoming a Fellow of All Souls College. He took some time to overcome American reservations about him, due partly to his pre-war association with the policy of appeasement and partly to his manner. Indeed, he wrote in his diary that he found the Americans 'very crude and semi-educated'.[71] However, his standing steadily improved. On his departure, the *New York Times* said he had 'left British affairs in the United States in excellent shape'.[72]

His successor, Archibald Clark Kerr, Lord Inverchapel, who was Ambassador from May 1946 to May 1948, did not do so well, although he arrived with a good billing – 'Great Britain's ablest career man', declared the *St Louis Post-Dispatch*.[73] According to Sir John Balfour, his Political Minister, he disliked Washington society, did not try to make friends with leading Americans and was bored by his work and his surroundings. He appeared played out. Moreover, he displayed an exhibitionist sense of humour which did not please a United States whose nerves were jangling in those early days of the cold war.[74] He conceded that his relations with the State Department were not good: 'The trouble is they lack a sense of humour, they don't like dirty stories.'[75] Nicholas Henderson observed:

> In a long career abroad he had become so bored with small talk and polite responses that he longed for the unusual and unexpected. He would say things in order to shock and so to produce some non-automatic reaction, a temptation he found irresistible in Washington's Victorian society.[76]

His statement to the press that he was 'just an old man come to do a job' noticeably failed to impress; understatement was not likely to work with Americans.[77] Moreover, he was the last Ambassador to adopt the old attitude to Washington in the summer. There had been a time when nearly the entire Embassy staff had left for Manchester, New Hampshire where there was 'a sort of American Simla'.[78] While that no longer took place, Inverchapel left the US capital for two months in the crucial summer of 1947.[79] In addition, he regarded Truman as at most 'an honest and intelligent mediocrity' or 'a bungling if well-meaning amateur'.[80] Franks's appreciation of him given in a speech after succeeding him as Ambassador provides an indication of Inverchapel's standing: 'He travelled widely in the United States and made many friends. He had a deep love of the countryside and of country life. This gave him an appreciation of the importance of the American rural community.'[81] An anonymous Foreign Office official minuted in the margin of this text: 'Well put.'

SIR OLIVER FRANKS

Oliver Shewell Franks, who served as Ambassador from May 1948 until December 1952, had an outlook and personal qualities that were altogether more helpful to good Anglo-American relations. Born in a village just outside Birmingham on 16 February 1905, he was the elder son and eldest of four children of the Reverend Robert Sleightholme and Katharine (née Shewell) Franks. His paternal grandfather, William James Franks, of Redcar, Yorkshire, was also a clergyman who lived from 1838 to 1929. His father, who was born on 1 April 1871 and died in January 1964 was educated at St John's College, Cambridge, qualifying brilliantly in mathematics and physics, then at Mansfield College, Oxford where he trained as a minister. In 1900–04 he was minister at Prenton Congregational Church in Birkenhead. During this period he married Katharine Shewell of Redcar, Yorkshire on 3 September 1902. Between 1904 and 1910 he was Theological Lecturer at the Friends' Settlement for Religious and Social Study, Woodbrooke, Birmingham. It was during this period that Oliver was born. When the child was 5 years old, in 1910, Reverend K. S. Franks became Principal of Western College, Bristol, where he remained until 1939.[82]

Oliver attended Bristol Grammar School. According to one profile of him, he had raced through most of the weighty philosophical volumes in his father's vast library by the age of 12. Meanwhile, at school, his flashy brilliance won him so many book prizes that 'old Franks and his books' became a school joke. 'He had a mind', said one of his teachers, 'that was so logical it was frightening.' He also displayed a quality which admirers call purposefulness and his critics call opportunism. So, for instance, he had no interest in athletics, but when he realised that he should be seen on the playing fields to be an 'all-round star', he proceeded to captain his rugby team to the school championship. Here was encapsulated the calm, deliberate quest for achievement that was to mark Franks's whole career.[83]

He won a classical scholarship to The Queen's College, Oxford in 1923. In 1925 he was awarded a First Class in Classical Moderations and in 1927 he was awarded a First in Literae Humaniores, in the same year as the distinguished classicist Ronald Syme. That same year also saw him secure the John Locke Scholarship in Mental Philosophy.[84] On his final examinations, Queen's extended 'ceremonious congratulations' and promptly appointed him (at 22) a Fellow and Praelector in Philosophy,[85] a post he held until 1937. Franks accepted, explaining to a journalist much later, 'I said "yes" because at the time I was more interested in philosophy than in anything else.'[86] He then spent a year on the continent studying German, French and Italian and attending occasional lectures at Heidelberg and Berlin universities. Returning to Oxford he settled down to teach, becoming a tutor in 1933 and a university lecturer in 1935, holding both posts until 1937. On 3 July 1931 he married Barbara Mary Tanner, one of his students and a graduate in Politics, Philosphy and Economics, who was a Quaker and the daughter of Herbert George Tanner of Bristol. They were to have two daughters, Caroline born in April 1939 and Alison born in January 1945.[87]

In 1935 he took up the post of Visiting Professor at the University of Chicago where he spent three months teaching. This first contact with the United States made an impact on him. He said of the experience: 'It was very important for a small islander like me to spend some time in Chicago, 1000 miles from the sea where the natural horizons are New York and San Francisco.'[88] Then, at the age of 32 in 1937, he was appointed Professor of Moral Philosophy at Glasgow University, a chair once held by Adam Smith.[89] He remained in the post officially until 1945. Franks's smooth ascent of the academic ladder suggested that he was on his way to becoming, in due course, Provost of Queen's or Vice-Chancellor of one of the major universities. However, 1939 was to change all that.

On the outbreak of the Second World War Franks was given leave of absence from Glasgow and became a temporary civil servant in the Ministry of Supply in London.[90] Here he learned, observed Geoffrey Murray of the *News-Chronicle*, the value of 'what he calls "diffusion of initiative"'. His first major task was to create the establishment division in the Ministry which he accomplished by his powers of despatch, coherent administration, tact and creative judgement. In 1942 he was promoted to Second Secretary and awarded a CBE. The following year he accompanied Redcliffe-Maud, the British representative, for the first council meeting of the United Nations Relief and Rehabilitation Administration (UNRRA) in Atlantic City.[91] His special concern was raw materials. In 1944 he was a representative at the Montreal meeting of UNRRA where *Time* reported, 'he held a deadlocked meeting in session most of the night, finally convinced Russia's delegates that they had misinterpreted their instructions from Moscow'.[92] It was at these UNRRA meetings that Franks first met Dean Acheson who was the US representative and thereby established the foundations for what proved to be a remarkable relationship between the Ambassador and Secretary of State.[93] Franks also served on the Advisory Committee on Atomic Energy which met between September 1945 and May 1947. Its brief was to advise on the general policy for the use of atomic energy. The new Labour government was anxious to establish continuity with the stance of the wartime coalition.[94] Thus, he was to secure a reputation for sage reflection on atomic questions which was to last up to and beyond his period as Ambassador. All these activities brought their reward when, in 1945, he was made Permanent Secretary of the Ministries of Supply and Aircraft Production and received a KBE. His final months as a civil servant saw him securing the merger of the two ministries. He left in April 1946 to become Provost of The Queen's College, Oxford.[95]

Yet within little more than a year Franks was recalled to government service to help organise the British and subsequently, the European, response to the Harvard speech of the US Secretary of State, George C. Marshall, in June 1947. Six months after this he was offered and accepted the post of Ambassador to the United States. It took a special range of qualities for so unassuming an outsider to government service to be so compelling a candidate for such important tasks.

He brought to his duties a rare combination of traits of temperament and bearing as well as of intellect. A tall (six foot three-and-a-half), austere, virtual teetotaller whose gravity of manner led to the undergraduate sobriquet 'Father Franks', he had considerable presence without appearing pompous or aloof. Yet he lacked small talk, not least because he had little interest in art or music or literature.[96] Moreover, he was a reluctant writer. He was to find the Reith lectures laborious and difficult to construct.[97] He displayed a strong sense of duty and moral fervour and had an underlying confidence that never veered towards arrogance, a cheerful imperturbability based on inner control. To these aspects of personality and appearance were added superlative qualities of intellect. He possessed a first-class analytical mind that could reduce to order a mass of information, however complex. The results of his mental exertions were then presented in a crystal clear and methodical manner via simple, direct language. Indeed, as one observer noted, 'when he speaks, whether in public or in private, he seems always to be thinking aloud; there are no ready-made phrases or patter; the words have weight'.[98]

Many academics have brought similar intelligence to their public service, if few of them have displayed the same qualities of character. However, what separated him from the others was his keen sense of the practical. In his duties he had to work with not only civil servants and politicians but also the military and business; and these last two were unlikely to be impressed by a donnish approach. He proved to be a talented negotiator. In the first place, he was a good listener, ready to learn from others and never overrating his own knowledge or competence. As he has said of his work on committees:

> I do enjoy it. I think the first reason is that I have always found myself with very able members of committees I have been on, with minds as good or better than my own very often bringing expert deep knowledge into it, and trying to match them; trying to keep up with their minds. And trying to bring them into some sort of agreed unity about the way to tackle a problem. It is to me an exciting form of endeavour. I do enjoy that.[99]

Underlying these words can be detected a second feature, his 'vigorous confidence that every problem, theoretical or practical, is soluble by the human intellect, given sufficient exercise of will to get the intellect working'.[100] He identified, in a lecture on his wartime experiences, some of the reasons why meetings failed. Apart from the failure of the chairman to keep to business, this could arise either because the meeting, though clear about what was to be done, was not clear about how, or because it failed to allocate responsibility for initiating action. The civil servant needs, Franks added, to take a line, expound it and persuade, to have a keen sense of what was practicable and of timing, and the strength of will to pursue a task to its completion.[101] A third attribute to his approach, then, was his attention to the end result – a sense of the instruments and circumstances needed to produce action. Indeed, he had limited intellectual curiosity; he preferred to think for a purpose. As one of his colleagues at Oxford observed, he was a great problem solver but he needed to be given the problem.[102] In order to secure a decision in favour of action along the lines he deemed appropriate called for subtle skills of persuasion. His fine mind allowed him to dissect the issues and '[s]everal moves ahead of his colleagues he would decide what ought to be done, and quietly use all his power of argument and moral authority to persuade; he very rarely failed'.[103] He would achieve this by 'the exercise of great restraint not to disclose too soon his own convictions which might only incite opposition and ... [by] his ability to raise doubts by questions and suggestions, nothing more, about any other solution'.[104]

The fresh enthusiasm he invariably brought to his duties was due to his aptitude for deploying his talents to their maximum effect. He understood how to delegate tasks, thereby reserving his energies for the major problems of policy. After he had made what he felt to be the best possible decision, he had the capacity to leave it behind him and not worry about it.[105]

Such an array of talents and personal qualities was to create a favourable impression in the United States; and in particular with Dean Acheson, who was US Secretary of State from January 1949 to

January 1953. Such personal relations between the Ambassador and Secretary of State were of great importance. Yet ambassadors were not independent forces. They were dependent upon their relations with their government and upon the relations between Britain and the United States and between the President and the Prime Minister.[106] The condition of postwar relations was clearly vital to the prospects of a successful ambassadorship.

NOTES

1. David Dimbleby and David Reynolds, *An Ocean Apart: The Relationship Between Britain and America in the Twentieth Century* (London: BBC/Hodder & Stoughton, 1988), p. 139.
2. Anderson, *United States, Great Britain and the Cold War*, p. 2.
3. For the Marshall–Dill relationship see A. Danchev, *A Very Special Relationship: Field-Marshal Sir John Dill and the Anglo-American Alliance, 1941–1944* (London: Brassey's, 1986). On the BJSM see S. J. Parker, 'The Attendant Lords' (PhD thesis, University of Maryland 1984). Anderson, *United States, Great Britain and the Cold War*, p. 2.
4. *Foreign Office List and Yearbook, 1920*; *Foreign Office List and Yearbook, 1939.*
5. Dimbleby and Reynolds, *An Ocean Apart*, pp. 139–40
6. Anderson, *United States, Great Britain and the Cold War*, pp. 2–3.
7. David Reynolds, *The Creation of the Anglo-American Alliance, 1937–1941* (London: Europa, 1981), p. 182.
8. W. H. McNeill, *America, Britain and Russia, their Cooperation and Conflict, 1941–1946* (London: Oxford University Press/RIIA, 1953), pp. 109–10.
9. H. D. Hall and C. C. Wrigley, *Studies on Overseas Supply* (London: Longman, 1956), pp. 360–1.
10. M. M. Gowing, *Britain and Atomic Energy* (London: Macmillan, 1964).
11. See F. H. Hinsley, *British Intelligence in the Second World War*, 4 vols (London: HMSO, 1979–90); also R. Lewin, *Ultra Goes to War* (London: Hutchinson, 1978). The official account has now been published: *British Security Co-ordination: The Secret History of British Intelligence in the Americas* (London and New York: Little, Brown, 1998).
12. H. D. Hall, *North American Supply* (London: HMSO, 1955), p. 353.
13. Theodore A. Wilson, 'Coalition: Structure, Strategy and Statecraft', in David Reynolds, Warren F. Kimball and A. O. Chubarian (eds), *Allies at War: the Soviet, American, and British Experience, 1939–1945* (New York: St Martin's Press, 1994), p. 89.
14. Alex Danchev, *Oliver Franks: Founding Father* (Oxford: Clarendon Press, 1993), p. 116.
15. See Hall, *North American Supply*, and A. P. Dobson, *US Wartime Aid to Britain 1941–1946* (London: Croom Helm, 1986).
16. Wilson, 'Coalition: Structure, Strategy and Statecraft', p. 81.
17. Alan P. Dobson, *Anglo-American Relations in the Twentieth Century* (London: Routledge, 1995), p. 81.
18. C. Thorne, *Allies of a Kind* (London: Hamish Hamilton, 1978); D. Reynolds, 'Competitive Co-operation: Anglo-American Relations in World War Two', *Historical Journal*, Vol. 23, No. 1, March 1980; R. M. Hathaway, *Ambiguous Partnership* (New York: Columbia University Press, 1981).

19. D. Brinkley, *Washington Goes to War* (New York: Alfred A. Knopf, 1988).
20. These observations are based on D. C. Watt, *Succeeding John Bull: America in Britain's Place, 1900–1975* (Cambridge: Cambridge University Press, 1984), pp. 77–8, 171–2; J. Charmley, *Churchill's Grand Alliance: The Anglo-American Special Relationship, 1940–1957* (London: Hodder & Stoughton, 1995), pp. 12–13; W. S. Miscamble, *George F. Kennan and the Making of American Foreign Policy, 1947–1950* (Princeton, NJ: Princeton University Press, 1992), pp. 354–5.
21. N. Henderson, 'The Washington Embassy: Navigating the Waters of the Potomac', *Diplomacy and Statecraft*, Vol. 1, No. 1, March 1990, p. 42.
22. J. M. Keynes to Sir Kingsley Wood (Chancellor of the Exchequer), 2 June 1941, quoted in Kathleeen Burk, 'American Foreign Economic Policy and Lend-Lease', in Ann Lane and Howard Temperley (eds), *The Rise and Fall of the Grand Alliance, 1941–1945* (Basingstoke: Macmillan, 1995), p. 63.
23. E. R. May, 'The American Commitment to Germany 1949–1955', *Diplomatic History*, Vol. 13, No. 4, Fall 1989, pp. 434–5.
24. David Reynolds, *Britannia Overruled: British Policy and World Power in the Twentieth Century* (London: Longman, 1991), p. 40.
25. David Reynolds, 'Roosevelt, Churchill and the Wartime Anglo-American Alliance, 1939–1945: Towards a New Synthesis', in H. Bull and W. R. Louis (eds), *The 'Special Relationship': Anglo-American Relations Since 1945* (Oxford: Clarendon Press, 1986), p. 19.
26. May, 'American Commitment', p. 435.
27. Henderson, 'Washington Embassy', p. 41.
28. May, 'American Commitment', p. 436.
29. *Foreign Office List and Diplomatic and Consular Yearbook, 1949*.
30. *Time*, 26 September 1949.
31. See R. Marrett, *Through the Back Door* (Oxford and London: Pergamon Press, 1968) and P. H. Gore-Booth, *With Great Truth and Respect* (London: Constable, 1974).
32. See PRO, FO 371/68028–68040 for these activities in 1948 – the year that B.29s were moved to Britain. See S. Duke, *US Defence Bases in the United Kingdom* (London: Macmillan, 1987) for the general issue.
33. See Jebb's memoirs, Lord Gladwyn, *The Memoirs of Lord Gladwyn* (London: Weidenfeld & Nicolson, 1972).
34. Max Beloff, *New Dimensions in Foreign Policy* (London: Allen and Unwin, 1961), p. 136.
35. David Reynolds, 'A "Special Relationship"? America, Britain and the International Order since the Second World War', *International Affairs*, Vol. 62, No. 1, Winter 1985–86, p. 16.
36. National Archives, Washington DC, (NA, Wash. DC) Record Group 59, State Department Decimal Files 1945–49, 841.02/12-3148.
37. NA, Washington, DC, Record Group 59, State Department Decimal Files 1945–1949, 841.01B11/5–1645.
38. Until 1947 these were the Admiralty, War Office and the Air Ministry. After 1947 the Ministry of Defence coordinated these three bodies. See *Cmd 6923 Central Organization of Defence* (London: HMSO, 1946); cited in John Baylis, *British Defence Policy* (London: Macmillan, 1989), pp. 12–13. See M. L. Dockrill, *British Defence Since 1945* (Oxford: Blackwell, 1988) for an outline of developments.
39. This was called the North American Department until 1950. Thereafter it was known as the American Department. See Beloff, *New Dimensions in Foreign Policy*, ch. 5; and V. Cromwell, 'The United Kingdom' in Zara Steiner (ed.), *The Times Survey of the Foreign Ministries of the World* (London: Times Books, 1982).

40. Washington had four Ministers and four Counsellors. The Political Minister and the Political Counsellor were the senior figures in each category.
41. Lord Strang, *The Foreign Office* (London: George Allen and Unwin, 1955), pp. 99–100.
42. *Time*, 26 September 1949.
43. R. Cecil, *A Divided Life: A Biography of Donald Maclean* (London: Bodley Head, 1988), p. 70.
44. Sir I. Berlin, 'Introduction', to H. G. Nicholas (ed.), *Washington Despatches 1941–1946* (London: Weidenfeld & Nicolson (1981), p. xi.
45. Reynolds, 'A "Special Relationship"?', p. 10.
46. For an example of this during the talks on a North Atlantic Pact in February 1949, see PRO, FO 371/79227, Z1627/1074/72G.
47. Reynolds, 'A "Special Relationship"?', pp. 10–11.
48. Berlin, 'Introduction', p. xi.
49. W. P. N. Edwards Oral History, London 1970; quoted in Caroline Anstey, 'Foreign Office Publicity, American Aid and European Unity Mobilizing Public Opinion 1947–1949' in J. Becker and F. Knipping (eds), *Power in Europe? Great Britain, France, Italy and Germany in a Postwar World, 1945–1950* (Berlin & New York: Walter de Gruyter, 1986), p. 380.
50. *Time*, 26 September 1949.
51. Lord Franks, *Britain and The Tide of World Affairs* (London: Oxford University Press, 1955), p. 17.
52. See PRO, FO 371/99218, F19345/9 for evidence of this.
53. Strang, *The Foreign Office*, pp. 120–1.
54. Berlin, 'Introduction', p. xi.
55. Caroline Anstey, 'Foreign Office Efforts to Influence American Opinion, 1945–1949', (PhD thesis, London School of Economics, 1984), p. 244.
56. Ibid., p. 21
57. *Time*, 26 September 1949.
58. Lord Strang, *The Diplomatic Career* (London: André Deutsch, 1962), p. 33.
59. Strang, *The Foreign Office*, p. 121.
60. Ibid., p. 98.
61. D. Healey, *The Time of My Life* (London: Michael Joseph, 1989), p. 113.
62. The principal details have been taken from various editions of the *Foreign Office List and Diplomatic and Consular Yearbook*.
63. Sir Anthony Eden, *The Memoirs of Sir Anthony Eden: Full Circle* (London: Cassell, 1960), p. 118.
64. Healey, *Time of My Life*, p. 320. Evelyn Shuckburgh *Descent to Suez: Diaries 1951–56* ed. John Charmley (London: Weidenfeld & Nicolson, 1986), p. 33.
65. See his memoirs: John Balfour, *Not Too Correct an Aureole: The Recollections of a Diplomat* (Salisbury: Michael Russell, 1983).
66. PRO, FO 371/73074, Z6238/2307/72G, minute by J. W. Russell of a conversation with Charles Bohlen, 28 July 1948.
67. NA, Wash. D., RG59, State Department Decimal Files 1945–49, 701.4163/12-3147, Box 2960, Gallman (US Embassy, London) to Secretary of State, telegram A–1654, 31 December 1947.
68. PRO, FO 371/68045G, AN1678/183/45, various minutes, March 1948.
69. Sir Roderick Barclay, *Ernest Bevin and the Foreign Office 1932–1969* (London: published privately, 1975), p. 20.
70. Moreover, he devised a secret scheme, together with another Foreign Office official, Frank Roberts, almost identical with the one later adopted in 1954 to solve the problem. By it the Brussels Pact would be expanded to include West Germany who would also join NATO; and there would be a British commitment to station troops on the continent. Frank Roberts, *Dealing with*

Dictators: The Destruction and Revival of Europe 1930–1970 (London: Weidenfeld & Nicolson, 1991), pp. 158–59.
71. Robin Edmonds, *Setting the Mould: the United States and Britain 1945–1950* (Oxford: Clarendon Press 1986), p. 13.
72. *New York Times*, 29 May 1946.
73. HSTL, Harry S. Truman Papers, Official File, Box 215, 1945–48 folder, *St Louis Post Dispatch*, 23 June 1946.
74. Balfour, *Aureole*, p. 105.
75. Henry Brandon, *Special Relationships: A Foreign Correspondent's Memoirs from Roosevelt to Reagan* (London: Macmillan, 1989), p. 75.
76. Quoted in Ruth Dudley Edwards, *True Brits* (London: BBC Books, 1994), p. 130.
77. Interview with Leonard Miall 12 May 1983, who worked for the BBC in the United States in the 1940s; cited in C. Anstey, 'FO Efforts to Influence', p. 40. This approach remained throughout his ambassadorship. In a speech to the Yale Club of Washington in January 1948 he said, 'I ask for a firm understanding from you that I shall not be asked to come back here next year to explain why my prophecies were wrong', PRO, FO 371/68023, AN0314/19/45.
78. Rene MacColl, *Deadline and Dateline* (London: Oldbourne Press, 1956), p. 138.
79. NA, Wash. DC, RG59, Lot 54D224, Box 21, memorandum of conversation with Lord Inverchapel, 30 June 1947.
80. Quoted in Peter Boyle, 'America's Hesitant Road to NATO', in Joseph Smith (ed.), *The Origins of NATO* (Exeter: Exeter University Press, 1990), p. 76.
81. PRO, FO 371/68045G, AN3746/183/45, speech to the Pilgrims at the Waldorf-Astoria, New York, 13 October 1948.
82. Compiled from *Burke's Peerage and Baronetage* (London: Burke's Peerage, 1975), p. 1046; *Who's Who in America Vol. 27, 1952–1953* (Chicago, IL: A. N. Marquis Co., 1952), p. 846; *International Who's Who 1989–90* (London: Europa Publications, 1989), p. 514; entry for Franks in Anna Rothe (ed.), *Current Biography Yearbook 1948* (New York: W. W. Wilson, 1948), p. 228. See also letter by H. Carter Lloyd (of London Missionary Society) to *The Times*, 17 February 1948, p. 5, on Rev. R. S. Franks.
83. *Time*, 26 September 1949, p. 19.
84. *University of Oxford Calendar 1927, University of Oxford Calendar 1928, University of Oxford Calendar 1929*.
85. *Time*, 26 September 1949, p. 19.
86. Milton Shulman, *How to Be a Celebrity* (London: Reinhardt & Evans, 1950), p. 62.
87. *Burke's Peerage and Baronetage*, p. 1046.
88. Shulman, *Celebrity*, p. 63.
89. *Current Biography*, p. 229, *Time*, 26 September 1949, p. 19.
90. Danchev, *Franks*, pp. 39–54 provides the best available account of these years.
91. John Redcliffe-Maud, *Experience of an Optimist: The Memoirs of John Redcliffe-Maud* (London: Hamish Hamilton, 1981), p. 44.
92. *Time*, 26 September 1948, p. 14; see also *US News and World Report*, 27 February 1948, p. 35.
93. Interview with Lord Franks, 24 May 1990.
94. M. M. Gowing, *Independence and Deterrence. Britain and Atomic Energy, 1945–1952 Vol. I Policy Making* (London: Macmillan, 1974), pp. 24–5.
95. The main features of this paragraph are based upon 'Sir Oliver Franks', *Observer*, 10 August 1947 and *Current Biography*, p. 229.
96. In September 1946 he said that he had not had time to read or think in the last seven years, Danchev, *Franks*, p. 41.

97. Sterling Library, Yale University, Dean Acheson Private Papers, Box 12, Franks to Acheson, ? 4 August 1955.
98. Academicus (pseud.), 'Britain Sends a New Kind of Ambassador', *New York Times Magazine,* 2 May 1948, p. 12.
99. Quoted in Peter Hennessy, *Whitehall* (London: Secker & Warburg, 1989), p. 569.
100. 'Franks', *Observer* 10 August 1947.
101. Oliver Franks, *The Experience of a University Teacher in the Civil Service,* Sydney Ball Lecture, 3 May 1947 (London: Oxford University Press, 1947), pp. 11–12.
102. Danchev, *Franks,* p. 31.
103. Academicus, 'New Kind of Ambassador', p. 12.
104. Sir Nicholas Henderson, 'The Franks Way – Then and Now', *The Times,* 17 January 1983, p. 8.
105. Obituary notice, *The Times,* 17 October 1992, p. 17.
106. Brandon, *Special Relationships,* p. 320.

— 2 —

Postwar Relations

As THE SECOND WORLD WAR ended in 1945, so did the majority of the wartime Anglo-American structures. The various combined boards dealing with commodities were wound up and replaced by bodies with wider representation.[1] President Truman, who had succeeded Roosevelt on his death in April 1945, cancelled Lend-Lease.[2] In private, Whitehall worried that 'erratic' Americans would repeat their action after 1918. Richard Law of the Foreign Office in 1945 was fearful that the United States would 'swing back to … an expansionist isolationism of a highly inconvenient character'.[3] This seemed confirmed by the reductions in US forces from a total of 12 million, of which 3,500,000 were in Europe in June 1945, to a total of 1,500,000 of which 200,000 were in Europe in June 1947.[4] There was, moreover, no American commitment to help Britain or other West European countries if they were attacked.[5] Washington seemed more interested in the democratisation of Japan than in European developments.

Some writers have gone on from this to suggest that relations between Britain and the United States for the first 18 months or so of peace were cool and took some effort to improve.[6] However, the point should not be pressed too far. Over atomic questions, over Britain's position in the Middle East, more especially over Palestine, and over aspects of economic (mainly financial) policy there were strains. Nevertheless, in the period between the end of the war and Franks's appointment, the United States approved the Marshall Plan, and the intelligence services and military forces sustained closer co-operation than was made public at the time.

STRAINS: ATOMIC ENERGY, FINANCE AND PALESTINE

The British had particularly valued wartime collaboration on the atomic bomb and hoped to see it continue. They were soon to be disappointed. There were talks in Washington in November 1945 between Attlee, Truman and the Canadian Prime Minister, Mackenzie King. Although the British left Washington in good spirits, we should note that 'consultation' was substituted for the 'consent' stipulated in the Quebec Agreement. Moreover, the British Joint Secretary of the Combined Policy Committee, Roger Makins, later wrote of the meeting as 'something of a shambles'.[7] In a very short time, pressure grew from a nationalist and spy-scared Congress (in February 1946 the Ottawa communist spy ring was revealed) to cause Truman to re-think the pledges. Many in Congress were unaware of the secret understandings with Britain. In an attempt to overcome the growing difficulty, Attlee wrote to Truman a long letter, full of feeling, saying that 'our three governments stand on a special relationship to one another ... we believe we are entitled [to full information], both by the documents, and by the history of our common efforts in the past'.[8] But by this time British appeals were to no avail. The President had decided against further collaboration. In August the McMahon Act was passed by the United States virtually eliminating exchanges of nuclear information.

The British decided, in the face of this, to have their own nuclear programme. A Cabinet Committee took the formal decision to build a British bomb on 8 January 1947. It declared: 'We could not afford to acquiesce in an American monopoly of this development.'[9] The rationale behind the decision was partly strategic and partly a question of international status. In other words, it was aimed at impressing both the Soviets and the Americans. If the atomic project was aimed at deterring possible Soviet pressure and at a time of possible American neo-isolationism, it was also designed to have an impact upon the United States. Attlee explained, many years later:

> We had to hold up our position vis-à-vis the Americans. We couldn't allow ourselves to be wholly in their hands, and their position wasn't awfully clear always. At that time we had to bear in mind that there was always the possibility of their withdrawing and becoming isolationist once again.[10]

The British felt they were still a great power, as Bevin indicated in the House of Commons on 16 May 1947: 'His Majesty's Government do not accept the view ... that we have ceased to be a Great Power.'[11] Given such pretensions, they could hardly afford to opt out of nuclear status or become wholly dependent upon the United States. Franks not only shared this outlook but contributed to its maintenance; in the last days of 1948, when Ambassador, he wrote:

> the whole question of our relations with the Americans on atomic energy questions seems to me to be increasingly bound up with the larger issue of the extent to which the Americans are prepared to treat us on more or less equal terms as a first class power.[12]

Britain thus set about its programme hindered by the restrictions of the McMahon Act – it took longer and was more costly. But as Roger Makins, the member of the Foreign Office chiefly responsible for atomic matters, said much later: 'the door to collaboration was *almost,* though *not quite,* hermetically barred by the passage of the McMahon Act', for it persisted in 'two important fields – raw materials and intelligence, where the machinery of collaboration continued without interruption'.[13] Yet the Americans were concerned about the British programme. Should 'the Soviets overrun Western Europe during 1948', they could seize British materials, laboratories and industrial plants.[14]

There was then, a certain coolness in Anglo-American atomic relations until an improvement came with the January 1948 *modus vivendi*. It was the product of talks almost solely between officials.[15] The Americans were keen to obtain British supplies of scarce raw materials as inexpensively as possible, for they expected their own stocks to be exhausted by the end of 1949.[16] It is clear that they also wanted to remove the British veto.[17] By not signing the agreement, they avoided the need to register it with the United Nations or to inform Congress. Instead, the representatives of the three member countries of the CPC declared, at the 7 January meeting, their intention to proceed along the lines of the document. It superseded all previous agreements, with certain exceptions.

So the British calmly forewent the secret right of veto under the Quebec Agreement and even the right of consultation contained in the 1945 memorandum. Recognising that the wartime level of co-operation could not be restored, they hoped that the *modus vivendi* would bring valuable exchanges of information. The British official historian of atomic energy noted that, just six months before the arrival of US B.29 aircraft in England made control of the atom bomb quite critical, British officials casually threw away national rights: 'neither officials nor Ministers showed any concern or interest in the surrender of Britain's veto, or right to consultation on the use of the bomb'.[18]

The second area where wartime co-operation seemed, at least to British eyes, to be replaced by a cooler attitude concerned finance. The economic costs of the war for Britain were immense. The total deficit in the balance of payments on current account, 1939–45, was £10,000 million. More than half of this had been covered by Lend-Lease, leaving nearly £5,000 million to be raised by borrowing or by selling foreign investments.[19] Overseas assets worth £1,118 million had been sold.[20] Most of the borrowing was in sterling. These sterling balances totalled £3,355 million in 1945.[21] Keynes outlined the sombre circumstances for the Cabinet in August. Britain was facing a deficit of £1,200 million per year. During the war this had been met by Lend-Lease arrangements. But now Britain had to pay on the nail for raw materials, food and manufactured goods. The country confronted over the next three years a 'deficit of the order of $5 billion which can be met from no other source but the United States'.[22]

Besides the need to increase production and have marketable goods, there was an extra problem for the British. In 1938 imports from Canada and the United States had been four times greater than exports to them. By 1945 the difference was near to tenfold. This had arisen because the United States and Canada, undamaged by the war, were the world's main suppliers. Unless exports to the United States could be increased, there would be a shortage of dollars to pay for the goods imported from the United States. So the annual shortfall for Britain resolved itself into a shortage of dollars, for there was 'ample sterling around the world to pay for exports from Britain; but if payment was made in sterling, Britain was no further on in finding the means to settle accounts with United States her principal supplier.'[23] Britain thus had the choice of securing credit or facing economic anaemia.

So Keynes went to Washington in September 1945.[24] He asked for $5,000 million plus whatever was needed to settle Lend-Lease, hoping for a grant-in-aid or, at the very least, an interest free loan. Hard bargaining resulted in a US offer of $3,750 million at 2 per cent interest repayable over 50 years from December 1951 with a provision for waiver of interest (but not capital repayments) in years when British overseas earnings fell below certain levels. The second part of the agreement was a generous settlement of Lend-Lease. The net debit of $20,000 million was cancelled; $650 million was charged for US property and goods in transit which Hathaway has estimated were worth more than $6,000 million.[25] Canada provided a loan of $1,250 million. A grand total of $5,650 million was being lent to Britain.

The Loan Agreement, finally signed in Washington on 6 December 1945, had two main conditions. The first involved non-discrimination. US goods must be allowed to enter Britain as freely as similar Commonwealth goods and without quotas. The United States wanted a system of open multilateral trade and non-discriminatory international payments. Wartime talks resulted in the final agreement of the conference at Bretton Woods, New Hampshire on 22 July 1944 which created three institutions: the International Monetary Fund (IMF), the International Bank for Reconstruction and Development, more commonly known as the World Bank, and the International Trade Organisation.[26] The last institution was still-born and replaced in effect by the General Agreement on Tariffs and Trade (GATT) concluded in Geneva in October 1947. The British Parliament's delay in confirming Bretton Woods led the United States to make ratification of the Final Act of Bretton Woods a condition of the loan. Central to Bretton Woods was currency convertibility.[27] Full convertibility within 12 months, then, was the second major condition of the loan. Hence, 15 July 1947, one year after the loan passed Congress, became a most significant date.

The Americans wanted the British to wipe out the sterling balances, just as they had cancelled the Lend-Lease debt. The British did not want to do this. It seemed wrong to renege on debts to very poor countries like India and Egypt. The balances formed part of the reserves of the Bank of England and were available to the Bank, thereby helping to preserve sterling as an international currency. At this time something like half the world's trade was conducted in sterling.[28] Moreover, the balances were seen as assets, as balances not debts, for Whitehall viewed them as reserves of future purchasing power for British exports.

At first, things went quite well for Britain. In the final quarter of 1946 exports reached 111 per cent of the pre-war level. Only $600 million of the loan was withdrawn in 1946.[29] By 1947, however, the situation had worsened. The worst winter since 1881 brought transport, industry and coalmines to a virtual halt for several weeks. The US government's inflationary policies allowed US prices to rise by 40 per cent between settlement of the loan and mid-1947. In 1947, 36.3 per cent of British imports were from the dollar area.[30] There was an increasing cost for the British share of feeding Germany which rose from $5 million per month in 1946 to $20 million a month in 1947. This item alone threatened to take one-tenth of what was left of the US Loan.[31] The onset of the cold war caused continued defence spending. So, at the height of the financial worries, Parliament approved in April 1947 the maintenance of conscription for a period of 12 months service, extended in 1948 to 18 months and in 1950 to 2 years.[32] Drawing on the loan, therefore, accelerated in 1947. Dalton warned the Cabinet, 'we were racing through our United States dollar credit at a reckless and ever-accelerating speed' and predicted 'a looming shadow of catastrophe'.[33]

Confronted with such problems, the Cabinet decided to reduce

Britain's commitments and, where possible, secure the help of the United States. In July 1946 there was Anglo-American agreement to fuse their two zones of occupation in Germany into the Bizone which became effective in January 1947.[34] Then in February 1947 the Cabinet decided to leave India by June 1948, actually accomplished by Mountbatten in August 1947; to refer Palestine, which was under British rule, to the United Nations; and to confirm its decision to end aid to Greece by 31 March 1947. The British Embassy in Washington stressed the importance of Greece and Turkey in the growing tension with the Soviet Union. This led to President Truman's address of 12 March 1947 to Congress. He persuaded them to approve $400 million of aid for Greece and Turkey.[35]

So the difficulties facing Britain were serious even before full convertibility was introduced on 15 July 1947. But catastrophe quickly followed. On 20 August Dalton, the Chancellor of the Exchequer, suspended convertibility. Only $400 million of the loan was left.[36] It was not until their mission arrived in Washington on 18 August that the British revealed to the Americans the gravity of the crisis. The British government, according to Cairncross, had displayed 'extraordinary insensitivity to the need to carry American opinion with them and delayed an approach until the very last minute without putting in hand a credible programme of self-help'.[37] Nevertheless, in two days of talks agreement was reached on an exchange of notes which declared suspension to be 'of an emergency and temporary nature'.[38] In the event it lasted until December 1958. This ended the financial chaos; but it was only with the advent of Marshall Aid, first made available in 1948, that the problem began to ease.

At the very time when Britain's financial problems had reached an acute phase, there came new hope from Washington. In the spring and summer of 1947 the Americans came to appreciate two things about Britain: its importance as an ally in the developing tension with Soviet Russia; and how fundamentally weak was the British economy. This had led to the enunciation of the 'Truman Doctrine'. On 5 March 1947 Dean Acheson, the US Under-Secretary of State, noted that Greece and Turkey were 'only part of a much larger problem growing out of the change in Great Britain's strength'. He then proposed that they study 'situations elsewhere in the world which may require analogous financial, technical and military aid on our part'.[39] George F. Kennan, head of the newly formed Policy Planning Staff of the State Department, said in a memorandum of 16 May that a programme 'be designed to encourage and contribute to some form of regional political association of Western European States' which would aid the economic restoration of Western Europe. He wanted the plan to be agreed in advance with Britain.[40] On 8 May Acheson gave a speech in Cleveland, Mississippi on Europe's dollar shortage and the need for reconstruction.[41]

Meanwhile, Acheson lunched with three British reporters to stress the significance of the impending speech by Marshall at Harvard. In his memoirs Acheson wrote:

> Getting hold of my British friends Miall, MacColl and Muggeridge … I explained the full import of the Harvard [speech] … asking that they cable or telephone the full text and have their editors send a copy to Ernest Bevin with my estimate of its importance. This they did while Miall broadcast the story to Britain from Washington.[42]

So on 5 June Marshall spoke at Harvard and launched the proposal that the European nations prepare a plan for their own recovery and reconstruction which the United States would help to finance.[43]

Bevin's response was immediate. He visited Bidault, the French Foreign Minister, in Paris. They invited Molotov, the Soviet Foreign Minister, to a meeting on 27 June to consider Marshall's offer. Prior to this there were five Anglo-American meetings held in London involving both ministers and officials. Both parties wanted to secure a joint understanding prior to the meeting of 27 June. Bevin suggested an Anglo-American partnership, saying that Britain with its Empire was on a different basis from the rest of Europe. He continued that if Britain were considered 'just another European country this would suit Russian strategy … the Russians in command of the Continent, could deal with Britain in due course'. Clayton for the United States countered by saying that the United Kingdom, acting 'as a partner in the Marshall Plan rather than as a part of Europe, with special assistance to the UK partner would violate the principle that no piecemeal approach to the European problem would be undertaken'.[44] But Bevin maintained that the British 'did not want to go into the programme and not do anything – that would sacrifice "the little bit of dignity we have left"'. This, however, was to no avail. The British had to accept the American position.[45]

On 27 June talks began in Paris between Bidault, Bevin and Molotov. By 2 July the negotiations had broken down, as the Soviets were not prepared to enter into any scheme which involved the disclosure of information about their production plans. As Molotov put it, 'No outside interference in these matters would be acceptable to sovereign states.'[46] Thus did 3 July see Bidault and Bevin invite all the European countries west of the Soviet Union, except Germany and

Spain, to join them in producing a response to Marshall; 14 states accepted and so the representatives of 16 nations met in Paris on 12 July 1947 under Bevin's chairmanship. The conference set up a Committee of European Economic Co-operation (CEEC) to produce a report on what Europe needed to get back on its feet. By an Anglo-French compromise the CEEC met in Paris but had a British chairman.[47] For this task the British government succeeded in prevailing upon Sir Oliver Franks to take temporary leave from his duties as Provost of The Queen's College, Oxford. He arrived in Paris as head of the British delegation and was then made chairman of the CEEC. On 16 July, Bevin made an opening statement to the CEEC and then left matters to Franks. His brief was to identify the main economic needs of the participating nations, establish how these countries could help themselves, and estimate the amount of dollar aid from the United States that would be needed. Franks used his high administrative skills to pursue these goals. He recognised that a committee of all 16 nations would be unwieldy. So he established a six-nation executive committee and four technical sub-committees: Food and Agriculture, Fuel and Power, Iron and Steel, and Transport. Questionnaires were sent out to member countries calling for four-year production programmes for basic industries and services and balance of payments projections, both overall and with the dollar area. Throughout the summer these committees proceeded and the CEEC had little direct consultation with the Americans. Nevertheless there was a consciousness of the US outlook, particularly on the matter of closer European co-operation and the emergence of institutions reflecting such a stance. Indeed, the initial report was subject to some amendment as a result of American reservations about arrangements for including the German Bizone and about the need to produce a more integrated approach.[48] On 22 September the final report was signed. It comprised an 86-page general report and a 355-page second volume containing the reports of the four sub-committees. It recommended $22,400 million aid over four years. Franks's achievement in producing this report was recognised by British and foreign colleagues alike. Edwin Plowden, head of the Central Economic Planning Staff, wrote: 'There is no doubt that the successful conclusion of the report owes much to the way he was able to secure agreement on such a difficult subject from governments holding such divergent views.'[49] Ernst van der Beugel, Dutch representative on the CEEC, observed, 'My generation was spoilt for the rest of our lives by serving under the very best chairman in the very beginning of our careers.'[50]

The production of the report, however, was not to be the end of

Franks's contribution. He was asked to lead a CEEC delegation to the United States to persuade American opinion to accept the proposed aid. Shortly before his departure one observer noted that 'He looked tired but seemed in good form', but added, 'He is very gloomy about the prospects for the UK until we realise how bad everything is.'[51] So he arrived in the United States in October with 'an appreciation that political compromise would then be necessary to persuade the US Congress to appropriate such vast sums'.[52] He made quite an impression. *Time* noted: 'To a spellbound conference of US officials. Franks put on a show they have never forgotten: he talked for $2^1/_2$ hours on the whole European recovery program without notes, pause or repetition.'[53] He was equally adept with individuals, managing to convey the urgency of the need for assistance with tact and a sense of exactly the right tone to adopt with US officials.[54] As a result of his endeavours, President Truman sent a European Recovery Plan (ERP) Bill to Congress on 19 December proposing aid of $17,000 million over four years – less than the $22,400 million of the CEEC report but still a considerable achievement.

As with the question of atomic energy, the turn of 1948 therefore saw an easing of Anglo-American strains over finance. Yet each was to be the source of intermittent irritations throughout the years 1948 to 1952. Perhaps what gave a certain piquancy to these frictions was their association with the wider issue of Britain's place in the world. For behind the British stance on each of these matters was the determination to remain a great power. As Bevin said to Attlee in September 1947: 'I am sure we must free ourselves of financial dependence on the United States as soon as possible. We shall never be able to pull our weight in foreign affairs until we do so.'[55] When the Americans pressed for closer European ties for Britain, for integration, one of the principal economic authorities in the Foreign Office noted how this would be at the cost of links with the Commonwealth which, if carried too far, might lead to the disintegration of the sterling area. This, in turn, might well spell the beginning of the end of the United Kingdom as a world power, for British political power was firmly based on economic foundations: remove the foundation and the political structure would totter.[56]

In the third area of contention between the two powers, Britain's status as a world power also underlay its approach; for the Middle East came to be regarded as an area of paramount importance, particularly after the withdrawal from India. Sir Orme Sargent, Permanent Under-Secretary, felt that if the British Empire were to continue as a 'world power' then it must retain its hold in the Middle East and the Mediterranean.[57] This outlook was reflected in the periodic assessments of British strategic interests. It was not until the global strategy paper of May 1950 that Western Europe overtook the Middle East in importance. It was now argued: 'If we lost the Middle East we would still survive: if we lost Western Europe, we might well be defeated.'[58]

Until doubts arose on a continued British presence in Palestine, the Suez Canal Zone together with Palestine were usually seen as the heart of British power in the region.[59] Interestingly enough, both Churchill, in his last weeks as Prime Minister, and Attlee, had reservations. Churchill felt that Palestine had brought not 'the slightest advantage' to Britain; it would be better to let the Americans take it over. But the Chiefs of Staff argued that the Britain would be seen to have abandoned its predominant position in the Middle East; that protection of its strategic interests in the area 'would virtually depend upon the policy pursued by the United States in Palestine'; and that the Soviets might see an American presence in Palestine as a threat and come to support the Arabs if the Americans adopted a Zionist policy.[60] Attlee's doubts were more wide-ranging. He talked of 'deficit areas', of the need to reassess strategic conceptions and of the importance of avoiding sentimental attachment to past stances. The Chiefs of Staff maintained that the Soviets would take over the ready-made base area of Egypt–Palestine and prejudice the British position in north-west Africa and the Indian Ocean; that Britain needed to remain so as to protect its access to Middle Eastern oil; and that here was an important centre for political influence on southern Europe.[61] When it was clear that the Palestine mandate would be ended, the COS shifted their emphasis to Egypt: 'if we abandon Egypt, we must abandon our status in the Middle East altogether'.[62] Attlee came to accept that there was, after all, a need for a continued British presence in the region. What might have persuaded him was contained in a minute by Gladwyn Jebb, then Assistant Under-Secretary at the Foreign Office. Jebb identified two alternative consequences of withdrawal: either support from and therefore growing dependence on the United States; or US reluctance to continue protecting the British Isles, thereby reducing Britain to a client state of the Soviet Union. He continued:

> In either case the idea of 'Social Democracy', which represents our own 'way of life', would be snuffed out between the rival forces of Capitalism and Communism, and our only role would merely be that of the grain (or perhaps chaff?) between the millstone [*sic*].[63]

Moreover, the Foreign Office (and the Prime Minister tacitly) eventually accepted the COS arguments that the Egyptian base was irreplaceable. The Permanent Under-Secretary's Committee declared in 1949: 'the strategic key to this area is Egypt, to which there is no practical alternative as a main base'.[64]

When the Palestine issue produced Anglo-American discord, then, it affected a central feature of British strategy in the Middle East. After the collapse of the Ottoman Empire in the First World War, Britain assumed control of the territory under a League of Nations mandate.[65] In 1917 the Balfour Declaration talked of allowing 'a national home for the Jewish people', though it stipulated that 'the civil and religious rights of existing non-Jewish communities' must not be put at risk. Increasing Jewish immigration produced an Arab revolt in 1937–39. As the Second World War ended and Jewish suffering in it was revealed, there were high expectations that large-scale immigration by Jews would now be permitted. Truman, on 31 August 1945, urged Attlee to sanction the immediate admission of 100,000 Jews to Palestine. While the British and Americans sought a solution, Palestine saw considerable violence. The most notorious example of this was the bombing of the British military headquarters at the King David Hotel in Jerusalem with the loss of 91 lives. Besides the terrorist pressure, the 100,000 British troops in Palestine had to cope with the steady flow of illegal immigrants by sea many of whom were intercepted and diverted to Cyprus and other locations.

The year 1946 saw unsuccessful attempts at a solution. In a speech on 4 October Truman called for the immediate and unconditional admission of 100,000 Jews to Palestine. According to Morgan, this 'reduced Anglo-American relations to a new, glacial level'.[66] In January and February 1947 the Cabinet tried and failed to find a solution. Bevin, on the advice of his officials, believed that the United Nations would not accept partition: the Soviet bloc plus the Arab states would be able to defeat any such proposal.[67] Left without any other alternative, the Cabinet authorised Bevin to refer the issue to the United Nations which he announced to the House of Commons on 18 February 1947.[68] In May a UN Special Committee was set up. Tension grew in Palestine as ships continued to try and bring illegal immigrants. Meanwhile, the UN Special Committee recommended in August that Palestine be partitioned, with Jerusalem under UN administration. Recognising the multiple difficulties of such a solution, the Cabinet on 20 September accepted Bevin's proposal that Britain surrender the mandate and withdraw its troops by 1 August 1948.[69] The UN General Assembly voted on and accepted the partition scheme on 29 November, by 33 votes to 13 with 10 abstentions (including Britain). British authority in the territory began to wither away as violence escalated. By early 1948 there was virtual civil war.

Palestine was indeed the issue that brought the greatest degree of friction between Britain and the United States. Yet the Middle East did see improved understanding between the two countries. In the face of the growing breakdown in relations between the United States and the Soviet Union the Americans turned to the British on matters of common interest and outlook. By the later months of 1947 this included the Middle East. The 'Pentagon talks' of October–November 1947 saw Palestine 'regarded as a thing apart and not to be debated in these discussions'.[70] The talks covered economic and social as well as political and military aspects of policy towards the Middle East. The discussions were proposed by Bevin, who suggested:

> a joint review of the whole position in the Middle East ... for the purpose of aiming at a gentleman's understanding in regard to a common policy and joint responsibility throughout the area, with Britain acting as the front and ourselves [the Americans] supplying the moral support.[71]

Both the President and the British Cabinet accepted all that their officials had agreed in the talks. Michael R. Wright, Assistant Under-Secretary at the Foreign Office and one of the leaders of the British delegation, summed up: 'The principal result of the Washington talks is that for the first time American policy has crystallised on the line of supporting British policy. It is not the Americans who have altered our policy, but we who have secured American support for our position.'[72] This spirit of co-operation was maintained in a series of letters between British and US officials – first between Wright and Loy W. Henderson, Director of the Office of Near Eastern and African Affairs of the State Department, and then between other officials.[73]

The Middle East was one of four topics discussed on 4 December 1947 by Bevin and Marshall at the US Embassy in London. Dixon, Bevin's private secretary, recorded them as concluding: no agreement or understanding between the two governments on the problems discussed at Washington was agreed; it merely happened that each had presented recommendations that substantially coincided. Dixon added that the Foreign Secretary intended telling Molotov, the Soviet Foreign Minister, that the Middle East was a vital area for Britain but that he would not mention the Middle East talks. By 9 December Marshall agreed that Bevin could refer to the Middle East as a vital area for the British and omit mention of the Anglo-American talks in

Washington.[74] Two days later Attlee reported to the four Dominion Prime Ministers that the government had been disturbed at the attitude of the US government on the Middle East and the eastern Mediterranean. This had led to Foreign Office and Chiefs of Staff representatives visiting Washington in October for talks with their opposite numbers. Virtually identical conclusions on most points had been reached; the two powers had virtually identical and parallel policies without having made an agreement. Both agreed that the area was vital to their security and world peace; that they needed each other to implement this and should thus co-operate; and that the United States would help the British strategic, political and economic position in the Middle East and co-operate with the British government in assisting the countries of the region in their social and economic reform and progress. He urged the premiers to keep this secret.[75]

This theme of Anglo-American partnership should not be pressed too far. The British may have needed US economic and military aid but they did not want to lose their liberty of manoeuvre. Bevin said he 'wanted to keep the Middle East predominantly a British sphere and to exclude the United States militarily from the area'. There was suspicion about what role US military missions would play and about how American economic influence in the region might be wielded. Concern that help in the Middle East might be traded for support of the Americans elsewhere led to British reluctance to discuss additional regional agreements. Furthermore, there were the questions of American reliability and diffusion of 'policy'. Wright said of the 'Pentagon talks':

> American decisions are still apt to be taken piecemeal; it is often the case that various Divisions and various levels of the State Department have different and uncorrelated views on policy, and that the American Service Departments hold different opinions from the State Department (if the State Department has a single view). In the background is the White House where pressure from party managers (e.g. over Palestine) may cut across the advice of the State Department and Service Departments.[76]

CO-OPERATION IN DEFENCE AND INTELLIGENCE

If, after 1945, there were strains over atomic and financial questions and over Palestine, there were two areas of continued collaboration in peacetime. First, there was co-operation between the armed forces and, secondly, there was co-ordination of intelligence activities. In the area of military relations some of the wartime machinery continued. In May 1941 the two countries agreed to exchange missions representing their Chiefs of Staff. In Washington there was the British Joint Staff Mission, at one stage numbering over 4,000 members. Comprising representatives of the services and supply organisations, its central task was to service the Combined Chiefs of Staff, the committee of British and US military chiefs which ran the war. This involved multifarious activities covering tactics, equipment design, exchange of technical information and so on, which would have been beyond the capabilities of the service attachés alone. The Americans had a similar mission in London. Most of these organisations survived the war. The American naval mission continued in London. A US Naval Officer of flag rank was attached to the London Embassy in April 1941. A year later the officer holding this post was also given operational command as Commander of US Naval Forces, Europe. In November 1947 the headquarters of the Commander-in-Chief of US Naval Forces, Eastern Atlantic and Mediterranean was established in London.[77] The BJSM also survived and even managed to secure offices at the Pentagon. Alone among the combined boards, the Combined Chiefs of Staff survived after 1945.

The British were keen to see the same kind of collaboration continue as had existed during the war. The Americans, however, were somewhat evasive. The Combined Chiefs had undertaken two main categories of work: first, the elaboration of joint strategies and tactics; secondly, exchanges of technical and scientific information and training exercises. After the war the first of these activities largely ceased: the Combined Chiefs were divorced from the American postwar planning process. Yet the leader of each of the US services was interested in continued co-operation with his British counterpart. General Eisenhower, Chief of Staff of the US Army from early 1946 onwards, Admiral King and Admiral Nimitz, successive chiefs of naval operations, recorded their support for mutual collaboration, as did Generals Spaatz and General Vandenberg, consecutive chiefs of the US Air Force. The British tried to build on this and secure a level of co-operation similar to that in wartime. The Americans replied, however, by saying that 'it would be impossible for the United States administration to recognise officially a special degree of United States/British collaboration'.[78] Best has summed up the situation:

> In essence the Americans considered that interservice collaboration was acceptable and useful but co-operation on larger questions of defense strategy had to be handled on an ad hoc basis when crises

> arose. In any event, it was not possible to proceed further on major issues of combined defense strategy as long as no consensus existed on American military policy.[79]

There was, therefore, only a limited amount of combined planning for contingency operations. The Trieste crisis in 1946 over the Italo-Yugoslav border produced co-ordinated activities. In October 1946 Eisenhower visited London and held informal talks which were based on the assumption that the British and Americans would be 'in together' in any future world war.

The bulk of postwar co-operation, then, did not concern planning. It covered exchanges of information and various schemes for liaison between the services of the two powers. There were few obstacles to the free flow of information. On 27 February 1946 President Truman approved a 'Basic Policy Governing the Disclosure of Classified Information to Foreign Governments' which allowed the military of the two countries to arrange the passage of data.[80] A December 1946 directive by the Co-ordinating Committee of the US War and Navy Departments said that 'all classified information ... to which the United Kingdom had contributed could be released to the United Kingdom'. It omitted atomic energy but included 'intelligence, technical and scientific information on weapons' and so on – so long as the information was not passed to third countries.[81] Moreover, chemical and biological warfare programmes were 'virtually integrated'.[82]

With regard to service liaison, more far-reaching arrangements were made. The extent to which these were approved by the politicians has been the subject of historical debate. Hathaway maintains that:

> working without the knowledge of their civilian heads, even contrary to the desires of their superiors, a small group of officers took it upon themselves to enter into arrangements with the British which had the effect of tying their two countries together far closer than all but a few imagined.[83]

Best has challenged this view, saying that Truman and successive Secretaries of State were familiar with and involved in continuing schemes for co-operation with the British and Canadians; and that Attlee, at least, was also *au fait* with developments.[84] What seems to have happened is that President and Prime Minister favoured the general principle of liaison at the operational level and then left the detailed tasks to the military. Consequently the Foreign Office and Washington Embassy were often unaware of the arrangements. It took a parliamentary question on the US Naval headquarters in London for the Foreign Office to discover the papers on the matter.[85] In May 1948 Denis Allen, Counsellor at the Washington Embassy, told London he had discovered from speaking to Wailes of the State Department that there was at least one informal agreement on the use of British airfields by USAF aircraft dating from 1945 which was regarded by each side as being in force. He said that it had been recently confirmed in an exchange of letters by the head of the RAF delegation in Washington and General Vandenberg, Chief of the US Air Staff. It was, he continued, the general impression, at least in USAF quarters, that aircraft movements could be arranged directly between the two air forces.[86]

The most significant of these agreements came in mid-1946. In March 1946 the Strategic Air Command, the bomber component of the United States Air Force, was established. Its main task was nuclear warfare. The USAF chief, General Spaatz, had kept in regular contact with the British Air Marshal, Sir Arthur Tedder. Their particular concern was to have effective air strength in Europe to compensate for the weaknesses of ground forces facing the Soviets. Not a single British airfield, however, was equipped to receive the US heavy bomber, the B.29. So Spaatz held talks in England on 25–28 June and 4–6 July 1946 to make arrangements that would allow these atomic-capable bombers to use British bases. The agreement reached, known as the Spaatz–Tedder Agreement, declared that the RAF would prepare four or five East Anglia bases by mid-1947 for the use of US bombers in time of emergency. On 17 August, Colonel E. E. Kirkpatrick of the US 'Manhattan Project' arrived in Britain to supervise the construction of the aprons, loading pits and various buildings necessary, at the chosen bases – Mildenhall, Lakenheath, Bassingbourn, Marham and Scampton. By July 1947 there were regular tours to Europe by bombers of Strategic Air Command. All this had resulted from arrangements that were handled as routine by officials and not through the two governments. There was no public discussion or political debate on the major issues involved.[87]

Meanwhile, in December 1946 the two air forces agreed on the continuation of the wartime collaboration in staff methods, tactics, equipment and research.[88] The following month saw a further agreement concerning officer exchanges for training and visits by senior US Air Force officers to British counterparts.[89] Similar contacts were maintained between the two armies and navies. By early 1948, then, there was extensive liaison between the British and US services. As the Foreign Office files show,[90] diplomats were aware of most of the arrangements. However, they did voice two concerns. First, they were anxious to see that schemes were properly cleared. Hence, Allen's concern in his talk with Wailes in May 1948. But in some ways it was the military departments of state who were most concerned about higher level clearance of locally arranged schemes. So, in February 1948, the Air Ministry was reported as being unhappy that US P.47 flights to Malta and US survey flights of the Middle East were not cleared. Burrows of the Foreign Office minuted, however, that they should avoid a bureaucratic attitude. The last thing we want, he continued, was to appear reluctant to let the Americans into our preserves.[91] Secondly, Bevin said in February that he had no objection to goodwill missions but added that exchanges of visits might be interpreted as tending towards a military alliance. But by the end of the same month, and after the communist seizure of power in Czechoslovakia, he approved a plan involving RAF aircraft going to the United States and Canada, and B.29s visiting Britain.

There were, therefore, many promising features for Britain in its military relations with the United States. The shared outlook of officers from both countries which had emerged during the war had not disappeared. With the end of conflict each power had begun to pursue its own interests rather than those of an alliance. Yet the continued existence of the wartime machinery – the Combined Chiefs and the BJSM – meant the British had access to the higher echelons of the US military. Inevitably, this meant a reasonable likelihood that the British would have some influence. At the lower levels of the military hierarchy there was the continuation into peacetime of Anglo-American co-operation through the exchange of information on staff methods, tactics, equipment and research; and via a whole series of arrangements for training exercises and visits of goodwill, principally by aircraft but also by ships. These contacts were kept informal but did produce what one officer called 'healthy hanky panky' between the two nations.[92] This meant that, if a political decision was taken to pursue a joint defence strategy, it would be easier to proceed, for the foundations were already laid. Moreover, circumstances were moving towards such an outcome. Britain came to assume an increasingly important position in US planning for war in the Western hemisphere: East Anglian air bases were included in schemes to launch an air offensive.[93] Indeed, Admiral Moore of BJSM writing to officials in London urged the achievement of a common appreciation of the defence problem, saying the seasoned British outlook could influence the Americans for the common good.[94]

If Anglo-American defence co-operation was, by spring 1948, better than at any time since the end of the Second World War, collaboration in intelligence undoubtedly contributed to the situation. A good deal of this resulted from the informal contacts between the military. There was also the continuation and development of wartime arrangements. In 1943 Britain had begun supplying the United States with intelligence estimates prepared by the Joint Intelligence Committee and this persisted after the war.[95] After VJ Day the Americans halted the flow of their own estimates. The year 1943 had also seen the BRUSA agreement which aimed at a co-ordinated interception of communications. With the coming of the cold war renewed co-operation was mutually beneficial. The British possessed intelligence services of a size they found difficult to finance, while the Americans had dissolved the wartime Office of Strategic Services and was rebuilding in 1947 with the Central Intelligence Agency (CIA). 'America could therefore use British expertise, staff and installations; Britain needed US financial support.'[96] As a result, the June 1948 UKUSA agreement was concluded.[97] It divided interception of the world's communications between the English-speaking powers – Britain and the United States plus Canada, Australia and New Zealand. Liaison between the British Government Communications Headquarters (GCHQ) near Cheltenham and the US became most effective after the October 1952 foundation of the National Security Agency (NSA) headquarters at Fort Meade, Maryland. And the British received substantial US funds for the GCHQ and other intelligence activities; for the British were felt to have something to offer:

> Since there are many areas, particularly parts of Europe, the Near East and the Middle East where the British sources of information are superior to those of the United States, it is believed desirable that the United States JIC (Joint Intelligence Committee) continue to receive such estimates. This view is reinforced when the present world situation is considered.[98]

It was to take until September 1948, however, before the US Joint Chiefs of Staff would agree to a limited release of US intelligence reports to the British after 'thorough re-editing'.

The CIA was less reticent. It instituted co-operation with a number of different countries, especially Britain. In May 1946 General Vandenberg, the second director of the Central Intelligence Group, as the CIA was known from January 1946 until mid-1947, was given information on British intelligence reorganisation by Commodore Tully Shelley of US naval intelligence from London. He added that Sir Kenneth Strong, the director of the British JIC, was enthusiastic about Anglo-American co-operation and intended coming to Washington in June to present a scheme for a joint intelligence bureau to Eisenhower,

Strong's former commander during the war and now the US Army's Chief of Staff. By 1949 the CIA and British intelligence were involved in regular liaison in both Washington and London. There was also co-operation in the monitoring of foreign broadcasts which was achieved by negotiating arrangements with the British Broadcasting Corporation.[99]

By the beginning of 1948, then, Anglo-American relations were showing signs of improvement. The United States' desire for atomic exclusiveness was a continuing cause of regret but not a daily source of friction. The *modus vivendi* brought a small advance in relations. With the emergence and subsequent passage of the European Recovery Programme financial discord had been lessened, though the associated American interest in greater European integration was to prove a recurring difficulty for the British. On the Middle East in general a common outlook had been achieved. However, Palestine remained a running sore and was, perhaps, the greatest obstacle to better relations between the two governments. While the areas of contention had, with the exception of Palestine, been reduced, the field of co-operation had grown. Military and intelligence collaboration provided a substantial addition. It was upon this increasingly promising foundation that ever closer co-operation was to emerge in 1948–49. The catalyst for this development was the breakdown in relations with the Soviet Union which happened progressively and reached a climax at the collapse of the London Conference of Foreign Ministers in December 1947. In that same month Franks was invited by Attlee to become Ambassador to the United States.

NOTES

1. McNeill, *America, Britain and Russia*, pp. 678–79.
2. H. Pelling, *The Labour Governments 1945–51* (London: Macmillan, 1984), p.54. The Second World War ended at midnight 14/15 August British time.
3. Reynolds, *Britannia*, p.159.
4. Anderson, *United States, Great Britain and the Cold War*, p. 152.
5. Gowing, *Independence and Deterrence* I, p. 94.
6. See, for example, Hathaway, *Ambiguous Partnership* and Anderson, *United States, Great Britain and the Cold War*.
7. Lord Sherfield (formerly Roger Makins), 'On the Diplomatic trail with LBP: Some Episodes, 1930–1972', *International Journal*, Vol. 39, No. 1, 1973–74, p. 77. See also for these developments, James Gormley, 'The Washington Declaration and the "Poor Relation": Anglo-American Atomic Diplomacy, 1945–1946', *Diplomatic History*, Vol. 8, No. 2, Spring 1984.
8. Quoted in Francis Williams, *A Prime Minister Remembers* (London: Heinemann, 1961), p. 117.

9. PRO, CAB 130/18, GEN 163, 1st Meeting, 8 January 1947; cited in Warner, 'Anglo-American Special Relationship', p. 481.
10. Williams, *A Prime Minister*, pp. 118–19.
11. *House of Commons Debates*, Vol. 437, col. 1965.
12. Quoted in Gowing, *Independence and Deterrence*, I, p. 265.
13. Lord Sherfield, 'Britain's Nuclear Story 1945–52: Politics and Technology', *Round Table*, Vol. 65, No. 258, 1975, pp. 194–5.
14. Duncan Campbell, *The Unsinkable Aircraft Carrier: American Military Power in Britain* (London: Paladin, new edn, 1986), p. 98.
15. Jill Edwards, 'Roger Makins: "Mr. Atom"', in John Zametica (ed.), *British Officials and British Foreign Policy 1945–50* (Leicester: Leicester University Press, 1990), pp. 31–2.
16. Edmonds, *Setting the Mould*, p. 89.
17. FRUS, 1950, VII, p.1463; cited in Campbell, *The Unsinkable Aircraft Carrier*, p. 98.
18. Gowing, *Independence and Deterrence*, I, p. 251.
19. Alec Cairncross, *The British Economy since 1945: Economic Policy and Performance, 1945–1990* (Oxford: Blackwell, 1992), p. 47.
20. Ritchie Ovendale (ed.), *The Foreign Policy of the British Labour Governments, 1945–1951* (Leicester: Leicester University Press, 1984), p. 3.
21. *Cmd 6705, Statistical Material presented during the Washington Negotiations* (HMSO, 1945).
22. PRO, CAB 129/1, CP(45)112, Appreciation by Lord Keynes of 'Our Overseas Financial Prospects', 13 August 1945; circulated by Chancellor of the Exchequer, 14 August 1945. Attlee presented the main facts to Parliament, *House of Commons Debates*, Vol. 413, Col. 956 (24 August 1945).
23. Cairncross, *British Economy*, p. 50.
24. See Richard N. Gardner, *Sterling–Dollar Diplomacy* (London: Clarendon Press, 1956), chapter 11.
25. Hathaway, *Ambiguous Partnership*, p. 196.
26. *Cmd 6546, United Nations Monetary and Financial Conference, Bretton Woods, New Hampshire, USA, July 1 to July 22, 1944, Final Act* (London: HMSO, 1945).
27. *Cmd 6708, Financial Agreement between the Governments of the United States and the United Kingdom* (London: HMSO, 1945).
28. Edmonds, *Setting the Mould*, p. 106.
29. Ibid., p. 104.
30. Kathleen Burk, 'Britain and the Marshall Plan', in Chris Wrigley (ed.), *Warfare, Diplomacy and Politics : Essays in Honour of A.J.P. Taylor* (London : Hamish Hamilton, 1986), p. 212.
31. Peter Calvocoressi, *The British Experience 1945–1975* (London: Penguin, 1979), p. 15.
32. Reynolds, *Britannia*, p. 161.
33. Sir Richard Clarke, *Anglo-American Economic Collaboration in War and Peace: 1942–1949*, ed. Alec Cairncross (Oxford: Clarendon Press, 1982), p. 156.
34. On the origins of this decision see G. Warner, 'The Study of Cold War Origins', *Diplomacy and Statecraft*, Vol. 1, No. 3, November 1990, pp.17–19.
35. For the background to the address see Daniel Yergin, *Shattered Peace. The Origins of the Cold War* (New York: Penguin, new edn 1990), Ch. 11; and Robert Frazier, 'Did Britain Start the Cold War?: Bevin and the Truman Doctrine', *Historical Journal*, Vol. 27, No. 3, September 1984, pp. 715–27.
36. Alec Cairncross, *Years of Recovery: British Economic Policy 1945–51* (London: Methuen, 1985), p. 139.
37. Ibid.
38. Ibid.

39. FRUS, 1947, V, pp. 94–5.
40. FRUS, 1947, III, p. 221.
41. J. M. Jones, *The Fifteen Weeks February 21–June 5, 1947* (New York: Viking, 1955), pp. 274–81.
42. Dean Acheson, *Present at the Creation My Years in the State Department* (New York: W. W. Norton, 1969), p. 234. See also MacColl, *Deadline and Dateline*, pp. 173–5 and L. Miall, 'How the Marshall Plan Started', *The Listener*, 4 May 1961.
43. Royal Institute of International Affairs, *Documents on European Recovery and Defence, March 1947–April 1949* (London: Oxford University Press/RIIA, 1949), pp. 8–10.
44. FRUS, 1947, III, pp. 268ff. contain summaries of these meetings by Douglas, US Ambassador in London.
45. FRUS, 1947, III, pp. 284–8.
46. PRO, T236/1890, 'UK Draft Record of Conference of Foreign Ministers', 3 July 1947; cited in Pelling, *Labour Governments*, p. 189.
47. FRUS, 1947, III, pp. 338–470, Paris Conference, 12–15 July, 1947.
48. See Bullock, *Bevin*, chapters 10 and 11 on the whole process, and p. 460 on the question of amendments to the report.
49. Edwin Plowden, *An Industrialist in the Treasury: The Post-War Years* (London: André Deutsch, 1989), p. 29.
50. Ernst van der Beugel, 'Comment' in OECD, *From Marshall Plan to Global Interdependence* (Paris: OECD, 1978), p. 27.
51. Alec Cairncross (ed.), *The Robert Hall Diaries 1947–1953* (London: Unwin Hyman, 1989), p. 7.
52. Peter Boyle, 'Oliver Franks and the Washington Embassy, 1948–52', in John Zametica (ed.), *British Officials and British Foreign Policy, 1945–50* (Leicester: Leicester University Press, 1990), p. 190.
53. *Time*, 26 September, 1949, p. 20.
54. See, for example, Franks to C. H. Bonesteel (State Department), 21 October 1947 in NA, Wash. DC, RG59, State Department Files, Lot 54D170, Records of the Office of British Commonwealth and Northern European Affairs, Labouise File (Economic), 1942–51, Box 1.
55. PRO, FO 800/444, Bevin to Attlee, 16 September 1947, quoted in John Kent, 'The British Empire and the Origins of the Cold War', in Anne Deighton (ed.), *Britain and the First Cold War* (London: Macmillan, 1990), p. 177.
56. PRO, FO 371/68013B, AN669/6/45, minute by Sir E.Hall-Patch, 9 March 1948. The minute was a response to the Washington Embassy's 1947 Annual Report on US foreign policy. A copy of the minute was sent to the Embassy on 27 April.
57. W. R. Louis, *The British Empire in the Middle East, 1945–1951: Arab Nationalism, the United States, and Postwar Imperialism* (Oxford: Clarendon Press, 1984), p. 31.
58. *DBPO*, 2nd Series, IV, pp. 411–31 for the paper; *DBPO*, 2nd Series, II, No. 43, p. 164n for discussion of it.
59. Figures on expenditure confirmed this: 40 per cent of overseas spending went on Palestine and Egypt in early 1948. PRO, CAB 129/25, CP(48)61, 'Overseas Military Expenditure', Joint Memorandum by the Chancellor of the Exchequer and the Ministry of Defence, 23 February 1948.
60. *DBPO*, 1st, I, No. 15, p. 25 (Churchill to Colonial Secretary and to COS, 6 July 1945) and No. 109, p. 28 (minute by General Ismay to Churchill, 12 July 1945).
61. Louis, *The British Empire in the Middle East*, p. 28.
62. Quoted in Edmonds, *Setting the Mould*, p. 120 (Minute to Prime Minister by

Secretary of War (Shinwell) of 9 December 1949). Harvey, Assistant Under-Secretary at the FO, noted 'The Chiefs of Staff will always object to evacuating anything where they have been for some time, just as they will always object to occupying anything where they have not hitherto been', quoted in Louis, *The British Empire in the Middle East*, p. 23.

63. Quoted in Louis, *The British Empire in the Middle East*, p. 31.
64. PRO, FO 800/455, Def/49/20, PUSC(19) Final, memorandum, 'Near East', 30 April 1949.
65. The main features of this outline of the Palestine question are based on Louis, *The British Empire in the Middle East*, Part IV, pp. 383–571, and Ritchie Ovendale, *Britain, the United States and the End of the Palestine Mandate 1942–1948* (Woodbridge, Suffolk: Boydell Press, 1989).
66. K. O. Morgan, *Labour in Power, 1945–1951* (Oxford: Clarendon Press, 1984), p. 123.
67. PRO, CAB 128/9, CM 18(47), CM 22(47) and CM 23(47) for the discussions in Cabinet on 7, 14 and 18 February 1947. See PRO, CAB 129/16, CP(47)28, 'Palestine Reference to the United Nations', memorandum by E. Bevin, 13 January 1947 for advice about partition.
68. *House of Commons Debates*, Vol. 433, Cols. 433, 985–989.
69. PRO, CAB 128/10, CM(47)76, 20 September 1947.
70. FRUS, 1947, V, pp. 488–626. See also PRO, FO 371/68041, AN1197/45/45G, G. Lewis Jones (US Embassy) to M. R. Wright, 9 December 1947, enclosing records. On the talks, see also Richard A. Best, *'Co-operation with Like-Minded Peoples': British Influences on American Security Policy 1945–1949* (New York: Greenwood Press, 1986), pp. 136–41.
71. Quoted in Edmonds, *Setting the Mould*, p. 129.
72. PRO, FO 371/68041, AN556/45/45G, minute by M. R. Wright, 20 January, 1948.
73. See PRO, FO 115/4355, G17/8/48 for the 'Michael-Loy' Letters, 27 November 1947–3 February 1948 which referred to operation 'Handclasp'; and later letters, 12 February – 14 April 1948.
74. PRO, FO 371/68041, AN45/45/45G contains Dixon memorandum on 'The Middle East' and his minutes of contacts with the US Embassy and their replies.
75. PRO, FO 371/68041, AN46/45/45G.
76. Louis, *The British Empire in the Middle East*, p. 112, Bevin's view is in FO 371/61558, minutes of meeting of 8 October 1947, Wright's minute of 14 November 1947 is in FO 371/61559.
77. PRO, FO 371/68025, AN350/20/45G.
78. Best, *Co-operation with Like-Minded*, p. 34.
79. Ibid., p. 36; the main lines of this paragraph are based on Best, pp. 27–43 and Hathaway, *Ambiguous Partnership*, pp. 263–72.
80. Ibid., p.41.
81. Baylis, *Anglo-American Defence Relations*, p. 36.
82. Ibid., p. 37.
83. Hathaway, *Ambiguous Partnership*, pp. 263–4.
84. Best, *Co-operation with Like-Minded*, p. 41n.
85. PRO, FO 371/68025, AN350/20/45G contains the search for papers on the arrangements so as to answer a parliamentary question in January 1948.
86. PRO, FO 371/68034, AN2034/38/45G, Chancery (Allen) to FO, 20 May 1948.
87. This paragraph is based upon Simon Duke, *US Defence Bases in the United Kingdom*. pp. 19–24 and Campbell, *Unsinkable Aircraft Carrier*, pp. 27–8.
88. Hathaway, *Ambiguous Partnership*, p. 270.

89. Notes of the Month, *World Today*, Vol. 16, No. 8, August 1960, p. 319.
90. See PRO, FO 371/68028–68040 for details on military liaison.
91. PRO, FO 371/68016, AN652/15/45.
92. Baylis, *Anglo-American Defence Relations*, p. 37.
93. Duke, *US Defence Bases*, pp. 26, 27.
94. PRO, FO 371/68013B, AN6/6/45, Admiral Moore, Notes on recent talks in Washington, 19 December 1947.
95. Richard Aldrich and Michael Coleman, 'The Cold War, the JIC and British Signals Intelligence, 1948', *Intelligence and National Security*, Vol. 4, No. 4, October 1989, p. 540. See also A. Thomas, 'British Signals Intelligence After the Second World War', *Intelligence and National Security*, Vol. 3, No. 4, October 1988, pp. 103–10.
96. David Reynolds, 'A "special relationship"?', p. 11.
97. C. Andrew, 'Anglo-American-Soviet Intelligence Co-operation', in A. Lane and H. Temperley (eds), *The Rise and Fall of the Grand Alliance* (London: Macmillan, 1995), p. 130. On this agreement see J. Bamford, *The Puzzle Palace: Report on America's Most Secret Agency* (New York: Penguin, 1983); Jeffrey, T. Richardson and Desmond Ball, *The Ties that Bind: Intelligence Co-operation Between the UKUSA Countries* (London: Allen and Unwin, 1985), Campbell, *Unsinkable Aircraft Carrier*.
98. Campbell, *Unsinkable Aircraft Carrier*, p. 125.
99. Trevor Barnes, 'The Secret Cold War: the CIA and American Foreign Policy in Europe, 1946–1956. Part I', *Historical Journal*, Vol. 24, No. 2, June 1981, p. 401.

— 3 —

New Ambassador

WHEN FRANKS returned to government service to chair the CEEC in the summer of 1947 he may have regarded it as merely a task for the Oxford summer vacation.[1] However, even before his trip to the United States as leader of the CEEC delegation in October to November, he seems to have changed his mind. The diary entry for 27 September of Robert Hall, Director of the Economic Section to the Cabinet, recorded a conversation with Franks in Oxford:

> I think that he is very anxious to get back into public life if he can (a) square Queen's, (b) time his reappearance so that he can pull us out of our troubles. He thought that the 40s should replace the 60s – at least the former had some ideas and some knowledge of how to carry these out.[2]

By 15 October Hall's reflections on the matter had led him to act, as he recorded in his diary: 'Saw Plowden later and suggested Oliver Franks as the US Ambassador – he could be just the man to keep the conditions for the loan tolerable. Plowden very favourably impressed and will "float it" as he says.'[3] Edwin Plowden, Chief Planning Officer and Chairman of the Economic Planning Board, approached Franks: 'Both he and his wife were dismayed at the prospect of giving up working with and guiding young people.'[4] Hall noted that 'After a good deal of difficulty … and after a good deal of hesitation, Franks accepted.'[5] On the Saturday before Christmas (20 December), while visiting his parents in Somerset, he was telephoned by Attlee who asked to see him at 11 a.m. on Monday 22nd at 10 Downing Street. At the meeting he was offered and accepted the post of Ambassador.[6]

At the same time the incumbent Ambassador, Lord Inverchapel, was informed of the government's plan to replace him. Franks's name was not mentioned. The Ambassador answered: 'I am only too glad to fall in with your plan. Indeed I had been myself about to make this very suggestion to you.' He added that he wanted to stay long enough to see the Marshall Plan through which he felt would take until the middle of 1948; 'let us aim roughly at June.'[7] Bevin, however, had not planned on a changeover until the autumn.[8] So the timing of Franks's arrival was brought forward to accommodate Inverchapel.[9]

CHOOSING AN AMBASSADOR

There do not appear to be any records of the thinking behind Franks's appointment. It is possible, though, to extrapolate from the facts. After the lacklustre performance of Inverchapel, there was a certain reluctance about choosing another career diplomat. Only Makins of the Foreign Office staff seemed to combine deep familiarity with US affairs with expertise in the key fields of economics and atomic energy. But Makins had encountered the disapproval of Attlee during the war while they attended an International Labour Organisation (ILO) conference in the United States. The then Lord Privy Seal told Dalton: 'He was supposed to be my Secretary, but he tried to run me on a Foreign Office string. I wasn't having it.' Makins had prepared a draft, without first discussing it with Attlee, that proposed Van Zeeland, Belgian Prime Minister 1935–37, to preside over an ILO commission to study postwar problems. Attlee tore up the paper.[10] Moreover, the Washington Embassy had a tradition of receiving appointees from outside diplomatic circles, such as Inverchapel's immediate predecessors, Lord Halifax 1941–46 and Lord Lothian 1939–41. Sir Oliver Franks had already made a favourable impression with the Americans and in the vital area of economics.[11] As with any position, the good opinion of those who chose was important. Much has been made, rightly, of Franks's connexions with Bevin. During the Second World War the then Minister of Labour was most impressed by the civil servant from the Ministry of Supply. Their common background in Bristol also helped to create a personal rapport between them.[12] In addition, there was a certain similarity in their respective approaches to work. Bevin 'could speak beautifully and he could marshal his thoughts ... But he couldn't write.'[13] While Franks could write with great clarity, economy and with force when needed, he too laid emphasis on conducting business orally.[14] Officials traditionally committed their ideas to paper and referred to such papers in discussion. But Franks, like Bevin, was at ease analysing the issues orally; he did not need to look up documents or make notes in order to retain command of his subject. Turning to the relations between Franks and Attlee, less has been made of this connexion. Temperamentally they may have felt in harmony, since both had a somewhat austere demeanour and were not given to wasting words.

Attlee 'was philosophically inclined'[15], something that was likely to bring him closer to the former Professor of Moral Philosophy. Furthermore, they had contacts in the vital area of atomic energy where the Prime Minister 'exercised an especially close personal surveillance.'[16] For the first 12–15 months after the war the key committee helping him in this task was the Advisory Committee on Atomic Energy. Franks served on the committee until he left the civil service in April 1946.[17]

No other candidate could compete with this combination of assets. Although he was comparatively young (being 43 in February 1948), he was a man of weight in the eyes of the Prime Minister and Foreign Secretary and was highly regarded in US government circles. His knowledge of economics and advice on atomic questions were respected. It was felt that his grasp of the functioning of bureaucracies and his talents as a negotiator would be crucial in advancing British policies. The drive he brought to the securing of Marshall Aid, it was hoped, could be directed to other needs. As events unfolded in early 1948, one of the most urgent of British needs was US military support in the form of an Atlantic Pact. Bevin told Franks that: 'he regarded this as probably the most important task of your Ambassadorship; and he relied on you to push this through with the same resolution and speed as you showed over E.R.P.'[18]

The first indication in public of Franks's appointment came in the *New York Times* of 5 February 1948. Sulzberger wrote from London that it was considered almost certain that Inverchapel would be replaced, and that rumours had suggested that his successor would be either Earl Mountbatten, Lord Ismay or Franks. 'However', he continued, 'this correspondent has now been told by a most responsible source that Sir Oliver has been selected.'[19] On 13 February the *New York Times* carried Matthews's report on the Foreign Office announcement of the 12th that Franks was to succeed Inverchapel as Ambassador to the United States. Matthews described Franks as having one of the most brilliant minds in Britain, saying that nobody in his country knew more about the Marshall Plan, and that he was quiet, unassuming, not very sociable.[20]

He was a popular choice among US political circles. An editorial in the *New York Times* at the time of his arrival in the United States in late May referred to 'A Welcome Ambassador.' It continued:

> Seldom has an Ambassador of a foreign nation been so well equipped to deal with the most important specific business at hand as is Sir Oliver Franks ... he came to know, as possibly no other man in Europe, the aims, the possibilities, and the attendant

> responsibilities of the Marshall European Recovery Program. He may, in a sense, be regarded as almost a co-author of that program.[21]

Yet some US diplomats recorded their reservations. Ambassador Caffery from Paris noted that Franks's move to Washington 'has been interpreted as meaning British Government places more reliance on its relationships [in] that city than through CEEC which Franks could undoubtedly have headed on permanent basis'.[22] The implication was clear: the appointment signalled an attempt by the British to deal directly with the Americans rather than as a part of European organisations, as US officials preferred.[23] Douglas telegraphed later from London: 'Personally, I felt that the British made a mistake in sending Oliver Franks to Washington instead of giving him this job in Paris [permanent head of CEEC].'[24] The British had this criticism drawn to their attention in late June by the American journalist, Walter Lippmann. Frank Roberts, Bevin's Private Secretary, rejected the charge that the British were likely to bypass the Organisation for European Economic Co-operation (as the CEEC became in April). Sir Orme Sargent, the Permanent Under-Secretary at the Foreign Office, doubted that this was a cause of concern for the Americans.[25]

Meanwhile, Franks had been busy with preparations for his new post. He wrote to Sargent saying he needed a personal assistant who knew about Washington, Congress and so on.[26] The Ambassador-designate knew the United States but not Washington. Sargent suggested the man who had done the job for Lord Halifax – Angus McDonnell. When Franks met him, he realised he was too old. So Sargent then proposed a bright young Foreign Office man. As he seemed to know no more than Franks, he too was rejected. In consequence of this, Sargent wrote to John Wheeler-Bennett, who had worked for British Information Services (BIS) during the war. After consulting his wife, Wheeler-Bennett decided against considering the position for himself, but, unwilling to disappoint Franks, he suggested Aubrey Morgan who had ended the war as head of BIS in New York and had then retired with his American wife to a farm in Oregon. Wheeler-Bennett later wrote of him:

> With his wide knowledge of the American scene he would be an invaluable adjunct to any ambassador and his extensive wartime experience had given him a powerful insight into the machinations and bewildering byways of the world of public relations.[27]

Sargent was persuaded that Morgan might be the right man. On 22

April, Morgan lunched with Franks and Wheeler-Bennett at New College, Oxford as the guests of Isaiah Berlin, the distinguished philosopher who had worked in the Washington Embassy during the war. After eating, Morgan and Franks had a long stroll in the gardens. Franks felt he had found the right man for the job of helping him to understand the US political process and how political relationships operated; and of 'humanizing . . . [him] for popular consumption.'[28] He said afterwards of their arrangement: 'We had a marvellous relationship.'[29]

MARSHALL PLAN DUTIES

Before he could devote himself more fully to arrangements for his ambassadorship, Franks still had to complete certain duties associated with ERP. On 3 April 1948 the Economic Co-operation Act embodying the programme of Marshall Aid was signed into law by President Truman. An Economic Co-operation Administration (ECA) was established in Washington with Paul G. Hoffman, a Republican industrialist, as Administrator. Averell Harriman, formerly Secretary of Commerce, was appointed as United States Special Representative in Europe. Since late 1947 the Americans had wanted a permanent body to emerge from the CEEC to act as a European counterpart to the ECA; and they wanted it to be a strong organisation with powers of review and criticism.[30] The British, however, took a different view. The London Committee, chaired by R. W. B. Clarke of the Treasury, set up to handle issues concerning the Marshall Plan, reported on 2 March. Its findings were circulated to Ministers on the 6th and discussed by the Cabinet on the 8th. The committee accepted the need for some restrictions on the British so as to pursue worthwhile European co-operation. It saw as the principal target of the new permanent organisation the removal of the 'dollar gap' with the United States. So the committee was ready to see the reduction of intra-European barriers as a way of creating a system of European trade that could function with the minimum use of dollars. There was reluctance to go further than this. The committee recommended that the machinery for achieving these goals 'should be in the hands of the national delegations ... to prevent the secretariat (or an "independent" chairman) from taking action on its own'. This intergovernmental formula was endorsed by the Cabinet.[31]

The CEEC then met in Paris between 15 March and 16 April to try and settle the question of the permanent organisation. Proceedings began with a plenary session of the Foreign Ministers of the 16 nations on 15–16 March. The work of drafting a multilateral agreement on the continuing organisation was then handed over to a Committee of Alternates, chaired by Sir Oliver Franks, which met on 17–18 March. The Alternates in turn set up a Working Party, co-chaired by Berthoud for Britain and Marjolin for France, to reach a solution.[32] On 15 April the Committee of Alternates met again to consider the findings of the Working Party. The next day the Foreign Ministers assembled to give formal approval to the unanimous proposals of the Working Party which represented a triumph for the British point of view. A permanent organisation, the Organisation of European Economic Co-operation (OEEC), would be based in Paris. The Secretary-General would be Robert Marjolin of France; the chairman of the Executive Committee would be Sir Edmund Hall-Patch, Deputy Under-Secretary and leading economic expert in the Foreign Office; and the Chairman of the Council would be Paul-Henri Spaak, the Belgian Prime Minister. Bevin's survey of the successful completion of the CEEC conference ended with a tribute to Franks:

> I think it would be appropriate for me to conclude by mentioning to my colleagues the great debt owed by all the countries concerned to Sir Oliver Franks and his team of assistants and advisers for the part they played in bringing this enterprise so successfully to the end of its first stage.[33]

LEARNING ABOUT ANGLO-AMERICAN RELATIONS

In the month between the end of the CEEC conference and his departure for the United States in late May, Franks was able to turn his undivided attention to considering the state of Anglo-American affairs. His work on the Marshall Plan had brought him into regular contact with Americans. Now he was able to have discussions with officials from the American and other departments of the Foreign Office who had familiarity on a daily basis with the principal aspects of relations between the two powers. He found an improving picture; 1947 had witnessed many causes for concern by the Americans. The harsh winter and its concomitant economic problems, the failure of sterling convertibility and the Grimethorpe miners' strike combined to produce a view from the Middle West that 'John Bull is no longer a heroic figure of sacrifice, but a lazy, inefficient bum.'[34] On 2 September 1947 Robert A. Lovett, Acting Secretary of State, had telegraphed to the London Embassy: 'There is a growing feeling here that there have been too many occasions of British lack of co-operation in the past few months.' He had concluded that the United States 'does not expect gratitude but it does expect friendly co-operation and the exercise of good sense and good faith. We wonder whether we are getting this.'[35] But the Pentagon talks on the Middle East and the conclusion of the *modus vivendi* on atomic questions had helped restore harmony. On a visit to London in December, John D. Hickerson, Director of the Office of European Affairs in the State Department, had been able to tell Michael Wright of the Foreign Office that he thought Britain had floated off the bottom.[36]

Franks was able to read in late April and early May 1948 a series of mainly encouraging reports from the Washington Embassy on the US outlook on international affairs and on US assessments of Britain which covered both her strengths and weaknesses and her stance on various foreign policy issues important to the United States. The Embassy's Annual Survey for 1947 was written by Sir John Balfour, the Political Minister, and forwarded to London in several parts in February. It was recognised by Roger Makins as a superb analysis. The report explained that Americans had recognised since 1945 their country's power and position in the world, but in 1947 it had become widely appreciated among those who helped mould public opinion that the United States had to assume the responsibilities attendant upon its position as the leading world power. This led the average American to accept that his country had a stake in Europe – the earlier call for withdrawal of US troops from the continent had given way to calls for their reinforcement. In the face of what were seen as Soviet attempts to fill the political and economic vacuums left by the Second World War, the Americans felt the need to exert themselves, to build up their military strength so as to be able to resist pressure. F. B .A. Rundall of the Foreign Office American Department minuted that he felt that this was a permanent change in the US outlook, for this new-found power was to the American taste.[37]

The Americans were confirmed in their stance by what was widely recognised as the Soviet-inspired communist takeover in Czechoslovakia in late February[38] and by the announcement of the death in mysterious circumstances of Masaryk, the Czech Foreign Minister, on 10 March.[39] This latter development produced a heightened sense of crisis and led President Truman to address a joint session of Congress when he urged further measures of military preparedness.[40]

In this atmosphere of growing tension the United States quite naturally looked for support from other powers – and turned first to Britain. The Washington Embassy pointed out how British prestige had risen steadily since September; and that by the end of the year

'Britain had to a large extent been restored in the opinion of intelligent Americans as a valuable partner in world affairs.' The despatch added that:

> it is virtually taken for granted by responsible Americans that the destinies of Britain and of the United States are inseparably bound together by the coincidence of the moral and strategic interests. This attitude is particularly marked among members of the Administration with whom the most pleasant and harmonious relations now exist.[41]

The Foreign Office felt this was possible because Americans still viewed world affairs in terms of British interests, through a 'British window'.[42] In his final comprehensive review, which Franks saw just before leaving for the United States, Lord Inverchapel declared that Great Britain had a unique asset now that the risk of war bulked large in the American consciousness:

> in the event of hostilities, our partnership would be more greatly needed, more certainly forthcoming that that of any other foreign power and far more substantial … [this] offer[s] an opportunity to approach the United States Government on a franker, more intimate and trustful basis than is possible for other countries, or even for ourselves within the confines of the European Recovery Programme.[43]

The closeness of Anglo-American ties is confirmed by an evaluation from the US Embassy in London. It noted that the 'US–UK relationship is virtually unbreakable and … we have every reason to be satisfied with development Anglo-American solidarity in last few months.' Yet it added that too much must not be taken for granted: delays in ERP or attachment of conditions offensive to British pride might endanger this solidarity and might even lead to the British having no alternative but rapprochement with the Soviet Union.[44]

However, there were two aspects to the American outlook that were a cause for concern in the Foreign Office. An important change in the US government's attitude to Britain's status was observed: 'Our needs are usually admitted to be greater than those of any other European country, but are not considered so much more urgent as to entitle us to the preferred treatment accorded as a matter of course at the time when the United States loan was made.' Britain was 'now part of the European queue'. Hall-Patch in an important minute said that the Americans did not understand the mechanism of the Commonwealth and of the sterling area; and that their stress on European integration would be at the expense of economic links with the Commonwealth which might lead to the disintegration of the sterling area and which, in turn, might spell the beginning of the end for the United Kingdom as a world power. Makins felt that, if the British wanted to keep ahead of the queue, they must take the lead in western Europe and be seen to take the lead.[45]

In addition there were misgivings about British economic strength. Lord Inverchapel reported that many Americans 'are inclined to question whether any permanent solution can be found for difficulties of balance of payments as deep-seated and intractable as those of the United Kingdom'.[46] Douglas, the US Ambassador in London, was making in private even harsher judgements. He told Harriman that, though the war had aggravated the British problem, the heart of the difficulties was the failure to modernise machinery. Added to this, he continued, was the new commitment to social services amounting to more than a third of the total budget, which needed to be cut so as to facilitate modernisation. He noted a final infirmity, namely the drain of dollars for sterling area expenditures outside the United Kingdom. In the previous year they had reached $1,064 million.[47] The American news media were also drawing a pessimistic picture of the British economy. In discussing a survey of US opinion, officials drew attention to the extent that the British themselves had helped worsen matters. C. J. Child of the Foreign Office Research Department observed that too many members of the English Speaking Union criticised socialist Britain to American friends. M. A. Hamilton of the American Information Department declared that pieces like *The Economist*'s 'On the Rocks' did an amount of harm that it was very slow to offset. Rundall of the American Department enunciated what was to be a central theme of Franks's early ambassadorship: 'We must get across to US public that we need economic help, yet at the same time convince them that we are a good long-term investment.'[48]

Here lay a central feature of discussions which Franks had in the Foreign Office in May. C. F. A. Warner chaired a meeting on 10 May of Franks, Michael Wright, Philip Broad, Alan Dudley and M. A. Hamilton which considered how best to deal with the current American outlook. Discussion was centred on a letter of 9 April by W. P. N. Edwards, head of BIS in the United States. He pointed out that, since June 1947, Britain had stressed its need for ERP. Now that ERP was secured (for the first year at least), he felt Britain should concentrate on building up again the idea of the ultimate strength of Britain and the Commonwealth. Since many Americans had lost sight of Britain's importance as a world power, he maintained that it was increasingly important to develop the themes of its political stability, still considerable military power and industrial potential. He concluded:

> Our aim should be, I think, to cause Americans to regard us, not as a purely European power to be lined up with the rest of the queue of supplicants for US aid, but as the third member of the 'Big Three', whose world-wide position, economic, political and military, is a vital factor in world prosperity and world peace.[49]

In discussion of the letter, there was general acceptance of its central emphasis. It was also emphasised that in speaking of relations with the Commonwealth and with Europe *and* not *or* should be kept constantly in mind. It is interesting that Franks, the most economically astute member of the meeting, should have added a note of caution:

> We shall become sound and have done a lot but we must not suggest that prosperity is 'round the corner'. It is not; and we want United States Aid for the next four years. Willy, nilly, the economic aspect remains dominant.[50]

Franks departed for the United States in the last week of May and, as he recollected, with broadly no guidance from the Foreign Office. Sargent, the Permanent Under-Secretary, told him: 'You'll find out when you get there.'[51] Nevertheless, he took with him a number of ideas that helped shape his stance on arrival. Central to these was the notion that Britain was a world power and not just a member of the European queue. Shortly before leaving he lunched with Churchill who told him of the three circles of the Empire, the United States and Europe. The former Prime Minister added that we should never let the British government get too heavily into one circle.[52] This perspective was confirmed for Franks by his talks with Foreign Office staff. Britain was involved in Europe to an unprecedented extent; indeed it was taking a leading role through the OEEC. But it could not restrict itself to the affairs of the continent, for it had world-wide commitments via the Commonwealth and the sterling area. The Commonwealth, moreover, was essential to Britain's great power status – particularly important now that Britain wished to stress its strength to the United States whose support was seen as a *sine qua non*. All the same, the Foreign Office emphasised that

> while Anglo-American relations must of course be very close, it is essential that the impression should not get about that we in

> Britain are tied to the American chariot wheel. This impression is of course strengthened if American foreign policy appears to shift with every wind, and we are expected to shift with it.[53]

At Cabinet on 27 May, Bevin insisted, and secured the support of his colleagues, that he was not prepared to let American objections to the flow of Britain's dollars to the Arabs, who might use them in the conflict with the Jews, to deflect British domestic policy.[54] At least one senior American seemed to share the British view on an independent line. Dean Acheson, Deputy Under-Secretary of State 1945–47, told Balfour of his high regard for two of the authors of a pamphlet which maintained that Britain would be better acting as a free agent rather than as 'a mere tail on the American kite'.[55]

Accordingly, when Franks set sail for the United States on board the *Queen Elizabeth* on 22 May, he was, as Robert Hall recalls, 'full of ideas about what he will do'.[56] He was conscious of the need to walk the tightrope between economic dependency and independence as a third global power: he had to convince the Americans that the British were an important and reliable force in international politics, that their support was vital to future peace and prosperity but that they needed economic assistance to overcome temporary difficulties.

NOTES

1. Boyle, 'Oliver Franks', p. 190.
2. Cairncross (ed.), *Hall Diaries 1947–1953*, p. 7.
3. Ibid., pp. 12–13.
4. Plowden, *An Industrialist*, p. 28.
5. Cairncross (ed.), *Hall Diaries 1947-53*, p. 20n.
6. Interview with Lord Franks, 24 May 1990.
7. PRO, FO 800/514, US/47/76, Lord Inverchapel to Foreign Office, telegram No. 7140, 22 December 1947.
8. PRO, FO 800/515, US/48/3, Foreign Office to Lord Inverchapel, telegram No. 95, 3 January 1948. Bevin added that, despite rumours, he would prefer not to announce Inverchapel's retirement. Such announcements were not usually made until agreement was granted for a successor, and this was not normally done until one to two months before the changeover.
9. See NA, Wash. DC, RG59, State Department Decimal Files 1945–49, Box 2958, 701.4111/2–548 and 701.4111/2–948 for British pursuit of US agreement to Franks's appointment. President Truman's endorsement was conveyed to the British on 9 February.
10. B. Pimlott (ed.), *The Second World War Diary of Hugh Dalton 1940-45* (London: Jonathan Cape/LSE, 1986), pp. 320–1 (entry for 19 November 1941).
11. There was a Foreign Office appreciation of his work at the CEEC meetings: FO records list it as located at UR 654/21/98. This should be found in PRO, FO 371/71785, since this file covers items UR 589–706. It is not there; it must have been weeded as there is no record of its removal.

12. Boyle, 'Oliver Franks', p. 189.
13. Gladwyn Jebb's recollection in Michael Charlton, *The Price of Victory*, (London: BBC, 1983), p. 46.
14. Franks wrote of his wartime experience: 'Most of my time was spent talking or listening rather than writing', Franks, *University Teacher*, p. 11.
15. Gladwyn Jebb's observation in Charlton, *The Price of Victory*, p. 44.
16. Gowing, *Independence and Deterrence* I, p. 24.
17. Attlee played a larger role in foreign affairs than some accounts suggest. See Raymond Smith and John Zametica, 'The Cold Warrior: Clement Attlee reconsidered 1945–7', *International Affairs*, Vol. 61, No. 2, Spring 1985, pp. 237–52.
18. PRO FO 800/454, Def/48/65, Sir I. Kirkpatrick to Sir O. Franks, 29 November 1948.
19. *New York Times*, 5 February 1948, p. 5.
20. *New York Times*, 13 February 1948, p. 17; see also *The Times*, 13 February 1948, p. 4.
21. *New York Times*, 28 May 1948, p. 22.
22. FRUS, 1948, III, p. 396, Ambassador in France to Secretary of State, 20 March 1948.
23. See p. 33 above.
24. Library of Congress, Manuscript Division, Washington, DC [hereafter L of C], W. Averell Harriman Papers, container 266, Finletter folder, Thomas K. Finletter to W. A. Harriman (US Special Representative in Europe for ERP), 8 September 1948 forwarded text of Douglas to Secretary of State, 31 August 1948; see also FRUS, 1948, III, p. 1119.
25. PRO, FO 800/515, US/48/40, W. Lippmann to P. Jordan (Downing St), 21 June 1948; US/48/41, minute by F. K. Roberts, 26 June 1948; US/48/43, minute by Sir O. Sargent, 29 June 1948.
26. This account is based on interview with Lord Franks, 24 May 1990 and John Wheeler-Bennett, *Friends, Enemies and Sovereigns* (London: Macmillan, 1976), pp. 94–8.
27. Wheeler-Bennett, *Friends, Enemies*, p. 95.
28. The observation of Alan Davidson, the Ambassador's private secretary, Danchev, *Franks*, p. 113.
29. Interview with Lord Franks, 24 May 1990. See also *The Times*, 12 May 1948, p. 3.
30. FRUS, 1948, III, pp. 384–5, Secretary of State to Embassy in the United Kingdom, 29 February 1948; and ibid., pp. 387–8, memorandum by W. T. Phillips for Nitze, 4 March 1948.
31. PRO, CAB 129/25, CP(48)75, 'European Economic Co-operation', memorandum by Bevin and Cripps, 6 March 1948, which contained the London Committee Report; see also Clarke, *Anglo-American Economic Collaboration*, pp. 192–201. PRO, CAB 128/12, CM 20(48), 8 March 1948.
32. PRO, CAB 129/26, CP(48)98, 'The Second Meeting of the CEEC held in Paris from 15th to 18th March', Memorandum by Bevin, 1 April 1948. See also FRUS 1948 III, pp. 395–423.
33. PRO, CAB 129/26, CP(48)109, 'European Economic Co-operation', memorandum by Bevin, 21 April 1948; FRUS, 1948, III, pp. 423–5.
34. PRO, FO 371/61050, AN 3154/28/45, Monthly Political Report Section IV: Sentiment towards Britain, August 1947; see also Anstey, 'Foreign Office Publicity', p. 381.
35. NA, Wash. DC, RG 59, State Department Decimal Files 1945–49, Box 3296, 711.41/9–247, R. A. Lovett to L. Douglas (London), 2 September 1947.
36. PRO, FO 371/68013B, AN 6/6/45, minute by M. R. Wright of 22 December 1947.

37. PRO, FO 371/68013B, AN 667/6/45 and AN 668/6/45, Inverchapel to Foreign Office, 14 February 1948, Annual Survey for 1947, Parts I and II.
38. PRO, CAB 129/25, CP(48)69 of 27 February 1948 and CP(48)71 of 3 March 1948 reported Czech developments for the Cabinet.
39. PRO, FO 371/68018, AN 1118/26/45, Washington to the Foreign Office, 12 March 1948, contains the American reaction.
40. PRO, FO 371/68013B, AN 1198/6/45, Washington to Foreign Office, 17 March 1948.
41. PRO, FO 371/68013B, AN 669/6/45, Inverchapel to Foreign Office, 16 February 1948.
42. PRO, FO 371/68045G, AN 1678/183/45G, minute by A. A. Dudley, 11 March 1948.
43. PRO, FO 371/68014, AN 1997/6/45, Inverchapel to Bevin, 13 May 1948.
44. FRUS, 1948, III, Chargé in UK (Gallman) to Secretary of State, 30 January 1948, p. 1075.
45. PRO, FO 371/68013B, AN 669/6/45, minute by Makins, 8 March 1948 and minute by E. Hall-Patch, 9 March 1948, which was sent to Balfour in Washington on 27 April. Danchev, *Franks*, p. 128 suggests that the Ambassador's later usage of 'the European queue' was Franksian language; but clearly it was not his coinage, for it was already circulating in the Foreign Office before he assumed his mission.
46. PRO, FO 371/68014, AN 1997/6/45, Inverchapel to Bevin, 13 May 1948.
47. L of C, Harriman Papers, container 266, Finletter folder, L. Douglas to A. Harriman, 11 May 1948. Douglas emphasised that the letter 'be handled with great discretion, and receive no circulation'. On the question of the drain of dollars from the sterling area see J. Tomlinson, 'The Attlee Government and the Balance of Payments, 1945–1951', *Twentieth Century British History*, Vol. 2, No. 1, 1991, pp. 47–66.
48. PRO, FO 371/68045G, AN 1678/183/45; *The Economist*, 14 February 1948.
49. PRO, FO 953/156, PAN 557/56/945 contains W. P. N. Edwards to M. A. Hamilton, 9 April 1948, together with minutes on it; and minutes of meeting at FO of 10 May.
50. Ibid.
51. Interview with Lord Franks, 24 May 1990.
52. Ibid.; Lord Franks, 'The "Special Relationship" 1947–1952', in W. R. Louis (ed.), *Adventures with Britannia: Personalities, Politics and Culture in Britain* (London: I. B. Taurus, 1995), p. 56.
53. PRO, FO 371/73070, Z464/2307/72G, F. K. Roberts minute for Sir O. Sargent, 31 May 1948.
54. PRO, CAB 128/12, CM 33(48), 27 May 1948.
55. PRO, FO 371/68013B, AN 156/6/45, Sir J. Balfour to M. Wright, 3 January 1948.
56. Cairncross (ed.), *Hall Diaries 1947–1953*, p. 25 (entry for 20 May 1948).

PART II:
ESTABLISHING A REPUTATION

'There has survived, not by design or by forethought, but almost by accident, a kind of working partnership … There is no alliance now, or political agreement. There is simply the habit of talking over together the main points of common interest and concern … the impression sometimes gains ground that because there is discussion or disagreement that something is wrong with Anglo-American relations … who would wish that two vigorous peoples, each with their own traditions and outlook, could always see eye to eye, or even could always agree readily after discussion.'

Sir Oliver Franks's speech to The Pilgrims, 13 October 1948

'J. W. Davis, as chairman, rose to speak at the close of the Ambassador's address and was visibly moved and said that it was the voice of Bryce speaking once more.'

Aubrey Morgan on Franks's speech, 14 October 1948

— 4 —

First Impressions

FRANKS'S ARRIVAL in New York on 27 May 1948, delayed for 12 hours by fog, coincided with a number of annoyances to smooth Anglo-American relations. The first of these concerned the alleged sale of British jet aero-engines to the Soviet Union. The Washington Embassy reported that administration officials were concerned about the reaction of Russophobes in Congress. It also recorded Harriman's warning about the possible effects upon the British position with regard to ERP. An immediate press release, through BIS, was sanctioned. This announced that no aircraft had been supplied to the USSR since 1945; that no jet engines had been supplied under the Anglo-Soviet Trade Agreement of December 1947; that the Soviet government last year purchased from Britain 55 jet engines which were not on the secret list and were consequently available for general sale; and, finally, that no jet engines on the secret list had been made available and that there was no intention of supplying aircraft or any further jet engines to the Soviet Union.[1]

Secondly, there were the exchanges between Molotov, Soviet Foreign Minister, and Walter Bedell Smith, US Ambassador in Moscow. The Americans asked that these attempts to clarify basic problems in Soviet–American relations remain secret. But, on 11 May, Molotov announced the exchange of messages. Bevin told Washington of his bewilderment and very grave doubts arising out of the failure to inform the British of the intended communication. Inverchapel had a long meeting with the US Secretary of State, Marshall, and two of his senior officials, Kennan and Bohlen. The Americans pointed out that Molotov's announcement from Moscow was misleading and tendentious. They went on to explain that the United States government, concerned about both extreme anti-Soviet feeling in Congress and the growing viciousness of Soviet propaganda, wanted to clarify their position so as to avoid any miscalculation by the Soviet Union which might lead to conflict. Smith was instructed to say that US policy was set and determined but was not intended to infringe upon the legitimate rights and interests of the USSR. Kennan and Bohlen explained that it had been due to an unhappy mishap in the State Department that a telegram had not been sent to London explaining the approach to the Soviet government. Marshall concluded by saying there was no question of Soviet–American discussions. Balfour told Wright on 12 May that, as seen from Washington, one of the reasons why the State Department had made their views known in the Smith–Molotov exchange was British reluctance to respond to their earlier suggestion that the US, French and British governments in concert should place on record at Moscow their attitude in face of Soviet attempts to dislodge them from Berlin. On 14 May Marshall sent a personal message to Bevin explaining the misunderstanding and assuring him that there had been no intention to initiate unilateral talks with the Soviet government on any matters in which Britain or other third parties were involved. This message had arisen from British prompting. Kennan told Balfour that Marshall had reluctantly consented and that it had distressed him that Bevin should cast doubts on American intentions. It was, perhaps, for this reason that the message lacked any sense of apology.[2]

This incident highlighted two recurrent concerns for the British. There was anxiety lest the two superpowers negotiate directly and ignore British interests in any bilateral agreements. In addition, there was the question of the manner in which Anglo-American relations were conducted. As Harriman had noted in 1945 of unilateral American actions:

> They [the British] were ready to support American policies provided they had a chance to thrash out questions before we took decisions, but it was very embarrassing for … their new Labor [*sic*] Government when they had to defend matters with which they did not agree and on which they had not had a chance to express their views.[3]

A far more serious example of US failure to consult arose out of the British withdrawal from Palestine. The gravity of the matter was obvious to Franks the moment he landed:

> Sir Oliver Franks arrived here today in circumstances as unlucky as any new Ambassador has known. The British Consulate and British business offices … were being picketed by Zionists … The newspaper contempt for official British policy and the personal vilification of Mr. Bevin might make Sir Oliver mistake himself for Ribbentrop if he had returned to London after Munich.[4]

On 14 May Truman had disowned the US delegation to the UN and recognised the State of Israel. Bevin received the news with 'extreme displeasure'.[5] Douglas, US Ambassador in London, reported:

> I am convinced that crevasse widening between US and Britain over Palestine cannot be confined to Palestine or even the Middle East. It is already seriously jeopardising foundation-stone of US policy in Europe – partnership with a friendly and well-disposed Britain. Irrespective of rights and wrongs of question, I believe worst shock so far to general Anglo-American concept of policy since I have been here was sudden US *de facto* recognition Jewish State without previous notice of our intentions to British Government.[6]

A Foreign Office appreciation warned that the Soviet Union might benefit from the Anglo-American rift. It might 'gobble up Iraq and make Turkey a satellite, and oil, one of the great resources essential for the material and political recovery will be gone, and enormous power will be placed in the hands of Russia'.[7]

Franks had to face Zionists and others suggesting that retention of ERP aid or a boycott of British goods might be used to coerce the United Kingdom into following the American line. Fortunately for the new Ambassador this was not endorsed by what the Embassy called 'responsible Americans.'[8] A week later the Embassy could say that, despite intense anti-British agitation in New York and other centres of Zionist influence, the country at large, especially the south and the west, did not appear to be taking a great interest in the complexities of the Palestine issue.[9]

Although this was the most pressing cause for concern, there were many other topics that demanded Franks's attention. On 28 June he noted that his first four weeks had been strenuous but enjoyable. He added that he had seemed to have met people from 9 a.m. until 11.30 p.m.[10] Despite this welter of meetings he knew it was important to tackle Palestine and to try and foster a more favourable view of British policies. In a speech he gave without notes to the National Press Club in Washington on 8 June he pursued these ends to great effect. He began by saying that he did not think he would always succeed in saying things which would please all of them, that he would not always be able to tell them all the things they would like to know or think he could tell. But he felt sure that there would be times when they would give him an uncomfortable time which he accepted as 'part of the rules of the game'. Having established his respect for the press, and thereby endeared himself to the reporters, he turned to his task as Ambassador. He wisely stressed his hope of faithfully interpreting American views back to London by acquainting himself with the different spheres of interest and policy and action. Then he directly addressed the question of Palestine. He hoped that it would be possible to find from their different approaches a common solution, and in an atmosphere rather different from that of the last few weeks. He accepted that Britain during the period of its mandate had failed to find a solution:

> Who has not made mistakes? Surely that is not the thing that most matters for the time being. What matters is that we should try to find an atmosphere in which there is not recrimination but an approach to the problems as they are in which, by frank and critical discussion, something can be hammered out.
>
> I do not ask that there should not be criticism. There should be criticism where the proposals that one country or the other has in mind do not seem sensible to the other or the one, but surely no-one is helped – neither country is helped – if bad faith is imputed.

He closed by saying that his first job was to learn more about the United States and that to do that effectively he needed to visit the various regions of the country. He looked forward to learning lessons, a refreshing change from the lectures he had been giving these past few years, when not interrupted by government. He then agreed to take questions from the audience and handled them with a wit and aplomb that impressed his interlocutors. When the final questioner asked whether the British regarded themselves as mediators or partisans in the United States-Russia 'cold war scrap', he answered: 'we were with you on this issue ... I do not wish to be understood ... that the whole of the rest of our attitude ... would be exactly the same as yours part for part but on the big issue the answer all the way down the line is "Yes".'[11]

In a personal letter to Franks on 18 June Bevin praised him, saying that it was quite clear from several reports that the Ambassador had already earned golden opinions in Washington and started his mission there as well as the Foreign Secretary was sure that he would. He added that he was particularly glad about the handling of the Palestine issue. It was no good avoiding big issues and, in any case, the Americans usually responded to explanations of our policy when given in the right way. The Foreign Secretary also reassured him about the parliamentary question of 14 June on Franks's remark that Britain was on the American side in the cold war.[12]

Within weeks of his arrival Franks had made three important advances. By declaring support for the United States in the cold war with the Soviet Union he was able to hearten members of the 'foreign policy public' and government officials at a time when tensions were developing over Berlin. His direct and open approach to Palestine created a calmer climate for discussion of the issue in the United States. He advised London to downplay criticism of the boycott of British goods in the United States when confronted by a parliamentary question on the matter. He added that the less that was said the better, if the British were to squeal too much it would only encourage the instigators.[13] The Anglo-American policy difference remained, but the animosity associated with it had been lessened. Finally, the new Ambassador had succeeded, by his easy and receptive demeanour, in laying the foundations for establishing a good reputation.[14]

The first six months or so of his ambassadorship were dominated by three major issues. First, there was the question of European recovery. This involved high-pressure negotiations for a bilateral agreement on ERP which were completed by the end of June. Thereafter, there were intermittent exchanges about integrating the sterling area and the extent of British commitment to closer ties with Europe, and the working of the ERP machinery. Secondly, there was the German question, or, more precisely, the Soviet blockade of the British, French and US sectors of Berlin. This was handled mainly between the Foreign Office and the US Embassy in London. Thirdly, there was the pursuit and then conduct of negotiations for a North Atlantic treaty which was eventually signed in April 1949. The talks took place in Washington and provided the principal task for the Ambassador and his senior staff up to early 1949.

THE BILATERAL AGREEMENTS ON ERP

Once ERP aid had passed Congress in April 1948, an elaborate machinery was constructed to help run the project. The Economic Co-operation Administration (ECA), led by Hoffman, controlled matters from Washington. The OEEC, based in Paris, was its European counterpart. To help in this task Averell Harriman acted as the US Special Representative in Europe for ECA. In addition the Americans had a mission to each country receiving ERP aid. Thomas K. Finletter was the leader of the London Mission, which was attached to the US Embassy. On top of this, each country had its own organisation. Britain had the London Committee which liaised with the country mission and the Paris Committee which liaised with the OEEC. Before this bureaucracy could begin effective operations, agreement had to be reached on the allocation of aid. During the Congressional debates it had been decided that the money would be voted annually. Each of the participating governments had to reach bilateral agreements with the United States so as to release the funds for the first year.

Draft master Economic Co-operation Agreements were circulated to missions in OEEC countries by the State Department on 30 April. But by 2 June, Lovett, Under Secretary of State, was expressing his concern about the slow progress of these missions. He urged the US representatives to make clear to the governments to which they were accredited that, if agreement was not concluded by 3 July, the EC Administrator would have no choice but to suspend assistance until such time as an agreement was concluded.[15] Franks therefore arrived in America at the very time when the issue was at its most pressing. He was an appropriate individual to handle the bilateral agreement talks. In August 1947 when he had been chairing the CEEC and when it had been expected that there would be a general European agreement with the United States, he had proposed that Britain should hold bilateral negotiations with the United States over ERP and take advantage of its special position with the Americans.[16]

Before Franks's arrival, his predecessor, Lord Inverchapel reported to London that the Embassy had considered the draft among themselves and at the weekly informal meeting with the representatives of the other participating countries. He noted that there was a general feeling, which the Embassy fully shared, that the wording of the draft was unfortunate in certain respects and neglected the susceptibilities of the European parliaments. But this was unhappily common, he continued, in a document drafted by US lawyers and, short of rewriting the whole of it, there was little they could do about it. He concluded that 'we think that in general we should be well advised to swallow the blemishes of form and to limit our objection to points of substance'.[17] Meanwhile the London Committee had set up a Working Party chaired by Berthoud to study the draft and prepare a submission to ministers on important matters of principle. Its findings were to be presented to the London Committee on 2 June.[18]

The Cabinet Economic Policy Committee met on 3 June to consider the US draft and hear from the chairman of the London Committee, Leslie Rowan. He felt that the 'tone of the draft is unfortunate', that the wording of the text could give rise to differences of interpretation and that there were certain articles which were 'definitely unacceptable'. Further objections were raised at a second meeting of the Economic Policy Committee on 8 June.[19] In a minute for Franks by Hoyer Millar, Minister at the Embassy, on 10 June all the major British concerns were outlined.[20] The British wanted the deletion of three articles. First, was the obligation to 'locate and identify' British assets in the United States and put them and their earnings 'into appropriate use', a matter on which the government felt it had done as much as it could. Secondly, was what seemed like an attack on nationalisation – US citizens' claims for compensation, when their property or interest had been affected by government action, could be put to the International Court of Justice. Thirdly, there was the important worry that the stipulation that Britain maintain a 'valid' exchange rate and consult the United States would allow the Americans to put special pressure on the government to alter the exchange rates. There were also four clauses that the Ambassador sought to amend. First, was the matter of the colonies which were defined as part of the United Kingdom in the draft. It was proposed that the colonies be consulted and that an accession clause be included. Secondly, were the undertakings to do things in the internal economy and in trade relations with the rest of the world – 'balancing the budget' and 'reducing private and public barriers to trade'. The objection related mainly to the form of article, to ensuring that its language did not provoke political difficulties. Thirdly, there was the American ability to terminate or suspend aid at any time, while Britain could not terminate its obligations before 30 June 1953. The government wanted the right for both parties to be able to terminate the agreement on six months' notice. Fourthly, there was the question of most favoured nation status which proved a major stumbling block in negotiations.[21] The Americans proposed it for Anglo-American trade in a way that would limit British tariffs without placing restrictions on American ones. It seemed as though the US Treasury was continuing its fight against the position of the pound and British trading policies. The Americans also wanted most favoured nation treatment for certain of its occupied territories. Britain was ready to accept this for Germany but was opposed to the inclusion of Japan and Korea; it did not seem logical to link Japanese trade with the ECA; and Commonwealth governments were strongly opposed to granting most favoured nation (MFN) rights to Japan in advance of a peace treaty.

The British were concerned not only about the substance of the terms, but also about their tone and their likely political impact. Hoyer Millar pointed out that the bilateral agreements were as much political as economic. It was important that they were drafted in a way that took full account of the susceptibilities of participating countries and that they 'should not be worded in a way which will give a handle to those sections of opinion, or to those hostile countries which profess to see in the Marshall Plan an instrument of American economic penetration of Europe'.[22] Bevin told Franks that very close Anglo-American relations were necessary, but if the impression were created that, whenever US foreign policy shifted, the British were expected to shift with it, there may be an outcry against Britain falling to 'the position of a vassal state'. Then, referring to ERP difficulties, he said that they should draft agreements in a way that avoided the appearance of US domination. He ended by saying that he knew Marshall liked straight talk and that, unless Franks saw any objection, he would be glad if these remarks were passed on orally more or less in the language used.[23] The Ambassador replied that he did not want to send a message via Lovett, Under-Secretary of State, but preferred to see Marshall privately.[24] Clearly he felt this was not the type of message that should be passed via a deputy but he was not able to do so until 14 June.

Before that, Franks saw Thorp and others at the State Department on the morning of 11 June, when he outlined the general British attitude to the US draft, emphasising in particular the provisions which gave rise to acute difficulty in substance and presentation so far as Britain was concerned. He concluded of the meeting: 'My general impression is that we shall find the State Department sympathetic and understanding of our difficulties but that their hands will be largely tied by what Congress has written into the act and by legislative history.'[25]

It was agreed that a Working Party, made up of representatives from the State Department, the French, the Danes and the Swedes, should examine the issues. The first meeting took place on the afternoon of 12 June and lasted 4 hours. The Embassy's account of proceedings said that the Swedes were silent, the British took the lead and were well supported by the French and Danes. It was agreed that discussions be informal and without commitment on either side, the object being to produce a report to be considered by Thorp and the ambassadors as soon as possible, showing articles on which agreement could be reached at the Working Party level and on an *ad referendum* basis, and questions of principle on which no agreement could be reached at that level. The telegram observed that the Americans were friendly and understanding of British difficulties, but repeatedly emphasised the extent to which they were bound either by the terms of the act or by legislative history. The meeting was devoted to a general survey of the agreement (both US and French texts were being considered), with a view to isolating the main points of difficulty and to seeing on which articles agreement could possibly be reached at the Working Party level subject to drafting changes. There were more meetings on the 13th to pursue this programme and try and secure a Working Party text.[26]

Franks finally saw Marshall on the 14th when he communicated essentially the same words as used by Bevin.[27] During their conversation the Ambassador was able to say that he had already had a satisfactory talk with Willard L. Thorp, Assistant Secretary of State for Economic Affairs, on the ECA bilateral agreement. Although Thorp would not be able to make all the changes in the draft which the British might have liked, nevertheless, he had indicated that he was ready to meet the British views as far as possible.

By 15 June a further set of exhausting meetings had resulted in a revised draft being produced for submission to the four Ambassadors and Thorp. The Embassy reported the general position as being complete impasse at the Working Party level on three major points: the articles concerning exchange rates, Germany and Japan and the termination clause. On other points the revised text had been agreed *ad referendum* at the Working Party level, subject to reservations on specific points by the British, French and Danish representatives and to the inclusion of various points in an interpretative minute. Although the Americans had agreed to treat most favoured nation status for Germany outside the agreement, the Embassy failed to secure any of the major safeguards it wanted on this question. The Embassy noted that the discussions had been friendly but it had been difficult to secure any substantial concessions owing to State Department fear of criticism by Congressional representatives if they appeared to weaken the original draft from the form shown at the watch-dog committee. It concluded:

> We judge that when the Ambassadors see Thorp we will get satisfaction on some of the reservations we have made on relatively minor points. We find it difficult to predict the American attitude on the major points but our feeling, though we are not optimistic, is that concession on or even withdrawal of Article X may not be so difficult to secure by determined negotiation as any modification of attitude about Germany or Japan or concession about the termination clause.[28]

Before meeting Thorp and other State Department officials to try to thrash out these differences, Franks sent a telegram marked for Roger Makins. He said that they could not tell how the meeting with Thorp would go but that they would try to get a position by that evening, when the major points would have been isolated, and on which progress could be made pending receipt of fresh instructions from the governments. He added that they would be sending a telegram that night indicating points on which ministerial guidance from London would be necessary. He guessed that they would be pressed to resume discussions on the morning of 19 June, particularly as the Scandinavian representatives were anxious to get an agreed text by 22 June. He suggested that they might wish to take preliminary steps to enable ministerial instructions to be obtained the next day and telegraphed to the Embassy in time for the further meeting with Thorp on the morning of the 19th.[29]

There was also a sympathetic attitude from US representatives in London. Bevin saw Finletter on 17 June and stressed that it was essential to avoid the impression that the US government was seeking to impose particular solutions upon European countries. Finletter agreed.[30]

Yet sympathy and a friendly relationship did not remove real difficulties on substantive questions. The negotiations came close to breakdown on 17 June following six hours of talks. Franks summed up:

> the concessions to which the Americans have been brought today after a difficult struggle clearly do not go as far as you want. Throughout the discussion the Americans were for the most part reasonable and understanding of our standpoint but were constantly dominated by their apprehension of Congress past, present and future. They regarded themselves as rigidly bound by the specific provisions of the Act ... They were also terrified of the effect on Congress of any manifest weakening on their part – either immediately in the short period before Congress goes into recess or in the critical period when the second appropriation is under discussion. And although Thorp was throughout reasonable and inclined to accommodation he was (as so often happens) hagridden by the fears of the lawyers.
>
> My general feeling is that we may be able to get further limited concessions but that ... the number of other substantial points on which we can reasonably hope to get concessions ... is limited.[31]

The Foreign Office answered that more time was needed to consider these important questions in a meeting which could not be held before 21 June.[32] Meantime, on the afternoon of the 18th there was another meeting of the Working Party.[33] There was a further meeting with Thorp on the 19th. The Americans agreed to drop Article V (concerning exchange rates) with the hope that when the agreements were debated by the parliaments of participating countries a common line would be taken, namely, that there was provision for general consultation, which included consultation relating to the establishment of a valid exchange rate. The Embassy also secured some textual improvements on certain articles. Most favoured nation status for Germany and Japan remained an open issue, although the Americans had agreed to a limitation in time. They said, however, that they would have to stand firm on Japan. [34]

But, after some serious reflection, the State Department issued on 19 June a revised draft, meeting some of the British concerns. The most important concession in British eyes was acceptance of a termination clause for both parties.[35] This eased the situation but did not resolve it.

On the morning of 21 June British ministers met and went through the Bilateral Agreement, raising objections to a number of articles in their current form – including the proposal that each country declare a readiness to include consideration of exchange rates in general consultation which was offered as a replacement for Article V.[36]

There were further inconclusive meetings with Thorp on 22 and 23 June.[37] Franks assessed how matters stood. He felt they had arrived at a very difficult phase as regards time. The other powers had no further points to raise. So when they met the next day Britain would be alone which, if it became public, might have adverse political repercussions; and the agreement as it stood was sure to be published in some country in the following two to three days. Thorp told Franks privately after the meeting of 23 June that the United States had reached the limit of concession.[38]

The British now decided that an initiative needed to be taken in London. On 22 June Hector McNeil, Minister of State at the Foreign Office and responsible for the bilateral negotiations, saw the US Ambassador, Lewis Douglas. McNeil appreciated the excellent work done by Thorp and Franks in Washington, but he felt 'over-riding political considerations' had emerged justifying talks with the Ambassador and their transmittal to the US Secretary of State. In fact, McNeil was hoping that he could secure the support of someone who was both friendly to Britain and influential in Washington; and Douglas was both of these things. McNeil said that there were three 'breaking points'; unless the Americans could meet these points, there was no likelihood of Parliament approving the agreement. First was the unwillingness to accept most favoured nation status for Japan and Korea. Secondly, the British could not accept the phrase 'will take all possible steps' in the article on general undertakings. This would impinge upon British sovereignty. The Cabinet would accept a phrase like 'will use their best endeavours'. Thirdly, was the need to include with the clause on locating remaining British assets in the United States an interpretative minute explaining that Britain had already done all that was required on this point. Douglas forwarded these observations to Marshall with the remark that a postponement of the parliamentary debate, owing to a failure to reach a bilateral agreement, might well 'aggravate the relatively strong feeling here that the US is behaving precisely as Molotov predicted we would behave'.[39] Undoubtedly, Douglas's attitude was further influenced to make this report by Sir Roger Makins, who accompanied the US Ambassador from Oxford to London on the evening of the 23rd and went through the Agreement clause by clause.[40]

Meanwhile, Sir Stafford Cripps, Chancellor of the Exchequer, circulated to the Cabinet a memorandum which Plowden says was drafted three months earlier by the Cabinet Economic Section. It warned of the serious consequences of a failure to secure an agreement. There would be no Virginia tobacco, cuts in food rations, and perhaps 1.3 million unemployed in industry because of raw materials shortages. Moreover, the reserves would be reduced to the dangerously low level of £270 million by the year's end in order to finance the balance of payments deficit.[41] When the Cabinet considered Cripps's memorandum on 24 June the situation remained grave; and it was noted that Franks had telegraphed to say that Britain could no longer look for support from other participating countries in obtaining a better draft, for they had all reached agreement.[42] However, the deadlock was about to be broken. After the Cabinet, Attlee and Cripps saw Douglas. They said the Agreement had never been discussed from the political point of view. Parliament was unlikely to accept it in its present form. Rejection would inevitably lead to the breakdown of the Western Union and give impetus to the communist advance in Europe and gravely prejudice close collaboration with the United States. Douglas undertook to telephone Marshall at 2.30 p.m. BST.[43] Their demarche worked, for US negotiators in Washington were subsequently more willing to meet British concerns – Franks reported good progress in talks on 24 June.[44] As a result, only one difficulty remained – most favoured nation status for Japan. After further meetings with British Ministers,[45] Douglas urged strongly that this point not be pressed and Hoffman felt 'the economic recovery program should not be jeopardized by insistence' on this article. These thoughts were conveyed to the White House personally by Thorp. They secured the President's approval. With that, a bilateral agreement was reached on 26 June. Its formal signature took place in London on 6 July.[46]

Although under considerable economic pressure to gain ERP aid, the British had managed to stand out for better terms. The willingness of the United States to compromise reveals the importance they attached to even an economically straitened Britain. As a State Department Policy Statement said on 11 June: 'British cooperation is not only desirable in the United Nations and in dealing with the Soviets; it is necessary for American Defense.'[47] In January, Gallman, Chargé at the London Embassy, had warned of the dangers of attaching conditions to ERP that were offensive to British pride, for that might lead to the British having no alternative but to pursue rapprochement with the Soviet Union.[48] With the communist coup in Czechoslovakia and the growing Soviet restrictions on movements to and from Berlin culminating in a full blockade on 24 June, there seemed little prospect of Britain turning to the Soviets. However, there was a certain wariness that Britain might be cool towards the United States if treated harshly over the bilateral agreement.

Given these broader political considerations, it is not surprising that the breakthrough came in London and not in Washington. What persuaded Washington was evidence that Parliament would not accept the terms of the draft of 19 June. Only the first-hand reports of Douglas could convey this. Franks had greatly helped the completion of the agreement by establishing a congenial atmosphere for the talks and by a creative and constructive approach to drafting. Thus had the texts of most of the difficult clauses been settled. It took movement at the highest level to overcome the final obstacle, and the main credit for this must go to Douglas.

This episode helps to identify the scope of influence open to ambassadors. Whatever their abilities, they cannot achieve their countries' goals if the crucial lever for movement is not in their control. In this case, what was decisive was first-hand knowledge of the true state of British opinion which was something the United States would want to see established by its own representative and not reported to them by the British. Moreover, that representative needed to be someone held in high esteem by his government. Douglas fulfilled both these requirements – as did Franks in other, converse circumstances. The negotiations for a bilateral agreement on ERP reveal how an ambassador's energies could frequently be directed to persuading his own government to change its mind.

NOTES

1. PRO, FO 371/68018, AN 1801/16/45, Washington to FO, 30 April 1948; PRO, FO 115/4361, G35/8/48 Inverchapel to F0, 30 April 1948 and G35/9/48, BIS Press Release, 30 April 1948.
2. PRO, FO 115/4361, G35/19/48, G35/20/48, G35/23/48, G35/24/48, G35/29/48, G35/30/48, G35/36/48, G35/48/48, G35/49/48 contain details of the issue. C. E. Bohlen, *Witness to History 1929–1969* (New York: W.W. Norton & Co., 1973), pp. 276–7.
3. W. Averell Harriman and Elie Abel, *Special Envoy to Churchill and Stalin 1941–1946* (London: Hutchinson, 1976), p. 509.
4. *Manchester Guardian*, 29 May 1948, p. 4, report by Alistair Cooke.
5. PRO, FO 371/68655, E6758, minute by M. R. Wright, 15 May 1948.
6. FRUS 1948, V, Part II, p. 1031, Douglas to Lovett, 22 May 1948.
7. PRO, FO 371/68650, E7032/G; see also Louis, *The British Empire in the Middle East*, p. 113.
8. PRO, FO 371/68018, AN2134/16/45, Washington to FO, Weekly Political Summary, 28 May 1948.
9. PRO, FO 371/68018, AN2164/16/45, Washington to FO, Weekly Political Summary, 4 June 1948.
10. PRO, FO 800/515, US/48/42, Franks to Bevin (letter), 28 June 1948. Franks delivered his credentials to President Truman on 3 June. See PRO, FO 371/68045G, AN2195/183/45 and Harry S. Truman Library, Independence, Missouri [hereafter HSTL], Official File (hereafter OF], Vol. 48, Box 215.
11. PRO, FO 371/68045G, AN2275/183/45, D. Allen to M. R. Wright, 8 June 1948 enclosed the text of the speech and noted the praise on all sides for the Ambassador's grasping of the Palestine nettle.
12. PRO, FO 800/515, US/48/38, Bevin to Franks (letter), 18 June 1948; Parliamentary Debates, *House of Commons*, Vol. 452, Col. 22–24.
13. PRO, FO 371/68072, AN2408/2408/45, Franks to FO, 26 June 1948.
14. See *New York Times*, 9 June 1948 p. 2 and *Washington Post*, 9 June 1948 for favourable assessment, the latter praised Franks for being 'free from prepossessions'. See also Beverly Smith, 'Britain Tries a New One on US', *The Saturday Evening Post*, 13 November 1948 pp. 30, 180, 182. The author notes 'He got off to a good start. He spoke without notes and answered hard questions extemporaneously, without once dodging behind the screen of "off the record"... And he relaxed an audience braced for icy intellectuality, with unexpected slants of humor.'
15. FRUS, 1948, III, p. 445. A copy was delivered to the British Embassy on 13 May, ibid., p. 1108n.
16. PRO, FO 371/62576, UE7598/6169/53, memorandum by R. W. B. Clarke, 16 August 1947. See also, Anstey, 'Foreign Office Publicity', p. 383.
17. PRO, FO 371/71897, UR1646/1511/98, Washington to FO, Tel. No.2373, 19 May 1948.
18. PRO, FO 371/71897, UR1848/1511/98, minute by P. H. Gore-Booth, 26 May 1948.
19. PRO, CAB 134/216, EPC(48) 20th Meeting, 3 June 1948, CAB 134/218, EPC(48)48, T. L. Rowan, 'Draft Economic Co-operation Agreement between the United Kingdom and the United States', 2 June 1948; CAB 134/216, EPC(48) 21st Meeting, 8 June 1948. Also at PREM 8/768. See also, Cairncross (ed.), *Hall Diaries 1947–1953*, p. 26 (entry for 9 June).
20. PRO, FO 115/4417, 'Bi-lateral Agreements', minute by F. R. Hoyer Millar, 10 June 1948.

21. The clause in a trade agreement between two countries stating that each will accord to the other the same treatment on tariffs and quotas as they extend to the most favoured nation with which each trades. *Oxford Dictionary for International Business* (Oxford: Oxford University Press, 1998).
22. PRO, FO 115/4417, 'Bi-lateral Agreements', minute by F. R. Hoyer Millar, 10 June 1948.
23. PRO, FO 800/515, US/48/35, Bevin to Franks, 3 June 1948.
24. PRO, FO 371/73070, Z4673/2307/72G, Franks to FO, Tel. No. 2634, 4 June 1948.
25. PRO, FO 371/71898, UR2185/1511/98, Franks to FO, Tel. No. 2764, 11 June 1948.
26. PRO, PREM 8/768, Franks to FO, Tel. No. 2796, 13 June 1948.
27. FRUS, 1948, III, pp. 1108–9.
28. PRO, FO 371/71899, UR2271/1511/98, Franks to FO, Tel. No. 2836, 15 June 1948; see also ibid., UR2278, Franks to FO, Tel No.2837, 15 June 1948 which contains the text of the draft as amended by the Working Party.
29. PRO, FO 371/71900, UR2323/1511/98, Franks to FO, Tel. No. 2877, 17 June 1948.
30. PRO, FO 800/515, US/48/37, Record of a conversation by R. Makins, 17 June 1948. See Cairncross (ed.), *Hall Diaries 1947–1953*, p. 25 (entry for 20 May 1948) on Finletter: 'We could not have had a more sympathetic appointment.'
31. PRO, PREM 8/768, Franks to FO, Tel. No. 2898, 17 June 1948.
See PRO, FO 115/4410–4416 and FO 371/71897–71906 for detailed reporting on the talks in Washington.
32. PRO, FO 371/71900, UR2348/1511/98, FO to Washington, Tel. Nos 6606 and 6607, 18 June 1948.
33. PRO, FO 371/71900, UR2371/1511/98, Franks to FO, Tel. No 2916, 18 June 1948.
34. PRO, PREM 8/768, Franks to FO Tel. No. 2940, 19 June 1948.
35. FRUS, 1948, III, p. 454n; Cairncross (ed.), *Hall Diaries 1947–1953*, pp. 28–9 (entry for 21 June 1948): 'US have been very conciliatory and most of the points are settled, especially the termination clause which was most difficult for us.'
36. PRO, FO 371/71900, UR2348/1511/98, FO to Washington, Tel. No. 6699, 21 June 1948.
37. PRO, FO 371/71901, UR2476/1511/98, Franks to FO Tel. No. 3008, 22 June 1948; ibid., UR2510/1511/98, Franks to FO, Tel. No. 3050, 23 June 1948.
38. PRO, FO 371/71901, UR2521/1511/98, Franks to FO, Tel. No. 3048, 23 June 1948; PRO, PREM 8/768, Record of a Conversation (Franks's telephone call at 11 p.m. on 23rd) by Sir Roger Makins, 24 June 1948.
39. FRUS, 1948, III, pp. 1109–13, Douglas to Secretary of State, 23 June 1948.
40. PRO, FO 371/71902, UR2543/1511/98, minute by Sir Roger Makins, 23 June 1948.
41. PRO, CAB 129/28, CP(48)161, Chancellor of the Exchequer, 'Economic Consequences of Receiving No European Recovery Aid', 23 June 1948; Plowden, *An Industrialist*, p. 42.
42. PRO, CAB 128/13, CM 42(48), 24 June 1948.
43. PRO, FO 371/71902, UR2539/1511/98, FO to Washington, Tel. No. 6805, 24 June 1948.
44. Ibid., FO to Franks, Tel. No. 3086, 24 June 1948. PRO, CAB 128/13, CM 43(48), 25 June 1948.
45. PRO, FO 371/71902, UR2539/151/98, FO to Washington, Tel. Nos. 6881 and 6903, 25 and 26 June 1948.

46. FRUS, 1948, III, pp. 457–8, memorandum by the Secretary of State to President Truman, 26 June 1948; PRO, FO 115/4410, 1514/244/48 Franks to FO, Tel. No. 3144, 26 June 1948; *Cmd 7446*, Economic Co-operation Agreement between the Governments of the United Kingdom and the United States of America, initialled ad referendum, 26 June 1948.
47. FRUS, 1948, III, p. 1091.
48. Ibid., p. 1075, Gallman to Secretary of State, 30 January 1948.

— 5 —

Cold War Allies

NO SOONER HAD FRANKS declared at the National Press Club on 8 June 1948 that Britain was on the US side in the growing cold war than the confrontation intensified. The two remaining major issues – once the bilateral agreement was reached – in the first phase of Franks's ambassadorship were related aspects of this development. There was a breakdown of relations with the Soviet Union on Germany. Crisis point came with the Berlin blockade of June 1948 to May 1949. Communist takeovers in Eastern Europe and fears of them in France and Italy, as well as anxieties over the Near and Middle East, had already produced a desire for enhanced military security. It was increasingly felt, particularly by the British, that economic aid had to be augmented by US military assistance. The communist takeover of February to March in Czechoslovakia and the end of Allied co-operation over Berlin heightened the pressure for talks on defence arrangements between Europe and the United States.

THE BERLIN BLOCKADE

As Bevin told the House of Commons in October 1946, agreement on Germany was 'the touchstone of relations between the four powers'.[1] At the Yalta and Potsdam conferences Germany was divided into four zones of occupation to be administered by an Allied Control Council, comprising the commanders-in-chief of the four zones. Berlin was split into four sectors and governed separately by an Allied Kommandatura. Each power could take freely from its own zone and the Soviet Union was authorised to take certain proportions of materials from the Western zones. Absent from Yalta and Potsdam, France not surprisingly distanced itself from the decisions. It obstructed the creation of a central administration with its pursuit of the annexation of the Saar and the separation of both the Ruhr and the Rhineland from Germany. Before long, however, Soviet obstructionism in Berlin and looting of its own zone and a failure to supply other zones were causing difficulties.[2]

A series of Councils of Foreign Ministers (CFMs) revealed increasingly irreconcilable differences. Failure to agree on a settled economic regime for Germany resulted in the establishment of the Anglo-American Bizone in January 1947. By the Moscow CFM of March 1947 differences had grown sharper, a situation made clear by the announcement, two days into the meeting, of the Truman Doctrine which promised US assistance for Greece and Turkey (and by implication other peoples) which faced subjection by armed minorities or outside pressures. The launch in June of the idea of the Marshall Plan, which treated Germany as part of the European economy, produced a hardening of the division between East and West. The London CFM of November–December 1947 constituted a watershed. Four-power co-operation over Germany collapsed amid bitter recrimination. With no progress on the question of recreating a united Germany, the US Secretary of State, Marshall, felt that there was no point in debating the other items on the agenda and moved that the meeting be adjourned. Immediately following this, Bevin, Marshall and Georges Bidault for France met informally to discuss their next moves.[3]

From the breakdown of the London CFM there flowed two sets of developments. First, there were the British-inspired efforts towards Western consolidation – what Bevin called the 'Western Union' – in response to the perceived danger of Soviet expansionism. This led to the Brussels Treaty of March 1948; and then to talks about US support for European security, that is, for some type of North Atlantic Pact. These were pursued by the Washington Embassy and formed the principal diplomatic task for Franks between June 1948 and March 1949. Secondly, there was the deepening cleavage over Germany. As the Western powers set about establishing a politically and economically distinct Western Germany out of their three zones, relations had quickly moved to a climax by the summer of 1948. In the first major crisis of the cold war Britain was on the side of the United States less than three weeks after Franks's speech. Developments over Germany provided the vital background to the conversations on a pact, for the timing and pace of those talks were influenced by the breakdown over Berlin.

Talks on the future of Germany took place in London between February and June 1948, and involved Britain, France, the United States and Benelux. Despite stern Soviet disapproval, agreement was reached by all the powers. A communiqué of 7 June announced what became known as the London Programme: the integration of West Germany into the European economy; an international authority, with German representation, to control the Ruhr which would remain part of Germany; the continued presence of British, French and US troops; and the establishment of a constituent assembly to draft a constitution for a federal government.[4]

The adoption of the London accords meant the effective end of four-power co-operation on Germany. Events moved rapidly to a conclusion. On 16 June Sokolovsky left the Kommandatura. On 18 June the three Western Military Governors told the Soviet Military Government that on 20 June a new currency would replace the Reichsmark in the Western zones, except for Berlin. The next day the Soviets introduced new travel restrictions for Berlin. On the 23 June they distributed their own currency in their zone and Berlin. Clay, US Military Governor, without consulting Washington, but after talking to the British Military Governor, who fully agreed, and to the French deputy Military Governor, who reluctantly acquiesced, announced that West German marks would now be circulated in Berlin on 24 June. The Soviet response was a complete surface blockade – road, railway and water – of Berlin from 6 a.m. on the 24th.[5]

It took a little while for an Allied policy to emerge. In the first days, Shlaim notes, 'Washington seemed almost paralysed by crisis-induced stress' while France exercised 'virtually no influence over American policy'; it was Britain who 'moved with greater speed and decisiveness in making its basic choice to stay in Berlin'. From the beginning, Bevin advocated a firm stance, advising that Berlin be supplied by air. He established a special committee of ministers, the Berlin Committee, to oversee the problem. On 6 July the British, Americans and French sent a joint note largely on the lines recommended by Bevin.[6] It maintained that the Berlin agreements were being violated; that the Western Allies would not surrender their rights; but that they were ready to enter talks to solve difficulties, provided the transport routes were reopened.

Although Britain and the United States were acting as cold war allies over Berlin, Franks and the Embassy did not play a central role. On 26 June Bevin proposed to the US Ambassador, Douglas, that London be the centre for discussions (by the Allied Ambassadors) rather than using 'the circuitous method of communicating directly with the British Embassy in Washington which in turn communicates with US'.[7] Marshall accepted the procedures the next day.[8] There seem to have been two reasons behind Bevin's thinking. First, he wanted to keep London as the centre for consideration of Germany. The CFM of 1947 and the conference of 1948 had both addressed the German question in London. The Foreign Secretary did not want to see all Allied policy discussion move to Washington. While this might have been motivated by national pride, Bevin's second reason lay in his belief that this was the best way to tackle the problem. If the US capital became the centre for decision-making, then Allied policy might be affected by the hesitations and uncertainties of US officials. Marshall accepted London as the location for co-ordination, for he felt that handling the question in both Washington and London would produce confusion.[9]

This meant, then, that Franks did not play a crucial role in handling the crisis. He largely confined himself to clarification of Bevin's position. His conversation of 11 September with Marshall and Bohlen was typical. The Ambassador said he had nothing to add to the message he had delivered from Bevin, since he knew the Americans were familiar with its views. He added, though, that 'in thinking it over he thought he might be able to make somewhat plainer the thoughts that lay behind Mr. Bevin's position'.[10]

There was, however, one major decision arising out of the blockade that did involve Franks – the question of moving US bombers to Britain. This issue was handled not through the Ambassadors' committee, but bilaterally through the two Ambassadors, Douglas and Franks. At their meeting on 26 September Bevin had raised with Douglas the possibility of sending more heavy bombers to Europe, for this would show 'that we are in earnest'. Marshall had then suggested that two or three B.29 bomber groups might be moved to Britain, which the Berlin committee approved on the 28th.[11] But Bevin was in no hurry to see the despatch of the aircraft, lest it be construed as aggressive. He wanted the diplomatic response to be settled before any military action was taken.[12] By 12 July, however, Douglas had agreed with the British that they need not await the Soviet reply to the note of 6 July. The Berlin Committee decided on the 13th that the United States should be asked to send the two squadrons at once. The request was conveyed to Marshall not by Douglas but by Franks after receiving strictly personal instructions from the Foreign Secretary which were to be kept on the Ambassador's private files. Bevin urged his envoy to stress to Marshall that publicity about the move of the aeroplanes 'should carefully avoid direct connexion with present situation over Berlin and should take the line that these are long range heavy bomber exercises'.[13] By the time Franks was able to see the Acting US Secretary of State, Robert Lovett, the next day, the Soviet reply to the 6 July note had been received.[14] Yet this did not deflect the Americans from deciding in the National Security Council on the 15th to send the B.29s.[15] The first two groups arrived on 17 July; a third one arrived in August. The *New York Times* of 16 July announced their despatch and added that they were nuclear-capable.[16] We now know, however, that they were neither adapted to such payloads nor were there the bombs available for deployment.[17]

The arrival of the bombers suggested to both the United States' allies and to the Soviet Union that the United States was prepared to consider bombing Moscow. Yet in Parliament the government maintained that the movement was the result of 'informal and long-standing arrangements between the USAF and the RAF for visits of goodwill' and that they were 'to carry out long-distance flying training in Western Europe.'[18] This was, indeed, partly true. On 10 February Bevin approved a USAF request for on average once monthly B.29 flights from Germany over the United Kingdom. France had refused this request the previous summer and the Americans were reluctant to approach them again.[19] On 27 February the Air Ministry sought approval for RAF aeroplanes to visit Canada and the United States in July and for US B.29s to visit Britain. Earlier in the month Bevin had declared that he had no objection to goodwill missions, though he felt that exchanges of visits might be interpreted as tending towards a military alliance. But now, following the communist coup in Czechoslovakia, he was less circumspect. He approved the plan but added 'don't let Russia become an obsession'.[20] On 3 April the Foreign Office declared that, in view of recent political developments, there was no longer a need to approach them over each joint exercise.[21] So acceptance of the aircraft emerged from training exercises but the decision was a conscious development of them and was timed to have an impact on the blockade. Bevin sought the best of both worlds: to make the Soviet Union wary of a bomber force within reach of its capital, while declaring that it was there for exercises only and not for sabre rattling.

Bevin explained the situation to the Cabinet Defence Committee in September:

> the intention was that all three groups of aircraft should remain in the United Kingdom as long as the Berlin crisis continued. No definite proposal that one or more of the groups should be stationed in this country on a more permanent basis has yet been made … this is a question that can only be considered at a later date in view of the political situation then existing … it is no part of the intention of the United States Government to maintain their Air Force in this country if their presence is not desired.[22]

The Americans, however, were already thinking of a permanent presence. The US Secretary of Defence, James Forrestal, has an entry in his diary for 15 July saying 'We have the opportunity now of sending these planes, and once sent they would become somewhat of an accepted fixture.'[23] By 13 September the Americans wanted to investigate with the British the possibility of having buildings capable of holding atomic bomb components at two British airbases, Lakenheath and Scunthorpe.[24]

While Franks had been the channel for conveying the decision about B.29s, he had not contributed to the decision. He was, however, to be centrally involved in subsequent attempts to negotiate an understanding about American use of the bases which, by 1949, could include launching an atomic bomb attack. In December 1950 Attlee visited Washington when there was talk of the United States using nuclear weapons in the Korean War and secured an oral undertaking to consult on atomic matters. In September–October 1951 the Ambassador achieved an agreement, endorsed by Churchill in January 1952, which has remained the essential basis for United States use of the airfields and related establishments.[25]

Meanwhile, efforts were made to talk with the Soviets. Charles Bohlen, head of the Berlin group in the State Department, visited Britain and France to investigate the possibility of conversations with Stalin. It was agreed that the three powers' Ambassadors should make a co-ordinated approach to Moscow.[26] On 2 August they met Stalin who suggested lifting the blockade if there was a simultaneous introduction in Berlin of the Soviet zone mark in place of the Western mark. He added that he would no longer ask, as a condition, for the deferment of the implementation of the London decisions. Washington's response, however, was cool, an outlook confirmed by the long, gloomy and uncompromising talks between the three envoys and Molotov on 6, 9, 12 and 16 August, leavened only by a convivial discussion with Stalin on the 23rd.[27] The seven meetings of the four Military Governors between 31 August and 7 September served to reveal the major obstacles. They were unable to agree on a joint report.[28] The deadlock lasted until January 1949, despite submission of the issue to the UN Security Council in October.[29]

TALKS ON A NORTH ATLANTIC PACT

If the involvement of Franks and the Washington Embassy in the crisis over Berlin was limited, the contribution to the setting up and pursuit of talks on a North Atlantic Pact placed the Ambassador and his staff at the centre of Anglo-American developments. For the main task was to persuade American opinion – in government, in Congress and among the public – that military arrangements with the Europeans were crucial. The main burden of such work had to be undertaken in the United States.

After the collapse of the London CFM in December 1947 Bevin spoke to Bidault and Marshall about arranging some sort of federation of the West as protection against Soviet advance.[30] The Foreign Secretary developed these ideas in a Cabinet Paper, 'The First Aim of Foreign Policy', on 4 January 1948. Russian encroachment could only be prevented through some form of Western Union, a Western democratic system with the backing of the Dominions. He added: 'We in Britain can no longer stand outside Europe and insist that our problems and position are quite separate from those of our European neighbours.'[31] On Bevin's instructions, Inverchapel sent Marshall a summary of the Cabinet paper and said that as a first step the Foreign Secretary was proposing to Bidault that Britain and France jointly offer a treaty to Belgium, Holland and Luxembourg.[32] In a letter of 20 January to the British Ambassador, Marshall said 'we heartily welcome European initiative' and 'I wish to see the United States do everything which it properly can in assisting the European nations.'[33] With this encouragement Bevin publicly announced his ideas to the House of Commons on 22 January. The deterioration of relations with the Soviet Union, he maintained, necessitated a drawing together of the free nations of Western Europe. Talks would soon begin with France and Benelux to conclude a treaty for self defence. Although he did not refer to US participation, he suggested that other historic members of European civilisation might be included.[34] For the next two months he sought to involve the Americans, proposing very secret talks with them on the whole question of Western security.[35]

The context of the pursuit of these talks lay not only in the breakdown of the London CFM but also in the search for worldwide co-operation with the Americans. The Washington Embassy was at the centre of activities. October–November 1947 saw conversations on the Middle East.[36] Admiral Moore of BJSM, reporting on the atomic energy talks which resulted in the *modus vivendi* of January 1948, lamented the lack of a common assessment of the defence problem. He proposed that the Combined Chiefs of Staff be instructed to draw up an appreciation of the time factor and the defence problem as a whole. It could be the foundation for discussion of atomic policy, but also for strategic planning arising out of the Middle East talks and any other subsequent conversations. Our 'seasoned' outlook, he maintained, could be an influence for the common good. Makins, the Foreign Office representative at the talks, supported the idea. On 23 December 1947 Bevin agreed to it.[37] Meanwhile Alexander, Minister of Defence, investigated how Far Eastern questions could be examined on the model of the Middle Eastern ones. A report of 6 January 1948 proposed three different types of discussion: by the BJSM on current topics; Foreign Office-led political-strategic ones; and more detailed military planning involving the Joint Planning Staff. The Chiefs of Staff maintained that Western European talks were more urgent and instructed their staffs to prepare briefs for both Western European and Far Eastern talks. Having examined the Middle East, Far East and Europe, they believed, it might be possible to 'produce one complete world-wide survey on which to base co-ordinated strategic plans for war'. On 28 January Bevin said he hoped the Far Eastern talks would not be extended to include discussion of Western Europe. The aim was to show the United States that Britain was not only interested in Western Europe, which was being raised separately.[38]

As over ERP, Britain was keen to be a partner of the United States and not just one of the European queue. US military assistance was seen, like US economic aid, as a temporary necessity. Bevin wanted to build up a Western Union separate from the Americans. When he sent a summary of 'The First Aim of Foreign Policy' to Marshall, he omitted the references in the original to how 'the countries of western Europe ... despise the spiritual values of America' and

> Provided we can organise a Western European system ... backed by the resources of the Commonwealth and the Americas it should be possible to develop our own power and influence to equal that of the United States of America and the USSR. We have the material resources in the Colonial Empire, if we develop them, and by giving a spiritual lead now we should be able to carry out our task in a way which will show clearly that we are not subservient to the United States or to the Soviet Union.[39]

This omission seems to have come largely as a result of the advice of Sir Norman Brook, the Secretary to the Cabinet. In a note to the Prime Minister, he observed, 'Can we be confident of securing American support for a policy which is based on overseas publicity designed to show that the policies of the British government represent a golden mean between the disastrous extremes of Russian communism and American capitalism?'[40] At least one American, John D. Hickerson, Director of the Office of European Affairs, favoured this independent (though not antagonistic) approach. He felt that there might be a US role in the European defence scheme provided it was at the Europeans' request, for the 'important aspect of this question was ... that any such concept should be and should give the impression that it is based primarily on European initiative'. Moreover, 'he had envisaged the creation of a third force which was not merely the extension of US influence but a real European organization strong enough to say "no" both to the Soviet Union and to the United States.'[41]

Marshall and his Under Secretary, Robert Lovett, however, were more cautious; the latter being wary about the possible consequences of the British proposal within the United States.[42] But the prospects for the British suggestions were promising because of the nature of the State Department under Marshall, which gave Hickerson the opportunity to promote the case for an Atlantic pact. It had been neglected by President Roosevelt. Although Truman turned to the Secretary of State as his main source of advice, the department did not thrive under his first appointee, James Byrnes. It was George Marshall who brought order and efficiency to it. The State Department never returned to its previous administrative practices, its report of 1970 concluding that Marshall had done more than any other secretary since the war to improve its organisation.[43] An austere man of great stature who personified a sense of duty,[44] he established more effective channels of communication and achieved a clear line of command. 'Believing in staff work and deeply secure in himself, Marshall willingly placed responsibility for policy-making on subordinates from whom he invariably garnered loyalty and respect.'[45] He preferred difficulties to be resolved before they reached him, for his under secretary to bring him more or less completed proposals. This led US foreign policy to be partly a product of bureaucratic struggles at the second echelon of government. Figures below the secretary could play an important role.

So Marshall left matters in the hands of his deputy, Robert A. Lovett. Franks had seen a lot of him in 1947 during his American visit to promote the CEEC report. A Texan educated at Yale and Harvard Law School, he was '[u]rbane and genial, of physical spareness'. Although his 'tongue … could cut with suavity', he displayed great skill in his dealings with Congress. He enjoyed a remarkable rapport with Marshall, a closeness 'similar to the mental processes of identical twins'.[46] It was Hickerson, however, who played the crucial role. He had developed an enthusiasm for close and powerful Anglo-American relations during the Second World War. More than any other US official, he was sympathetic to Bevin's ideas. The Office of European Affairs became under him 'an institutional bastion of support for a security pact in which the Americans would participate'.[47] Moreover, he proposed the form for the pact that was to shape the eventual agreement: a regional collective security pact like the Treaty of Rio whereby an attack on one should be regarded as an attack on all. As he lacked Lovett's close access to the Secretary of State, Hickerson had to deploy his considerable talents as a bureaucratic in-fighter to secure his goals.

When Bevin outlined his ideas in an aide-memoire to Marshall on 11 March he advanced three schemes: a British–French–Benelux system with US backing; an arrangement for Atlantic security with which the United States would be even more closely concerned; and a Mediterranean security system which would particularly affect Italy.[48] In practice, this meant two schemes, since the Mediterranean concept was given less stress in this forum. Britain, therefore, wanted to develop a Western Union, with US backing, that would be equal to and independent of the United States. But they also wanted to be the United States' special partners.[49]

By this time events were helping the British case for talks. The communist coup in Czechoslovakia and General Clay's claim on 5 March that 'war may come with dramatic suddenness' led Truman to ask 'Will Russia move first?' On 8 March Hickerson favoured US involvement in a North Atlantic–Mediterranean regional defence arrangement and suggested talks in pursuit of such a scheme.[50] Thus on 12 March the Americans agreed to talks.[51] On the 17th, Britain, France and Benelux concluded the Brussels Treaty of Self-Defence;[52] and Truman told Congress, while proposing new measures of military preparedness, that Brussels deserved the full support of the United States.[53]

Highly secret talks took place in Washington from 22 March to 1 April between the British, Americans and Canadians. While they were held in the Pentagon building to ensure secrecy, civilian and military officials played a secondary role. Military planning did not have a prominent place in US foreign policy-making. 'During much of 1948 the American military turned in on itself in the so-called unification battle . . .[between] the Army, Navy, and Air Force ... Nor did the Joint Chiefs of Staff offer substantive advice.'[54] During these talks London continued to stress the need to treat the Atlantic Pact and Brussels separately. Indeed, Kirkpatrick, Deputy Under-Secretary at the Foreign Office, rebuked Jebb, Assistant Under-Secretary and chief negotiator in Washington, saying that there was 'no need to abet the Americans in blocking our idea of two defence systems'.[55] But the agreed text at the end of the discussions, subsequently called the Pentagon Paper, visualised a single set of negotiations. It also raised the possibility of a declaration by the US President saying that the United States would consider an armed attack against any of the Brussels powers as an armed attack against itself.[56] Throughout April and May Britain tried unsuccessfully to develop the Pentagon recommendations in a new set of talks.

Franks, therefore, took up his duties as Ambassador when progress towards a North Atlantic Pact had slowed. He sought to persuade the Americans to begin conversations with Britain, France and Canada in the face of three obstacles. First, there were the doubts of Kennan and Bohlen within the State Department about a Pact. Bohlen felt a pact would provoke the Soviets, while Kennan believed that a formal pact was unnecessary when there were US troops in Europe. Both thought that a Senatorial Resolution would be enough – though Kennan also favoured military aid to fill European gaps.[57] But this was less of an obstacle than the British thought: 'Too much had been agreed already – with Vandenberg, with the British and Canadians – for Kennan to block the momentum towards an alliance. Similarly, the continued reservations of the Joint Chiefs of Staff were ineffective.'[58]

The second hurdle, the need to carry Congressional opinion, was more of a cause of delay than an obstacle. In this Lovett took the key part. He saw the President, the first time that Truman had been approached seriously about the suggested pact, and obtained his approval for conversations with prominent Congressmen. Vandenberg, chairman of the Senate Foreign Relations Committee, was then coaxed by Lovett into sponsoring a resolution backing the idea of US support for European defence. The Vandenberg Resolution received the unanimous backing of the Senate Foreign Relations Committee on 19 May and was passed by the full Senate, 64 votes to 6, on 11 June 1945.[59] The third difficulty centred on the US need for evidence of European military co-operation. Lovett suggested that the way ERP had been handled could serve as a model: the Brussels powers might devise a scheme for common defence and then have discussions with the Americans. Prior to these talks, he added, the United States wanted the Europeans to answer a questionnaire on their military plans.[60] The Brussels powers formed a military committee on 30 April and answered the questionnaire on 14 May.[61] In the face of a further request to commence quadripartite talks, Lovett told Balfour that 'there is no possibility of completing the necessary negotiation of these matters in time to permit Congressional consideration at the present session'. He proposed exploratory talks between the adjournment of that session (mid-July) and its reconvening in January 1949.[62]

The first days of his ambassadorship saw Franks pressed by London to secure a date for quadripartite talks,[63] but he did not want to send yet another letter to Lovett to this effect. He preferred to wait to see Marshall personally who was tied up with ERP.[64] The resulting delay caused impatience in the Foreign Office, which Franks answered by saying the State Department had been approached twice daily and was apologetic about the hold-up.[65] Eventually on 14 June

Franks met Marshall and Kennan. He said he inferred from them that the Americans were ready to enter discussions about a treaty in the near future but that they were undecided about its form and the exact timing of the talks.[66] Franks's personal involvement seemed to work, for on 24 June the Americans proposed beginning talks on the 29th or 30th, later postponed to 6 July. They favoured British representatives taken from their Washington staff. They felt that bringing Jebb over from London would only heighten interest.[67]

Between 6 and 9 July there were five meetings of the Washington Exploratory Talks, or Ambassadors' Committee as it was known to officials. Franks was joined by his fellow Ambassadors: Bonnet for France, Van Kleffens for Holland, Silvercruys for Belgium and Luxembourg, Wrong for Canada. Lovett was the senior US representative, and he acted as chairman, though the Foreign Office wanted Franks to take the initiative.[68] This was made easy by Lovett's reluctance to take a lead: he was content to let the British and Canadians make the going. At the second meeting Franks suggested, and the committee accepted, a procedure for security of records known as Metric. This involved sending only 18 copies of agreed minutes (brief summaries of the principal points) or other documents by accompanied bag to the Metric registry of the Foreign Office which would then distribute them elsewhere.[69] Franks assumed the role of drafter of these documents; he was, in the words of the Foreign Office, 'the guardian of the Metric shrine'.[70] At the same meeting he proposed that the 'whole agenda should be considered from the point of view of the community of interest on both sides of the North Atlantic'.[71] He thereby managed to establish an approach that largely pervaded the talks right up to the signature of the Pact, though the French were to put it under strain at times. In the Ambassadors' Committee he gently prodded the Americans along. After the first meeting he reported that Lovett did not exclude a pact but had by no means set his compass in that direction; but by the third session he could observe that, with Lovett speaking of a pact on the model of the Rio Treaty, the 'orchestra is beginning to play the piece we have in mind'.[72] Nevertheless, he felt 'it seemed hopeless to try to get agreement on texts in the full meeting of Ambassadors and on my suggestion the detailed work has been left to a working party ... This way of proceeding has speeded things up a lot.'[73]

Franks sought to achieve what he had done during the Paris talks on Marshall Aid in 1947: to establish a sub-committee of second rank representatives working in a spirit of co-operation and feeling less hidebound by national interest. He explained to London how he believed the Europeans should stress partnership and not appear as though they were out to secure advantages from the North Americans. He added that the British representatives should, as with ERP, take the lead but that the meetings would go better if they had a free hand. Moreover, he thought it wiser for the Brussels Five not to act as if they had doubts about US intentions, for the Americans could not go any further until the new Congress met in January 1949.[74] The meetings of the Working Group were made more informal and freer by this approach and by the lack of agreed records. The memoirs of Theodore Achilles, Chief of Division of West European Affairs, capture the sense of these meetings in their description of Hoyer Millar's approach, acting undoubtedly on Franks's instructions:

> The NATO spirit was born in that Working Group. Derick Hoyer Millar started it. One day he made a proposal which was obviously nonsense. Several of us told him so in no uncertain terms and a much better formulation emerged from the discussion. Derick said: 'Those were my instructions. All right. I'll tell the Foreign Office I made my pitch and was shot down and try to get them changed.' He did. From then on we all followed the same system. If our instructions were sound and agreement could be reached fine. If not, we'd work out something we all, or most of us, considered sound, and whoever had the instructions undertook to get them changed. It always worked, though sometimes it took time.[75]

Franks's success in moving the talks along, so soon after his completion of the Bilateral agreement did not go unnoticed by the Foreign Office. Russell noted that the Ambassador was 'rapidly acquiring a strong personal position'.[76]

The Working Group held 13 meetings between 12 July and 2 September. It had an agenda of four items : the European situation; security measures by the Five; the security relations of the seven powers with the other West Europeans; and the nature of the US association. The principal members were Taymans for Belgium, van Reuchlin for the Netherlands, Le Gallais for Luxembourg, Berard for France, Hoyer Millar for Britain and Hickerson for the United States (except when Bohlen or Kennan attended). Unlike in the Ambassador's Committee, the Americans took the lead. Hickerson, assisted by Achilles, pursued a pact: 'Perched high on the edge of his chair, he would dispose of difficulties, drastically, like a man swatting flies, and when confronted by new suggestions he would welcome them eagerly in the manner of an auctioneer receiving bids.'[77]

There was only one major difficulty, the French desire for prompt US aid. In the third week of August Bonnet intervened, saying France wanted the immediate despatch of military supplies and of US troops before his government could go any further on the question of a pact. He added that he wanted a meeting of the Ambassadors' Committee to consider this. At the suggestion of Silvercruys an informal meeting was arranged for 20 August at Lovett's house so as to allow Bonnet to let off steam, which Hoyer Millar reported he did *ad nauseam*.[78] After this the US Ambassador in Paris, Jefferson Caffery, was instructed to speak pretty sharply to the Quai d'Orsay – the telegram began 'The French are getting in our hair.'[79] But what probably soothed the difficulty were long talks by Jebb in Paris with Robert Schuman, the French Foreign Minister, and Jean Chauvel of the Quai d'Orsay. He managed to convince them that everything possible was being done to meet French needs.[80] After this, there was smooth progress to a draft paper of 2 September, examined by the Ambassadors on 3 September and amended by the Working Group in the two further meetings on 7 and 9 September. The Washington Paper, as it was called, of 9 September was then accepted by the Ambassadors on 10 September.[81] This was achieved largely as a result of Franks's urging. He maintained that it would be difficult go further without reporting to governments.

The paper agreed that the seven should work to produce a regional or collective defence pact so as to deter the Soviets and boost West European confidence. Two different categories of member-state were proposed: those with limited commitments and those with maximum commitments. The original members should be the seven powers at the present talks and any other states bordering the North Atlantic who were willing to commit themselves. Norway, Denmark, Portugal, Iceland and Ireland were considered desirable additions. In the event of aggression, direct or indirect, against any other OEEC country, the original members would consult about taking measures. The Americans stressed they would need to consult Congress before committing themselves to war. So it was agreed that the question of whether an armed attack had occurred would be determined by each country. There was a clause encouraging economic, social and cultural collaboration. And there were to be arrangements for mutual assistance and for setting up machinery to implement the treaty. Finally, there was the most important provision regarding mutual assistance in the event of an armed attack. The Rio Treaty spoke of assistance against attack, while Brussels talked of all the military and other aid in the power of the members. A compromise was achieved that said that assistance by all military, economic and other means in its power would be offered by each party, in accordance with its constitutional processes.

There remained a number of issues to resolve: whether there should be different categories of members; who should join; definition of the area; the wording of the obligation clause; the nature of the agencies for consultation; and the degree of emphasis to be placed upon economic, social and cultural co-operation.[82] Franks observed of the talks thus far:

> The Americans walked so warily that they hardly came down to earth at all. They were reluctant to move fast because they were anxious to avoid the charge that they were committing Congress in advance of consultations and they were afraid to agree, however tentatively, to anything but an extremely vague Obligation clause, again because of their doubts about Congressional reactions.[83]

Further progress was not possible until early December. The participants had to await the outcome of the presidential election of 2 November. Once he was re-elected Truman gave his approval, at the National Security Council on 5 November, to further talks in pursuit of a pact. These conversations could not take place, however, until the Brussels Treaty machinery had assessed the 9 September Paper and given its Washington Ambassadors their instructions. On 26 November the Brussels Permanent Commission agreed to the text of a draft treaty. This together with instructions did not arrive until December because of fog.[84] All the Brussels missions agreed not to tell the press that they had received a draft text of a treaty. In agreement with the State Department, they announced only that they had received guidance. They told the Americans that they were ready to resume talks, but they all agreed on the importance of not appearing to 'gang up' on the United States or present them with a draft treaty in a take-it-or-leave-it manner.[85]

Matters now moved quickly. The Ambassadors' Committee met once more on 10 December.[86] The pre-election caution of the Americans had gone. Lovett said 'he wished to move as rapidly as possible'. So the Permanent Commission draft was circulated and it was agreed to regard it as a 'summary of suggestions.' At a further meeting on 13 December Franks suggested submitting the whole question to the Working Party which could draft some articles, while on others it would be able to clarify the alternatives. Moreover, it could list the principles in dispute, setting out the various arguments and indicating the best order for discussion by the Ambassadors. Finally, Franks stressed the need for speed and said the more that could be done that week and the next, the better.[87] In the course of the next week the Working Group addressed the issues of contention. By the time the Ambassadors met again on 22 December[88] the idea of graded membership had been dropped, an obligation clause had been produced, and the question of which powers to invite to join the pact had been settled by the Working Party. The Ambassadors accepted these solutions. Franks now took a leading role in pressing for results. He said that he would very much like to send something to his government by Christmas. By 24 December the Ambassadors had agreed to the draft treaty of the Working Group of the same date.[89] The main remaining obstacles were whether to include Italy, which France supported while Britain opposed, and French North Africa, towards which Britain was sympathetic while Benelux and Canada were doubtful. The matters of duration, agencies for consultation, and some form of protection for Greece, Turkey and Iran were also unresolved.

In a letter to Bevin on 29 December Franks gave his thoughts on the progress of the conversations. He felt that the rapid progress of the last two weeks had been largely due to the more forthcoming attitude by the Americans and by relying on a small group to do the work. He added that the Americans now talked about putting teeth into the pact; and he thought that the draft obligation clause 'seems to me to give us everything we really want'. But he closed with a note of caution. The State Department, in agreeing the texts, had consulted nobody outside – though he thought the military at some level had been kept informed. He expected, then, that the next stage would be consultations with selected senators and Congressmen. With this in mind he recommended that it would probably be as well if Britain avoided taking up any absolutely rigid positions until the reactions of the Senators and Congressmen were known.[90]

THE FIRST SIX MONTHS

The year 1948 came to a close, and with it the first phase of Franks's ambassadorship, on a reasonably promising note. Three issues had dominated Anglo-American relations. The successful completion of the Bilateral Agreement on Marshall Aid owed a great deal to Franks's negotiating skills – though the final obstacle had been removed by Douglas's advice from London. The Berlin Blockade witnessed effective collaboration as cold war allies, within weeks of Franks's commitment of Britain to the US side. But the Ambassador's role in this crisis was not crucial in shaping the response to the Soviet Union. For the British government sought to keep London as the centre for co-ordination of policy. So long as Britain could retain the status of a great power, then the role of the Washington Embassy would be of equal or less importance than that of the US Embassy in London. But with British decline the Washington Embassy grew ever more important, for the British were now seeking to enlist the assistance of the Americans. As Allen of the Washington Embassy said, they want to show that Britain and the Commonwealth were the USA's 'best, stoutest and most dependable allies'.[91] Douglas summed up the position:

> Britain has never before been in position where her national security and economic fate are so completely dependent on and at mercy of another country's decisions … While they do not expect to retain former relative supremacy, with help from US they are confident that in conjunction with British Commonwealth and Empire they will again become a power to be reckoned with, which associated with the US, can maintain the balance of power in the world.[92]

The pursuit of the North Atlantic Pact was a vital feature of this approach and provided the principal task for Franks in the first nine months of his mission. Progress was hastened by his adept handling. More than anyone else he shaped the environment for discussion. With his authoritative presence and deft chairmanship he set the tone and guided business. Paul Nitze has described him in action:

> he would summarise the discussion in a way which was so much clearer than anyone else had said that we were all entranced with the lucidity of the analysis … so that we rather looked at Oliver as being the preceptor, the professor of the class. So that everybody valued Oliver. He was much more than … he wasn't representing his country; he was, in effect, doing that but he did it in a way in which he became a US leader.[93]

Thus did Franks encourage a collective rather than narrowly nationalistic approach in the discussions. He was greatly helped in this by the able, congenial and co-operative Minister at the Embassy, Hoyer Millar. Both adopted a candid, co-operative approach. As with the CEEC, he proposed a sub-committee to deal with details. Finally, the Ambassador knew how to maintain the momentum. The summary paper in September and the draft treaty within the short period between Truman's re-election and Christmas owed a great deal to his prompting and helped bring the year to a promising close. All this would not have been possible, however, if the Americans had not been receptive. Hickerson above all contributed this. Indeed, 'without

Hickerson's unflinching faith in the Pact it is doubtful whether the Working Party would have made the progress it did in the summer and whether any scheme would have been worked out in time for early consideration in the New Year'.[94] Nevertheless, in the final weeks of the year it was Franks who was, in essence, in charge of the talks as he led his fellow Ambassadors to accept the draft treaty.

NOTES

1. *House of Commons Debates*, Vol. 427, Col. 1510 (22 October 1946).
2. *FRUS: The Conferences at Malta and Yalta*, pp. 549-987; *FRUS: The Conference of Berlin* (The Potsdam Conference), 1945 2 Vols; *DBPO*, 1st series I.
3. FRUS 1947, II, pp. 337-414 (Moscow CFM), 728–72 (London CFM) and 811–30 (post-CFM talks).
4. FRUS, 1948, II, pp. 141–3, 313–17 and 883–7; PRO, CAB 129/27, CP(48)138, Bevin, 'Talks on Germany: Resumed Session', 4 June 1948.
5. FRUS, 1948, II pp. 908–9; L. D. Clay, *Decision in Germany* (London: Heinemann, 1950), pp. 362–5; PRO, CAB 128/13, CM 42(48), 24 June 1948.
6. Avi Shlaim, *The United States and the Berlin Blockade, 1948–1949: A Study in Crisis Decision-Making* (Berkeley and Los Angeles, CA: University of California Press, 1983), p. 198; PRO, FO 800/467, Ger/48/37 to 39; M. Carlyle (ed.), *Documents on International Affairs 1947–1949* (London: Oxford University Press for RIIA, 1952), pp. 568–88.
7. FRUS, 1948, II, pp. 921–6, Douglas to Secretary of State, 26 June 1948.
8. Ibid., pp. 926–8, Secretary of State to London Embassy, 27 June 1948. See also PRO, CAB 128/13 CM 46(48), 1 July 1948, when Bevin reported that the US and French governments had accepted that a committee of Strang of the Foreign Office, Douglas and Massigli, the French Ambassador, should be formed to review the Berlin situation.
9. Shlaim, *United States and Berlin Blockade*, p. 310.
10. HSTL, Truman Papers, PSF, Subject File, Box 171, memorandum of conversation, 11 September 1948.
11. PRO, FO 800/467, Ger/48/33, Bevin to Franks, 28 June 1948.
12. PRO, FO 800/467, Ger/48/39, Bevin to Franks, 2 July 1948.
13. PRO, FO 800/467, Ger/48/41, Bevin to Franks Tel. No. 7709, 13 July 1948.
14. FRUS, 1948, II, pp. 965–6, memorandum of a conversation by Lovett, 14 July 1948.
15. HSTL, Truman Papers, PSF, Subject File, Box 220, NSC Meeting of 15 July 1948, Summary for President, 16 July 1948.
16. *New York Times*, 16 July 1948.
17. Gowing, *Independence and Deterrence*, I, p. 311, says that no nuclear-capable bombers came to Britain until 1949.
18. *House of Commons Debates*, vol. 454, cols 122–3, Written Answers, 29 July 1948.
19. PRO, FO 371/68016, AN497/15/45G.
20. Ibid., AN712/15/45G.
21. Ibid., AN1291/15/45G.
22. PRO, CAB 131/6, DO(48)59, Bevin, 'United States Heavy Bombers', 10 September 1948, quoted in Edmonds, *Setting the Mould*, p. 181.
23. W. Millis (ed.), *The Forrestal Diaries* (New York: The Viking Press, 1951), p. 457.

24. A. Shlaim, 'Britain, the Berlin Blockade and the Cold War', *International Affairs*, Vol. 60, No. 1, 1983–84, p. 12. Campbell, *Unsinkable Aircraft Carrier*, p. 30 and Gowing, *Independence and Deterrence* I, pp. 309–21 say that in November 1948 the USAF told the RAF they would like a permanent place in Britain; this was accepted by the Air Ministry but not, apparently, submitted to the Foreign Office for political decision until a year later.
25. See chapters 10 and 11 below.
26. PRO, CAB 128/13, CM 53(48), 22 July 1948 and CM 54(48), 26 July 1948; FRUS, 1948, II, pp. 968–88, 989–993; Bohlen, *Witness to History*, pp. 178–279. Walter Bedell Smith, *Moscow Mission 1946–1949* (London: Heinemann, 1950), pp. 229–32.
27. See FRUS 1948 III, pp. 999–1014 and 1065–1097 for the exchanges.
28. Ibid., pp. 1099–1140, Millis (ed.), *Forrestal Diaries*, pp. 480–1, 485–6, PRO, CAB 128/13, CM 59(48), 10 September 1948, and CM 61(48), 22 September 1948, saw Bevin report on the progress of the talks.
29. See FRUS, 1948, II, pp. 1212–81.
30. FRUS, 1947, II, pp. 811–30.
31. PRO, CAB 129/23, CP(48)6, 4 January 1948. The Cabinet approved the memorandum, adding that Britain should not be too anti-Soviet; see PRO, CAB 128/12, CM 2(48), 8 January 1948.
32. PRO, FO 115/4359, G 31/1/48 and G 31/3/48 Bevin to Inverchapel, Tel. Nos. 437 and 438, 13 January 1948; FRUS, 1948, III, pp. 3–6.
33. FRUS, 1948, III, pp. 8–9.
34. *House of Commons Debates*, Vol. 446, Cols. 383–409.
35. FRUS, 1948, III, pp. 14–16, Inverchapel to Lovett, 27 January 1948.
36. See p. 38, nn 70–3.
37. PRO, FO 371/68013B, AN10/6/45.
38. PRO, FO 371/68041, AN517/45/45G, Alexander to Bevin, 19 January 1948 enclosing Chiefs of Staff, 'Subjects for Discussion with the Americans. Report by the Joint Planning Staff', 6 January 1948; Bevin to Alexander, 28 January 1948.
39. PRO, CAB 129/23, CP(48)6; these omissions are pointed out in J. Kent and J. W. Young, 'The "Western Union" Concept and British Defence Policy, 1947–8', in R. Aldrich (ed.), *British Intelligence, Strategy and the Cold War* (London: Routledge, 1992), pp. 170–1.
40. PRO, CAB 21/2244, note by Sir N. Brook to the Prime Minister, 7 January 1948. Interestingly, Roger Makins described Bevin's talk of creating a 'spiritual union' of like-minded powers as vacuous nonsense. FO 371/73045, Z809, memorandum from Roger Makins to Sir Orme Sargent, 21 January 1948; cited in Roger Woodhouse, *British Policy to France, 1945–51* (London: Macmillan, 1995), p. 127.
41. FRUS, 1948, III, p. 11, memorandum of Conversation by Hickerson, 21 January 1948.
42. Miscamble, *Kennan*, p. 119.
43. Forrest C. Pogue, *George C. Marshall: Statesman 1945–1959* (New York: Penguin, 1989), p. 151.
44. Franks described him as a very revered, austere man who only revealed the relaxed side to his nature outside the State Department. They had a more formal relationship than that which developed between the Ambassador and Acheson. Interview with Lord Franks, 24 May 1990. Roy Jenkins suggests, however, that though Marshall was not intimate with foreigners, Franks was the exception, for he 'has something of Marshall's own qualities of calm authoritative incisiveness', R. Jenkins, *Truman* (London: Collins, 1986), p. 98.

45. Miscamble, *Kennan*, p. 5.
46. Pogue, *Marshall*, pp. 149–50.
47. Miscamble, *Kennan*, p. 118.
48. PRO, FO 115/4348, G3/6/48, British aide-memoire, 11 March 1948.
49. See PRO, FO 371/68067, AN1214/1195/45G, FO to Washington, Tel. Nos. 3164 and 3208, 19 and 20 March 1948 where Bevin said he wanted Atlantic Pact talks separate from those between Brussels and the United States.
50. Miscamble, *Kennan*, p. 120; FRUS, 1948, III, memorandum by Hickerson, 8 March 1948, pp. 40–2.
51. PRO, FO 115/4348, G3/9/48, Marshall to Inverchapel, 12 March 1948; FRUS, 1948, III, p. 48.
52. *Cmd 7376 (1948)*; also at FO 800/515, US/48/2.
53. PRO, FO 371/68013B, AN1198/6/45, Washington to FO, Tel. Nos. 1261 and 1262, 17 March 1948.
54. Miscamble, *Kennan*, pp. 124–5.
55. PRO, FO 371/68067, AN1355/1195/45G, Bevin to Inverchapel, Tel. No. 3486, 30 March 1948.
56. FRUS, 1948, III, pp. 59–61, 64–7, 69–75 (Pentagon talks) and 72–5 (Pentagon Paper).
57. PRO, FO 115/4349, G3/124/48, Inverchapel to Sargent, 1 May 1948; PRO. FO 371/73069, Z4188/2307/72G, minute by Balfour, 4 May 1948.
58. Miscamble, *Kennan*, p. 130.
59. Ibid., p. 127 for Lovett's 7 and 8 April meetings with Truman; FRUS, 1948, III, pp. 82–4 (11 April) and 92–6 (18 April), Lovett's talks with Vandenberg; ibid., pp. 135–6, Vandenberg Resolution.
60. PRO, FO 371/68068A, AN1665/1195/45G, Inverchapel to FO, Tel. No. 1884, 19 April.
61. FRUS, 1948, III, pp. 123–6, Douglas to Marshall, 14 May 1948.
62. PRO, FO 371/73070, Z4467/2307/72G, Washington to FO, Tel. No. 2524, 28 May 1948; FRUS, 1948, III, pp. 132–4.
63. PRO, FO 371/73070, Z4467/2307/72G, FO to Washington, Tel. No. 5904, 1 June 1948; ibid., Z4674, Bevin to Franks, 3 June 1948.
64. Ibid., Z4673, Washington to FO, Tel. No. 2634, 4 June 1948.
65. PRO, FO 371/73071, Z4880, FO to Washington, Tel. No. 6306, 10 June 1948 and Washington to FO, Tel. No. 2749, 10 June 1948.
66. Ibid., Z4883, Washington to FO, Tel. No. 2814, 14 June 1948.
67. Ibid., Z5174, FO to Washington, Tel. No. 6966, 25 June 1948; Ibid., Z5226, Washington to FO, Tel. No. 3145, 26 June 1948; FO 371/73072, Z5260, Washington to FO, Tel. No. 3170, 28 June 1948.
68. Ibid., Z5502/2307/72G, FO to Washington, Tel. No. 7300, 5 July 1948.
69. PRO, FO 115/4380, G118/2/48; FRUS, 1948, III, p. 152.
70. See n74; see also A. Danchev, 'Taking the Pledge: Oliver Franks and the Negotiation of the North Atlantic Treaty', *Diplomatic History*, Vol. 15, No. 2, Spring 1991, p. 208n.
71. FRUS, 1948, III, p. 153.
72. PRO, FO 371/73072, Z5616, Washington to FO, Tel. No. 280(S), 6 July 1948, FO 371/73073, Z5669, Washington to FO, Tel. No. 282(S), 7 July 1948.
73. PRO FO 115/4429, G1/1/49, Franks to Bevin, 29 December 1948.
74. PRO, FO 371/73073, Z6053, Franks to FO, Tel. No. 3636, 23 July 1948; FO 371/73074, Z6137, Franks to FO, Tel. No. 3687, 27 July 1948.
75. T. C. Achilles, Draft Memoirs, p. 424G; quoted in E. Reid, *Time of Fear and Hope: The Making of the North Atlantic Treaty 1947–1949* (Toronto: McClelland and Stewart, 1977), p. 57.
76. PRO, FO 371/73074, Z6238, minute by J. W. Russell, 28 July 1948.

77. N. Henderson, *The Birth of Nato* (London: Weidenfeld & Nicolson, 1982), p. 59.
78. PRO, FO 371/73075, Z6826, Franks to FO, Tel. No. 341(S), 17 August 1948; Ibid., Z7002, Hoyer Millar to Jebb, 21 August 1948, FRUS, 1948, III, pp. 214–21.
79. PRO, FO 371/73075, Z7092, Hoyer Millar to Jebb, 25 August 1948.
80. Ibid., Z6947, FO to Washington, Tel. No. 9467, 25 August 1948.
81. See FRUS, 1948, III, pp. 148–250 passim for records of the seven Ambassadors' Committee meetings and the 15 meetings of the Working Group; the Washington Paper is at pp. 237–48.
82. PRO, FO 371/73077, Z7564, brief for Secretary of State by Jebb, 10 September 1948; ibid., Z7592, Washington to FO, Tel. No. 393(S), 13 September 1948.
83. PRO, FO 115/4429, Gl/1/49, Franks to Bevin, 29 December 1948.
84. PRO, FO 371/73081, Z9295, FO to Washington, Tel. No. 12567, 26 November 1948, ibid., McNeil to Franks, Tel. No. 1689, 29 November 1948.
85. PRO, FO 371/73082, Z9936, Washington to FO, Tel. No. 5510, 6 December 1948; ibid., Z9976, Washington to FO, Tel. No. 5548, 6 December 1948.
86. FRUS 1948, III, pp. 310–14. So swift were developments that Franks was away in the Mid-West and could not attend the meeting; Hoyer Millar deputised for him.
87. Ibid., pp. 319–20.
88. Ibid., pp. 324–32.
89. Ibid., pp. 333–43.
90. PRO, FO 115/442G, Gl/1/49, Franks to Bevin, 29 December 1948.
91. PRO, FO 371/68045G, AN2193/183/45, D. Allen to North American Department, FO, 4 June 1948.
92. FRUS, 1948, III, p. 113, Douglas to Secretary of State, 11 August 1948.
93. Quoted in Peter Hennessy and Caroline Anstey, *Moneybags and Brains* (Glasgow: University of Strathclyde, 1990), p. 34.
94. Henderson, *The Birth of NATO*, p. 59.

PART III: ACHIEVEMENTS

'There is no shallower delusion than the idea that we could get along without the United States, or indeed that the United States could get along without us: our interdependence is a fact. I am glad that our Governments since the war have accepted this fact and acted on it. For I also believe that close and effective co-operation between Britain and the United States is the basic condition of an orderly world, the best chance of avoiding another world war, and our hope of peace.'

Sir Oliver Franks, *Britain and the Tide of World Affairs*, 1955

— 6 —

Dean Acheson

IN JANUARY 1949 Dean G. Acheson succeeded George C. Marshall as US Secretary of State and served until the end of Truman's term in January 1953. They formed a remarkably close and loyal relationship. The President chose him because he valued his loyalty, displayed after the Democratic Congressional defeats in 1946, respected his intelligence and competence, shared the same general belief in the need for a firm response to the communist threat, and knew that they would be able to work well together because they had done so when Acheson was Under-Secretary of State between 1945 and 1947. His experience in the State Department meant that he had a sound grasp of the main issues of the day. Acheson realised that Truman did not want to make foreign policy from the White House; rather, he wanted close consultation and the right to veto final decisions. They held daily meetings or, if away, the Secretary of State sent the President a report at the close of each day. While very different in experience and talents, Acheson 'possessed a temperament so similar to that of his chief that he easily functioned as an alter ego in charge of foreign policy'.[1]

Truman also chose James E. Webb, former Director of the Budget, to replace Lovett as the new Under-Secretary. Acheson readily accepted because he realised that the President was at ease with him and because this would thereby help deepen presidential confidence in the State Department. The new Secretary of State hoped that Webb might assist in establishing the pre-eminence of the department over the NSC and the Pentagon in the making of foreign policy. He recognised that Webb's strength lay in administration. So he turned for policy guidance to Philip Jessup, Professor of International Law at Columbia University, whom he made an ambassador-at-large, and to Dean Rusk, whom he appointed to the new post of Deputy Under-Secretary for substantive matters.

Tall, striking in appearance and elegantly dressed, Acheson had a sharp tongue and an air of self-confidence that many took to be arrogance. Yet his working habits showed that he sought not to impose his preconceived ideas but to get to the heart of the problems. As Miscamble says, 'His confidence resided in his belief that he could develop appropriate policies and did not rest on any delusion about himself as an oracle'; what he sought was 'to debate the strengths and weaknesses of various positions and to forge the best course for the United States'. He recognised that this could only be done with the assistance of others. Consultation was to extend beyond members of the State Department.[2]

With Acheson's arrival there began a new and rich phase in Franks's ambassadorship. For the remaining four years the Ambassador and the Secretary of State were to enjoy a working relationship that was exceptional, if not indeed unique, in the history of the two countries since 1945. Despite the many difficulties and disagreements that were to arise, they established and sustained a confidential habit of consultation that was only revealed publicly in Acheson's memoirs:

> Not long after becoming Secretary of State, I made him an unorthodox proposal. On an experimental basis I suggested that we talk regularly, and in complete personal confidence, about any international problems we saw arising. Neither would report or quote the other unless, thinking that it would be useful in promoting action, he got the other's consent and agreement on the terms of a reporting memorandum or cable. The dangers and difficulties of such a relationship were obvious, but its usefulness proved to be so great that we continued it for four years. We met alone, usually at his residence or mine, at the end of the day before or after dinner. No one was informed even of the fact of the meeting. We discussed situations already emerging or likely to do so, the attitudes that various people in both countries would be likely to take, what courses of action were possible and their merits, the chief problems that could arise. If either thought that his department should be alerted to the other's apprehension and thoughts, we would work out an acceptable text setting out the problem and suggested approaches.[3]

The scale of this practice is revealed in Acheson's appointment books which show that he saw Franks more often than all the other ambassadors combined.[4]

A British journalist, Henry Brandon of the *Sunday Times*, was able to view the relationship at fairly close quarters. He has identified a number of Franks's qualities that so appealed to Acheson: 'He had the capacity to home in on the essentials of a problem … his training in clear thinking, his ability to speak his mind in simple, direct and morally honest ways, and having a vision of the future that was closely tied to existing realities ... made him such an outstanding ambassador.' He added:

> All these qualities made a deep impression on Dean Acheson. He saw in Franks not only an equal intellectually – an unusual concession on his part – but a man who could mentally dissociate himself from his own interests, put himself into Acheson's shoes and provide him with detached advice on almost any problem, however remote from Anglo-American affairs.[5]

As Brandon observes, the secrecy of these meetings was not as great as Acheson has claimed. The existence of the procedure was made known to Brandon by Acheson: 'I consult Oliver on problems that have nothing to do with Anglo-American relations', he confided, 'and if you write this, I'll cut your throat'.[6] Moreover, in a profile of the British Embassy in *Time* magazine in September 1949 it was claimed that the Ambassador and George Kennan were accustomed to having confidential discussions in the evening.[7]

While the level of secrecy about these confidential talks was not as great as Acheson later claimed, it is also clear that the Embassy was initially a little wary of the new Secretary of State:

> Acheson though also a man of high character and standing is essentially a lawyer and a person who, if confronted with a difficulty will examine it from all sides in the hope of finding some compromise way round it rather than give a clear cut yes or no.[8]

The telegram to London added that, given the increased personal influence of the President, Acheson's suppleness and responsiveness to American public opinion, the doubtful future of the bi-partisan idea, and likelihood that the State Department would be less influenced by strategic considerations, the British might find that policy agreement with the State Department might be less in line with their own ideas than would have been the case with Marshall and Lovett.

At first these reservations seemed justified. The talks on a North Atlantic Pact hit difficulties. However, these were resolved as was the Berlin blockade. In the two major issues of his first months as Secretary of State, Anglo-American co-operation produced substantial achievements.

CONCLUDING THE NORTH ATLANTIC PACT

January 1949 saw steady progress towards solving the remaining difficulties concerning the North Atlantic Pact. This took place principally in the Working Group, for there was only one Ambassadors' Committee meeting, on the 14th. The issues arising concerned the nature of the agencies of consultation; the inclusion of Italy; the addition of French North Africa; the duration of the treaty; and the question of a statement about Greece, Turkey and Iran. At the Working Party on the 11th the French and the Americans argued over the French suggestion that the defence committee of the pact should be involved in detailed military planning. The Americans insisted upon the December draft which visualised it as a mainly formal body of all the participating countries. Eventually the French agreed this.[9] However, there were further Franco-American strains over North Africa. At the Working Group on the 10th, Berard for France said he would now accept the inclusion of Algeria alone.[10] Pursuit of this goal the next day produced heated exchanges. Berard implied that without Algeria being covered, France would not sign a pact. This led Franks to observe of the French: 'They seem characteristically unable to look at the matter from anything but their own selfish point of view and almost to take the line that it is they who are conferring a favour on the Americans by joining the pact.'[11] However, this problem was soon resolved. At the Working Group on 13th the Americans suggested an approach to defining the area covered by the pact that should include Algeria. They suggested that the obligation should cover armed attack on the occupation forces of any party in Europe, any of their islands in the Atlantic north of the Tropic of Cancer, and, in the case of France, Algeria.[12] When the Ambassadors' Committee met the next day the inclusion of Algeria was all but accepted. Franks sympathised with the French position, but said that the United Kingdom did regard it as a vital issue and that if any solution could be formed the United Kingdom would be glad to agree. Lovett shared this desire. Although the US military doubted the wisdom of including Algeria, he felt it was necessary to find some way of meeting the views of all the various parties.[13]

Similarly, the question of the duration of the pact seemed on the point of settlement. Franks told his colleagues that the original European proposal of 50 years had been said without too much deep thought. His government preferred 25 to 30 years. Lovett had spoken of 10 or 12 or 20 years. In reporting the discussion Franks maintained that it was unlikely that the United States would agree to a term of more than 20 years. The Canadian idea of a provision for review of progress at a half-way stage in the 20 years seemed to persuade the Americans to accept their own upper limit as the duration.[14]

The inclusion of Italy in the treaty was also virtually settled before the end of January. At the Working Party on the 10th it was clear that the crucial question was whether Italy wanted to be invited.[15] On the evening of the 12th the Italian Ambassador in Washington, Tarchiani, gave the Americans a memorandum saying his government would like to join the pact. Hickerson of the State Department told the Working Group of the request on the 13th, saying he regretted that the Italians had precipitated matters, but he hoped that this could be discussed when the Ambassadors met the next day.[16] Since it was too late to receive instructions from their governments in response to this, it was not possible for them to decide the question. At the Working Party on the 18th, however, Hickerson said he thought Italy should join, although he did point out that the State Department had not discussed these views with Acheson as yet. He hoped to do so the following week. He added that he would like to see a declaration about Greece, Turkey and Iran by Britain and the United States, and by France if possible, at the conclusion of the pact.[17] Bevin had, for some time, opposed Italian inclusion, because of the implied exclusion of Greece, Turkey and Iran. The idea of a declaration eased this worry. He could now agree if the Americans insisted.[18]

Thus far Acheson had not been involved in the deliberations, and as a consequence the Ambassadors had held only one meeting. The arrival of a new Secretary of State brought with it necessary delays. There was the matter of the confirmation hearings on his appointment, the inauguration of the President, the need to address other urgent issues, and the task of familiarising himself with the progress of the talks on a North Atlantic Treaty. On 28 January Franks reported that Acheson had been so rushed in his first week of office (he assumed duties on the 20th) that the State Department had been unable to have serious talks with him about the pact. The next day he could telegraph that Acheson had discussed the pact with his officials and that there would be a further meeting on the Monday (1 February). The State Department said it would then be possible to hold an Ambassadors' meeting on 1 or 2 February.[19] However, when Franks met Acheson about the delay in the negotiations he was told that, while the need for an early resumption was recognised, he (Acheson) wanted to study the topic further, discuss it with the President and have further talks with Senators Connally and Vandenberg.[20] The need to delay meeting the Ambassadors was reiterated by Hickerson at the Working Group, but he thought that the next meeting could settle all the outstanding points.[21] Henderson, deputising for Hoyer Millar, wrote to Russell of the Foreign Office the next day saying that one of the reasons for the break in the negotiations was Acheson's belief that further groundwork on Capitol Hill was necessary. Hickerson had said the United States was wary because of the League of Nations experience.[22] Franks wrote later:

> I think Acheson was almost certainly taken aback that not more preliminary work had been done with the Senate. Lovett and the State Department officials told us on frequent occasions during the latter part of December and in January that they were in touch with the Senate leaders, who were in broad agreement with the implications of the Pact ... it looks very much as though these consultations were only in general terms.[23]

This failure to keep Congressional leaders more fully informed was to result in the emergence of a major obstacle in the talks. When Acheson met Senators Connally and Vandenberg on 3 and again on 5 February and showed them the draft treaty they objected to the obligation clause, article 5, which they felt was tantamount to an automatic American commitment to go to war. Connally wanted the removal of 'forthwith', 'military' action and 'as may be necessary'. This was passed on to the Embassy by a State Department official.[24] Bevin telegraphed from London, expressing concern at changes that would detract from the value of the pact, but said he had no objection to the omission of 'forthwith' which Franks was authorised to propose if he wished.[25] But the Ambassador was too shrewd a diplomat to volunteer a concession, unless it was needed to break a deadlock.

So the first meeting of the Ambassadors' Committee with Acheson took place in the face of a serious snag to the progress of the talks, made worse by the impression Acheson gave of accepting the Senators' points. The Secretary of State cited, and seemed to endorse, the Senators' claim that the language of article 5 'gave an impression of crescendo and haste which perhaps overstated the problem'. He felt they needed to find 'more neutral language than that contained in the present draft', for the phrase 'military or other action' was 'an unnecessary embellishment'.[26] Escott Reid of the Canadian Department of External Affairs wrote in his later assessment of the negotiations:

> Acheson was the new boy at the negotiating table ... it was only 10 days since he had been able to look at any of the papers ... Yet he spoke to the ambassadors not as a neophyte but as a teacher lecturing not very intelligent students ... Acheson may, of course,

> have decided that the more arrogant the language he used … the more likely he was to break down the opposition of the ambassadors and their governments.[27]

In his memoirs Acheson declared: 'Safety required the use of the ambassadors to urge on the senators, and the senators to hold back the ambassadors.'[28] Acheson's words produced a calm, restrained but powerful argument for the original text by Franks.

> In a sense, the substance of the Treaty was what mattered and the words were of secondary importance. But there was another angle to this. It was not just a matter … of what would happen if one of the Parties to the treaty was attacked. There was also … the effect which the Articles of the Treaty would produce themselves … the words of the Pact, while sober in tone, should make it plain beyond misunderstanding what would happen in the event of trouble … It was therefore necessary to balance what opinion in North America might be prepared to accept with what those on the Eastern shores of the Atlantic would regard as necessary. Wording which erred on the side of understatement might make the Pact look weaker than it really was and thereby detract from its value in maintaining peace.[29]

Yet the tide continued to flow in favour of the changes. On 12 February Acheson was quoted by the *Kansas City Times* as telling Norwegian Foreign Minister, Lange, that the pact 'would be interpreted as a moral commitment to fight' even though only Congress could declare war. This produced a debate on the 14th in the Senate which gave vent to isolationist sentiment.[30] Concern about this led Hume Wrong, the Canadian Ambassador, and Franks independently to consider suggesting that Vandenberg and Connally be invited to join the Ambassadors' meeting. They agreed that Franks might put the idea to Acheson, which he did on the 14th. When the Secretary of State raised this with Truman they decided not to sanction such a course of action.[31]

Franks did not appear unduly disturbed by Congress. He reported that, in the face of such a radical reversal of traditional US foreign policy, there was bound to be such a debate. He urged the Foreign Office to do what it could to persuade British newspapers to adopt restraint in their coverage. He added that the State Department had not succeeded in carrying the Senate with them. It was only after Acheson came to office and started discussing matters with Connally and Vandenberg that their objections to the wording of article 5 were heard. Here was implied sympathy for Acheson's position. The Ambassador viewed the two Senators quite differently. Connally he regarded as 'a man of lesser calibre and may not fully understand the issues involved. But I suspect that he is jealous of Vandenberg and disposed to be difficult about the North Atlantic Pact because it derives largely from the Vandenberg Resolution.' He added that 'Connally's intervention was lamentable.' He was not worried about Vandenberg, however, for '[i]t is part of his technique, if he wants something badly, to avoid showing his feelings too obviously in the early stage. He may have felt yesterday that he would only have stultified his position had he disclosed his full support for the pact.' Yet Franks thought the Senators might be hard to shift, and that Acheson might ask the ambassadors to consider revised texts on the lines desired by the Senators.[32] Indeed, Connally and Vandenberg maintained their tough stance in a meeting with Acheson immediately after the debate. The former suggested inserting 'as it may deem necessary' to stress that the type of action in response to an attack should be a matter for individual determination.[33] The next two days saw the State Department, in effect, give way to the Senators' proposals. Counselor Charles Bohlen, who was now the department's 'number one man on the North Atlantic Pact',[34] sent Acheson what he called the Department's minimum text. It read: 'The Parties ... will take, forthwith, individually and in concert with the other Parties, the measures it deems necessary to restore and maintain the security of the North Atlantic area.'[35]

Franks now played a crucial role. Bohlen recommended himself to approach the Ambassador in private to ascertain his personal opinion about the probable effect of the new draft on the other countries involved. He then proposed that 'if Sir Oliver believes that this draft would not seriously impair the objectives of the pact and would therefore be generally acceptable to the other countries', the President and Acheson should see Connally alone to secure his support for the draft.[36] But Acheson decided to see Franks with Bohlen that same afternoon, 16 February. They met for 15 minutes before the signature of the Anglo-American Consular Convention. Franks said he did not know his or the other governments' views and so could only speak personally. When asked about 'as it may deem necessary' to replace 'as may be necessary', he said he preferred the original but did not see any great objections provided it would not preclude joint consultations, military staff talks, advance planning and so on. He added that he could not agree to the revised wording unless 'military or other' be reinserted before 'measures', because to omit them would have an unfortunate effect on public opinion in Europe where it was now known that it had originally been intended to include these words. Acheson asked if the reinsertion of 'forthwith' would make matters easier? Franks said he would welcome this but it would not make up for the omission of 'military or other'.[37]

In the light of this conversation Bohlen presented three new drafts of the article. All omitted 'forthwith', but the first two included 'military or other action' while the third referred only to 'action'.[38] When Acheson saw the President on 17 February he produced a further draft, a variant of the first of these new drafts but with 'forthwith' added and 'action including the use of armed force' to replace 'military or other action'. The President said he would recommend it to Senator Connally.[39] Neither the British nor the US records reveal who devised the phrase 'including use of armed force'. It could well have been Franks at his meeting with Acheson, for throughout his time as chairman of the CEEC and as Ambassador he was called upon to find the right form of words to convey an agreed outlook. What is certain is that this formulation expressed the burden of his representation to Acheson and Bohlen on the 16th. Moreover, it provided the breakthrough.

On the afternoon of 18 February Acheson appeared before the full Senate Foreign Relations Committee. The next morning he called an informal Ambassadors' meeting. He said the session had gone well and the senators now proposed 'action including the use of armed force' to replace 'military or other action', and 'as it deems necessary' to replace 'as may be necessary', while 'forthwith' was retained.[40] At the next meeting of the Ambassadors' Committee on 25 February, Franks recommended acceptance of the new version of article 5, saying that, whilst he felt they (and he) would have preferred the original wording, they had achieved a good text bearing in mind its reference to armed forces. No one demurred.[41] He told Bevin that he thought they had achieved an obligation clause better than anything they could have reasonably expected.[42]

Within three weeks the remaining issues were settled. At the Ambassadors' meeting on 25 February the Americans proposed that Norway join the talks. The next day Bevin telegraphed his approval. When the Ambassadors met again on 1 March this was accepted by them and Norway joined their next meeting on 4 March.[43] The meeting on the 1st also considered Italian inclusion. Franks maintained that Britain preferred that it not be included but that this was not a breaking point and would be guided by other views expressed. By the next Ambassadors' meeting on the 4th, Franks said he was prepared to follow the weight of opinion favouring admission of Italy.[44] When they convened again on the 7th it was agreed to invite not only Italy but Denmark, Iceland and Portugal to be original signatories, if the Ambassadors' governments concurred. The State Department, however, told these four countries before the envoy's stance had been confirmed. Shuckburgh of the Foreign Office minuted that the Americans had 'treated us with scant courtesy'. It was decided not to make a fuss.[45] There were two further meetings on 11 and 15 March and the text was published on 18 March. It was agreed that both Britain and the United States would, simultaneously with the publication, make announcements declaring their interest in the security of Greece, Turkey and Iran.[46] The formal signature of the Treaty would take place in Washington on 4 April.

Success has many parents. Several claims of authorship have been made for the Pact. Henderson feels that it was a British invention, while Battle claims it as an American achievement.[47] Its origins lay in Bevin's response to Soviet behaviour in the London CFM and the Czech coup. His was the initiative for an Atlantic alliance against the growing danger from the Soviet Union, a response which chimed with US concerns; and he provided the main impetus towards this goal in the first half of 1948. The Soviet blockade of Berlin gave added urgency to his policy and made the United States more responsive. The US reaction, however, was the pivotal consideration in realising the initiative, for Bevin's central aim was to secure US adherence. Without US involvement there could be no alliance. Two figures played crucial roles in leading the United States to a treaty. Once Truman and Marshall approved talks, the much under-rated Hickerson took the lead for his country. He replaced Bevin's original idea of interlocking alliances with the Rio Treaty model which was more congenial to American opinion. Moreover, he was a powerful force for progress in the Working Party. In the later stages of talks both Acheson and Bohlen were valuable in finding procedures and formulas acceptable to both the negotiators and Congress. But no one figure fulfilled a more important task than Franks in the negotiations. He set the tone for discussion, encouraging his colleagues to follow his example. His advocacy of a community spirit helped lessen argument on national grounds. The main administrative procedures were his invention. He was the driving force to produce results – both the September paper and the December draft treaty emerged from his prompting. The fertility of his mind in devising workable phrasing for key ideas was deployed to solve the problem over article 5; a solution that was only used, however, because he had so effectively established himself in Acheson's eyes. The completion of the Treaty, therefore, promised a better future for both the strategic relationship and co-operation between Franks and Acheson.

ENDING THE BERLIN BLOCKADE

The need to be in Washington for the signature of the North Atlantic Treaty gave Bevin the opportunity to propose talks with Acheson. It would be the first time the Foreign Secretary (and Schuman also) had met Acheson. It was agreed that Bevin and Acheson should meet on 31 March, and that the three Foreign Ministers should have talks on 1 and 6–8 April.[48] The principal topic was Germany. The talks on the future of Western Germany occurred at an auspicious time, for the deadlock over Berlin was about to be broken.

The breakthrough had come in January when the US Ambassador in Moscow, Bedell Smith, told an influential American journalist, Kinsgbury Smith, that the Soviets 'wanted to get off the hook in Berlin but did not know how to'. The journalist asked Stalin if the Soviet Union would end the blockade if the West postponed the establishment of a West German state until there had been another meeting of the Council of Foreign Ministers. Stalin answered that he would remove the blockade if the West also lifted its counterblockade. No reference was made to the currency question, which had triggered the crisis. Philip Jessup, the deputy chief of the US Delegation to the United Nations, was instructed to ask Malik, the Soviet UN representative, if this omission had been significant. A month later, on 15 March, in Jessup's Park Avenue office, Malik replied that the answer was 'not accidental'. On 21 March, Malik said that if they could decide a definite date for the CFM, there could be a simultaneous lifting of the blockade and the counter restrictions before the CFM met. Cadogan, the British UN representative, and Chauvel, the French one, were then informed of the secret talks. Such was the position when the Foreign Ministers met.[49]

Bevin, Franks and Barclay, Bevin's newly appointed Principal Private Secretary, met Acheson, Murphy and Jessup on 31 March. The Americans gave details of the Jessup–Malik confidential exchanges. At this and the meeting of 1 April, which also included the French, the Foreign Secretary was wary about developments. The Soviets might drive a wedge between the Western allies. It was not clear that Malik had acted officially. Nevertheless, he was persuaded that here lay the best course of action to end the blockade. So it was agreed that Franks and Couve de Murville for France should join Jessup in drafting a statement that the American would send to Malik.[50] Once again Franks's skill in devising a suitable form of words was being utilised. The Ambassador's talents were admired by Barclay:

> I also enjoyed seeing Oliver Franks in action. He did not bother

> about briefs or records and at times seemed somewhat detached, but if, as sometimes happened, the Ministers got into a tangle over some complex problem he had a remarkable gift for sorting out the issues and listing (A, B and C) the possible courses open to them. Even Dean Acheson, who was not lacking in intellectual clarity, used to listen admiringly to these Franks interventions.[51]

Acheson's memoirs confirm this, describing Franks as 'one of the most creative minds I have worked with'.[52]

Jessup's statement was given to Malik on 5 April. It made clear that the Western governments would not accept the suspension or postponement of preparations for a West German government as a condition for ending the blockade.[53] While an answer was awaited from Moscow, the three Western Foreign Ministers resolved the remaining issues on Germany in talks on 6–8 April. The Western Powers would no longer seek to govern Germany, but would allow the Germans to run their own political and economic affairs, subject to certain provisos.[54] By 5 May an unconditional agreement about the blockade had been reached with Malik. The restrictions would end at midnight on 11 May. Although a CFM met in Paris on 23 May it only produced an impasse. Meanwhile, the Parliamentary Council in Bonn on 8 May had approved a Federal Constitution for West Germany.

The first five months of Acheson's incumbency as Secretary of State had produced two solid achievements in the completion of the negotiations for the North Atlantic Pact and in the ending of the Berlin blockade and the allied establishment of a West German state. In talks on the Pact Franks had played a vital role. On the resolution of the blockade and the setting up of political institutions the Ambassador had helped to smooth the course of developments. In doing this he had built up a sound relationship with Acheson. Each came to respect the other. Franks recognised the important job Acheson had performed in carrying Congress with the draft pact, while the Secretary of State appreciated the help of the Ambassador in securing acceptable words for the vital article 5. That mutual understanding, however, was about to be tested by another British financial crisis.

NOTES

1. Alonzo L. Hamby, *Man of the People: A Life of Harry Truman* (New York: Oxford University Press, 1995), p. 510.
2. These two paragraphs are based on Melvin P. Leffler, *A Preponderance of Power: National Security, the Truman Administration, and the Cold* War (Stanford, CA: Stanford University Press, 1992), pp. 268–70 and Miscamble,

Kennan, pp. 154–7 (quotation from p. 156).
3. Acheson, *Present at the Creation*, p. 323.
4. Gaddis Smith, *Dean Acheson* (New York: Cooper Square, 1972), pp. 194–5.
5. Brandon, *Special Relationships*, p. 75.
6. Ibid., p. 76.
7. *Time*, 26 September 1949, p. 20.
8. PRO, FO 371/74174, AN135/1023/45G, Washington to FO, Tel. No. 213, 11 January 1948; Franks did not draft this telegram but felt 'it would more or less do', interview with Lord Franks, 24 May 1990.
9. PRO, FO 371/79222, Z497/1074/72G, Franks to FO, Tel. No. 14(S), 12 January 1949.
10. PRO, FO 371/79221, Z283, Franks to FO, Tel. No. 196, 10 January 1949.
11. Ibid., Z337, Franks to FO, Tel. No. 243, 12 January 1949.
12. Ibid., Z365, Franks to FO, Tel. No. 273, 13 January 1949.
13. FRUS, 1949, IV, p. 32, minutes of Eleventh Meeting of the Washington Exploratory Talks on Security, 14 January 1949.
14. Ibid., p. 33; PRO, FO 371/79221, Z422, Franks to FO, Tel. No. 301, 14 January 1949.
15. See note 9 above.
16. PRO, FO 371/79221, Z362, Franks to FO, Tel. No. 270, 13 January 1949; see ibid., Z363 for Italian memorandum.
17. PRO, FO 371/79222, Z555, Franks to FO, Tel. No. 384, 19 January 1949.
18. Ibid., Z519, FO to Washington, Tel. No. 940, 22 January 1949.
19. PRO, FO 371/79223, Z866, Franks to FO, Tel. No. 573, 28 January 1949; ibid., Z868, Franks to FO, Tel. No. 594, 29 January 1949.
20. Ibid., Z962, Franks to FO, Tel. No. 942, 1 February 1949.
21. Ibid., Z963, Franks to FO, Tel. No. 943, 1 February 1949.
22. PRO, FO 371/79224, Z1184, Henderson to Russell, 2 February 1949.
23. PRO FO 115/4429, Gl/141/49, Franks to Bevin, 17 February 1949.
24. PRO, FO 371/79224, Z1053, Franks to FO, Tel. No. 692, 3 February 1949; NA, Wash. DC, RG 59, State Department Decimal Files, 1945–49, 840.20/2–349 and 840.20/2–549, Box 5661, Memoranda of Conversation, 3 and 5 February 1949.
25. PRO, FO 371/79224, Z1055, FO to Washington, Tel. No. 1528, 7 February 1949.
26. FRUS, 1949, IV, pp. 74, 85.
27. Reid, *Time of Fear and Hope*, p. 150.
28. Acheson, *Present at the Creation*, p. 277.
29. FRUS, 1949, IV, pp. 77–8.
30. Acheson, *Present at the Creation*, p. 281.
31. Public Archives of Canada, Department of External Relations [hereafter PAC, DEA] File 283(s), North Atlantic Security Pact, Vol. 6, Wrong to Secretary of State for External Affairs, Tel. No. WA 361, 10 February 1949; ibid., Wrong to DEA, Tel. No. WA 393, 14 February 1949; *Official Conversations and Meetings of Dean Acheson, 1949–1953* (Frederick, MD: Microfilm Project of University Publications of America, 1980), reel 1, frame 111, memorandum of conversation with the President, 14 February at 12.30 p.m., 15 February 1949.
32. PRO, FO 371/79225, Z1416 and Z1418, Franks to FO, Tel. Nos. 938 and 939, 15 February 1949.
33. FRUS, 1949, IV, p. 109, memorandum of conversation, 14 February 1949.
34. *Acheson Official Conversations*, reel 1, frame 107, memorandum by M. S. Carter, 14 February 1949, conveying Acheson's instructions; they included that 'He wants it stressed in the strongest possible language that no actions,

discussions, correspondence etc ... be taken by other Department officers without clearance with the officer assigned ultimate responsibility.'

35. FRUS, 1949, IV, pp. 114–15, enclosure in Bohlen to Acheson and Webb, 16 February 1949.
36. Ibid., p. 114.
37. PRO, FO 371/79226, Z1463, Franks to FO, Tel. No. 965, 16 February 1949; FO 115/4429, Gl/141/49, Franks to FO, 17 February 1949. Danchev in *Franks*, p. 104 suggests they met alone but cites no record of the meeting. Franks's letter of 17 February to Bevin in FO 115 (not mentioned by Danchev) says he saw Acheson *and* Bohlen.
38. FRUS, 1949, IV, pp. 115–16.
39. Ibid., p. 117.
40. PRO, FO 371/79226, Z1544, Franks to FO, Tel. No. 1022, 19 February 1949; PAC, DEA, File 283(s), North Atlantic Security Pact, Vol. 7, Wrong to DEA, Tel. No. WA 446, 19 February 1949, microfiche No. 2268, Leeds University; Ibid., Wrong to DEA, Tel. No. WA 450, 21 February 1949.
41. PRO, FO 800/455, minutes of Thirteenth Meeting of Washington Exploratory Talks on Security, 25 February 1949; the Brussels Permanent Commission had said, on 23 February, that the text of article 5 was acceptable, FO 371/79228, Z1718, FO to Washington, Tel. No. 2155, 23 February 1949.
42. Ibid., Z1778, Franks to FO, Tel. No. 1151, 26 February 1949.
43. Ibid., Z1754, FO to Washington, Tel. No. 2263, 26 February 1949; FRUS, 1949, IV, pp. 126–35.
44. Ibid., pp. 132–3; ibid., p. 51.
45. Ibid., pp. 166–74; FO 371/79232, Z2081, Shuckburgh minute, 9 March 1949, FO to Washington, Tel. No. 2739, 9 March 1949.
46. See Henderson, *Birth of Nato*, pp. 119–21, for Treaty text, and pp. 106–7 for the British and US declarations on Greece, Turkey and Iran. This book is the published version of the author's contemporary (May 1949) account; see PRO, FO 115/4430, Gl/395/49 for the original text. See also HSTL, Acheson Papers, Box 64, Memorandum of Conversation with Franks, 15 March 1949.
47. Peter Hennessey, *Never Again: Britain 1945–1951* (London: Vintage, 1993), p. 366.
48. PRO, FO 800/516, US/49/15, 18 and 19, Franks to FO, Tel. Nos. 1516, 1707 and 1759, 15, 23 and 28 March 1949.
49. Acheson, *Present at the Creation*, pp. 267–70; Shlaim, *United States and the Berlin Blockade*, pp. 380–3; Philip C. Jessup, 'Park Avenue Diplomacy – Ending the Berlin Blockade', *Political Science Quarterly*, Vol. 87, No. 3, September 1972, pp. 377–400.
50. PRO, FO 800/483, NA/49/10, Acheson–Bevin meeting, 31 March 1949, Acheson–Bevin–Schuman meeting, 1 April 1949; see FRUS, 1949, III, pp. 156–8, 709–12 for US records.
51. Barclay, *Ernest Bevin*, p. 56.
52. Acheson, *Present at the Creation*, p. 288.
53. FRUS, 1949, III, pp. 712–6.
54. PRO, FO 800/483, NA/49/10, meetings of 6–8 April 1949.

— 7 —

Devaluation of the Pound

ONE OF THE REASONS why Franks was appointed to the Washington Embassy was his expertise in economics. Even before the North Atlantic Treaty was approved by Congress (it was ratified on 21 July and came into effect on 24 August 1949) the British economy was encountering difficulties. It was natural, therefore, that he should assume a prominent position in the British response to the problem. For the only time during his ambassadorship he was to become involved in talks on the handling of a crisis in London as well as in Washington. With the help of an allocation of $1,293 million of Marshall Aid for the year 1948–49 the balance of payments on current account moved into surplus in 1948 for the first time since the end of the war.[1] But in early 1949 it moved back into deficit. The basic problem lay in a shortage of dollars in the sterling area to pay for the imports of American goods, which at that stage were not available elsewhere. The British economy was not earning enough dollars to cover these imports. Too many British exports went to soft currency countries; they were what were called unrequited exports. Then the US economy suffered a mild recession, thereby reducing the opportunities for increased dollar earnings. The US economy contracted from November 1948 to October 1949. Industrial production fell by 10 per cent and GNP dropped by a little over 5 per cent.[2] There was a sharp fall in US raw material and foodstuff purchases from Malaya, Ceylon, Australia and New Zealand; and the British trade deficit with the United States, Canada and Latin America increased.[3] The dollar shortage due to exports to soft currency areas was a problem for all the European countries but the British difficulties were the key ones, for something like half the world's visible and invisible trade was then conducted in sterling.[4]

PRESSURE ON EXCHANGE RATES

These dollar shortages led the US Treasury, State Department and

ECA to maintain that, to improve competitiveness, an adjustment in European exchange rates was required, and, in particular, in that for sterling which assumed so important a role. The American fear was that European production might collapse when Marshall Aid ended in 1952. Press speculation surfaced in Britain and the United States. *The Economist Intelligence Unit Foreign Report* of 24 March said 'The Pound may be Devalued';[5] while the *Journal of Commerce* of 4 April claimed 'United States seen moving to speed devaluation in ECA nations.'[6] By this time Southard, the US Executive Director, had tabled, on 1 April, a resolution at the IMF calling for a review of existing European rates. Franks had been busy with the formal signature of the North Atlantic Pact which took place on 4 April. The next day he spoke to the US Secretary of the Treasury, John W. Snyder. Recognising the strength of the American desire for the resolution, that the harm had already been done by raising the issue, and that 'it would be most unfortunate if the Board should be formally divided with ourselves and the other Europeans on our side and the Americans on the other', he counselled acceptance of the resolution. Moreover, Martin, Snyder's deputy, told Sir Sydney Caine, Head of the Treasury and Supply Delegation at the Embassy, that Snyder was inclined to view this as a test of 'whether we are prepared to go on working on the basis of the Fund'. So the Ambassador concluded:

> judging the situation admittedly from an American angle, I believe that the least harm will be done by accepting as inevitable the adoption of some resolution of the kind proposed and concentrating on getting it into the least obnoxious form possible.[7]

In another telegram, Franks sought to explain American practices and the circumstances facing Snyder. The Americans were much more attached to solemn declarations of purpose even though they might be dilatory in carrying them out and were apt to be suspicious of those who refused to subscribe to such declarations of purpose. Since the National Advisory Council on Monetary and Financial Policy at least knew that things had reached this stage, Snyder would reckon that a failure to place anything on record might provoke further embarrassing and more public discussion in Congress.[8] The Chancellor of the Exchequer, Sir Stafford Cripps, replied that he regarded 'the American attitude as deplorable' but that he was prepared to defer to Franks's judgement, provided the resolution recognised that the initiative lay with members and that the IMF had no rights to bring pressure on them.[9] So on 6 April a resolution was passed at the Board of the IMF declaring:

> the West European payments problem as a whole ought to be considered through the Fund's established methods of consultation with members ... [and] attention should be given ... to the relation of existing exchange rates and exchange controls to the payments position and price situation.

Tansley, the British Executive Director, finally agreed 'with great reluctance' not to oppose the decision on the understanding that any discussions with the Managing Director on the UK position would take place under conditions of secrecy and only at a time agreeable to the British government. It was clearly understood, and much stress was laid on it, that the procedure whereby Gutt made a round trip in Europe and discussed many things which were definitely not revealed to the Board would continue to be followed.[10]

The value of Franks's contribution was recognised by Roger Makins, Head of the Economic Relations department of the Foreign Office, who described the Ambassador's reports as 'models of good sense and restrained judgement'. He felt that 'American methods and tactics are of the "bull in the china shop" variety'; but that the US position 'is a fact which no amount of bad temper or ostrich-like attitudes are likely to dissipate'. So there might well be a head-on collision with the Americans. He feared that 'this may become a very troublesome matter'.[11]

After passage of the resolution, Franks focused on how the issues might be pursued. He said that there were continuing American suspicions about whether the British were ready to use the Fund to talk about the issues arising from the resolution. He stated:

> I believe, therefore, that it is important that we should try in the next few months to get a closer community of thinking with the Americans on the proper functions of the Fund as well as, if possible, on the matters of substance which are likely to arise from any further examination of the general monetary and balance of payments position in Europe.

He thought it would be best to let feelings die down after the recent events and to consider further what could be done towards harmonisation of British and American views. Sir Sydney Caine would be visiting London to report in more detail but the Embassy would warn of 'any threat of these difficulties becoming more acute in the meantime'. Franks advised that at the present moment 'any proposal from us for direct conversation with the Americans would be misinterpreted as another attempt to bypass the Fund'.[12]

But the possibility of exclusive talks was raised on 14 April by the United States. Henry Wilson Smith, head of the Treasury's Overseas Finance Division, telegraphed Caine that Finletter, ECA head in Britain, had told them that Harriman, the Special Representative in Europe of the ECA, felt that IMF activity on exchange rates should be damped down and that, instead, the issues should be studied quietly and confidentially between the British and US governments. Wilson Smith had the impression that Harriman had himself in mind as the designated envoy but 'We strongly deprecated this last suggestion ... we do not want this topic translated to the ECA sphere.' Finletter was told that the idea of bilateral and highly confidential talks (preferably in Washington and with the US Treasury) had been in British minds but they had assumed that Snyder was strongly committed to working through the Fund.[13]

FRANKS'S TELEGRAM OF 20 MAY 1949

That is where matters rested for the next month. Just as Franks had counselled, no attempt was made by the British to seek bilateral talks. But once passions had subsided, Franks gave, on 20 May, his appreciation of the situation in a thoughtful and wide-ranging telegram for the Foreign Secretary and the Chancellor. He addressed the possibility and desirability of informal and confidential talks with the Americans. He felt that there was a widespread feeling in the United States that the next year should see the taking of definite steps or, at least, definite decisions towards the establishment of the structure of economic and financial relations between the countries of the non-Soviet world. As most of those in responsible positions would admit, the Americans had not thought out at all fully the programme they ought to take. Franks thought that this was equally true of the British themselves. The general pressure of American opinion thus far had been canalised into pressure for exchange rate adjustments. There could be no doubt that the talk about devaluation on both sides of the Atlantic has aggravated the situation. Some American buyers of sterling had deferred purchases because of hope or fear that devaluation in the near future might make these products available at lower prices. So it would clearly be of benefit if they could reach agreement with the Americans on a line of policy which would persuade them definitely and openly to withdraw their pressures for early devaluation. Such an agreement was much more likely if they could reach an understanding on specific and urgent issues such as the inter-European payments scheme. 'If the Americans go on feeling that a general attitude on these questions is negative and defensive rather than open-minded and constructive, they will deliberately increase their pressure.'[14] He favoured an early agreement on general principles. He argued that they should do their utmost to convince the Americans of three things: that they wanted to build up one economic world outside the area of Soviet influence and not to build up either a sterling or western European autarchic or self-sufficient trading area; that we were willing to discuss quite openly the best methods and stages of progressing towards that ideal; and that our immediate decisions, for example, in relation to the inter-European payments scheme and our import policy, were consistent with these general principles.

Turning to the conduct of conversations, Franks believed that there were two conditions that needed to be fulfilled. They should be of a dual character, 'ranging both over the philosophical or economic policy involved, and over the immediate practical issues such as the payments scheme or current monetary arrangements'. Secondly, the participants must be prepared to talk with the maximum of freedom and to be as open-minded as possible. He suggested that, if talks were to be arranged in the near future, there might be an advantage if any representatives from the Treasury in London be accompanied by someone, for example, Robert Hall, Director of the Cabinet Economic Section, who could speak on the general economic problems involved in a manner which would carry weight with the Americans. He maintained: 'I regard it as of great importance and urgency to arrive at some community of mind with the Americans ... we are at a psychological moment the seizing of which may produce very valuable results: but the moment may pass quickly.' Recently there had been a tendency to discuss such matters in international bodies such as the IMF or OEEC, but there was a growing feeling among responsible Americans that it was only by getting agreement to direct conversations that we could make substantial progress. This was partly because there could be no doubt that, after the United States, the United Kingdom and the countries associated with us represented the largest and most stable economic unit in the world. He concluded: 'The present moment therefore appears to present a real opportunity of beginning to establish in the economic sphere a parallel to the Anglo-American partnership in leadership which is already yielding fruit in the political sphere.'[15] Even in times of crisis there was talk of an Anglo-American partnership.

Cripps quickly replied to 'your timely and valuable appreciation of the general position', saying that the present intention was to send Wilson Smith and Hall to Washington at the end of the week. He agreed that both sides might secure maximum benefit if the representatives arrived without specific instructions but, as Franks suggested, be ready to discuss all current economic and monetary problems with the fullest frankness. The Ambassador replied that he was pleased that both the Chancellor and Foreign Secretary shared his belief in the desirability of wide-ranging talks, but that Snyder appeared to have certain hesitations; and that it would clearly be undesirable for Wilson Smith and Hall to leave London until he let them know that the Americans agreed to conversations. By 30 May Franks was able to telephone and telegraph that, after an hour's discussion with Snyder, the latter would be happy for Wilson Smith and Hall to visit. So Franks urged that they should be sent to the United States to talk about the economic situation and to try and persuade the Americans to restrain their comments on devaluation. There should be no publicity, if possible. The visit was for routine talks which were to be of a general and exploratory character. He cautioned that they stick to this line and not introduce any element of negotiation: 'If not, we will find the Americans thinking that we are trying to pull a fast one.'[16]

INVOLVING THE AMERICANS

Robert Hall and Henry Wilson Smith held talks in Washington on 3–10 June. During their stay they benefited from the guidance of the Ambassador who proposed that they and their aides moved in small rather than large parties, that they entertained as much as possible, and that they aimed 'generally to try to establish a meeting of minds and not to discuss any current negotiations unless for illustration'. Hall felt this 'was very useful'.[17] They found the Americans to be concerned about continued British adherence to non-discrimination in trade. On their return they reported the view of Martin, Assistant Secretary at the US Treasury, that nearly all US government officials believed that devaluation of sterling was inevitable.[18] Moreover, both these British officials now shared this outlook.[19]

If American opinion increasingly favoured devaluation, it was clear that the attitudes of the Treasury and the ECA on the one side and the State Department on the other were different. The latter were far more sympathetic. Webb, Acting Secretary of State, cabled London on 28 May, saying that British exports were overvalued and that a moderate devaluation could take place without causing inflationary spiral. But he concluded: 'In view present strong Brit [*sic*] opposition to devaluation … "high pressure" or any action which wld [*sic*] force hands of Brit Govt wld be deeply resented.'[20]

By this time the position was becoming grave. On 16 June Douglas told Washington that Britain might have a major financial crisis that summer. He passed on figures given by Cripps, the Chancellor of the Exchequer, in the utmost secrecy. They showed an accelerating rise in dollar gold drain – from £82 million in the first quarter to £150 million in the second. Total reserves were expected to fall to £400 million by the end of June. He added that the publication of these figures, which would be necessary by mid-July, would constitute a strong psychological blow.[21] On 22 June he told Acheson that the figures would be published on 5 July and that Cripps was opposed to devaluation, favouring, instead, a sharp curtailment of imports from the dollar area. Douglas feared Anglo-American acrimony: 'a situation in which the UK blames adverse developments on the US recession and the US blames the UK for socialist mismanagement of its affairs'. He strongly urged secret, blunt and frank talks between the British, Americans and Canadians.[22] Meantime Attlee was suggesting to Bevin, who was attending the Paris CFM, that he try to persuade Acheson to visit London on his journey from Paris to the United States in order that he might thoroughly understand the position and the effect of failure to deal with the dollar position on the cold war.[23] This was a characteristic argument used by the British in this era: harm to sterling meant harm to Britain's capacity to act as the United States' principal cold war ally. In the event Acheson returned to Washington without detour. Yet he was sympathetic to Britain's plight and the government's arguments.

So Bevin asked Franks to give Acheson an urgent message proposing that Snyder, Secretary of the US Treasury, who was due to visit Europe shortly, should come to London for discussions with British and Canadian ministers. According to Acheson, Snyder was undecided about devaluation. Bevin's message contained the claim that 'Without firm action I fear much of our work on Western Union and the Atlantic Pact will be undermined and our progress in the cold war halted.' The next day the US Secretary of State sent a copy of Bevin's message to the London Embassy.[24]

FRANKS AND THE LONDON TALKS

While plans were underway for Snyder's visit, Franks was arranging a return to London, which he had been keen to make for the past six months.[25] On the evening of 27 June, Bevin telegraphed to say that, after discussion with his colleagues, he felt it desirable for the Ambassador to be present during the Snyder talks. He wanted Franks to arrive at the latest possible moment that would enable him to talk matters over with ministers before the talks started. He wanted him to come with the most up-to-date information about US policy and to 'be in a position to continue to influence the United States authorities in the formulation of such policy up to the last moment'.[26] Franks had been made a Privy Counsellor on 8 June, a move clearly designed to facilitate his full participation in the financial discussions.

Shortly after his arrival, the Ambassador attended the Economic Policy Committee of the Cabinet, chaired by Attlee, which held two sessions on 1 July. He reported Acheson and Hoffman, Administrator of ECA, as having told him to bear in mind Congressional feeling in July; it was important that the British government took no action which might prejudice Congress's consideration of the Atlantic Pact, the Military Assistance Bill, or the second appropriation under ERP. He added that it had been impressed upon him that the British government should avoid the impression that in times of crisis Britain always adopted a restrictive policy. As regards devaluation, the two Americans were more interested in British efficiency and competitive power than in devaluation as an isolated problem.[27] The Committee had before them a paper by Cripps offering three possible policies: severe deflation, devaluation and continuing improvement of competitive power.[28] Labour as a party was opposed to severe deflation, though Cripps was prepared to see it in a mild form. The Chancellor, backed by the Treasury and the Bank of England, opposed devaluation. So the meeting was left with only the current policy of import cuts and tighter control of public spending. Morrison, Lord President of the Council, was the only minister to favour devaluation.

On 6 July, Cripps announced the rise in the dollar deficit and restrictions on dollar purchases.[29] The next day the Economic Policy Committee met again to consider the impending talks with Snyder and Abbott. Franks also attended and stressed that the Americans did not see the crisis as being as serious as the British government did; they thought it was probably only a temporary phase.[30]

There followed two days of detailed talks on 8–9 July and another meeting at Chequers on the 10th with Snyder and Douglas C. Abbott, Canadian Minister of Finance.[31] Snyder found Cripps unwilling to contemplate devaluation and he reported his discouragement at this attitude. The difference between the British, on one side, and the Americans and Canadians, on the other, was brought out in the British attempt to include in the communiqué that neither the United States nor Canada considered devaluation of the pound an appropriate measure for present British difficulties. Neither Snyder nor Abbott would accept this. Instead, they agreed to say that devaluation was not explored during discussions. Moreover, the Americans accepted the idea of further talks in Washington in late August and September.[32] According to Douglas Jay, Economic Secretary to the Treasury, Franks helped save a frosty meeting with Snyder in which there was little understanding between them:

> However, Oliver Franks came to the rescue and left everybody feeling quite happy after about half an hour. The upshot was they would not give us advice in public anymore, but we would hold a meeting a bit later in the United States to see what could be done.[33]

Once more Franks's diplomatic skills had helped to smooth differences and produce action acceptable to both parties.

Immediately after the talks with Snyder there was a meeting of the Commonwealth Finance Ministers which agreed to cut dollar imports by 25 per cent.[34] However, as July progressed the inadequacy of such an approach was being recognised: opinion was shifting in favour of devaluation. Cripps's health deteriorated and caused him to enter a Swiss sanatorium on 19 July. Attlee entrusted Jay, Wilson, President of the Board of Trade, and Gaitskell, Minister of Fuel and Power, with the Chancellor's responsibilities. On 21 July they met and agreed (Wilson reluctantly) to advise devaluation. They persuaded Attlee on the 25th.[35] In two meetings of the Cabinet on 28 and 29 July, which Franks attended, the economic position was discussed. Ministers agreed to give Attlee the authority to take such further action as he thought necessary.[36]

The Prime Minister sent a letter, mainly drafted by Jay, to Cripps on 5 August, saying that all were agreed, including the responsible officials; they accepted that devaluation was a necessary step to stop the present dollar drain. He added that Franks confirmed that the Washington talks in September were unlikely to produce substantial help from the Americans to prevent the reserves from falling to a dangerously low level. The timing of devaluation, Attlee maintained, needed to be decided before Cripps and Bevin went to Washington:

> Sir Oliver Franks is clear in his view that we should not gain, but lose, with the Americans, if we appear to be trading an offer of devaluation for concessions on their part, or even if we had failed to make up our own minds. His view is that the Americans will expect us to have taken a decision ourselves on this crucial point of British policy; and I think we must accept his judgement.[37]

He closed by saying that they preferred 28 August or 4 September as dates for devaluation. The letter was taken by Wilson to Cripps in Switzerland. In a letter of 8 August Wilson reported the Chancellor's response. Cripps seemed to accept devaluation but wanted to decide its timing on his return in consultation with the Prime Minister, Foreign Secretary and President of the Board of Trade. He favoured an announcement on 18 September after the Washington conversations.[38]

Franks was clearly prominent in advising to ministers that they should arrive in Washington with a plan of action to present to the Americans. He told Hall on 11 July that a plan had to be found which he could put to Acheson. As regards the contents of such a plan he had some radical thoughts. He proposed abandonment of the sterling area and a return to convertibility which he felt would please the United States but really cost Britain nothing since with full convertibility the sterling area would become meaningless.[39] He maintained, in an 18-page memorandum on 20 July, that the sterling area had been draining off Britain's dollars.[40] On the next day, he spoke to Plowden and Hall about it. Hall observed of the meeting: 'At times he was very impressive and I began to wonder if he were our new Keynes. P[lowden] seemed a bit jealous at times.'[41] Nevertheless, nothing came of his proposal: it was too radical a challenge to financial orthodoxy and the scale of the sterling area's drain on dollars was doubted by Treasury officials. Yet, interestingly, Snyder, in his report on his London talks, wrote of a system that 'enabled these countries to run a heavy trade deficit with the United Kingdom which indirectly involves a substantial dollar drain on the United Kingdom'.[42]

As British thinking was moving towards a coherent policy, US official opinion remained divided between the sympathetic State Department who wanted to help and the more wary Treasury who felt it was up to the British to solve their own problems. Snyder said he was at the July talks for information, that he brought no recommendations. On the eve of these discussions he had told Acheson that the fall in dollar reserves 'should be viewed as a UK problem'.[43] Indeed, Martin, the Assistant Secretary of the Treasury, doubted the urgency of the problem for the British; and believed the government was not doing enough to cut costs.[44] A strong motif in the discussions in the US Treasury was the belief that the Europeans, and the British especially, were once again seeking more US aid.[45] Snyder declared that the British were relying on American help rather than their own efforts at eliminating rigidities in their economy to solve the problems.[46] As a result, at a meeting of the National Advisory Council on International Monetary and Financial problems, Snyder helped to block funds from the IMF or the Import-Export Bank to ease British financial pressures.[47] Acheson later observed that Snyder and the

Treasury did not want to be associated with the devaluation of sterling:

> the Treasury looks at these things from a very narrow point of view and John Snyder's great interest in this was not to get hooked for anything. He didn't want to be involved in the devaluation of the pound; he didn't want to be involved in making any concessions on the British loan agreement; he didn't want to be involved in loosening up any further credits or anything of that sort. Therefore, his whole tendency was to shrink back from discussion of anything. He was very bad from the point of view of our relations with the British, because whether we could do something or not, it was most important to talk about this, to talk it all out and understand one another and do what we could.[48]

Many American newspapers shared the Treasury outlook. The Washington Embassy reported that a 'large section of the press – which is predominately conservative – is increasingly impatient with recurrent British crises from which long-suffering Uncle Sam is called upon to rescue Socialist Britain'. The report also contained, however, the criticism by Walter Lippmann of the US Treasury for aggravating the crisis by promoting world speculation against the British reserves.[49]

The attitude of the State Department was more in keeping with Lippmann than with the conservative press. It was characterised by an understanding of British problems, a readiness to try and help and a recognition that harm to Britain meant problems for the United States. As Leffler said, 'Unlike Treasury officials who pressed the British to tackle their problems as if they were primarily financial … the State Department studied options in terms of their impact on the overall configuration of power between the United States and the Soviet Union.'[50] Kennan told his colleagues in the Policy Planning Staff that they needed to consider the consequences of the British abandonment of their military commitments abroad; and how many of them the United States might need to assume.[51] Acheson wholeheartedly shared this perspective. He maintained that 'Britain and the sterling countries of which she is the center are … our partners in the great co-ordinated effort to build a secure and prosperous world. They are indispensable to us, and we are indispensable to them.'[52] The State Department made its position clear to the British Embassy, no doubt to provide reassurance. Kennan said to Hoyer Millar that they 'were fully conscious of the necessity of looking at the problem from the political and not only from the economic point of view'.[53]

Not surprisingly, discussions between the Embassy and the State Department were at the core of future progress. When Franks returned to Washington on 9 August, he found an invitation from Acheson to talks. They met the next day for about an hour, together with Webb, the US Under-Secretary. The Ambassador reported that their conversation 'was so general and vague as to be difficult to record at all'. He identified three main strands. First, there was Acheson's anxiety to know what role Bevin would play. Franks gave his personal opinion that the Foreign Secretary would be *primus inter pares*. Secondly, the United States wanted to know whether broader issues would be addressed; and, interestingly, he gave as an example of such an issue the question of whether Britain was trying to build a third world outside the Soviet and dollar countries. The Ambassador again gave his personal opinion that wider matters would be considered. Thirdly, Acheson said he hoped the British were not coming with nothing to say except a request for help. He added that it would make all the difference if the British started the talks off with a really good analysis of the situation and its causes which would be generally acceptable. The main point Franks made was that, apart from the long-term policy issues, there was a need for immediate action, which he felt would have to include American help.[54] Since Acheson told the President on 11 August that he was working with Snyder on the nature of the long-term problems and of the necessity for short-term action, it seems likely that Franks's point registered.[55]

Acheson was also receiving advice from the London Embassy. The Ambassador, Douglas, now offered Acheson the same sage counsel as he had given Marshall over ERP. On 15 August Douglas sent a personal letter to the Secretary of State. He estimated that the British would be 'sensitive, very suspicious and perhaps unreceptive'. He suggested that the United States show great self-restraint and refrain from asking the British what they proposed to do. He was anxious to avoid causing resentment that would lead, in the impending election, to the return of a government on an anti-American platform.[56] On the 18th, Bliss, the Counsellor for Economic Affairs at the Embassy, sent an extensive assessment of the subject. He repeated many of Douglas's points about the psychological delicacy of the matter and the risks to Anglo-American relations. He noted various measures which the British would need to take, but added that these alone would not be enough, for the United States had responsibilities too. He declared that 'intellectual honesty' required them to recognise that the United States favoured 'non-discrimination in areas of trade where we are in a strong competitive position; but resorts to subsidies … and discrimination in those areas where we are competitively weak'.[57] A telegram from Douglas on 23 August noted that Bevin was not in the best of health and was in a 'sensitive, chip-on-the-shoulder subtly anti-American mood'.[58]

Meanwhile, the British were finalising their own position. On 19 August Cripps, now back in Britain, attended a meeting of ministers at Chequers where his acceptance of devaluation was clearly tentative. He had to be persuaded that the British action would be accompanied by American supporting measures.[59] At Cabinet on 29 August it was agreed in principle that the pound should be devalued but with the proviso that 'satisfactory understandings on consequential United States policy could be reached'. Bevin and Cripps were authorised to tell the US and Canadian governments of this decision at the Washington talks and to discuss with them the extent to which the pound should be devalued.[60] The Foreign Secretary and Chancellor then sailed for the United States. In the brief prepared for their guidance they were reminded of Franks's advice:

> it is very likely that the attitude of the United States Ministers in the forthcoming discussions will be to sit back and not make any suggestions themselves, unless and until they are satisfied that this country is determined to do everything in its power to extricate itself from the present difficult situation.[61]

This proved to be accurate advice. The paper also listed a series of short-term measures which would be requested of the United States: more favourable administration of ERP; resumption of stockpiling; loans from the Export-Import Bank; drawings from the IMF; reciprocal tariff reductions.

WASHINGTON TALKS BETWEEN OFFICIALS

While the ministerial party was *en route*, talks between US, British and Canadian officials took place in Washington. They met five times under the chairmanship of Webb, 27 August–2 September, and were designated as meetings of the Combined Official Committee.[62] At first the conversations did not go well. Hall noted in his diary that 'the whole feeling was one of shadow boxing'. On the 29th Webb gave a dinner for the participants who 'got on much better' and agreed to hold smaller meetings in future.[63] The return of Franks to Washington on 1 September cheered up Hall, for the Ambassador 'has taken hold'. After the last meeting on Friday 2 September, Hall could observe 'it was something to have got through the week at all in so friendly an atmosphere'. He added:

> At the last small meeting ... Wilson Smith was fairly frank about our position and said that the US and Canadians were not to be gloomy, because it had been inevitable that we could not say what we were going to do. But they need not suppose from this that our Ministers would do the same. Webb replied in the same spirit and said frankly how important it would be to them to know what we intended to contribute.[64]

In these first days of September before the ministerial talks began on 7 September there was a good deal of informal contact between Acheson and Franks. It is no accident that, in the section of his memoirs covering the devaluation, Acheson should have revealed the confidential relationship that he had established with the Ambassador. In the discussions about article 5 of the North Atlantic Treaty the Secretary of State had discovered the value of Franks's advice. It was during the British financial crisis that private discussion was first used to help solve a major problem. On 3 September Franks and Acheson dined alone and had a long conversation. Acheson said that the real American anxiety concerned whether the British wished to work towards a free world or whether they wished to build up a soft currency world centred around sterling and cut themselves off from North America. He added that the British attitude would be judged by the readiness to undertake short-term measures like import cuts, devaluation and a serious dollar export drive; and by the commitment to long-term goals such as improving productivity and minimising the dollar drain of the sterling area upon the central reserves. In reporting this to London, after the Washington talks, Franks recorded Acheson as saying that the US attitude would be sympathetic and helpful but the extent of US help would depend upon what the British had to say.[65] Franks did not reveal Acheson's observation that he did not really trust Cripps on the issue of one world.[66]

On the day he saw Acheson to talk things over, Franks telegraphed London. He said that the President's speech in Philadelphia on 29 August had been designed to create a favourable atmosphere for the talks, and had been specially composed to this end by Acheson and Kennan. Franks hoped the Prime Minister would use his speech to the Trade Union Congress at Bridlington on the day the Washington conversations began as an opportunity to complement Truman's speech with some appreciation of the President's words and of the equal determination of Britain to pursue 'mutual concession and co-operation'. He concluded by saying that it would strike at the heart of the matter if Attlee said Britain was not there 'to seek charity or gifts of dollars from the United States Government but to make its contribution to the solution of a world problem which particularly affects the three great trading nations represented at the talks'.[67] Attlee agreed to Franks's suggestions.[68]

WASHINGTON MINISTERIAL TALKS

The Washington talks on financial matters were held 7–12 September.[69] The principal delegates were Acheson, Snyder and Hoffman for the United States; Bevin, Cripps and Franks for Britain; and Lester Pearson, Secretary of State for External Affairs, Douglas C. Abbott, and Hume Wrong, Ambassador in the United States, for Canada. Snyder was appointed to lead the US team. But Kennan reassured the Embassy by saying that his own initial concern about this choice was removed when he realised that this arrangement would make it easier to secure the support of Congress and would allow Acheson to hold political discussions on the side with Bevin.[70] Acheson later observed of the first few days that they 'were everything a conference should not be, and too many are – a complete waste of time with rising exasperation among the conferees'.[71] On the eve of the meetings he told Franks that the preparation was the worst he had known and it must not be allowed to happen again: 'They have been, like us, so busy preparing a great mass of documentation that no one has had time to consider or use it.'[72] To a degree, however, this was understandable, since 'all the preliminary work … in the United States were [*sic*] quite meaningless and quite useless, because nobody could or would talk about the devaluation of the pound'.[73]

According to Franks, the conference began with the US delegation looking grave but not saying a word, and they 'persisted in this course until we British made up our minds what to do'.[74] Matters were not helped by an exchange between Bevin and Hoffman. The ECA Administrator urged the British to turn from the easy markets of the sterling area, reduce costs and pursue a dollar export drive. Irked by this self-righteous peroration, Bevin responded by asking Hoffman whether he would guarantee that Congress would allow these products into the United States if Europe sought to boost its exports to the United States?[75] It was clear that the British would have to reveal what they were planning. So the six ministers and Hoffman met alone and were told of the decision to devalue. Franks told London that the Chancellor's utterance made a profound impression both in content and manner. It was responsible for the evident goodwill and helpfulness of attitude by both the Americans and Canadians thereafter. He added that 'it forthwith became possible to treat the whole problem of trade between the sterling and dollar areas within the group as "our" problem'.[76] The subsequent meetings also owed a great deal to Franks's organisational powers:

> An early meeting at the Embassy where (at Oliver's insistence) a paper was produced giving all the subjects that might be discussed and suggesting which should be referred to Committees and which discussed by the Ministers . . . If Oliver were not here I wonder very much how the thing would have got itself organized.[77]

There still remained the question of the actual amount by which to devalue the pound. This was finally decided in Franks's study at the Embassy on the night of 12 September in a meeting that included Bevin, Cripps, Plowden, Wilson Smith, Hall, Makins of the Foreign Office, and the Ambassador. A reduction of 30 per cent from $4.03 to $2.80 was accepted, although Cripps had to be persuaded from seeking US and Canadian advice about what rate they might propose.[78] By this time the talks had closed with the Americans promising a number of helpful measures: lower tariffs, more overseas investment, simpler customs procedures and arrangements to allow the use of ERP dollars to purchase Canadian wheat.[79] On 18 September Cripps announced the devaluation. The impact of the decision is difficult to assess, but Britain had a current account surplus for every year from 1950 to 1954, except 1951.[80]

There was one other decision of the meetings that boded well for good Anglo-American relations. It was decided to have a permanent economic council of the three participating powers so as to ensure better co-ordination of policy in the future. Sir Leslie Rowan, Second Secretary at the Treasury, was appointed Economic Minister to the Washington Embassy in order to perform this task. Meetings began on 16 November.[81] Here was a scheme that had first been proposed by the Embassy in spring.[82] On 4 September Franks had spoken eloquently in favour of a combined board to Hall, who believed Acheson wanted the same.[83] It seems probable that the emergence of such a body owed something to collaboration between Ambassador and Secretary of State.

In assessing the Washington discussions, Franks gave a positive verdict. Interestingly, he felt Snyder had been a 'good sympathetic chairman'. He believed that all the ministers involved achieved 'a new degree of frankness and friendliness in their ability to discuss difficult questions'. He had seen the 'creation of an entirely new spring of goodwill and confidence towards us on the American and Canadian sides'. Moreover, it was clear that the Americans had decided 'once more to regard us as their principal partner in world affairs and not just as a member of the European game'.[84]

To British eyes, 1949 had brought two advances towards an Anglo-American partnership: in the field of security with the North Atlantic Pact and in the economic sphere with the resolution of the sterling crisis and establishment of machinery for close economic consultation in the future. Indeed, at the height of the crisis, British officials spoke about creating a financial counterpart to military arrangements.[85] Franks had been at the heart of the successful completion of the tasks. This achievement was all the more pleasing given the doubts expressed in the Foreign Office in the summer when Roger Makins had described the September meetings as Britain's last chance to secure a role as the United States' global partner.[86]

NOTES

1. Plowden, *An Industrialist*, pp. 35, 39; Cairncross, *Years of Recovery*, pp. 27, 201.
2. S. Newton, 'The 1949 Sterling Crisis and British Policy towards European Integration', *Review of International Studies*, Vol. 11, No. 3, July 1985, p. 172.
3. Leffler, *Preponderance*, p. 314.
4. Newton, '1949 Sterling Crisis . . .', p. 174.
5. PRO, T236/2398, OF110/10/16 has an extract from the article and a copy of FO to Washington, Tel. No. 3437, 24 March 1949 alerting the Embassy.
6. PRO, T236/2398, Washington To FO, Tel. No. 1944, 4 April 1949.
7. PRO, FO 371/75577, UE2132/150/53G, Franks to FO, Tel. No. 2004, 5 April 1949.
8. Ibid., UE2133/150/53G, Franks to FO, Tel. No. 1949, 5 April 1949.
9. Ibid., FO to Washington, Tel. No. 3888, 6 April 1949.
10. Ibid., UE2179/150/53G, Washington to FO, Tel. No. 65 EAGER, 6 April 1949. See also A. S. Milward, *The Reconstruction of Western Europe 1945–51* (London: Methuen, 1984), p. 289; Plowden, *An Industrialist*, p. 54; Cairncross, *Years of Recovery*, p. 171. At the same time, ECA Finance Officers, meeting in Paris on 4–6 April, raised the need to examine exchange rates, especially that of the pound; the representatives from London, at least, were at that point reluctant to favour devaluation. NA, Wash. DC, RG59, Records of the State Department, Lot 54D224, General Records of the Office of British Commonwealth and Northern European Affairs, Subject Files, H–20(A)–ERP, OEEC since January 1948 folder, Meeting of ECA Finance Officers in Paris, 4–6 April 1949.
11. PRO, FO 371/75577, UE2264/150/53G, note by Roger Makins for Sir W. Strang, 7 April 1949.
12. PRO, T236/2398, Franks to FO, Tel. No. 2097, 8 April 1949.
13. PRO, T236/2398, FO to Washington, Tel. No. 4254, 14 April 1949.
14. PRO, FO 371/75577, UE3176/150/53G, Franks to FO, Tel. No. 2764, 20 May 1949.

15. Ibid.
16. PRO, FO 371/75577, UE3176/150/53G, Franks to FO, Tel. No. 2764, 20 May 1949; ibid., FO to Washington, Tel. No. 5497, 24 May 1949; FO 371/75578, UE3224/150/53G, Franks to FO, Tel. No. 2809, 24 May 1949; FO 371/75578, UE3361/150/53G, Franks to FO, Tel. No. 2891, 30 May 1949. See also Cairncross (ed.), *Hall Diaries 1947–1953*, p. 58, (entry for 5 June); P. Hennessy and M. Brown, 'Deciphering the "Rose" Code', *The Times*, 3 January 1980; Cairncross, *Years of Recovery*, p. 172.
17. Cairncross (ed.), *Hall Diaries 1947–1953*, p. 59 (entry for 5 June). See NA, Wash. DC, RG 59, Lot 54D224, Office of British Commonwealth and Northern European Affairs, Subject Files, H–20(A)–ERP, OEEC since January 1948 folder, memoranda of conversation, 3, 4 and 7 June 1949; FRUS, 1949 IV, pp. 781–4, memorandum of conversation, 9 June 1949.
18. Cairncross, *Years of Recovery*, p. 173; Plowden, *An Industrialist*, p. 54.
19. Cairncross, *Years of Recovery*, p. 171; Plowden, *An Industrialist*, p. 56.
20. FRUS, 1949, IV, p. 398, Webb to Embassy in UK, 28 May 1949.
21. FRUS, 1949, IV, pp. 784–6, Douglas to Webb, 16 June 1949.
22. Ibid., pp. 787–90, Douglas to Acheson, 22 June 1949.
23. PRO, FO 800/516, US/49/30, FO to Luxembourg (repeated to Paris), Tel. No. 81, 18 June 1949.
24. Ibid., US/49/31 and 32, FO to Washington, Tel. Nos. 6396 and 6397, 22 June 1949; FO 371/75578, UE4007/150/53G, Franks to FO, Tel. No. 3299, 25 June 1949 confirming delivery of message to Acheson on 22nd; FRUS, 1949, IV, pp. 790–1, Acheson to Embassy in UK, 23 June 1949.
25. See PRO FO 115/4429, Gl/1/49, Franks to Bevin, 29 December 1948: 'I feel that I have already been away too long and am risking losing touch. It is always a very good asset out here to be able to say one has talked to people in London fairly recently.'
26. PRO, FO 800/516, US/49/44, FO to Washington, Tel. No. 6586, 27 June 1949; before he left Washington, Franks had talks with Acheson about the Snyder mission, see FO 371/75578, UE4007/150/53G, Franks to Makins, 24 June 1949 and FRUS, 1949, IV, p. 797.
27. PRO, CAB 134/220, EPC (49) 24th and EPC (49) 25th, 1 July, 1948; B. Pimlott (ed.), *The Political Diary of Hugh Dalton, 1918–1940, 1945–1960* (London: Jonathan Cape, 1986), pp. 451–2.
28. PRO, CAB 134/222, EPC(49)72, Chancellor of the Exchequer, 'The Dollar Situation', 28 June 1949.
29. *House of Commons Debates*, Vol. 466, Cols. 2149–55.
30. PRO, CAB 134/220, EPC (49) 27th, 7 July 1949.
31. PRO, T269/1, Record of Discussions held by United Kingdom Ministers with Mr Snyder and Mr Abbott on 8, 9 and 10 July 1949; FO 371/75580, UE4291–4293/150/53G, minutes by R. Makins of 8 and 9 July 1949.
32. FRUS, 1949, IV, pp. 799–802, Snyder to Acheson, 9 July and 10 July 1949.
33. Lord Jay in 'Witness Seminar: 1949 Devaluation', *Contemporary Record*, Vol. 5, No. 3, Winter 1991, p. 491.
34. H. Pelling, *Britain and the Marshall Plan*, (London: Macmillan, 1988), p. 82.
35. Plowden, *An Industrialist*, pp. 58–9.
36. PRO, CAB 128/16, CM 50(49) and CM 51(49), 28 and 29 July 1940.
37. PRO, PREM 8/1178 Part 1, Attlee to Cripps, 5 August 1949. See also Cairncross (ed.), *Hall Diaries 1947–1953*, p. 68 (27 July entry) which records Franks (at Hall's suggestion) telling a group of officials on 22 July that we should go to Washington with action already taken.
38. Ibid., Wilson to Attlee, 8 August 1949.
39. Cairncross (ed.), *Hall Diaries 1947–1953*, pp. 64–5 (11 July entry).

40. PRO, T269/1, Sir Oliver Franks, 'The Dollar Crisis of Summer 1949', 20 July 1949.
41. Cairncross (ed.), *Hall Diaries 1947–1953*, p. 68 (21 July entry).
42. HSTL, John W. Snyder Papers, Box 32, European Trip of the Secretary of the Treasury, July 2 through July 25, 1949 Report, n.d.
43. HSTL, Snyder Papers, Box 108, Trip File, France folder, Snyder (Paris) to Secretary of State, Cable No. 2793, 6 July 1949.
44. HSTL, Snyder Papers, Box 34, UK General 1946–49, Martin memorandum: 'British Monetary and Price Policy', 30 August 1949. Franks afterwards described Martin as 'doctrinaire' in his opinions; see HSTL, Oral History No. 194, Oliver Franks, 27 June 1964, p. 9.
45. HSTL, Snyder Papers, Box 33, Trip File, Europe – summary folder, William Hillman to Snyder, 3 August 1949.
46. HSTL, John W. Snyder Papers, Box 32, European Trip of the Secretary of the Treasury, July 2 through July 25, 1949 Report, n.d.
47. NA, Wash. DC, RG 56, Treasury, General Records of the National Advisory Council, Briefing Books, 1946–53, Box 33, Price of Gold folder, NAC Meeting No. 134, 11 August 1949.
48. *Princeton Seminars*, microfilm of discussion between Acheson and advisers, 1953–54, 10 October 1953, roll 3, frames 754–5.
49. PRO, FO 371/75581, UE4539/150/53, Washington to FO, Tel. No. 329(S), 15 July 1949.
50. Leffler, *Preponderance*, p. 315.
51. NA, Wash. DC, RG 59, State Department, Lot 64 D 563, Records of the Policy Planning Staff, Country and Area Files, Box 17, Great Britain 1947–53 folder, PPS 132nd Meeting, 2 September 1949 and 137th Meeting, 12 September 1949 and Memorandum for Secretary of State by John M. Ohly, 'The Need for an Assessment of the Full Implications to American Security of the Current British Dollar Crisis', 1 September 1949.
52. HSTL, James Webb Papers, Box 25, Department of State file – Secretary of State, notes for speech to Business Advisory Council 14 September 1949.
53. PRO, FO 371/75586, UE5526/150/53G, F. R. Hoyer Millar to R. Makins, 24 August 1949.
54. PRO, FO 800/516, US/49/42, New York to FO, Tel. No. 88, 11 August 1949.
55. HSTL, Acheson Papers, Box 64, memorandum of conversation with the President, 11 August 1949.
56. *Acheson Official Conversations*, reel 1, frames 681–3. See also Seeley G. Mudd Library, Princeton NJ, Lippmann Papers, Series III, Box 67, Douglas to Lippmann, 11 July and 10 August 1949, which show his scepticism about the British economic position.
57. FRUS, 1949, IV, pp. 806–20, 'Implications of the Sterling Area Crisis to the UK and the US', 18 August 1949.
58. NA, Wash. DC, RG 59, State Department Decimal Files 1945–49, Box 5980, 841.002/8–2349, Douglas to Acheson, 23 August 1949.
59. PRO, T269/1, Minutes of a Meeting of Ministers held at Chequers at 5.30 p.m. Friday 19 August 1949; Plowden, *An Industrialist*, p. 61; Cairncross, *Years of Recovery*, pp. 184–5.
60. PRO, CAB 128/16, CM 53(49), 29 August 1949.
61. PRO, CAB 129/36, CP(49) 185, Chancellor of the Exchequer, 'Brief for Ministerial Talks in Washington', 29 August 1949.
62. There were also several meetings of five sub-committees. It was agreed that there would be no verbatim record but only short summaries. See NA Wash. DC, RG 56, Records of the Treasury, NAC, Briefing Books 1946–53, Box 35, Tripartite Economic Talks folder, Minutes of the Combined Official

Committee, 27 August–2 September 1949.

63. Cairncross (ed.), *Hall Diaries 1947–1953*, p. 72 (31 August entry).
64. Ibid., p. 72 and pp. 73–4 (4 September entry).
65. PRO, FO 800/516, US/49/49, Franks to FO, Tel. No. 4555, 19 September 1949.
66. Cairncross (ed.), *Hall Diaries 1947–1953*, p. 74 (4 September entry).
67. Bodleian Library, Oxford, Attlee Papers, dep 87, Washington to FO, Tel. No. 4197, 3 September 1949. The FO and Treasury prepared a brief for the Prime Minister to deliver.
68. PRO, FO 371/75586, UE5572/150/53. FO to Washington, Tel. No. 8439, 6 September 1949.
69. PRO, FO 371/75587, UE5670, 5674, 5704, 5781, and 5781/150/53 contain Washington to FO, Tel. Nos. 4234, 4229, 4262, 4324, and 4337 reporting the discussions.
70. PRO, FO 371/75586, UE5526/150/53G, F. R. Hoyer Millar to R. Makins, 24 August 1949.
71. Acheson, *Present at the Creation*, p. 324.
72. Cairncross (ed.), *Hall Diaries 1947–1953*, p. 77 (6 September entry).
73. *Princeton Seminars*, roll 3, frame 752, Acheson, 10 October 1953.
74. HSTL, Franks Oral History, pp. 9–10.
75. Acheson, *Present at the Creation*, pp. 324–5; Bullock, *Ernest Bevin*, p. 717.
76. PRO, FO 800/516, US/49/49, Franks to FO, Tel. No. 4555, 19 September 1949; see also Acheson, *Present at the Creation*, p. 325.
77. Cairncross (ed.), *Hall Diaries 1947–1953*, p. 79 (9 September entry).
78. Ibid., p. 83 (15 September entry); Plowden, *An Industrialist*, pp. 63–64.
79. FRUS, 1949, IV, pp. 833–9, text of Joint Communiqué, 12 September 1949; Plowden, *An Industrialist*, p. 64.
80. On the economic consequences of devaluation see Cairncross, *Years of Recovery*, pp. 207–11.
81. Acheson, *Present at the Creation*, p. 325; *DBPO*, 2nd Series, II, No. 2, p. 3n.
82. Cairncross (ed.), *Hall Diaries 1947–1953*, p. 70 (9 August entry).
83. Ibid., p. 77 (6 September (evening) entry).
84. PRO, FO 800/516, US/49/49, Franks to FO, Tel. No. 4555, 19 September 1949. The copy of the telegram at FO 371/75590, UE5984/150/53 reads 'as a member of the European queue'.
85. PRO, T236/2400, Sir Sydney Caine, 'Note on the Anglo–American Canadian Talks', 15 August 1949. In sending this to London, he said he did not think that Franks would be in serious disagreement with the general analysis.
86. PRO, FO 371/75594, UE6686/150/53G, R. Makins minute, 'Anglo–American Canadian Talks. General Considerations', 26 August 1949.

— 8 —

Part of the European Queue or Special Partners?

THE CRISIS over the devaluation of the pound caused the British in London and at the Washington Embassy to reflect a good deal on their status. In the period between summer 1949 and the outbreak of the Korean War in June 1950 the British deliberated on their position in the world and their relations with both the United States and Europe. Franks played a prominent role in this process of reassessment. Debate was characterised by a concern to ensure that Britain be regarded not just as a part of the European queue but as the United States' special partner in world affairs.

ASSESSING RELATIONS

In July 1949, as the sterling crisis mounted and while Franks was in London, the North American Department prepared a paper entitled 'Co-operation between the United Kingdom and the United States'. It had originally been called 'Ideas for Promoting the General Principles Behind the North Atlantic Treaty'. The change is perhaps a revealing one about the view from London. The paper did not attempt to deal with the broad questions of strategic, political and economic co-operation. Instead it listed various aspects to Anglo-American collaboration through bureaucratic consultation, service liaison, the work of official bodies and of semi-official and private bodies. The main theme was:

> In their day to day political relations Britain and the United States are often drawn together less by formal treaties and agreements than by mutual understanding of the common problems and by a desire to promote the common ideals of democracy and justice.

As regards the future, it suggested that the successful development of the North Atlantic Treaty would depend upon the effective continuation of the Anglo-American partnership. Franks felt the memorandum was on the right lines. With this observation, it was sent to the Washington Embassy for comment.[1]

Within a fortnight, Denis Allen, the Political Counsellor at the Embassy, sent a redrafted version of the paper to the Foreign Office. He said that the Americans were ready to receive British advice and help, provided it was tactfully offered, and were ready to recognise Britain as their strongest and most reliable partner. But he identified three reasons for caution. First, the Americans tended to see Britain in different guises 'according to whether they are dealing with us in our role as the centre of the Commonwealth, as their chief partner in the cold war, as the leading Western European country or as the country with whom they hold many ... traditions in common'. Secondly, they were reluctant to admit to their special relationship with Britain, given domestic American prejudices about socialism. Thirdly, he warned

> we must be careful not to appear more concerned with using the North Atlantic Treaty as a means of developing our special relationship with the United States rather than with developing our own co-operation with the Western European countries. There have recently been signs over matters such as the exchange of military information ... that the United States are becoming increasingly disinclined to grant to ourselves facilities which they might not in principle be equally willing to accord to other members of the North Atlantic community.[2]

The paper was received in the Foreign Office registry on 24 August, but no further action was taken on the survey of Anglo-American relations until the anxieties of the winter led to reappraisals in spring 1950. The Permanent Under-Secretary's Committee then prepared a paper which was designed as an aid to talks with the Americans in April and May.[3]

In the immediate aftermath of the successful handling of the financial crisis, both the Foreign Office and the Embassy were optimistic about Anglo-American relations. Even Hoffman, the ECA Administrator, had called the devaluation a bold and imaginative move.[4] The arrangements for economic co-operation between Britain, Canada and the United States helped lead to an Atlantic rather than European outlook by the Cabinet. On 27 October ministers approved two Cabinet papers stressing this line. The first, on the Council of Europe, spoke of 'our new relationship with the United States' and how Britain was 'different in character from other European nations and fundamentally incapable of wholehearted integration with them'. The second memorandum declared that economic ties with Europe were secondary to the 'new relationship with the United States and the Commonwealth which had followed the Washington talks'.[5]

This outlook seemed to be confirmed on the American side by the observations of George Kennan at the Combined Policy Committee on 13 September:

> an attempt should be made to link the United Kingdom more closely to the United States and Canada to get the United Kingdom to disengage itself as much as possible from Continental European problems. While the United Kingdom would continue to be a staunch ally of Western Europe, it should assume more nearly the role of advisor to Western Europe on its problems and less the role of active participants.[6]

No doubt such thoughts encouraged the British. However, they would have been wise to treat them with circumspection. By the end of the year Kennan had resigned as head of the Policy Planning Staff. Moreover, Acheson did not take such a view; nor did US Ambassadors in Europe meeting on 21–22 October. Indeed, in a letter to the envoys Acheson said the 'key to progress towards integration is in French hands … France needs to take the initiative promptly and decisively'.[7] Here was an interesting premonition of the Schuman Plan of May 1950.

Acheson's thoughts were repeated to Franks in a private lunch on 26 November at Sandy Spring, the Secretary of State's farm outside Washington.[8] In response to a question, Acheson said he had been thinking a good deal about Franco-German rapprochement, both political and economic. The United States would do all it could to press this forward, since it afforded the only chance of keeping Germany with the West and giving it an economic outlet. Acheson also urged British acceptance of the idea that Spaak, the former Prime Minister of Belgium, be a politically authoritative Director-General of the OEEC, what was dubbed the OEEC 'Superman'. Britain was completely opposed to the idea of giving the OEEC political powers.[9] The Americans felt that their continent-wide market and federal system of government had benefited them and would do the same for the Europeans. The British were ready to pursue inter-governmental co-operation but did not want to surrender sovereignty. In addition, they felt schemes for European integration would diminish Britain's global status: the country was more than just another European power.[10] Acheson, however, agreed with Franks's suggestion that steady quiet attention be given to the tripartite conversations arising out of the September financial talks. They agreed that the whole issue of the sterling balances needed to be tackled.

A further difficulty arose in Anglo-American relations over the Mutual Defence Assistance Programme, a scheme designed to provide the North Atlantic Treaty members with sufficient forces to defend themselves against a Soviet attack. It was signed into law by Truman on 6 October 1949. Part of the arrangements was a bilateral agreement between Britain and the United States governing the financial contributions of each power. Franks saw Acheson on 14 December to explain that the British Cabinet was deeply concerned about the proposed agreement. It seemed to include less assistance than expected and to make heavy demands on British spending.[11] The Ambassador's advocacy managed to ease the problems for Britain, to some degree. On 17 December he met Acheson again.[12] The Secretary of State accepted alterations to certain clauses along British lines, and to make clear in the bilateral that the British contribution to mutual assistance should not be made to such an extent as would cause a conflict with the principle that economic recovery must have a clear priority. On 27 January 1950 Franks signed the bilateral agreement on behalf of the British government.[13]

The strains in the relationship over Europe and military assistance were noted on both sides of the Atlantic. Acheson saw Truman on 20 December 1949 and reviewed what he called 'the uneasy situation in the British–American relationship'.[14] That same day, Strang, Permanent Under-Secretary at the Foreign Office, wrote to Franks saying that ministers had

> a growing sense of irritation, amounting at times to resentment, at the lack of consideration and understanding too often shown by the United States authorities in their dealings with us and with other European countries; and at the implicit assumption by too many Americans that there is nothing in the world that dollars cannot buy, that the European Recovery Programme gives United States agents the right to press for changes in internal policy, and … European governments must toe the line.[15]

He added that he realised there was a good deal of confidential intimacy between the two countries, but the resentments and humiliations lingered. Bevin wanted Franks to come to London for talks on this and other subjects in early February. The Foreign Secretary also wanted the Ambassador to see if he could secure a visit

1. Franks at the White House, 13 January 1949. (Harris & Ewing, photograph courtesy of the Harry S. Truman Library)

2. Sir Gordon Munro of the British Embassy, Oliver Franks, President Truman and Sir Stafford Cripps in the rose garden of the White House, 2 October 1948. (Harris & Ewing, photograph courtesy of the Harry S. Truman Library)

3. Sir Stafford Cripps, Lady Cripps, Lady Franks and Oliver Franks on the terrace of the British Embassy, 26 August 1948. (Harris & Ewing, photograph courtesy of the Harry S. Truman Library)

4. Ernest Bevin, the Foreign Secretary, on the podium at the signing ceremony for the North Atlantic Treaty, with Franks to the left, 4 April 1949. (State Department, photograph courtesy of the National Archives)

5. Oliver Franks presenting the UK's instrument of ratification of the North Atlantic Treaty to acting Secretary of State, James E. Webb, 7 June 1949. (State Department, photograph courtesy of the National Archives).

6. President Truman greets the arrival in Washington of Clement Attlee, the Prime Minister, with Franks to their right, December 1950. (White House photographer Abbie Rowe, photograph courtesy of the National Archives)

7. Prime Minister Clement Attlee speaking to the press, with Franks to his right, Washington, December 1950. (White House photographer Abbie Rowe, photograph courtesy of the National Archives)

8. British Commonwealth Ambassadors in Washington on visit to USA of Princess Elizabeth, 1 November 1951. *Back row:* Percy C. Spender (Australia); Sir Carl Berendsen (New Zealand); Oliver Franks; G. C. S. Corea (Ceylon); B. J. Jarvie (Chargé d'Affaires, South Africa). *Front row:* M. A. H. Ispahani (Pakistan); Hume Wrong (Canada); Princess Elizabeth; Prince Philip; Madame Vijaya Lakshmi Pandit (India). (State Department, photograph courtesy of the Harry S. Truman Library)

9. President Truman greeting Winston Churchill, the Prime Minister, on his arrival in Washington, January 1952; Anthony Eden (holding hat) and Franks are on the aircraft steps. (White House photographer Abbie Rowe, photograph courtesy of the US National Archives)

10. *Back row:* Walter Gifford, US Ambassador to Britain; General Omar N. Bradley; Oliver Franks; Lord Cherwell; Lord Ismay; Averell Harriman. *Front row:* Anthony Eden, British Foreign Secretary; Winston Churchill, Prime Minister; President Truman; Dean Acheson, US Secretary of State; John Snyder; Robert A. Lovett. 5 January 1952. (US Army and Acme, photograph courtesy of the Harry S. Truman Library)

by Acheson to Britain for this would 'give an opportunity for renewing understandings and re-setting courses'.

Franks replied on 31 December. He said he had seen Acheson the previous day and told him of his intended visit to London in early February to discuss some of the issues causing Anglo–American friction. The Ambassador then added that there was justification for ministerial disquiet about the attitude of the United States. He believed that there was 'a sort of imperialism in the efforts made by the Americans to assert their ascendancy' in international organisations like the IMF. Because they did not see the way that they were enforcing their views, they were 'insensitive to the consequences of their actions'. He felt a good deal of the trouble lay in the domestic political situation of the two countries. He concluded by recommending: 'an absolutely consistent endeavour should be made to raise questions between us to the level of reasonable discussion. I do not think this will be easy, but we shall have all the assistance here that our friends like Acheson can give.'[16]

Before leaving for London Franks arranged to see both Hoffman and Acheson. Bevin was worried about Hoffman's proposed visit to Paris which might involve his pressing for penalties against countries that failed to achieve greater trade liberalisation and for acceptance of an OEEC superman. Franks and Caine, head of the Treasury delegation to the Embassy, met Hoffman on 23 January and had 'a very thorough and most friendly talk'. The American was anxious to be helpful and accepted the Ambassador's suggestion that using the language of penalties and threats should be excluded.[17]

Acheson was forewarned of British concerns by Holmes, Chargé d'Affaires in London, whose account of Anglo-American frictions was very similar to that presented in the correspondence between Strang and Franks. He noted the 'growing number of differences, and recent signs of strains and stresses on Anglo-American relations'. While there had been several periods of strain since the Second World War, the 'present strain strikes us as being potentially more serious'. He identified four main causes of difficulty: continuing economic problems; annoyance at 'our prodding, pressure and criticism'; the impending general election; and the physical and mental exhaustion of many ministers and civil servants. In such circumstances 'there is bound to be irritation when we hammer away indiscriminately on whole range of problems regardless of their importance, lay down deadlines, or ignore the human element'. The London Embassy was clearly aware of the crucial role Franks played in relations, for Holmes suggested that Acheson consider a general talk with Franks to reassure him that 'our guiding principle too is to maintain close, harmonious and co-operative relations'.[18]

Franks saw Acheson on 20 and 24 January. In a memorandum for the second meeting, Perkins, Assistant Secretary of State for European Affairs, said that they had been told by the British that there was a feeling currently in the United Kingdom that 'we are trying to push them around and there is reaction against us for that reason'. He proposed that 'we should ask that responsible Government officials try to take a longer range viewpoint and to discount as much as possible the election fever'.[19] On the 26th Acheson and Franks met once more and the Ambassador again raised Bevin's desire for the Secretary of State to visit London. Acheson said he fully intended coming in March or April but the timing of his arrival would depend upon preparations. He wanted to make sure that major decisions could be taken after the discussions.[20]

FRANKS'S VISIT TO LONDON, FEBRUARY 1950

Arriving in Britain on Saturday 4 February, Franks went straight to Oxford. He visited Hall on the Sunday staying all the morning and having lunch. They talked mainly about current economic issues. He told Hall that 'the difficulties in Anglo-US relations were much exaggerated and thought that we would be all right and get about $500mn which would be enough'.[21] On 6 and 7 February he had informal contacts with officials in London, and on 8–10 and 13–15 February he attended various informal meetings.[22]

On the 8th he discussed the Far East.[23] Franks first sought to explain American delays in concluding a Japanese Peace Treaty. At the end of the war Japan was placed under an occupation regime that quickly became exclusively American. General Douglas MacArthur governed the country as appointed Supreme Commander Allied Powers (SCAP), instituting a series of political and economic reforms. Meanwhile, the Far Eastern Commission (FEC) was established to represent the nations who had fought the Japanese. It debated policy to Japan, including the matter of a peace treaty. MacArthur enjoyed good relations with the British representative, Gascoigne. By 1948, however, concerns were growing about the continuing weakness of the Japanese economy which was proving a drain on US finances and a hindrance in arranging western defences in the cold war. Britain favoured an early peace treaty with Japan and pressed this case in 1949. But the dispute between Acheson and Louis Johnson, Secretary of Defence, was an obstacle to progress. While both MacArthur and Acheson sought a peace treaty, Johnson wanted to retain US forces in Japan in the face of the communist takeover of China in October

1949.[24] The United States, Franks said, felt vulnerable in the Pacific, seeing their position in Japan as their main protection. So they were tempted to stay either in occupation or with access to bases so long as fear of the Soviet Union remained.

He then turned to the question of the British recognition of Communist China on 6 January. The Americans had been kept informed of British thinking on the possibility of such a move. On 8 December Acheson told Franks:

> I appreciated that the arrangements had been made to consult but that no commitment had been made necessarily to act unitedly, it being recognized that the interests of states differed and that in matters of recognition they would, in the final analysis, be governed by their views of immediate and long term self-interest.

Acheson asked only that 'if this decision were taken, I hope we would at least be given as much advance notice as possible so as to minimize the effects that misunderstanding might well create and cause repercussions on other Anglo-American concerns'.[25] After the Cabinet decided in favour of recognition on 15 December, the US Secretary of State sent a personal message to Bevin which showed what Tang called 'understanding rather than resentment'.[26] By 3 January, however, Franks was reporting that American opinion was less amenable than a month earlier: 'we shall probably be in for a sticky patch immediately after our recognition of Communist China'. He felt the Truman administration was partly responsible for this because of its failure to secure a bipartisan understanding on Asia. Franks recounted Walter Lippman's advice to a member of the Embassy that the British should persevere in exposing the inanity of the China lobby.[27]

Franks could report on 7 January that the initial American reaction was 'less violent than we feared', although the press was distinctly chilly. He added that '[There] is room to conjecture that Mr Acheson's strong statement on Formosa was designedly made on the day preceding British recognition in order to lessen the reaction against us.' H. A. Graves of the Embassy reported to London that it was a very astute move by Acheson to arrange for the President to make a statement about Taiwan on the 5th and to follow it up with some well-chosen 'extemporaneous' remarks of his own.[28] On 12 January Acheson spoke to the National Press Club, making what was meant to be an important statement of policy. Franks observed 'Acheson's advocacy that the United States disembarrass itself of its contact with Chiang Kai-shek'; and that 'the State Department have gone as far as they can towards dropping the Nationalist Government short of withdrawing from it their recognition'.[29]

In the February meeting Franks noted that, immediately after recognition, the US government went out of its way to be helpful. According to Warren Cohen, Acheson was willing to ignore his subordinates' advice, as well as the pressures from the Pentagon, anti-administration forces in Congress and the China lobby; Franks 'in whose judgement Acheson had supreme confidence, reinforced his approach consistently'.[30] Dean Rusk, Deputy Under-Secretary of State, claimed in his memoirs that he and the Ambassador

> speculated privately that our policies would come together, depending upon the behaviour of Peking. If China entered the world community and acted reasonably in foreign affairs, American policy would move toward Britain's. But if China acted aggressively, Britain might move toward the United States and break with China.[31]

Reading the US press at that time Franks had the impression that US recognition might not be more than about three months off. Optimism, however, was very short lived. On 13 January the Chinese Communist government seized all foreign barracks, which had been granted by a 1901 protocol to each of the nations who had suppressed the Boxer rebellion. Despite American protests that their barracks only contained consular offices, the communists insisted on ending this symbol of China's degradation. But to Acheson this was a humiliation. On the 14th he ordered the withdrawal of all US official representatives from China.[32] In the circumstances, Franks told the February meeting, no US recognition was likely in the foreseeable future. Having removed their diplomats, the Americans could only return them as a result of an overt act of considerable importance. They would be unprepared to make this decision until US opinion had settled down and this would not happen before the November elections. Franks's outlook was shared by Hume Wrong, the Canadian Ambassador in Washington:

> Recognition of Communist China is a dead issue at the moment in the United States. A month ago one might have been justified in predicting that public opinion could have been conditioned to accept recognition within a period of three to six months. The seizure of United States consular property in Peiping on January 14th, resulting in the withdrawal of United States officials from China, has eliminated the possibility of any action in the near future, and with the elections coming up in November it is most

> unlikely that the Administration would consider it politic to raise the question, even if it wished to do so, before the end of the year.[33]

With the benefit of hindsight, Franks, Acheson and Wrong appear to have been overoptimistic about the prospects of shifting US opinion before the barracks incident. After years of support for the nationalists of Chiang Kai-shek, it was improbable that the American public would readily extend recognition to their conquerors, especially when they were so vociferously communist and anti-American. Indeed, opinion polls at this time gave two to one margins against recognition, an outlook no doubt cultivated by *Time* and *Life* who regularly criticised the administration for having 'lost' China.[34]

For the next meeting of his visit Franks joined a session of the Russia Committee on 14 February. When asked to comment on Acheson's speech of 8 February where he was reported as being willing to 'call off the cold war', Franks said that the statement was consistent with the outlook of the State Department in recent months. They believed that it might be possible to make local or limited arrangements with the Soviets. But, he added, they would not make such arrangements without consulting the United Kingdom and Western Europe. Moreover, Franks maintained that the general American attitude to the cold war was unchanged and unlikely to change.[35] There were further discussions on the Caribbean Commission, commercial staff problems in the United States, the ERP and on defence. On the 9th there was a meeting with the Permanent Under-Secretary's Committee on the basis for Anglo-American collaboration. The records for this meeting appear to be closed.[36] Franks also saw the Prime Minister who 'asked me many questions about the American attitude'.[37]

When Franks returned to the United States, he left a country in the middle of a general election campaign. Labour was returned to office on 23 February with a majority of only five seats. Moreover, both Bevin and Cripps were ill. Cripps retired in October 1950, but Bevin remained until March 1951. Yet between 1 May and 31 July 1950 the Foreign Secretary was absent for 85 of the 153 days.[38] The Prime Minister was compelled to play an important part in both economic and foreign affairs. The respect he had for Franks ensured that the Premier listened to the Ambassador's advice.

ANXIETIES FOR ACHESON

There were also domestic difficulties for the conduct of US foreign policy. Acheson noted the breakdown in bipartisanship in foreign affairs. Yet, as Hoyer Millar reported, the Secretary of State was to some extent to blame, for he did not suffer fools gladly in Congress.[39] Acheson was under pressure over his remark that he would not turn his back on Alger Hiss, who had just been convicted of perjury. Added to this were the hearings of a sub-committee of the Senate Foreign Relations Committee on Senator McCarthy's charges of communist infiltration of the State Department.[40] Aware of these pressures on him, Bevin sent, through Franks, a message of support for Acheson, declaring that his prestige in Britain was higher than ever.[41] The discovery that the Soviet Union had exploded its own atomic bomb in September 1949 undoubtedly contributed to the atmosphere of concern in Washington about communist activities. It touched Anglo-American relations when Klaus Fuchs, the British atomic scientist who had worked on the Manhattan Project, was arrested as a Soviet agent in January 1950. On 30 December 1949 Franks had submitted a draft proposal to the State Department for 'complete collaboration' in nuclear matters between the two countries. The Fuchs case forced their abandonment for the time being. Hoyer Millar reported that the talks had been 'completely wrecked'. To forestall a possible Congressional requirement that British and Canadian nationals be screened by the FBI, the Americans suggested that the British call a meeting to establish joint US–British–Canadian security procedures for atomic information.[42]

Shortly after arriving back in Washington Franks dined on 7 March with Douglas (who left early) and Acheson. It was one of the most fully prepared (on the American side) and reported (on the British side) of their confidential conversations. Prior to the meeting Acheson asked his officials to provide him with complete information on what they wanted him to say to Franks. A list of possible topics was made and a background memorandum was prepared which maintained: 'Among friendly powers, the UK is the one which best meets the test of being reliable, basically friendly, and having the same long-run objectives.' It continued that it was 'of major importance to have a clear understanding with the British as to whether we can count on a basic relationship of collaboration on long-run basic objectives'. It was felt best not to go into details with Franks, but discuss instead aims and their general application to certain specific situations.[43] In discussion with his officials, Acheson said that he proposed emphasising that the West had lost its momentum; it was 'necessary to find some new idea or new step which would regain the initiative'.[44]

In reporting their conversation Franks said that Acheson particularly asked that their talk should not be reported as he was talking very freely. At the same time the Ambassador wanted to share certain impressions of the discussion. So he hoped the letter would be kept private and personal, for it would be difficult and embarrassing, if Acheson or Douglas discovered that their conversation had been reported to London. Acheson, Franks noted, was troubled about the course of events in the world in the previous six months and wanted policies that would offset and indeed reverse this trend. The American did not think that such major policies could be formulated or made effective except in partnership with Britain. Furthermore, he seemed to want to do this fairly quickly, that is, in the spring. But he was troubled about how to do this. Franks identified what he took to be the problem. Acheson felt that the right policies should be pursued irrespective of economic considerations. Franks, however, pointed out that Britain wanted 'to play our part as a world power … but … we were bound to count the cost'. He told Bevin that a good deal of misunderstanding would be removed if they were able to keep what they and the Americans would like to see done in foreign affairs in a separate phase of discussions from the issues of cost and how they should be borne between us. Finally, he declared:

> The Americans seem to me to be groping desperately for ideas on foreign policy … If we have ideas, their minds are wide open to them. I think in the next few weeks we have the opportunity to take advantage of this attitude of combined eagerness and frustration.[45]

Franks returned to the economic costs of policies in a telegram to the Foreign Office on 30 March. He maintained that the 'Americans feel that major policies in the foreign field can be formulated and carried out only with the aid of Britain'; that the British wanted to play a full part in shaping and executing policies with the Americans; that 'our ability to do so depends on our economic condition. We cannot adopt foreign policies without counting the cost.' Consequently, there were 'two interconnected priorities – that of effective action in foreign policy and that of building long-term economic strength without which our foreign commitments cannot be supported'. Thus:

> We need a full recognition of this position and of its application in practice by the Americans, i.e. given they want our active partnership in the world, they must be prepared to make changes which will give us long term economic strength.[46]

Despite this appeal, such considerations were not addressed at the meetings. Bevin preferred to regard conferences as political.[47]

THE LONDON CONFERENCES, 1950

The London Conferences of 9–18 May 1950 were elaborate affairs. They involved two days of Anglo-American talks followed by two days of negotiations between Britain, France and the United States, and, finally, a meeting of the 12 power North Atlantic Council. The last week of April and the first week of May saw extensive preparatory talks between officials. While these were taking place, Franks sent his observations. On 19 April he told Strang that he had had an after-dinner talk with Webb, Under-Secretary of State, and Perkins, Assistant Secretary of State for European Affairs. They told the Ambassador that, with 1952 an election year, they would need to go to Congress in the first eight months of 1951 to handle any long-term policy to meet the situation after ERP. He felt that the Americans were aiming to get things done in the next 12 months. So, he added, if anything could be done on the political side, it would have to be confined to what could be started at the May meetings and in the autumn.[48] Six days later, in a hand-written letter to Bevin, Franks sent Acheson's off-the-record supplement to his public speech to the Conference of Editors of American Newspapers which 'reveals more simply than anything else the state of Washington in the last few weeks'. It showed the US Secretary of State having 'to defend himself & his Department ... before in effect a public audience'. Franks wanted Bevin to understand that this was the Washington background for Acheson at that time.[49] On 28 April the Ambassador wrote again to Strang, reporting a conversation with Acheson. The American was anxious to find policies that would satisfy his main objectives. He was particularly keen to tie Germany to the West. Franks apologised for the lack of clarity in his account of their talk, but Acheson was 'very far from crystallised in the views which he holds'. Nevertheless, their talk seemed to reveal a difference of approach. For Acheson the end of ERP aid in July 1952 was not so vital, but Franks regarded it as important:

> what we want are new American policies which will enable us with the United States to play our part as a world power in a condition of world affairs which permits us to take a longer view than temporary help and yearly Congressional approval can ever permit.[50]

Several points emerged in American thinking prior to the London meetings. In a paper of 19 April entitled 'Essential Elements of US–UK Relations', the main lines of the US position were set out. The United

States needed allies in the cold war. 'No other country has the same qualifications for being our principal ally and partner as the UK.' A 'serious impairment' of Anglo-American relations 'would require a whole reorientation of US foreign policy, since the achievement of many of our objectives ... depends upon the British agreeing with those objectives and taking the necessary action to accomplish them'. But the paper added that the British 'are inclined to wish to make this relationship more overt than we feel desirable'. Moreover, the British 'react strongly against being treated as "just another European power"'. In response to this, it was proposed that the British be made to recognise that 'it is necessary for us, when we are dealing with a generalized European problem, not to make overt distinctions between them and other European countries.' While acknowledging that the 'special close relation' of the two countries was one of the premises of US policy, the memorandum concluded that the British 'will have to recognize that in the European context, we must deal with them as a European country'.[51] Further American qualifications to an Anglo-American special partnership were revealed in a memorandum by the Chief of Staff of the US Army commenting on the State Department paper. This proposed two alterations. First, that Britain be deemed 'an important' rather than 'our principal partner' in strategic planning. Secondly, that there be a 'Continuance of close military collaboration with the United Kingdom wherever appropriate.' This would water down the original formulation which spoke of 'intimate discussion, consultation and collaboration'.[52]

On 7 May, Douglas sent his reflections to Acheson, who had gone to Paris prior to the conference. He considered two questions: whether there was a 'peculiar relationship' between Britain and the United States; and whether, assuming it existed, this should be disclosed to the British. He felt that there was 'no country ... whose interests were so wrapped around the world as the UK' and that the British pursued policies and had interests in common with the United States. This made a special relationship 'inescapable'. But, he added, 'a special relationship' was not 'necessarily exclusive of, or precludes special arrangements with other countries'. He felt there could be bilateral arrangements over certain matters but there had to be a multilateral approach to others. As regards admitting the special relations, he believed a degree of caution was needed, lest the British were to lean too heavily on the relationship. Finally, he rejected the idea that British pursuit of closer Anglo-American ties was aimed at avoiding greater participation in Europe: 'Her principal motive is to buy insurance.'[53]

British expectations of the conference were rather more hopeful. As the brief for the preparatory talks declared, 'It is the first time since the war that they have approached us as a partner on the most general issues of policy.' It added that one reason for this was that the United States 'cannot get the main lines of their foreign policy right, whether in Europe, the Middle East, or Asia, without our help'.[54] In the light of this the British government became more avowedly Atlanticist. In a revision of its paper, 'A Third World Power or Western Consolidation', the Permanent Under-Secretary's Committee (PUSC) reasserted that the Commonwealth could not form a third world force equivalent to the United States or the USSR. The future lay in a consolidated West in which Britain sought 'to maintain its special relations with the United States'.[55] This outlook was endorsed by the Cabinet on 8 May.[56] The PUSC also prepared a paper on 'Anglo-American Relations Present and Future'. It adopted a generally optimistic perspective: 'For the time being ... the United States is confirmed in its resolve to rely on the United Kingdom as its principal partner in world affairs.' But it warned that, if British power contracted, they would no longer be able to 'achieve a position, closely related to the USA, and yet sufficiently independent of her, to be able to influence American policy'.[57] Cripps provided a discordant voice among the general enthusiasm for partnership with the United States: 'I am not sure I agree with the implications which seem to me to be much nearer permanent subservience to the USA than anything else.'[58]

When Acheson and Bevin met on 9 and 10 May their talks did not produce the kind of results the British were hoping to achieve. The most interesting exchange occurred at the fourth Bilateral Ministerial Meeting on the 10th when a paper entitled 'Continued Consultation and Co-ordination of Policy' was put before the group. Acheson entirely agreed with the general content of the paper in 'its exposition of the need for close and continued consultation on all the parallel interests of the United States and United Kingdom'. However, he felt it was 'quite impossible to allow it to be known that any such paper had been drawn up or that it had been agreed to'. So he could not admit any knowledge of such a paper.[59] That was as far as acknowledgement of the special relationship went.

Shuckburgh, head of the Western Organisations Department of the Foreign Office and Secretary-General of the conference, summed up the meetings in a letter to Washington. The Americans, he felt, 'had not developed very clear ideas on most of the subjects under discussion ... we found the Americans somewhat plastic'. He added that some had been expecting that the United States was 'coming to these talks with the intention of establishing some very special and very close relationship with this country as a basis on which policy in all broad fields could be built'. There was a belief that there would be a return to something like the wartime relationship. He concluded:

> In any event, it became quite clear early on in the official talks that the Americans were not thinking along these lines. Although of course quite willing to subscribe to the doctrine of continuous close consultation in all matters between the two countries, they made it very clear that the value of this country to the United States, apart from our Commonwealth position and our influence in the Far East and other parts of the world, lay in the leadership which we could give in Europe; and they were not prepared to encourage us to think that we could establish, through any special relationship with them, an alibi for our duties in respect of European integration etc.[60]

Kenneth Younger, appointed Minister of State on 28 February and frequently in charge of the Foreign Office due to Bevin's absences, observed that the meetings 'have been largely futile … mainly occupied with platitudes'; this he attributed to Bevin's ill health and the lack of a lead from Acheson.[61]

THE SCHUMAN PLAN

Anglo-American harmony had undoubtedly been upset by the announcement on 9 May of the Schumann Plan to establish an authority to control steel and coal production in all those West European countries willing to join.[62] It became clear that Acheson had been told of this in advance, whilst in Paris. Although this initially soured relations, the British should not have been entirely surprised. After all, Acheson had raised the possibility of a Franco-German initiative in November when he spoke to Franks. Moreover, their conversation in March revealed an American desire for some new impetus. Franks has subsequently said that he was not surprised that Monnet had produced the plan for his Foreign Minister, but only at the timing.[63] At the time he advised London that the plan 'has struck the American imagination and is widely regarded as the most hopeful development in the direction of European cooperation'. He favoured issuing a communiqué that gave the Americans no 'easy excuse for once more accusing us of "dragging our feet" in the matter of co-operation with Western Europe'.[64] However, the British reaction to the scheme did not prove enthusiastic. On 5 June Franks was instructed to tell Acheson:

> Where matters of such vital importance are at stake, we cannot buy a pig in a poke, and he is pretty sure that if the Americans had been placed in a similar position they would have thought the same.[65]

On 14 July Franks wrote to Makins what he called 'a most unofficial epistle' about the plan. He believed that they should not be trying to water down the plan but, rather, seeing how they could ally or associate themselves with it in some limited way. He maintained that it was 'essentially a major political question' rather than an economic one. The plan might produce, Franks continued, an anchorman over 90 million Europeans which would be most worthwhile. He recognised this was a gamble, but one he believed to be worth taking.[66] The Ambassador's ideas were not pursued. This was hardly surprising, if Younger's diary accurately reflected thinking in the Foreign Office: 'Strang said frankly he thought the whole thing nonsense and a mere French attempt to evade realities.'[67]

In the nine months since the talks in September 1949 had ended with Franks's claim that Britain was the United States' principal partner in world affairs and not just a member of the European queue, there appeared, to the British, to have been real progress towards consolidating this position – despite the irritations voiced in December and January. Certainly they mutually acknowledged their habit of continuous close consultation, of military collaboration, and that Britain was the United States' chief cold war partner. But the more astute observers saw that this was only part of the picture. Americans viewed Britain in different guises. While accepting it as their chief cold war ally, they were not ready to extend special treatment in NATO. Moreover, exasperation at British failure to take a lead in schemes for closer West European co-operation had led the Americans to back the French in the Schuman Plan. Indeed, improved Franco-American ties were also emerging over French Indo-China, as the Americans showed a willingness to support the French struggle against the Viet Minh.

By July 1950 consideration of the Schuman Plan was overtaken by a far more pressing issue – the Korean War. It appeared to offer the beguiling prospect of wartime co-operation, the possibility of a resurrection of the special partnership of the Second World War. The striking disparity between the contributions of each nation was to reveal, however, how their comparative military and economic strength had shifted since 1945.

NOTES

1. PRO, FO 371/74187, AN2389/10510/45, North American Department to Chancery, Washington Embassy, 4 August 1949, enclosing the memorandum.
2. Ibid., AN2671/10510/45, D. Allen to P. Broad, 17 August 1949, enclosing re-drafted memorandum.

3. *DBPO*, 2nd Series, II, No. 27, pp. 81–7, PUSC(51), Final 2nd Revise, 'Anglo-American Relations: Present and Future', 22 April 1950.
4. PRO, FO 371/74197, AN2933/11114/45, Franks to FO, Tel. No. 4559, 20 September 1949.
5. PRO, CAB 128/16, CM 62(49), 27 October 1949; CAB 129/37, CP(49)204, Bevin, 'Council of Europe', 24 October 1949; CP(49)203, Bevin and Cripps, 'Proposals for the Economic Unification of Europe', 25 October 1949.
6. FRUS, 1949, I, p. 521.
7. FRUS, 1949, IV, p. 470, Acheson to Paris Embassy, 19 October 1949.
8. PRO, FO 371/81637, AU1053/1, Franks to Strang, 17 November 1949.
9. On this issue see FRUS, 1949, IV, pp. 425–6, 429–31, 435–7.
10. Dimbleby and Reynolds, *Ocean Apart*, pp. 207–8.
11. HSTL, Acheson Papers, Box 64, memorandum of a conversation, 14 December 1949; on the passage of Mutual Defence Assistance Act, see Acheson, *Present at the Creation*, pp. 307–13.
12. HSTL, Acheson Papers, Box 64, memorandum of a conversation, 17 December 1949.
13. See text of agreement in PRO, FO 800/517, US/50/3.
14. HSTL, Acheson Papers, Box 64, meeting with President, 20 December 1949.
15. PRO, FO 371/74183, AN3854/1053/45G, Strang to Franks, 20 December 1949; see also PRO, FO 800/516, US/49/63, FO to Washington, Tel. No. 11716, 23 December 1949.
16. PRO, FO 371/82937, UEE59/lG, Franks to Strang, 31 December 1949. Curiously, Danchev, *Franks*, p. 128 cites Strang's message but not Franks's response.
17. PRO, FO 371/86969, UR103/1, FO to Washington, Tel. No. 338, 17 January 1950; ibid., UR103/3, Washington to FO, Tel. No. 266, 23 January 1950.
18. FRUS, 1950, III, pp. 1599–604, Holmes to Secretary of State, 7 January 1950.
19. FRUS, 1950, III, p. 1611, memorandum by Perkins, 24 January 1950; ibid., pp. 1615–17, memorandum of conversation with Franks, 24 January which covered no significant points, other than that the United States would not raise the Superman question with Spaak.
20. PRO, FO 371/81637, AU1053/4, Washington to FO, Tel. No. 324, 26 January 1950.
21. Cairncross (ed.), *Hall Diaries 1947–1953*, p. 105 (15 February 1950 entry).
22. See PRO, FO 371/81778, AU1891/1 for outline arrangements for the visit.
23. PRO, FO 371/84528, FZ10345/3, notes of a discussion, 8 February 1950.
24. Peter Lowe, *Containing the Cold War in Asia: British Policies towards Japan, China and Korea, 1945–1953* (Manchester: Manchester University Press, 1997), pp. 11–27. See also Michael Schaller, *The American Occupation of Japan: The Origins of the Cold War in Asia* (New York: Oxford University Press, 1985).
25. FRUS, 1949, IX, pp. 219–20, memorandum of Conversation by the Secretary of State, 8 December 1949; PRO, FO 371/75826, F18481/1023/10, Washington to FO, 8 December 1949. Cited in James Tuck-Hong Tang, *Britain's Encounter with Revolutionary China, 1948–1954* (London: Macmillan, 1992), pp. 57–8.
26. Tang, *Britain's Encounter*, p. 58. FRUS, 1949, IX, pp. 241–2, the Secretary of State to Ambassador in the UK, 23 December 1949.
27. PRO, FO 371/83279, FC1022/26, Washington to FO, Tel. No. 17, 3 January 1950. The China lobby in Congress blamed Truman and Acheson for 'losing' China to communist control. It was exemplified by Congressman Karl Mundt who declared that the President had let 'red waters rush unchecked through the flood plain of Asia' (quoted in Dimbleby and Reynolds, *Ocean*

Apart, p. 184).
28. PRO, FO 371/83281, FC1022/72, Franks to Bevin, Despatch No. 15, 7 January 1950; ibid., FC1022/108, H. A. Graves to P. W. Y. S. Scarlett (FO), 9 January 1950.
29. PRO, FO 371/ 83013, F1022/5, Franks to Bevin, Despatch No. 37, 16 January 1950.
30. Warren I. Cohen, 'Acheson, His Advisers and China, 1949–1950', in Dorothy Borg and Waldo Heinrichs (eds), *Uncertain Years: Chinese American Relations, 1947–1950* (New York: Columbia University Press, 1980), p. 49.
31. Dean Rusk, *As I Saw It* (New York: Penguin, 1991), p. 158.
32. Ronald McGlothlen, *Controlling the Waves: Dean Acheson and US Foreign Policy in Asia* (New York & London: W. W. Norton, 1993), p. 154.
33. Greg Donachy (ed.), *Documents on Canadian External Relations Volume 16: 1950* (Ottawa, Department of Foreign Affairs and International Trade, 1996), p. 1176, Ambassador in United States to Acting Secretary of State for External Affairs, despatch 314, 4 February 1950.
34. Alonzo Hamby, *Man of the People: A Life of Harry Truman* (New York: Oxford University Press, 1995), p. 520.
35. PRO, FO 371/86761, NS1053/6G, Minutes of the Meeting of the Russia Committee, 14 February 1950.
36. The Permanent Under-Secretary's Committee was established on 1 February 1949 as a British counterpart to the American Policy Planning Staff; see NA, Wash. DC, RG 59, State Department Decimal Files 1945–49, Box 5909, 841.021/4–2049, London Embassy to Secretary of State, 20 April 1949.
37. See PRO, FO 800/517, US/50/8, Franks to Bevin, 8 March 1950; in citing his meeting with Attlee, Franks suggested that this letter be sent to him. It was.
38. Bullock, *Ernest Bevin*, p. 757.
39. PRO, FO 371/81615, AU1016//6G, Hoyer Millar to Wright, 6 March 1950.
40. Acheson, *Present at the Creation*, pp. 359–60; PRO, FO 371/81611, AU1013/5, Franks to FO, Tel. No. 59(S), 28 January 1950; ibid., AU1013/11 Franks to FO, Tel. No. 140(S), 10 March 1950.
41. PRO, FO 115/4478, 1018/2/5 and 6/50G, FO to Franks, Tel. No. 1586, 24 March 1950; Franks to FO, Tel. No. 1006, 28 March 1950 reported that Acheson 'was much gratified to get your message'.
42. PRO, FO 115/4514; FO 371/81611, AU1013/7, Hoyer Millar (for Franks) to FO, Tel. No. 86(S), 11 February. See also Robert Chadwell Williams, *Klaus Fuchs, Atom Spy* (Cambridge, MA: Harvard University Press, 1987), p. 100.
43. NA, Wash. DC, RG 59, State Department Decimal Files 1950–54, Box 2768, 611.41/3–650 and 611.41/3–750, Battle to Perkins, 6 March 1950, and Rusk memorandum enclosing list of topics and general background paper, 7 March 1950.
44. Ibid., Box 2768, 611.41/7–350, memorandum of conversation 7 March 1950.
45. PRO, FO 800/517, US/50/8, Franks to Bevin, 8 March 1950. This letter and one on 13 March say the conversation took place on the 6th but the US documents say the 7th. It seems likely that the 7th is correct given the number of US documents referring to that date.
46. *DBPO*, 2nd Series, II, No. 11, pp. 33–4.
47. Ibid., No. 74i.
48. PRO, FO 371/81615, AU1016/4, Franks to Strang, 19 April 1950.
49. PRO, FO 371/81644, AU10511/3, Franks to Bevin, 25 April 1950.
50. *DBPO*, 2nd Series, II, No. 48, pp. 186–7, Franks to Strang, 28 April 1950.
51. FRUS, 1950, III, pp. 869–81. Acheson was anxious to avoid any undue attention to a special relationship. When he arrived in London on 9 May he

discovered a paper, entitled 'Special Relationship between the United States and Great Britain', that had emerged from talks between State Department and Foreign Office staff while he was in Paris. He accepted the unique nature of Anglo-American relations but he feared that, in the hands of troublemakers, the paper 'could stir up no end of hullabaloo, both domestic and international'. He ordered that all copies be destroyed. Acheson, *Present at the Creation*, pp. 387–8. See also Lawrence S. Kaplan, 'Dean Acheson and the Atlantic Community', in Douglas Brinkley (ed.), *Dean Acheson and the Making of US Foreign Policy* (London: Macmillan, 1993), p. 32.

52. *Records of the Joint Chiefs of Staff, Part 2: 1946–1953. Europe and NATO*, reel II, frames 389–92, JCS 2128, 3 May 1950.
53. L of C, Harriman Papers, container 270, Country File: UK, Douglas to Paris, Cable No. 791, 7 May 1950.
54. *DBPO*, 2nd Series, II, No. 24, p. 70, brief for the UK Delegation, 21 April 1950.
55. Ibid., No. 20, pp. 54–63.
56. PRO, CAB 128/17, CM 29(50), 8 May 1950.
57. *DBPO*, 2nd Series, II, No. 27, pp. 81–7.
58. Ibid., No. 27i.
59. Ibid., No. 84, p. 293 (for Acheson's remarks), No. 67, pp. 242–4. See PRO, FO 371/81645, AU10512/2G for PUSC observations. See *Princeton Seminars*, microfilm, roll 3, frames 832–7 for Acheson's comments.
60. *DBPO*, 2nd Series, II, No. 117, pp. 388–393.
61. Kenneth Younger Diary, 14 May 1950.
62. *DBPO*, 2nd Series, I, No. 2, pp. 2–5, Note from French Ambassador in London to Mr Bevin, 9 May 1950.
63. Edmonds, *Setting the Mould*, p. 316n.
64. *DBPO*, 2nd Series, I, No. 54, pp. 105–6, Franks to Bevin, Tel. No. 1547, 29 May 1950.
65. Ibid., No. 88, pp. 54–155, Younger (Minister of State) to Franks, Tel. No. 2634, 5 June 1950.
66. Ibid., No. 140, pp. 259–60, Franks to Makins, 14 July 1950.
67. Younger Diary, 12 June 1950.

— 9 —

The Korean War

THE COMMUNIST North Korean invasion of South Korea on 24 June (25 June by Korean time) 1950 with what was generally assumed to be Soviet approval, if not indeed connivance, launched the most serious crisis since the Second World War. It occasioned one of the clearest examples of Franks's influence on both sides of the Atlantic. The attack occurred in an area where Anglo-American relations had faced difficulties, even during the Second World War. The 'loss', as many Americans saw it, of China to the communists had produced a good deal of pressure in Congress against Acheson who was blamed for the defeat of Chiang Kai-shek's nationalists. Even greater insistence was therefore laid on the US government to ensure Formosa (Taiwan), whither Chiang's forces had retreated, should be protected from falling to the communists. When Britain recognised the new Chinese regime on 6 January, Franks had hoped that the Americans might, in time, follow suit. But he had to report on his visit to London in February that such a development was highly unlikely. So there were clear Anglo-American differences about the best policy for the Far East when the Korean crisis arose. In the first months of the war the British were particularly concerned to ensure that the United States did not extend their action to involve Formosa and thereby risk the possibility of drawing China into the conflict.

Korea, annexed by Japan in 1910, was conquered in 1945 by the Soviets and Americans who divided their forces at the 38th parallel. They entered a country in the midst of a revolution which sought land reform and the removal of colonial practices. While the Soviets allowed the revolution to proceed in the North, the Americans set up in the South a military government, assisted by various right-wing politicians whose leading figure was Syngman Rhee. In October 1947 the Americans proposed elections. When the Soviets blocked the electoral committee's entry to the North, voting took place in the South on 10 May 1948. After his victory, Rhee formed a government which was recognised by the United Nations in December as the Republic of Korea. The Soviet Union recognised the Democratic

People's Republic of Korea, based in Pyongyang, as sovereign in the whole peninsula, on 12 October 1948. Both regimes thus claimed to be a national state. The Americans decided to end their occupation – the last troops left in July 1949 – and offer limited military and economic assistance to Rhee's government. As MacDonald says, 'The aim was to obtain containment at minimum cost. Rhee would hesitate to attack the North because he was unsure of American backing. Kim Il Sung would refrain from action against the South lest the US intervene.'[1]

Britain had not regarded Korea as strategically important before the outbreak of hostilities,[2] nor had the Americans. Indeed, in a speech of 12 January, surveying US policy in the Far East, Acheson had excluded Korea from the area within the US defensive perimeter. Franks alerted London to this, saying that Acheson classified Korea, Loochoos and the Philippines as areas of direct US interest but he did not include Korea, as he did the other two countries, in the US defensive perimeter in the Pacific. But the Ambassador did not think it significant enough to warrant a comment.[3] The invasion changed this outlook, as the Foreign Office believed that the 'Soviet Govt [*sic*] have connived at, if they have not instigated, the aggression.'[4] A similar stance was taken by the Americans. Cohen has admirably summed up the thinking behind the US response: 'stopping an aggressor, containing Soviet expansion, demonstrating American resolve to America's European allies, and to nervous Asians, preserving the credibility of the United Nations, protecting Truman at home'.[5] For Britain the imperative to act also included what might be called the 'Munich' syndrome: the need to be seen to be standing up to aggression.[6] For a long time after the Second World War the British were susceptible to charges that their policy of 'appeasement' and, in particular, the Munich settlement, had rewarded aggression and led to war. They were consequently anxious to ensure that they did not repeat this stance in the postwar era.

So the Americans immediately drew up two resolutions to present to the UN Security Council. The first one, which was passed by the Council on the evening of 25 June (the Soviet representative was absent), acknowledged a breach of the peace and demanded an immediate North Korean withdrawal.[7] The second one, which would be issued first in the form of a presidential statement on the 27th, announced the commitment of US air and sea forces to give cover and support to the South Koreans. It then called on UN members to give aid. It added that the attack 'makes amply clear centrally directed Communist Imperialism has passed beyond subversion in seeking to conquer independent nations'.[8] When the Cabinet met that day they agreed to support the US resolution but they did not want it to include the reference to 'centrally directed Communist Imperialism'.[9] Franks was asked to try and secure its omission, which he succeeded in doing.[10] When the Americans presented a second resolution to the United States that day, which was passed, it asked only for the assistance of UN members in repelling the armed attack.[11] Franks had made his first impact on the crisis.

There then arose the question of what assistance the British would offer. The Cabinet Defence Committee met on 28 June and accepted the suggestion of the Chiefs of Staff that Royal Navy forces in Japanese waters should be put at the disposal of the US Naval Commander for operations in support of South Korea.[12] The Foreign Office, under the guidance of the Minister of State, Kenneth Younger, during Bevin's illness, was not slow to see the potential of this move for its effect on wider questions. Franks was urged to use the prompt British response to counteract US criticism of British policy in relation to Europe and on the 'foot dragging' issue generally. The telegram continued:

> There could not be a more useful demonstration of the United Kingdom's capacity to act as a world power with the support of the Commonwealth. It may also be possible to suggest that the United Kingdom would not be free to play this part if, as some circles in the United States have often suggested, the United Kingdom were to be integrated with some form of Western European federation.[13]

The Embassy was also alive to the need to secure support for British interests in the Far East. The Ambassador and his staff asked US officials why Hong Kong had been omitted from American pronouncements. The State Department maintained that they believed that Britain could cope with the territory's defence.[14] In addition, Franks recognised the value of favourable press and radio coverage of the British position. He told Lord Tedder, head of the British Joint Services Mission (BJSM), on 5 July that now that US involvement in Korea and the struggle against communism were headline news, British participation in Korea as well as its commitments in Malaya (where there had been a communist uprising since 1948) and Hong Kong were important from the point of view of public relations.[15]

The Americans, however, were more interested in whether Hong Kong could provide forces. As early as 26 June the US Embassy in London speculated, on its own initiative, whether the British might send troops.[16] This was partly a reflection of the serious position facing the South Korean forces. On the same day, Truman approved air and naval support; Seoul fell on the 28th; the next day direct attacks on the North were sanctioned; and on the 30th he committed US ground troops, whose first elements arrived the following day.[17]

When the Defence Committee considered sending troops on 6 July, Slessor, Chief of the Air Staff, objected because of the consequent endangerment of Hong Kong. The Committee decided against sending British land forces, and the Cabinet endorsed this.[18] The Chiefs of Staff regarded the attack as Soviet 'war by proxy' and as a diversion; a more serious probe might occur nearer home. Despatching troops to Korea would expose such targets.[19] Yet the British wanted to adopt a constructive approach. Franks was asked to convey a message from Attlee to Truman proposing talks between the two powers to determine 'our common policy … in the event of further outbreaks'. He suggested that Lord Tedder could be joined by a representative of the Chiefs of Staff to act on behalf of the United Kingdom. Two days later the President sent his agreement, saying that Ambassador-at-large Jessup and General Bradley, Chairman of the Joint Chiefs of Staff, would represent the United States. Moreover, he accepted Attlee's view that the French and other governments need only be informed as and when the situation demanded.[20]

DISCORD: KELLY–GROMYKO TALKS – TAIWAN

There were, though, two sources of difficulty between London and Washington which called for Franks's skill in producing harmony. The first concerned the Kelly–Gromyko talks, in which the British Ambassador in Moscow had pressed the Soviet Foreign Minister (as the Soviets had declared their peaceful intentions), to use his country's influence to secure the withdrawal of the North Korean armed forces. For the Americans there was a clear need to be firm with the Soviet Union, since they were taken to have encouraged the North Korean invasion. Franks warned London that the Americans did not understand these proceedings.[21] Secondly, there was the matter of Formosa (Taiwan). Bevin, who was consulted in hospital, asked Franks to tell Acheson that the United States had the 'whole-hearted backing of world in the courageous initiative' in response to the invasion. But, he added, 'I do not believe they could rely on the same support for their declared policy … with Formosa.' He felt that many countries, particularly Asian ones, disliked the prospect of extending the dispute.[22] When Franks gave this message to Acheson on 8 July he thought he 'looked well but taut'. Acheson emphasised the need to be firm with the Soviets and the strategic dimension of the Formosa question. He could not contemplate the Far Eastern situation if China took Formosa and were well-equipped. The Ambassador told the Foreign Office that the Philippines had been invaded by Japan from Formosa.[23]

Acheson sent Bevin a frank and robust answer, which was delivered to the Foreign Secretary on the 11 July. He said he did not want to see the conflict expanded, but that the United States could not allow hostile forces to seize Formosa and use it as a base. In guidance to Douglas, he asked him to stress to the Foreign Secretary that he could not see the value of Britain wanting to get China into the Security Council and the return of the Soviet Union. Furthermore, he wanted Bevin to have 'no doubt of seriousness with which I view implications of his message and their possible effect on our whole future relationship'.[24] Bevin was clearly taken aback. He asked Franks to see Acheson as soon as possible and, while thanking him for his message, say that he was surprised by the last sentence of Douglas's letter. He added, 'I hope I may continue to feel free to express myself with complete frankness ... without exposing myself to a retort of this kind.'[25] When Franks put this to Acheson the next day, 13 July, he was told that 'we regarded most seriously the possibilities of our policies drifting apart and that there was no other meaning intended'.[26] The Ambassador's tactful approach was followed by Bevin in his considered response to Acheson's message of the 11th. The Foreign Secretary advised the drafters of the telegram to reply 'in a conversational tone, rather than argumentatively, which might give the sense that we are setting up a counter-barrage'. In the telegram of the 14th, given to Acheson by Franks on the 15th, Bevin said the US action in Korea was appreciated by all and the British were not willing to do a deal with the Soviet Union and would not be raising the issue of a Chinese seat at the United Nations. He recognised that the Americans attached great strategic importance to Formosa, but he wanted to avoid giving the Russians 'a chance to divide Asia from the West on an Asian problem'. He therefore suggested:

> Maybe the President in his own inimitable way could say something to remove any misapprehension by making it clear that the final disposal of Formosa is an open question which should be settled on its merits when the time comes.[27]

On 19 July Truman sent a special message to Congress on Korea and the issues arising out of the crisis. He declared that the military neutralisation of Formosa was without prejudice to the political questions affecting it. He did not want the island 'embroiled in hostilities' and desired that Formosan issues 'be settled by peaceful means as envisaged in the Charter of the United Nations'.[28] Since Acheson was anxious that the British reaction be favourable, he gave Franks, at the Ambassador's suggestion, advance sight of the text. Franks told London that it

> contains an important clarification of the US position on Formosa which I think goes some way to meet our worries in that it sharply distinguishes between the present temporary military necessity and the long term disposal of the island by orderly means.[29]

Thereafter the issue of Formosa was put on ice. General MacArthur, appointed by the Security Council as Commander-in-Chief of UN forces in Korea on 7 July, visited the island 31 July–l August, thereby causing speculation about US help. This concerned both Acheson and Truman, for the State Department had tried to dissuade him from making the visit.[30] But when Franks saw American officials he was told that the policy of putting Formosa on ice held firm without qualification. In January 1951 this commitment to keep the island in cold storage was reiterated by Acheson to Franks.[31]

If discord over Formosa eased, the visit pointed to a problem in the making – controlling MacArthur. A remote, forbidding individual, yet with considerable personal magnetism, MacArthur emerged from the war in the Pacific as a popular hero. As occupation commander he ruled Japan in an imperious style. Holding a vaunted view of his own talents, he did not welcome censure. The General and the President both believed that the United States should direct policy with the minimum of intrusion from allies. But MacArthur also wished to restrict the contribution of Washington. He took the same attitude to his command in Korea. On the day he became UN commander, John Foster Dulles, appointed special advisor to the State Department in March, wrote to Acheson:

> I suggest that the President might want to emphasize by personal message to General MacArthur the delicate nature of the responsibilities which he will now be carrying not only on behalf of the United States but on behalf of the United Nations, and the importance of instructing his staff to comply scrupulously with political and military limitations and instructions which may be sent, the reasons for which may not always be immediately apparent but which will often have behind them political considerations of gravity.[32]

Dulles's prescient advice was not followed. Instead, instructions to the General were usually too broad. Given his prestige, it was not easy to control him.

ANGLO-AMERICAN DISCUSSIONS

With the removal of Formosa as an issue of contention and the collapse of the Kelly–Gromyko talks the atmosphere improved. The Washington talks, which Attlee had suggested on 6 July, on the political and military implications of the Korean aggression on the world situation, took place on 20–24 July. Franks was told that ministers felt he should lead on the British side, for political issues were likely to be pre-eminent. It was left, however, to the Ambassador's discretion to decide how he would be associated with the talks.[33] Truman agreed that political questions were of great importance and consequently arranged for Jessup to act as a political adviser and to work in consultation with Franks who would associate himself with the conversations at his own discretion.[34] Tedder felt that the four lengthy meetings that he and the Ambassador held with Bradley and Jessup were 'extremely satisfactory', given American acceptance that 'the closest possible US and UK collaboration is vital'. Franks summed up by saying:

> I think we can be satisfied they have made progress, not only in persuading the Americans that they have something to gain by discussing Far Eastern problems with us, but also of the value of Anglo-American consultation over the whole area under discussion.[35]

The Americans also seemed satisfied. Jessup saw the talks as a continuation of Anglo-American talks on the Middle East in 1947 and 1949, and the May 1950 London conference, which resulted in a common conclusion concerning the identity of interest of the two powers generally throughout the world. The July talks did not produce agreed common plans of action but 'laid the groundwork for such joint planning'.[36] The editor of the Foreign Office official documents has concluded, however; 'Overall the results were modest in respect of both global strategy, where principles were agreed but little satisfactory action taken[,] and the conduct of operations in Korea, where the lack of a consultative or informing process remained a concern.'[37]

FRANKS AND THE DESPATCH OF BRITISH TROOPS

So the British left the talks feeling that some form of Anglo-American partnership had been re-established. However, the value of Britain in that arrangement would depend upon its contribution to the military effort in Korea.[38] Indeed, the question of the despatch of British land forces was raised by Bradley in the conversations. It was probably on this issue that Franks made his major contribution in the handling of the Korean War. In a series of communications he noted the importance of troops in American eyes. On 15 July he sent a handwritten letter to Attlee, while Bevin was convalescing. He did not suggest what the decision should be, since that lay outside his province. However, he wanted to raise certain aspects of the issue. He felt that the recent exchanges of messages between the two powers had witnessed the 'assertion by us + [*sic*] the acceptance by the US of our partnership in world affairs'. That would have been impossible three or even two years previously, when Britain was one of the queue of European countries. Now, though 'we are effectively out of the queue, one of the two world powers outside Russia'. He estimated that the Americans would, to some extent, 'test the quality of the partnership by our attitude to the notion of a token ground force'. Moreover, he thought that, if it was decided to send troops, it should be done quickly. Too often in the past the British had taken their time before acting and seemed to respond only under pressure. Consequently they received neither credit nor approval for their response. Finally, he maintained that the Americans saw their action as being on behalf of the United Nations. They 'inevitably look to see what their partner can offer'.[39]

From this it seems clear that Franks favoured token land forces being sent. He appeared to feel this was needed for the sake of the 'special relationship'. To this end he pursued twin aims: to encourage London whilst reassuring Washington. On 19 July he told Acheson that he 'sensed a growing feeling of realism in the messages … from London'. He attributed it partly to the return of General Slim to London from his trip to the East.[40] Once again Douglas, US Ambassador in London, seemed to share Franks's perspective. On 21 he said 'it would be better if British were to make offer on their own initiative instead of as result of *aide-mémoire* from us'.[41]

On 21 July Franks contacted London again, saying that they would know from Tedder that Bradley had raised the question at the political–military talks. It was clear that this issue was uppermost in American minds. By this time Attlee had passed Franks's letter to him on to the Foreign Office without comment. According to Farrar-Hockley, 'miffed that their man in Washington was approaching the Prime Minister direct, the Permanent Secretary asked Sir Oliver for a formal expression of his views'. So the Foreign Office told the Ambassador that militarily it would be very difficult to send troops, but they realised that this was at least partly a political question. They would be influenced if an offer of troops would strengthen the British hand with the US administration. Franks was asked to estimate (without consulting the Americans) the importance, primarily in terms of the likely reaction of the US government but also of US public opinion, of Britain's making a positive response to Bradley's suggestion.[42] This occasioned one of the most forthright messages he sent as Ambassador.

His telegram of 23 July began by stating that the Americans believed it was essential for the UN character of Korean operations that they should not be carried out solely by US forces. They believed many nations would follow a British decision and so awaited our decision as of more importance to them and their purposes than any other. He then identified two further influences on the Americans. First, beneath the 'difficulties and disagreements between us and them there is a steady and unquestioning assumption that we are the only dependable ally and partner'. Secondly, 'despite the power and position of the United States, the American people are not happy if they are alone'. The US public would think that, if they were alone on the ground, 'it shows coolness to them or even disapproval of what they are doing'.[43] Franks was repeating a theme raised by George Perkins, Assistant Secretary of State for European Affairs, who had stressed the psychological importance for the US of not being alone in Korea.[44] Sir Gladwyn Jebb, newly appointed as Britain's Permanent Representative at the United Nations, noted how the Americans seemed to have two 'separate and probably irreconcilable objectives': they did not want it to appear that they were 'fighting a lone battle'; but also they wished to avoid the impression that 'American troops are being forced into battle at the behest of some outside body', for this would not be well received by Congress.[45]

The next day the Defence Committee met and approved the sending of a brigade to Korea, a decision which was endorsed by the Cabinet on the 25th. The Prime Minister told Ministers that Franks had argued very strongly for the benefits of the despatch to Anglo-American solidarity.[46] The Americans were pleased by the decision but disappointed by the length of time it would take for the troops to arrive. For, by August, MacArthur's troops occupied a narrow perimeter around Pusan in the south-east. General Bradley explained that soldiers were needed immediately and not in October, as Britain planned. He declared, 'A platoon now would be worth more than a company tomorrow.' American pressure resulted in the Chiefs of Staff agreeing to send two battalions from Hong Kong immediately, thereby reversing the stance of the Cabinet on 25 July. Attlee supported their decision and the soldiers arrived on 29 August.[47]

Most accounts see the decision to send troops as part of the general pattern to British policy in Korea of succumbing to American pressure. According to Hastings, what principally motivated the British to support the United States in Korea was the 'fear that if she did not do so, America's sense of betrayal by her Western allies might have disastrous political and military consequences for Europe … if the US was left to face the burden of war alone and was humiliated, the American people would … revert to isolationism'.[48] MacDonald identifies another 'powerful lever to secure allied compliance': 'Congress would not support collective action outside Korea if the allies proved reluctant to pay the butcher's bill.'[49] But to the negative factors of financial pressure and fear of a weakened Nato must be added the opportunity of partnership which was especially emphasised by Franks. What shifted the Cabinet was not the argument that the troops were crucial for the military effort or merely that they felt obliged to concede the American request – though this played a part. The decisive consideration was the belief that it served British goals.

The discussions also reveal how an individual could exercise influence. Sir Oliver Franks was a respected figure with access to the highest political circles in Washington and London. But it was neither his status nor his connexions that was crucial. He secured the *volte face* because his proposal offered the best means of accomplishing a more important goal for the British government – partnership with the United States. Indeed, the opportunity provided by Korea had been foreseen by his predecessor, Lord Inverchapel, who had declared that Britain had a unique asset:

> in the event of hostilities, our partnership would be more greatly needed, more certainly forthcoming than that of any other foreign power and far more substantial … [this] offer[s] an opportunity to approach the United States Government on a franker, more intimate and trustful basis than is possible for other countries, or even for ourselves within the confines of the European Recovery Programme.[50]

REARMAMENT

The Americans, however, were thinking in even broader terms about the military response to the Korean War. In April 1950 the State

Department had produced NSC-68, a document which identified the Soviet Union as inherently expansionist, and called on the United States to resist communism everywhere. It proposed large-scale rearmament by the United States and its allies to meet the threat. But its suggested massive increase in the defence budget had caused hesitations. With the invasion of South Korea this position was adopted by the American government. Interestingly, the driving force behind this was Acheson, who maintained, on 14 July, that the President should 'ask for money and if it is a question of asking for too little or too much, he should ask for too much'. Following this guidance, Truman sought from Congress an increase of $10 billion on 19 July.[51]

On 22 July US diplomats around the world were told that President Truman proposed a large increase in the US military effort and hoped 'other free nations will also undoubtedly want to increase their defences and has expressed our willingness to give them further assistance'.[52] A working party led by Plowden, Chief Planning Officer, investigated the situation for Britain. It reported that defence expenditure in the period April 1951 to April 1954 could be increased by £800 million to a total of £3,400 million. This was provided that £550 million could be secured from the United States in 'free dollars' (i.e. the purchase of dollar goods without using dollars) to cover the cost of increased imports and reduced exports. The Cabinet agreed to the plan on 1 August.[53]

Douglas had told Attlee that there would be US help for 'any interruption in the economic plans for balance of payments which might be caused by the need for switching over from production of goods for exports to rearmament'. Looking back on events, Plowden felt he should have known better than to believe this, for such measures would rest with Congress not the US administration.[54] Certainly the British were over-optimistic, for the US Embassy in London deftly avoided committing themselves to the £550 million. They received this figure without comment, concentrating on persuading the British not to include references to the amount and to 'free dollars' in any press release.[55] Indeed, the US Embassy felt that the British programme was inadequate; and was shocked at the assumption that the programme depended upon £550 million of 'free dollars' – as the US taxpayer was unlikely to approve such subsidies.[56] Moreover, Charles Spofford, US Deputy and Chairman of the North Atlantic Council and responsible for co-ordinating increases in the NATO rearmament efforts, made clear on 24 August his feeling that the responses were inadequate and disappointing. The British expressed surprise because the President had said he was satisfied with the British effort. Spofford sought to emphasise his point. He wanted it made clear that he correctly stated the American view and that it was their considered opinion that Britain could devote substantially more of its resources to defence with much less dollar aid than requested. It is interesting that he thought the best way of persuading the British was for the State Department to take this line with Franks. When Acheson saw Franks on 31 August he told him that there was some feeling in London that Spofford was taking a position which did not represent the thinking of the US government. He wanted to assure Sir Oliver that this was not the case. Franks later asked Freeman Matthews, Deputy Under Secretary of State, whether the reference to the inadequacy of British defence efforts referred to the financial effort or to the question of increased military forces. Matthews replied that it applied to both.[57] British claims that they could not afford greater expenditure were undermined by the Cabinet, on 4 September, approving an extra £200 million to cover increased service pay, making the total £3,600 million.[58]

It was partly with a view to tackling such questions that Bevin and Attlee proposed a meeting between the Prime Minister and President in a telegram on 14 August. Bevin felt the international situation had grown more dangerous. He added that Britain had taken 'new and momentous decisions in defence'. The Prime Minister would be able to outline this situation to the President in a more intimate manner than was possible on paper. Attlee would not come 'to beg favours but to make clear that what we want to do is to make the utmost contribution within reason for the common purpose'. Franks was asked to discover whether the United States would welcome such a visit in the next fortnight and, if so, whether Attlee should take the initiative and propose a meeting or whether he could move the President to issue an invitation. Bevin and Attlee would prefer the latter.[59] Franks replied on the 16th, saying he had not mentioned the proposal to any Americans. He believed that a visit at that time would not be appropriate. Such an unexpected meeting would be viewed by the American public as dramatic and critical. Great things would be expected to flow from it. There would also be a tendency to believe that the world situation had grown worse. Secondly, he noted that once aggression had occurred in Korea, 'American opinion swung back from its post-war views about the economic weakness of Britain … to the older view of a Britain from whom much should be expected and demanded.' He implied that a visit by the Prime Minister, and the associated revelation of British efforts, might lead to disappointment and a return to the US view of an economically weak Britain. Moreover, he did not believe the Americans were ready to return to 'something like the wartime basis of our partnership, and this it seems to me, would be implied by your proposal'.[60]

While Bevin and Attlee accepted these arguments against an early visit, they still felt it would be a good thing if the Prime Minister and President were to meet. Franks was asked to talk to Acheson about such a scheme, which might include preparatory work for the meeting by Bevin and Acheson during the various meetings in New York in September.[61] The Ambassador spoke to Acheson after dinner on 25 August and again the following day. It is interesting to compare Franks's account with that prepared for Acheson. According to the Ambassador, Acheson seemed preoccupied with the fact that on most key foreign policy questions the American government had not made up its mind. In the American record, Franks maintained that the suggested visit did not make much sense 'unless we were sure what we had in mind for the two to talk about and were sure that progress could be made if there were discussions'. Since neither admission would probably have been welcomed by their two governments, it is perhaps not surprising that they were omitted. Taken together, though, they do indicate the openness of discussion between Ambassador and Secretary of State. In his account Franks said Acheson was sympathetic to the idea of a visit and seemed to have two possibilities in mind: either for Attlee to arrive in September and address the United Nations; or for him to visit after the November elections, which Franks preferred.[62] When Acheson and the Ambassador met again on 31 August the Secretary of State said that he and his colleagues favoured postponing any visit until after the November elections.[63]

KOREA: PREMATURE OPTIMISM

If concern about rearmament had led Bevin and Attlee to favour a prime ministerial visit, their interest in Korean developments had also been influential. In September there was spectacular movement by the UN forces. The successful Inchon campaign, launched on 15 September, quickly led to the retreat of the North Koreans. The issue then arose as to whether they should be pursued across the border – the 38th Parallel. In fact, the State Department had told Franks as early as 4 July that it was thinking of going beyond the Parallel.[64] Attlee had reservations about such a move, and the Chiefs of Staff opposed it.[65] However, the Prime Minister deferred to Bevin's judgement. The Cabinet approved crossing the border at its meeting of 26 September.[66] Indeed, Britain sponsored the UN resolution designed to sanction the move. It spoke of using 'all appropriate steps ... for ensuring conditions of stability throughout Korea'.[67] Nevertheless, there was a certain wariness. Franks was instructed to tell the Americans that the British were keen to do everything possible to confine the conflict to Korea. He saw Jessup and Dean Rusk, Assistant Secretary of State, who told him on behalf of Acheson, away in New Haven, that 'it continues to be US policy to localize the Korean fighting'.[68]

What gave London pause for thought were the Chinese warnings about expanding the war north of the 38th Parallel.[69] Yet the Americans seemed strangely unconcerned. This was evident at a meeting between MacArthur and Truman at Wake Island on 15 October, clearly called by the President to link himself with the Korean victories before the impending elections. MacArthur gave Truman what he wanted to hear. Chinese intervention was unlikely; but if they attacked, they would suffer the 'greatest slaughter'.[70] Acheson was equally bullish, dismissing the risks of Chinese entry by saying that what was required was firm and courageous action and not fright at the Chinese bluff. As Hamby says:

> The declaration was vintage Acheson – a telling indication of his rapport with Truman. Whether as successful businessman or victorious politician, Truman had never been daunted by risk. Both men demanded movement and accepted gambles. Neither sufficiently appreciated the magnitude of this particular one. They shared this unfortunate characteristic with Douglas MacArthur.[71]

By 31 October the presence of large numbers of Chinese forces was confirmed by the State Department.[72] The war had entered a new phase, as indeed had the Anglo-American relationship. A major crisis confronted Franks and the Embassy.

NOTES

1. This outline is based on A. Farrar-Hockley, *The British Part in the Korean War. Volume I: A Distant Obligation* (London: HMSO, 1990), pp. 2–31; and Callum A. MacDonald, *Korea: The War Before Vietnam* (New York: Free Press, 1987), pp. 3–17 (quotation at p. 16).
2. See chapter 1 of a first-rate thesis on Britain's involvement: C.P. Alcock, 'Britain and the Korean War 1950–1953' (University of Manchester PhD., 1986). See also P. Lowe, *The Origins of the Korean War* (London: Longman, 1986).
3. PRO, FO 371/83013, F1022/5, Franks to Bevin, Despatch No. 37, 16 January 1950. The Weekly Political Summary did not even mention Korea's exclusion; FO 371/81611, AU 1013/3, Franks to FO, Tel. No. 36(S), 14

January 1950. See also Alcock, 'Britain and the Korean War', p. 40.
4. PRO, FO 371/84058, FK 1015/62, FO Memorandum, 26 June 1950.
5. Warren I. Cohen, *The Cambridge History of American Foreign Relations. Volume IV: America in the Age of Soviet Power, 1941–1991* (Cambridge: Cambridge University Press, 1993), p. 68.
6. Peter Lowe, *Containing the Cold War in East Asia*, p. 190.
7. *DBPO*, 2nd Series, IV, No. 1 and note 5, p. 2.
8. FRUS, 1950, VII, p. 187 (text of statement); PRO, PREM 8/1405 Part I, Strang minute of PM–Douglas meeting, 27 June 1950.
9. PRO, CAB 128/17, CM 39(50), 27 June 1950.
10. PRO, FO 371/84057, FK 1015/40, FO to Washington, Tel. No. 2904, 27 June 1950; ibid., Franks to FO, Tel. Nos. 1771 and 1772, 27 June 1950; PREM 8/1405 Part I, Franks to FO, Tel. No. 1773, 27 June 1950; FRUS 1950, VII, p. 187 note 3.
11. FRUS, 1950, VII, pp. 187 and 207.
12. PRO, PREM 8/1405 Part I, DO(50), 11th Meeting, 28 June 1950. The force comprised a light fleet carrier, two cruisers and five destroyers and frigates.
13. PRO, FO 371/81655, AU 1075/1, FO to Franks, Tel. No. 2980, 30 June 1950.
14. PRO, FO 371/84040, FK 1022/2, Franks to FO, Tel. No. 1789, 28 June 1950; FRUS, 1950, VII, p. 268, memorandum of conversation, 30 June 1950.
15. PRO, FO 115/4486, 10233/53/50G, Franks to Lord Tedder, 5 July 1950.
16. PRO, FO 371/84057, FK 1015/54, Minute by Strang, 26 June 1950.
17. MacDonald, *Korea*, pp. 33–5.
18. PRO, PREM 8/1405 Part I, DO(50) 12th Meeting, 6 July 1950; CAB 128/17, CM 43(50), 6 July 1950.
19. Max Hastings, *The Korean* War (London: Pan, 1988), p. 73; *DBPO*, 2nd Series, IV, No. 141.
20. PRO, FO 371/84086, FK 1022/112G, FO to Franks, Tel. No. 3070, 6 July 1950; FRUS, 1950, VII, pp. 314–15, 335.
21. *DBPO*, 2nd Series, IV, p. 35 note 4.
22. PRO, FO 371/84082, FK 1022/56G, FO to Franks, Tel. No. 3092, 7 July 1950.
23. PRO, FO 371/84084, FK 1022/77G, Franks to FO, Tel. No. 1901, 9 July 1950.
24. FRUS, 1950, VII, pp. 347–51 (Acheson message to Bevin), pp. 351–2 (guidance to Douglas).
25. PRO, FO 371/84084, FK 1022/77G, FO to Franks, Tel. No. 3158, 12 July 1950.
26. HSTL, Acheson Papers, Box 65, Memorandum of Conversation, 13 July 1950. In reporting this meeting, Franks said Acheson was distressed at the concern caused to Bevin, PRO, FO 371/84086, FK 1022/117G, Franks to FO, Tel. No. 1946, 13 July 1950.
27. PRO, FO 371/84086, FK 1022/111G, 'Draft Notes by the S of S for the reply to Mr. Acheson's message of July 11th', FO to Washington, Tel. Nos. 3185 and 3186 (text of message), 14 July 1950; FRUS, 1950, VII, pp. 395–9.
28. FRUS, 1950, VII, p. 430.
29. PRO, FO 371/84088, FK 1022/153 and 154G, Franks to FO, Tel. Nos. 1981 and 1990, 18 July 1950.
30. *Acheson Official Conversations*, reel 3, frame 134, meeting with the President, 3 August 1950.
31. *DBPO*, 2nd Series, IV, No. 34, p. 97, Franks to Bevin, 10 August 1950; ibid., No. 103, p. 287, Franks to Bevin, 4 January 1951
32. Lowe, *Containing the Cold War*, p. 193.
33. PRO, FO 371/84087, FK 1022/137G, FO to Franks, Tel. No. 3203, 15 July 1950.
34. PRO, FO/124935, ZP6/7G, FO to Alexandria, Tel. No. 948, 21 July 1950, FO Memorandum by P. Dixon, 19 July 1950.

35. Ibid., ZP6/3G, Tedder to Ministry of Defence, Tel. No. AWT 24A, 25 July 1950, and Franks to FO, Tel. No. 2052, 25 July 1950.
36. FRUS, 1950, III, p. 1658, Jessup to Acheson, 25 July 1950; ibid., pp. 1661–9, Agreed United States – United Kingdom Memorandum of Discussions on Present World Situation, 25 July 1950.
37. *DBPO*, 2nd Series, IV, p. x.
38. Cairncross (ed.), *Hall Diaries 1947–1953*, p. 124 (18 July entry): Rowan on a visit to London said 'we had a good chance to be treated as partners if we did our stuff'.
39. PRO, PREM 8/1405 Part I, Franks to Attlee, 15 July 1950.
40. FRUS, 1950, VII, p. 431, Memorandum of Conversation, 19 July 1950. This was a prescient observation, for Slim helped influence the decision of the Defence Committee of 24 July to send forces. See note 36.
41. Ibid., p. 447, Douglas to Acheson, 22 July 1950; *Acheson Official Conversations*, Reel 3, frames 40–1, 13 July 1950.
42. PRO, FO 371/84090, FK 1022/198G, Franks to FO, Tel. No. 2022, 21 July 1950, FO to Franks, Tel. No. 3225, 22 July 1950. Farrar-Hockley, *Korean War. Volume I*, p. 103.
43. PRO, FO 371/84091, FK 1022/222G, Franks to FO, Tel. No. 2036 (later corrected to 2037), 23 July 1950.
44. FRUS, 1950, VII, p. 214, Memorandum of Conversation, 28 June 1950.
45. Hastings, *Korean War*, pp. 72–3.
46. PRO, CAB 128/18, CM 46(50), 25 July 1950. Franks afterwards noted he had needed to weigh the human element in this: 'I felt a weight of responsibility because I knew that I was dealing with other men's lives, but I decided in the end I'd got to put that from me and say what I thought', Hennessy and Anstey, *Moneybags*, p. 5.
47. *DBPO*, 2nd Series, IV, No. 38, pp. 108–11, minute by Air Marshall Sir William Elliot to Mr Attlee, 17 August 1950; ibid., No. 44 n3, pp. 127–8. See Farrar-Hockley, *Korean War.* Vol. I, pp. 447–50 for details of the movement of British forces. Britain eventually sent two infantry brigades, one armoured brigade, one and a half artillery regiments, one and a half engineer regiments and support staff, Lowe, *Containing the Cold War*, p. 194.
48. Hastings, *Korean War*, p. 219.
49. MacDonald, *Korea*, pp. 39–40.
50. PRO, FO 371/68014, AN1997/6/45, Inverchapel to Bevin, 13 May 1948.
51. MacDonald, *Korea*, pp. 337–8.
52. FRUS, 1950, III, p. 138.
53. PRO, CAB 129/41, CP(50) 181, Cripps, 'Defence Requirement and United States Assistance', 31 July 1950; CAB 128/18, CM 52(50), 1 August 1950.
54. Plowden, *An Industrialist*, p. 98. Plowden's record is confirmed in FRUS, 1950, III, p. 141, Secretary of State to Certain Diplomatic Offices, 26 July 1950 where Acheson's noted 'our [US] expression willingness make dollar compensation for loss exports.'
55. FRUS, 1950, III, pp. 1699–73, Douglas to Secretary of State, 2 August 1950 and Douglas to Secretary of State, 3 August 1950.
56. Plowden, *An Industrialist*, p. 100; FRUS, 1950, III, pp. 1373–8, Douglas to Acheson, 9 August 1950.
57. NA, Wash. DC, RG 59, Lot File 54D224, Box 24, Perkins to Acheson, 31 August 1950; State Department Decimal Files 1950–54, 795.00/8–3150, Box 4268, Memorandum of Conversation, 31 August 1950.
58. PRO, CAB 128/18, CM 55(50), 4 September 1950.
59. PRO FO 800/517, US/50/33, FO to Washington, Tel. No. 3663, 14 August 1950.

60. Ibid., US/50/33, Franks to FO, Tel. No. 2333, 16 August 1950.
61. Ibid., US/50/36, FO to Franks, Tel. No. 3787, 23 August 1950.
62. Ibid., US/50/37, Franks to FO, Tel. No. 2320, 26 August 1950; FRUS, 1950, III, pp. 1680–2, memorandum by L. D. Battle, Assistant to Secretary of State, 26 August 1950.
63. PRO, PREM 8/1156, Franks to FO, Tel. No. 2361, 31 August 1950; NA, Wash. DC, RG59, State Department Decimal File 1950–54, 795.00/8–3150, Box 4268, Memorandum of Conversation, 31 August 1950.
64. PRO, FO 371/84059, FK 1015/86G, Franks to FO, Tel. No. 1859, 4 July 1950.
65. *DBPO*, 2nd Series, IV, No. 50, pp. 144–5.
66. Ibid., No. 52, pp. 146–8; PRO, CAB 128/19, CM 61(50), 26 September 1950.
67. *DBPO*, 2nd Series, IV, p. 176.
68. PRO, FO 371/84100, FK 1022/401G, FO to Franks, Tel. No. 4456, 6 October 1950; Farrar-Hockley, *Korean War*. Vol. I, p. 224.
69. *DBPO*, 2nd Series, IV, Nos. 53, 60, pp. 148–50, 165–7.
70. MacDonald, *Korea*, p. 57.
71. Hamby, *Truman*, p. 543.
72. *DBPO*, 2nd Series, IV, No. 69, pp. 188–90, Franks to FO, Tel. No. 2950, 1 November 1950.

PART IV: DIFFICULTIES

'It is unfortunately true that Anglo-American divergence is news in this country whereas Anglo-American harmony is not.'

B. A. B. Burrows, 21 September 1951

'It is evident that during the past three months Anglo-American relations, upon which so much depends, have been subjected to strain.'

John Strachey, Minister of War, 1 January 1951

'[T]he people of Britain are greatly concerned by the possibility of an extension of the conflict in Asia … It is natural and inevitable that the business of working out the appropriate policies should involve discussion and at times argument with our friends.'

Sir Oliver Franks in *Look*, 19 June 1951

'Hands and Fists Across the Sea.'

Title of article in *Foreign Affairs* by Roy Harrod, October 1951

—10—

Anglo-American Tensions

NOVEMBER 1950 to January 1951 were months of crisis for the UN forces in Korea and for Anglo-American relations. The difficulties centred on the dramatic arrival of the Chinese, and differing views of the best response. After the initial shock in early November that large numbers of Chinese 'volunteers' were fighting for the North, there was a respite when they withdrew from the battlefield between about 4 and 24 November 1950.[1] Recognising the stakes involved in a large-scale Chinese intervention and taking advantage of their departure, the British Chiefs of Staff proposed that the UN forces withdraw to a line roughly along the 40th Parallel and establish a buffer zone. The Cabinet agreed and the next day, 14 November, Franks was asked to seek the views of Acheson.[2] The Ambassador, however, did not immediately present the suggestion, feeling it would 'be extremely difficult for Acheson ... to accept the proposal', given the recent mid-term election results. He added that it would appear to the American Mid-West to be a unilateral concession.[3]

Bevin, nonetheless, urged Franks to speak to Acheson. The US Secretary of State said he 'regarded the proposals with sympathy and active interest', but did not think that military operations in North Korea could be halted.[4] So General MacArthur's new offensive designed to push on to the Yalu river border with China was launched on 24 November. Within days the UN forces were confronted with over 200,000 organised Chinese forces. It led MacArthur to say 'We face an entirely new war.'[5]

KOREA: BRITISH FEARS OF ESCALATION

For the next two months, until the end of January 1951, there was uncertainty about the nature of strategy in Korea in the face of a series of devastating defeats. There was intense activity at the United Nations. The range of responses available to the US administration was narrowed by Republican successes in the Congressional mid-term elections. The Republican victories encouraged those most critical of US Asian policy. The administration came under attack for sacrificing American lives. Some called for Acheson's resignation. There seemed three choices: escalation, limiting the war or evacuation. Each option on different occasions seemed to be a real possibility. MacArthur, as ever, wanted to escalate the war. Washington decided to limit the war unless further provoked and to speed up its plans for European defence. This produced, according to MacDonald, 'a serious breach with MacArthur which was to end in his dismissal'. Truman was concerned at the likelihood of Republican attacks on the administration's European strategy. With the prospect of such an onslaught, neither he nor Acheson could afford to appear weak in Asia.[6] The situation was so serious for the US administration that there was talk of the need to replace Acheson as Secretary of State.[7] One way in which they could sound strong was by taking action in the United Nations. In any event, the Americans were extremely angry with the Chinese. So they now proposed a motion condemning the Chinese in the Security Council.

In London there was considerable alarm at the collapse of the UN position in Korea and at political developments in Washington. Passage of a UN resolution condemning Chinese aggression, it was feared, might make the US administration readier to yield to pressure from MacArthur to attack Manchuria,[8] an action which could result in a general war with China and thus to possible global war with the USSR.

Never was there, during his mission, a greater need for the deployment of the fundamental skill required of an ambassador of fostering a sympathetic understanding of each country's position. Franks needed to explain the nature of the US administration's difficult position: under severe domestic pressure to 'get tough' with communism and suffering military defeat in Asia, while proposing expanded commitments in Europe, they were being asked to show restraint by those very Europeans to whose problems they were giving priority and whose forces contributed such a small proportion of the UN effort in Korea. At the same time, he had to convey London's, indeed Europe's and the Commonwealth's, anxiety that matters not escalate into a global war. Achieving mutual understanding of contrasting circumstances in the making of policy and the pursuit of acceptable joint approaches called for the very highest talents. He was only partially successful: it is doubtful whether any other figure could have secured much more. It certainly was an matter of urgency. As Younger noted:

> the main trouble is the widening gap between US and UK policy. US policy has been 'hardening' and we are being accused of 'appeasement'. I do not think there is any justification for this. The word 'appeasement' is coming to be used for any attempt to reach agreement.[9]

When the Cabinet met on 29 November to review developments, Bevin said that he had been in contact with the Americans. He was apprehensive lest they take any precipitate action in response to the rout of the UN troops, or that MacArthur should pursue his previous request for authority to launch air attacks across the border into Manchuria. Acheson had assured him that he would continue to consult closely with the British government, and that he remained committed to localising the area of hostilities. Both Bevin and Attlee stressed that the Korean operations should not, in the Prime Minister's words, 'be allowed to draw more of their military resources away from Europe and the Middle East'. Attlee was also concerned that the Americans appeared to be intent upon advancing a resolution in the Security Council charging China with open aggression. This might involve full-scale military operations against China, at the expense of other areas. Yet the Cabinet recognised that 'If we were to withdraw our support for United States strategy in the Far East, the United States Government would be less willing to continue their policy of supporting the defence of Western Europe.'[10]

Moreover, on 30 November, Franks added to British concerns, when he reported Acheson's speech of the 29th to the National Council of Churches at Cleveland, in which 'for the first time Mr. Acheson openly placed upon the Soviet Union the ultimate responsibility for Korean aggression.'[11] In a further telegram that day the Ambassador said opinion in Washington was 'grave and anxious but neither despairing nor bellicose'. He felt that there was 'no clarity in general opinion about what to do next.' He added:

> I feel the situation here presents a major opportunity to British policy. If we can hammer out plans and objectives adequate to the situation ... I believe we could make steady headway. We shall encounter a good deal of unpopularity and criticism from those who are angry or frightened, but I feel sure that a constructive approach consistently and patiently advocated would yield dividends ... because of the changed situation in Korea and the shock to public opinion here a new approach is necessary and stands a real chance of achieving a welcome.[12]

Franks was trying to be positive, seeing the situation as an opportunity rather than as a cause for concern.

If the changed situation in Korea and fears about the likely US response heightened the tension in the Far East and in Anglo-American relations, then Truman's press conference on the morning of 30 November brought issues to crisis point. During questioning on the Korean War he was asked whether his readiness to use 'every weapon we have' meant there was active consideration of the use of the atomic bomb. He answered: 'There has always been active consideration of its use.'[13] A garbled version of Truman's remarks was transmitted on the press wires, which included the observation that MacArthur would take whatever steps were necessary, including use of the atomic bomb. Attlee's press adviser, Philip Jordan, told him that the President had been aiming to lessen pressure from the Republicans and that, although 'this does not make the reply any less dangerous … it does not contain, I think, all the implications that could be read into the first "flash" that appeared'. Franks, asked to secure reassurances from the Americans, telegraphed that senior officials had said that Truman's statement of clarification 'makes absolutely clear that no new action is under consideration and that there has been no change in the general situation in regard to the atomic bomb'.[14]

Before Franks's telegram arrived, however, the considerable consternation among MPs, who were holding a two-day debate on foreign affairs, led to pressure on the Prime Minister to act. An emergency Cabinet meeting was held at 6.45 p.m. on the 30th. Attlee told ministers that 'urgent action was necessary to allay public anxiety'.[15]

It would appear that concerns about resort to nuclear weapons were more well-founded than Franks seemed to suggest. The Ambassador afterwards maintained that the United States had never seriously considered the use of the atomic bomb. Hastings feels that Franks may have underestimated the pressures that might have developed had the Americans been driven out of Korea. From the outbreak of the war there had been consideration of its possible use, but only in time of direst emergency. In November more intensive scrutiny was given to its employment: on 28 November the Army's Plans and Operations Division suggested that the military should be ready to make 'prompt use of the atomic bomb … as, if and when, directed by the President'.[16] There is no evidence to indicate that Franks had any knowledge of such studies.

Attlee was deeply worried about the possible use of atomic weapons, for there were US nuclear bombers in Britain. The B.29s had originally arrived in 1948 as an earnest of American support during the Berlin blockade, but they were only made atomic-capable in 1949. In April 1950 an agreement was concluded to build four airfields at Upper Heyford, Brize Norton, Fairfield and Greenham Common. The Foreign Office, in arguing for this development, maintained that 'the establishment of secure air bases in this country ... would certainly constitute an important additional tie'. The Korean War led to the stockpiling of nuclear components at these sites. This had been arranged informally because the 1946 McMahon Act forbade exchange of atomic information with any other power. Likewise, Britain was given little information about the US plan for global war, Offtackle, which assumed that Britain would be the main European base for the US. This naturally irked the British. Sir John Slessor, Chief of the Air Staff, observed 'In a matter like this, which was of life and death for the country and Western Europe, we were entitled not only to know the details of the plan but also to be consulted about them[*sic*].'[17] The Korean War exposed for the first time the perils of the situation for Britain, which could be a prime target for Soviet attack and yet lacked mechanisms for effective consultation on these issues, much less operational control of bases on British territory. London was naturally keen to obtain clearer understandings and some manner of veto over American use of nuclear weapons and bases. As MacDonald remarked, 'It was no longer a matter of committing the US to British security but of restraining the indiscriminate use of American power.'[18] Attlee wanted to press the British position, feeling that they were being taken for granted.

So it was decided that the Prime Minister should visit Washington as soon as possible for a meeting with Truman. Franks was asked to gain the President's agreement, which was secured that same night.[19] Interestingly, the French asked to see the Prime Minister before he left. Talks were held between Attlee and Bevin and their French counterparts, Pleven and Schuman, in London on 2 December.[20] Clearly, Attlee would be representing more than just British concerns.

ATTLEE IN WASHINGTON: PREPARATIONS

At the Cabinet meeting, and in the telegram to Washington requesting the visit, a number of topics were identified as needing discussion. Attlee was keen to avoid the impression that the only purpose of the trip was to discuss use of the atomic bomb. Undoubtedly this was important, though, given the US bases in Britain. He also wanted to consider the general situation in the Far East, in the light of the Chinese intervention, and two further matters which were causing

Anglo-American difficulties: European defence arrangements, and the British rearmament programme and, in particular, the problem of raw materials. On this second issue Franks had an important contribution to make.

Concern that the North Korean invasion heralded the possibility of further communist probes in other parts of the world had led the United States to encourage greater defence expenditure by the NATO powers. The British had responded with their scheme costing £3,600 million. By September 1950 there was concern about the inadequacy of such programmes in the face of reports of major increases in the manpower and equipment of the military police force in the Soviet zone of Germany. Bevin feared 'that next year the Soviet Government will seek to repeat what they have done in Korea'. Although the Chiefs of Staff had advanced a plan for the gradual rearmament of West Germany, Bevin persuaded the Defence Committee that this was not viable at present. Ministers accepted, instead, that there should be mobile police forces.[21] Meanwhile, the Americans had developed similar ideas about West German rearmament. On 4 September Holmes, the US Chargé d'Affaires, told Bevin of the US 'one package' proposal that would be made at the tripartite and North Atlantic Council meetings of 12–26 September. The Americans suggested the formation of an Atlantic unified force under a US Supreme Commander and with more US troops in Europe; and German units would be integrated into this force.[22] The British were pleased about the ideas for a unified force and for a US Supreme Commander but more reticent about the immediate establishment of German units. Yet, as Bevin reported from the New York meetings, the Americans had presented a single scheme: if German rearmament could not be accepted, the increased US commitment to Europe was endangered. This led the Cabinet on 15 September to accept in principle that the Germans should participate in Western defence.[23]

The French reaction, however, was less forthcoming. They refused to sanction German forces. As a result, the final communiqué of the North Atlantic Council on 26 September said only that there was 'agreement that Germany should be enabled to contribute to the build-up of the defence of Western Europe'.[24] As an alternative the French devised the Pleven Plan. It called for a European army comprising units from the various national armies which would merge at the lowest possible level. Germany would be permitted to provide such units. The army would be controlled by a European Defence Council and be financed through a single European defence budget. This was revealed to the British and Americans on 24 October.[25] The Americans were strongly opposed to this idea and told the British of their objections in Political–Military conversations on 26 October that followed up the July talks on a similar basis.[26] The Americans produced the Spofford Compromise, named after the Chairman of the North Atlantic Council Deputies. This assumed that the American scheme and the Pleven Plan should be allowed to proceed in parallel. The British supported this approach.[27] Such was the position on the eve of Attlee's visit. The Prime Minister was anxious to move matters forward and secure the establishment of a unified force in Europe with a US Supreme Commander.

September 1950 was also an important month for the second Anglo-American difficulty – the question of American help for the British rearmament programme. According to Plowden, it was only then that the position became clear, revealing how misguided were the original expectations about US aid. He added: 'We were faced with a situation in which, instead of the full funds for our balance of payments we had been counting on, we could, at most, hope to receive one-sixth of the meagre amount of dollars available.'[28] As a consequence, British officials prepared a report suggesting that it might be possible to retain the £3,600 million programme with only £350 million of aid. Ministers in a Cabinet sub-committee were dubious about this and would not approve a lower figure.[29]

FRANKS'S MEMORANDUM OF 27 SEPTEMBER 1950

At this point Franks entered the debate with a memorandum of 27 September. Britain in mid-1950, he said, was, thanks to ERP and the efforts of the government and people, independent of extraordinary outside help. Indeed, 'we were becoming able for the first time since the war to sustain our world-wide commitments'. North Korean aggression, however, altered this radically. The new defence programme would cause great difficulties to the British economy. There would be a growth of debts to sterling area countries supplying raw materials, and the latter might well demand dollars from Britain because it could not export to them all that they would like. Franks then argued against direct US aid, causing Britain to become economically dependent upon the United States again: 'Once more we shall lose the position we were just attaining, the partner in world affairs of the United States.' He suggested an alternative form of US assistance: asking the Americans to underwrite British reserves to an extent roughly corresponding to the defence programme debts; a waiver of the capital and interest repayments on the 1945 loan; and assistance with stockpiling. Franks had had a 'secret, informal and wholly personal conversation' with Acheson about these ideas. After talking the ideas over within the State Department, Acheson said that the general feeling was that they were interesting but 'too bold and too difficult'.[30]

The response in London was similar. An inter-departmental meeting shared Franks's desire to escape dependence on direct American aid, but felt there were too many difficulties in the Ambassador's proposal.[31] Moreover, Hugh Gaitskell, Minister for Economic Affairs, questioned Franks's approach. He preferred to pursue the line in the memorandum of Paul Nitze, the Director of the Policy Planning Staff, which suggested that an equitable distribution of economic burdens could be achieved through an analysis of each country's military programme and its effects on their national accounts.[32] Gaitskell then left for the United States to seek answers to two questions: the methods for assessing contributions within NATO, and the need to control the spiral of raw material prices because of US purchasing policy. His meetings with Spofford and with Harriman proved inconclusive on these matters. He seems to have put his trust in the Americans. According to Cairncross, 'He accepted – although it came as news to the Prime Minister two months later – that the bid for £550 million should lapse and that it would be necessary to rely on the United States to make something available on account and provide additional aid under the agreed formula.'[33] A joint memorandum, signed by Bevin and Gaitskell, now Chancellor of Exchequer in succession to Cripps who was too ill to continue, summed up the British position on Gaitskell's return. It recommended acceptance of the US offer of interim aid of $84 million and collaboration with the other NATO countries in the Nitze plan.[34] By the time of Attlee's visit to Washington the raw materials aspect to the rearmament programme was a matter of serious concern. Attlee told the Cabinet that 'American action in this matter was seriously handicapping the efforts of other countries, including the United Kingdom'.[35]

Adding to British financial concerns was the reluctant recognition that Marshall Aid would have to end on 31 December. Rowan telegraphed from Washington, in the Ambassador's absence, to say on 20 October that Britain could not count on anything further, except some $200 million in the pipeline.[36] This was a response to the Economic Co-operation Administration's (ECA) declaration of 19 October that, on account of the strengthening of the sterling area's central reserves, ERP aid was likely to stop at the end of the year. After talks with the Americans Gaitskell had to tell the House of Commons on 13 December that Marshall Aid would be suspended as from 1 January 1951.[37]

In November the question of Franks's effectiveness as Ambassador arose. Sir Edward Bridges, Permanent Secretary at the Treasury, told Strang on 6 November that doubts were being raised in London about Franks. At a recent luncheon attended by Plowden, Jordan, press officer to Attlee, and Geoffrey Crowther, editor of *The Economist*, among others, someone had said that the Ambassador 'no longer cut any ice in Washington'. Bridges reported that the Prime Minister's secretary had told him that Attlee had not lost confidence in Franks. He also told Strang that Plowden had been speaking to Aneuran Bevan, Minister of Health, who maintained that Franks was 'sold on the American point of view'. Strang told Bridges that he felt certain that Bevin had complete confidence in Franks and 'there was no one in the Foreign Office who did not think he was doing a grand job'.[38] Although Bevin spoke to Attlee about this, nothing further developed. It seems probable that the doubts were part of the general atmosphere of concern about Anglo-American relations at the time. Indeed, James Cable, then a junior official in the Foreign Office, has noted how 'irreverent men in London' described Franks as 'the American Ambassador in Washington'.[39] Those like Bevan, who were more critical of the Americans, were inclined to blame those figures who seemed ready to reach accommodations with the United States. Yet, it is interesting to read Younger's diary for 19 November, which records that, after spending the weekend with Ambassador and Lady Franks, he had found him 'less alarming and didactic than I had been led to believe'.[40] Franks himself knew nothing of these doubts.[41]

ATTLEE IN WASHINGTON: DISCUSSIONS

In such circumstances the most important meetings thus far in his ambassadorship took place in Washington on 4–8 December. The main topics were: Korea and its implications for the general situation in the Far East; arrangements for European defence; the British defence effort and the raw materials question; the atomic bomb; and British proposals for improved liaison. The London Embassy sent Washington its appreciation of the mood of both government and public and of the key concerns that Attlee would be seeking to address. There was apprehension that the world might be drifting towards war; a desire to avoid dependence on the United States; irritation at the lack of appreciation of the British contribution to the world-wide struggle in Malaya, Hong Kong, Middle East and so on; and doubts about the wisdom of rearming Germany. The Embassy added that the British would probably be most sensitive in discussing raw materials and US aid.[42] Each country prepared briefs to cover the main themes.[43]

The meetings brought together two men who were not especially adept at getting on with those from unfamiliar backgrounds and whose experiences could hardly have been more different. Attlee was austere, exact, punctilious, not given to wasting words and ready to disclose the magnitude of British concerns. Truman preferred plain speaking to diplomatic niceties. They shared a desire for getting to the heart of problems in a way that could expose disagreements. Acheson seemed ambivalent about the Prime Minister. In his memoirs he said: 'December opened by bringing us Job's comforter in Clement Attlee.' But in a later interview with Kenneth Harris he maintained that 'Attlee was very adroit, extremely adroit, his grasp of the situation was masterly.'[44] A good deal of the progress in the talks was owed to Franks's talent for a conciliatory approach.[45] He clarified differences in a form likely to suggest the possibility of their resolution and he helped to improve personal relations between Prime Minister and President. Franks later told Roy Jenkins that dinner at the British Embassy on the 7th saw a breakthrough when Truman and Attlee sang First World War songs together.[46]

Attlee arrived on the morning of 4 December. Originally, the first meeting with Truman was to have taken place on the 5th but it was brought forward, at Acheson's request, to the late afternoon of the 4th.[47] The meeting began with General Bradley's survey of the situation in Korea. The American maintained that the defence of Europe was the primary objective but that Korea, Japan, the Philippines and Malaya were also of importance. There was discussion of the military prospects in Korea and of the possible diplomatic options. Franks then tried to summarise the discussion by saying there seemed to be three lines of thought. First, the Korean bridgeheads might not be held, leaving the UN position one of definite weakness. Secondly, the Prime Minister had tried to predict what would be in the mind of the Chinese if they came to negotiate. Thirdly, Acheson had outlined another possibility where the UN forces held on in Korea for as long as possible. Acheson explained that his proposal was to offer a ceasefire on condition that we would remain behind the 38th Parallel.[48]

It is clear that this first meeting did not go well. But the Chief of the Imperial General Staff, Field Marshal Slim, said, 'Franks finally summed up extremely cleverly and made it all sound not quite so bad.'[49] At a meeting on the evening of the 4th Franks and Acheson, together with a number of officials, sought to improve the atmosphere. Reviewing this meeting the next morning, Acheson said he had suggested to Franks that the first meeting had been rather too rigid and had too many people in attendance. He suggested that Attlee allow his subordinates to initiate discussions.[50] Franks and Acheson followed up their 4 December meeting with a discussion on the 5th prior to the next meeting of Attlee and Truman that afternoon. Franks felt the next set of talks should devote themselves first to the short-range problems. He hoped that the discussion could be kept vigorous and alive. Moreover, he did not feel that they needed to find a complete accommodation on the long-range results.[51]

The second meeting took place after lunch on the President's yacht on the 5 December. Again Korea was covered, together with the ramifications for the rest of the Far East. Discussions were drawn together once more by Franks's summary. He believed that they had found considerable agreement. First, that they would not contemplate a voluntary withdrawal from Korea and would try to keep their forces up to strength. Secondly, they were ready to negotiate if a ceasefire could be achieved. If, however, there was no chance of negotiation, Britain was far from convinced that the right course would be to maintain a state of war and to take measures like economic sanctions and subversive activities against China. Thirdly, if the chance of negotiations arose, the British 'were not convinced that their scope should be confined to Korea'. The withdrawal at least of recognition for Chiang Kai-shek and perhaps also the seating of Communist China might have to be considered. In reporting this to London, he observed that the Prime Minister's statement of the British case had made an impression on the Americans.[52]

Thus far the talks had been generally reassuring for the British on Korea and the dangers of its developing into a larger commitment in Asia. The two powers had agreed on the need for a ceasefire so as to concentrate on Europe. But Attlee was willing to consider a wider deal with China than the Americans, who were unwilling to link a Korean ceasefire with a general settlement in the Far East. Acheson made it clear, said Franks, that the administration 'were not reconciled to the concessions which would be necessary to make a negotiated settlement possible'.[53]

At the third meeting, 11.40–12.30 on the 6th, discussion turned to the British defence effort. Attlee tabled a British memorandum, 'United Kingdom Defence Programme', and outlined its main points. He said that no adequate defence programme could be carried out by his government unless sufficient supplies of raw materials were made available. He asked for immediate emergency action and also longer-term planning; there might be a need for something like the Combined Raw Materials Board set up during the Second World War. They agreed to establish a working group to explore these issues.[54]

Later that afternoon the fourth meeting considered the British rearmament programme and European defence arrangements. Attlee urged the Americans to establish a unified command structure and appoint a Supreme Commander and not be delayed by French reluctance over German rearmament. For their part the Americans pressed Attlee on the size of the British defence programme, Acheson 'emphasising that Britain was the United States' main ally'. They needed to know that the British would go along with them in their rearmament efforts, if they were to convince Congress to approve the new spending.[55] That evening, after a dinner at the British Embassy, Franks helped to organise a discussion involving Truman and Attlee and their senior advisers. In the course of consideration of the running of the Korean War, Field Marshal Slim and Lord Tedder 'urged very strongly both the feasibility and desirability of some regular and closer contacts between the Chiefs of Staff on both sides and stated their view that this could be arranged without formally reconstituting the Combined Chiefs of Staff'. Truman was sympathetic, feeling that only Britain and the United States could be relied upon. He felt certain that good arrangements could be achieved.[56] As a result, the British presented the Americans with a paper, 'US and UK Liaison Arrangements' at the fifth meeting on 7 December.[57]

At the fifth meeting Attlee raised the question of the atomic bomb. Truman said that Britain and the United States had always been partners in this matter and he would not consider the use of the bomb without consulting Britain. Attlee wondered if this might be put in writing. Truman responded: 'if a man's word wasn't any good it wasn't made any better by writing it down'.[58] This went further than Acheson felt the President was constitutionally entitled to go. When the final meeting took place on 8 December the joint communiqué, produced after Acheson and Franks had consulted, read: 'The President told the Prime Minister that it was also his desire to keep the Prime Minister at all times informed of developments which might bring about a change in the situation.'[59] But the British record of the conversation retained Truman's commitment to 'consult'. A compromise was reached by which this British record was sent to London in that form, and this was stressed to the Americans, but the copy sent to the United States referred only to the undertaking to 'inform'.[60] At this final meeting Truman repeated his belief that regular military contact between the British and Americans was a good idea.[61]

ATTLEE IN WASHINGTON: RESULTS

The Washington talks closed with some progress. Franks had helped to establish a congenial atmosphere of co-operation, so that the participants left the meetings feeling that the relationship was stronger. Farrar-Hockley has observed, 'it is doubtful whether there would have been such a clear understanding of each other's views without the personal contact of the principals and no less, their immediate subordinates'.[62] There had been achievements. On 19 December, Eisenhower was named NATO Supreme Commander. Attlee telegraphed Bevin, saying that the Americans 'implicitly and on occasion explicitly assumed that we are their principal ally'. He added that the 'United Kingdom was lifted out of "the European queue" and we were treated as partners, unequal no doubt in power but still equal in counsel'.[63] Asked for his comments on these observations, Franks gave them his qualified approval:

> Although the wartime partnership has been revived, it is undoubtedly accompanied on the American side by an increase in their expectations of our own performance. Not only do they consider this a reasonable requirement in itself but they pointed out that it will help the Administration's case domestically.[64]

This telegram was circulated to the Cabinet and seems likely to have influenced both Attlee's remarks and the Cabinet's decision of 18 December. The Prime Minister said he had persuaded the Americans to 'accept the Anglo-American partnership as the mainspring of Atlantic defence'. But this would be lost, he added, 'if we were now to be treated as merely one of the European countries which were being urged by America to make a larger contribution to the common defence effort. We should align ourselves with the Americans in urging the others to do more.' The Cabinet agreed to tell the North Atlantic Council that Britain had decided to increase and accelerate its defence preparations still further.[65] On 25 January 1951 the Cabinet agreed to increase the defence programme from £3,600 million to £4,700 million for the three years 1951–54.[66] The British had yielded over the defence programme but had not accepted the American proposal of £6,000 million. Once again the desire to be the United States' main ally led to greater exertions and commitments. It would appear that British efforts yielded some benefits, for Acheson told the National Security Council on 12 December that close relations with Britain were important since they could only bring US power into play with the co-operation of the British.[67]

As regards the Korean War, the need to localise the hostilities had been accepted. According to Farrar-Hockley, 'the event of meeting relieved a rising crisis of European and Commonwealth confidence in the conduct of the war by the United States'.[68] But there were no advances in pursuit of a negotiated settlement. Nor did they make much progress on MacArthur, although the British felt they detected encouraging signs. They were persuaded by the private comments of Bradley and other US figures recognising that they might soon have to restrain the General. Acheson wondered whether 'any government had any control over General MacArthur'.[69] On the atomic bomb, Attlee told the Cabinet on 12 December that 'Truman had entirely satisfied him about the use of [it]. . . The President ... had never had any intention of using the atomic bomb in Korea.' The Prime Minister added that Truman regarded it as 'in a sense a joint possession of the United States, United Kingdom and Canada', and would not authorise its use 'without prior consultation' with these two governments except in 'an extreme emergency'.[70] Attlee had secured a qualified success in the matter.

On the question of close Anglo-American liaison the aftermath of the Attlee visit was more promising. On 3 January 1951 Franks saw Acheson, saying that the previous talks between Jessup and the Ambassador had been useful, and that his government now wanted to put them on a more or less regular basis. He also intimated that Britain wanted to know about US war plans in connexion with the use of English airfields by US forces. Franks told Perkins that he did not feel it was necessary to have a fixed schedule of meetings but that it should be the right of either side to call meetings at reasonable intervals of time. He added that the British felt that perhaps they were entitled to, and certainly would be greatly helped by, having such periodic meetings.[71] Air Marshal Sir John Slessor, Chief of the Air Staff, arrived in the United States on 14 January and emphasised the same point. He felt that 'each country might be able to arrive at sounder decisions if it were aware in advance of the tentative thinking of the other'.[72] When Franks met Acheson, Jessup and Nitze on 31 January the Americans were ready to approve talks. They made clear that the talks would not be held at stated intervals; and that the aim would be to exchange ideas, without formal minutes, instead of seeking formal decisions or tentative agreements. When Franks suggested that some record should be kept, Jessup accepted that each side keep a memorandum of the conversation, but that there be no attempt to exchange these memoranda.[73] The next day Franks reported this to London, saying:

> The American suggestion probably does not give us quite all we should like but if we can made [*sic*] a success of it I think these meetings should grow into a regular habit and have a real importance ... the Americans attach the highest importance to the complete secrecy of these arrangements so that if ever asked, for example by the French, they will not be in difficulty ... We owe a lot to Jack Slessor for the result.[74]

THE UN RESOLUTION ON CHINA

On China, however, the British had to give way to American wishes – though not before coming close to a major rift on the issue. The end of the Washington talks coincided with a lull in the fighting on Korea and a return to activity in the United Nations. On 14 December the General Assembly approved the establishment of a Cease Fire Group to seek the basis for an armistice, but their efforts were rebuffed by the Chinese on the 22nd, who then launched a new offensive on the 31st. This caused the Americans to renew their quest for a condemnatory resolution against China. The British were unenthusiastic about this. Franks told Acheson on 4 January 1951 that the issue should be left open for the moment and that British 'support for a resolution condemning China as an aggressor was not to be taken for granted'. Acheson was persuaded to delay any action on the matter until the Commonwealth Prime Ministers' conference had completed its deliberations. Franks also conveyed British anxieties about the military campaign in Korea. He said the news was 'gloomy and seems almost to be preparing the public mind for the evacuation of Korea'. Acheson accepted that this was indeed the tone of comments but that MacArthur was under orders 'to resist and fight it out unless he were threatened with annihilation'.[75] On 6 January Franks asked for and gained a week's delay in action on the resolution, but not before having to endure, in his interview with Rusk, 'a half-hour's lecture on the deplorable effect that this delay would have on United Nations itself and on American public opinion'.[76]

Franks sent his personal reflections – 'his considered views' – on the matter on the same day. He emphasised that fluctuations in US public opinion might well alter the administration's response from its present one:

> American opinion on foreign affairs is generally volatile and uncertain at the present moment, and in particular because military happenings in Korea are obscure and when revealed in

> time by actual events may provoke major gusts of emotion and opinion which will limit the freedom of action of the administration.

He added that the administration was likely to be influenced by its belief that, since the turn of the year, opinion in the country had hardened against China. In conclusion, he noted that, besides the search for collective measures, such as economic sanctions against China, the Americans, if China were declared an aggressor, would be likely to argue the case in the Collective Measures Committee for more far-reaching measures against China.[77]

Although the American mood was toughening, the Commonwealth Prime Ministers felt that a further effort should be made to talk to the Chinese. As a result, the United Nations produced on 11 January an approach based on 'Five Principles'. Acheson was reluctant to accept them and did so only because he expected the Chinese to reject them, which they virtually did on the 17th.[78] The Americans now wanted the immediate introduction of their resolution, condemning China as an aggressor and demanding the withdrawal of its forces. They tabled it on 20 January. Franks explained to London why the United States was so insistent upon this action: it was needed to satisfy public opinion, for the American people liked to go to law and get legal decisions.[79]

Up to this point the British had been content to influence American thinking from the inside, hoping to evade a break. But now there emerged a growing challenge to this sentiment. The Minister of War, John Strachey, argued that US hostility to China could endanger world peace.[80] Within the Foreign Office opinion was somewhat divided. Younger now favoured opposing the resolution:

> One further reason why I think this may be the moment at which to assert our independence of [the] USA in foreign policy is that the Americans have clearly reached the frame of mind in which they count upon us always to 'go along' with them, no matter what our misgivings. We have got to stop this rot if we ever want to have real influence upon them, and we are not likely to get a better chance than this of doing so.[81]

Jebb was altogether more sanguine, feeling the passage of the resolution would not have any major effect.[82] Sir P. Dixon, Deputy Under-Secretary of State at the Foreign Office, believed that it would not be possible to change the minds of the Americans on this issue. So he felt that, 'If we cannot effectively change American Far Eastern policy, then we must, it seems to me, resign ourselves to a role of counsellor and moderator.'[83]

The critics of the US stance, however, seemed to be in the ascendant. On the 23rd Franks was instructed, in a forceful telegram, to inform Acheson of British dissatisfaction with the resolution and the American approach. It spoke of 'the United States Government seeking to impose on the United Nations a policy which is the direct result of past American failures'. Franks said, in reply, that he had spoken 'very plainly' to Acheson who had agreed to delay the vote. However, the Ambassador maintained the importance of supporting the resolution 'from the standpoint of relations between the United States and Britain'. He concluded, 'Our inability to do this would not be understood here and would lead to very considerable difficulties.'[84]

British concerns centred on three parts of the resolution. Paragraph 2 maintained that the Chinese rejected all proposals for a settlement which the British felt was not accurate. Paragraph 3 claimed that China engaged in aggression in Korea, while Britain preferred to condemn Chinese support for aggression. Paragraph 8 asked for the Collective Measures Committee of the United Nations to consider further sanctions against China; and the British worried about the scale and consequences of such measures.

The highpoint of resistance to the American position came when the Cabinet, with Bevin absent through illness, decided on the 25th that Jebb should vote against the resolution, if there were no alterations to paragraphs 2 and 8.[85] On hearing this, Sir R. Makins, Deputy Under-Secretary of State at the Foreign Office, declared: 'I do not think that this vote will be soon forgotten or forgiven by the American people'; he feared it would have 'a very adverse effect on British interests generally'.[86]

However, it was decided the next day to back the American resolution if acceptable final wording could be found for the paragraphs.[87] To Franks fell the task of securing these amendments. He spoke on the 27th to Acheson who made a concession on paragraph 8, saying that the Collective Measures Committee would take into account in its report the results of the efforts of the Good Offices Committee. The Ambassador explained that this would not suffice. So the Secretary of State consulted the President and agreed to change the wording to read that the 'committee is authorised to defer its report if the Good Offices Committee ... reports satisfactory progress'. Franks recommended that this be accepted as the best that could be achieved. It was, he maintained, still a good test to see whether the Canadians were with us or the United States; and they now supported the resolution. Moreover, he hoped that the government would be able to accept that China 'aggressed' in the resolution. The Ambassador's main worry lay in 'the differences between public opinion in the United States and public opinion in Britain' rather than in 'the arguments and differences at Lake Success'.[88] Franks was able to ensure that paragraph 2 was also amended to meet British wishes, now saying that 'China has not accepted United Nations proposals'.[89] Jebb voted for the resolution which was passed on 1 February.[90]

By this time the situation in Korea had improved. A fresh UN offensive was launched in late January by the new commander of 8th Army, General Matthew B. Ridgway, and its success removed the sense of imminent military disaster and so passions cooled. The danger of a wider war had been averted. As MacDonald says, this was due not to the restraining influence of Britain and the Commonwealth but to Ridgway's stabilisation of the front.[91]

NOTES

1. This was consistent with Mao's strategy in previous wars: offensives often came in stages, with various fits and starts, rather than all at once. William Stueck, *The Korean War: An International History* (Princeton, NJ: Princeton University Press, 1995), p. 112.
2. PRO, CAB 128/18, CM 73(50), 13 November 1950; *DBPO*, 2nd Series, IV, No. 74, pp. 202–4, Bevin to Franks, 14 November 1950. On the buffer zone proposal see Peter N. Farrar, 'Britain's Proposal for a Buffer Zone South of the Yalu in November 1950: Was it a Neglected Opportunity to End the Fighting in Korea?', *Journal of Contemporary History*, Vol. 18, No. 2, April 1983, pp. 327–51.
3. Franks to FO, Tel. No. 3079, 14 November 1950, quoted in Farrar-Hockley, *Korean War Vol. I*, p. 299.
4. Franks to FO, Tel. No. 3089, 15 November 1950, quoted in ibid., p. 300.
5. FRUS, 1950, VII, p. 1237, MacArthur to Joint Chiefs of Staff, 28 November 1950.
6. MacDonald, *Korea*, pp. 69–73 (quotation at p. 71).
7. PRO, FO 371/81616, AU1016/49, B. A. B. Burrows (Washington Embassy) to M. Wright (FO), 20 November 1950. Attlee was told on 30 November of 'the mounting pressure on him [Truman] to get rid of Acheson', *DBPO*, 2nd Series, IV, p. 223n.
8. M. L. Dockrill, 'The Foreign Office, Anglo-American Relations and the Korean War, June 1950–June 1951', *International Affairs*, Vol. 62 No. 3 (1986), p. 464; *DBPO*, 2nd IV, p. 219 n8.
9. Younger Diary, 26 November 1950. He flew to New York on 20 September and remained in the United States until 17 December.
10. PRO, CAB 128/18, CM 78(50), 29 November 1950, 10 a.m.
11. PRO, FO 371/84120, FK1023/202, Franks to FO, Tel. No. 3220, 30 November 1950.
12. Ibid., FK1023/207, Franks to FO, Tel. No. 3232, 30 November 1950.
13. FRUS, 1950, VII, pp. 1261–2.

14. Bodleian Library, Oxford, Attlee Papers, dep. 114, Note for Attlee, no date, no signature, Minute by P. Jordan for PM, 30 November 1950; also at *DBPO*, 2nd Series, IV, No. 81, pp. 222–3 which contains at note 2 the quotation from Franks's telegram.
15. PRO, CAB 128/18, CM 80 (50), 30 November 1950, 6.45 p.m.
16. Hastings, *Korean War*, pp. 218, 220 (quotation); MacDonald, *Korea*, pp. 70–1.
17. Dimbleby and Reynolds, *Ocean Apart*, pp. 187 (Shuckburgh quotation), 188 (Slessor quotation).
18. MacDonald, *Korea*, p. 75.
19. *DBPO*, 2nd Series, IV, No. 82, p. 224, FO to Franks, 30 November 1950 and Franks reply at note 3.
20. PRO, FO 371/83019, F1027/6G, Record of a meeting of the Prime Minister and Foreign Secretary with the French Prime Minister and Minister for Foreign Affairs, 2 December 1950.
21. *DBPO*, 2nd Series, III, No. 3i, Defence Committee, 1 September 1950.
22. Ibid., No. 2, pp. 4–9, Sir P. Dixon Record of Meeting between Mr Bevin and the US Chargé d'Affaires, 4 September 1950. See also Acheson, *Present at the Creation*, pp. 437–40.
23. *DBPO*, 2nd Series, III, No. 27, pp. 58–61, Cabinet Conclusions, 15 September 1950.
24. E. Fursdon, *The European Defence Community: A History* (London: Macmillan, 1980), p. 85. See also Saki Dockrill, *Britain's Policy for West German Rearmament 1950–1955* (Cambridge: Cambridge University Press, 1991).
25. *DBPO*, 2nd III, No. 80, pp. 206–7, Harvey (Paris) to FO, 24 October 1950.
26. FRUS, 1950, III, pp. 1689–91, US Minutes of US–UK Political Military Conversations, 26 October 1950.
27. *DBPO*, 2nd Series, III, No. 109, pp. 274–7, memorandum from UK Deputy on NAC to Mr Bevin, 20 November 1950.
28. Plowden, *An Industrialist*, p. 101.
29. Ibid., pp. 101–2; Cairncross (ed.), *Hall Diaries 19*, pp. 126–7 (entries for 7, 8, 12 September 1950).
30. PRO, FO 371/82878, UE11914/106, memorandum by Sir O. Franks, 27 September 1950. See also FRUS, 1950, III, pp. 1682–3, Franks-Perkins (Assistant Secretary of State) conversation, 29 September 1950.
31. *DBPO*, 2nd Series, III, No. 49i.
32. PRO, FO 371/82878, UE11914/106, Gaitskell memorandum for Attlee, 3 October 1950.
33. Cairncross, *Years of Recovery*, p. 218; see FO 115/4490, 1071/379–381, 392/50, for minutes of Gaitskell's meetings 10–12 October 1950.
34. *DBPO*, 2nd Series, III, No. 79, pp. 194–205, Bevin and Gaitskell memorandum 'The Finance of Defence', 23 October 1950.
35. PRO, CAB 128/18, CM 80(50) 30 November 1950, 6.45 p.m.
36. PRO, FO 371/86983, UR1027/3G, Washington to FO, Tel. No. 2841, 20 October 1950.
37. *DBPO*, 2nd Series, III, p. 199n.
38. PRO, FO 800/517, US/50/51, Strang minute, 6 November 1950. Bridges felt Franks should visit London soon, since his trip planned for the summer had been called off.
39. James Cable, 'Korea', in *FCO Occasional Papers No. 5: Korea* (London: FCO, 1992), p. 23.
40. Younger Diary, 19 November 1950.
41. Interview with Lord Franks, 24 May 1990.
42. NA, Wash. DC, RG 59, State Department Decimal Files, Box 4270, 795.00/12–350, London Embassy to Acheson, Cable 3241, 3 December 1950.

43. For Britain see PRO, PREM 8/1200, GEN 347/1 and GEN 347/2, briefs for Prime Minister's visit; FO 371/81637, AU1053/29G, 'General Survey of World Situation Between the Prime Minister of the United Kingdom and the President of the United States.' For the United States see, HSTL, Truman Papers, PSF, Subject File, Box 164, Briefing Book for Truman–Attlee Talks, December 1950.
44. R. Jenkins, *Truman* (London: Collins, 1986), pp. 180–1.
45. Lowe, *Containing the Cold War*, p. 216.
46. Jenkins, *Truman*, p. 182.
47. PRO, FO 371/84105, FK1022/539G, Franks to FO, Tel. No. 3281, 5 December 1950.
48. Ibid., FRUS, 1950, VII, pp. 1361–74, US minute of First Meeting, 4 December 1950. UK records of all the meetings are in PRO, PREM 8/1200.
49. PRO, FO 800/462, FE/50/49, BJSM to Ministry of Defence, 5 December 1950.
50. FRUS, 1950, VII, pp. 1374–7, 4 December 1950 meeting; ibid., pp. 1382–6, 5 December 1950 meeting.
51. FRUS, 1950, III, pp. 1720–3.
52. PRO, FO 371/84105, FK1022/548, Franks to FO, Tel. No. 3295, 5 December 1950; FRUS, 1950, VII, pp. 1390–408, US minute of Second Meeting, 5 December 1950.
53. *DBPO*, 2nd Series, IV, No. 87, p. 240, Franks to Bevin, Tel. No. 3282, 4 December 1950.
54. PRO, FO 371/124949, ZP3/3G, UK minutes of Third Meeting, 6 December 1950; US minutes are at FRUS, 1950, VII, pp. 1739–46 which includes the British memorandum.
55. *DBPO*, 2nd Series, III, No. 132, pp. 348–51, Franks to Bevin, 7 December 1950; FRUS, 1950, VII, pp. 1746–58, US Minutes of Fourth Meeting, 6 December 1950.
56. PRO, FO 371/124949, ZP3/1G, record of a conversation at the British Embassy, 7 December 1950.
57. FRUS, 1950, III, pp. 1782–3.
58. FRUS, 1950, VII, p. 1462, memorandum by Jessup, 7 December 1950.
59. Ibid., p. 1479, final communiqué, 8 December 1950.
60. *DBPO*, 2nd Series, IV, No. 111, pp. 310–1, minute by Sir Roger Makins to Mr Bevin, 19 January 1951. Bevin remarked on this minute: 'does not this leave us where we are now?'
61. PRO, FO 371/124949, ZP3/3G, UK minutes of Sixth Meeting, 8 December 1950.
62. Farrar-Hockley, *Korean War Vol. I*, p. 368.
63. PRO, FO 371/81637, AU1053/19G, Ottawa to Commonwealth Relations Office, Tel. No. 1287, 10 December 1950.
64. Ibid., AU1053/25G, Franks to FO, Tel. No. 3371, 11 December 1950.
65. PRO, CAB 128/18, CM 87(50), 18 December 1950.
66. PRO, CAB 128/19, CM 7(51) and CM 8(51), 25 January 1951.
67. HSTL, Truman Papers, PSF, 220, NSC Meetings folder, memos for the President, NSC, 74th Meeting, 12 December 1950; Dobson, *Anglo-American Relations in the Twentieth Century*, p. 99.
68. Farrar-Hockley, *Korean War Vol. I*, p. 368.
69. Dockrill, 'The Foreign Office ... and the Korean War', p. 466; *DBPO*, 2nd Series, IV, No. 90 n6, p. 249.
70. PRO, CAB 128/18, CM 85(50), 12 December 1950.
71. FRUS, 1951, IV, Part 1, No. 417, pp. 888–9, Memorandum of Conversation, 3 January 1951.

72. NA, Wash. DC, RG59, State Department Decimal Files 1950–54, Box 2769, 611.41/1–1851, Acheson to Lovett, 18 January 1951.
73. FRUS, 1951, IV, Part I, No. 427, pp. 914–16, memorandum of conversation, 31 January 1951.
74. PRO, FO 800/517, US/51/8, Franks to Strang (extract), 1 February 1951.
75. PRO, FO 371/92765, FK1071/16, Franks to FO, Tel. No. 33, 4 January 1951. The Commonwealth PMs met 12 times, 4–12 January.
76. PRO, FO 371/92765, FK1071/26, Franks to FO, Tel No. 45, 6 January 1951.
77. Ibid., FK1071/27, Franks to FO, Tel. No. 52, 6 January 1951.
78. PRO, FO 371/92767, FK1071/69, Franks to FO, Tel. No. 128, 12 January 1951; MacDonald, *Korea*, p. 82; *DBPO*, 2nd IV, No. 110i, Peking to FO, Tel. Nos 144 and 152, 18 January 1951, which reported the Chinese response to the Indian Ambassador, Panikkar, on the17th, who was encouraged by their moderate tone, and to the British on the 18th.
79. *DBPO*, 2nd Series, IV, p. 307, No. 109i, Franks to R. Makins, 13 January 1951.
80. PRO, FO 800/517, US/51/1, John Strachey, 'Anglo-American Relations', 2 January 1951.
81. Younger Diary, 21 January 1951.
82. *DBPO*, 2nd Series, IV, No. 115, Sir G. Jebb to FO, 24 January 1951, pp. 327–9.
83. Ibid., 2nd Series, IV, No. 121, Minute by Sir P. Dixon, 28 January 1951, p. 344.
84. Ibid., 2nd Series, IV, No. 114, pp. 322–6, FO to Franks, Tel No. 291, 23 January 1951; ibid., note 10, p. 326, Franks to FO, Tel. No. 233, 23 January 1951.
85. Ibid., 2nd Series, IV, No. 116, pp. 330–3, CM(51) 8th Conclusions, 25 January 1951.
86. PRO, FO 371/92771, FK1071/239G, minute by Makins to Minister of State, 25 January 1951.
87. *DBPO*, 2nd Series, IV, No. 118, pp. 335–6, CM(51) 9th Conclusions, 26 January 1951.
88. PRO, FO 371/92771, FK1071/220, Franks to FO, Tel. No. 276, 27 January 1951; FRUS, 1951, VII, pp. 136–7, memorandum of telephone conversation by Lucius D. Battle, January 29, 1951.
89. *DBPO*, 2nd Series, IV, p. 346, note 4.
90. See A. Farrar-Hockley, *The British Part in the Korean War Vol. II: An Honourable Discharge* (London: HMSO, 1995), pp. 423–4 for the text of the resolution.
91. MacDonald, *Korea*, p. 262.

—11—

A New Foreign Secretary

THE ATTLEE VISIT had helped to lessen fears of an extension of the war in the Far East and of the possible use of atomic weapons, while the stabilisation of the front in Korea had led to a steady improvement in the military position. Yet difficulties remained in Anglo-American relations. The last seven months of the Labour government, March–October 1951, proved troublesome. A new and less sure Foreign Secretary took office; Franks found that he was subject first to rumours and then to newspaper criticism about his effectiveness as Ambassador; and new problems emerged. A major crisis arose over Iran, there were tensions over Anglo-Egyptian relations, difficulties on a peace treaty with Japan, as well as the scandal over the defection of Burgess and Maclean.

HERBERT MORRISON

On 9 March, Herbert Morrison, the Lord President, was appointed Foreign Secretary. Kenneth Younger, the Minister of State, described it as 'a rather painful transition … Old Ernie [Bevin] … had clearly not been reconciled to handing it over to his arch-enemy Herbert.'[1] Molly Hamilton of the American Department declared herself 'a great admirer' of Morrison but added that 'I would not have cast him for this role, and have indeed begged him in the past to realise what a fearful chore its paperwork is.'[2] Doubts soon emerged about Morrison on his own account and not just as a result of unreasonable comparisons with his predecessor. According to Sir Roderick Barclay, his private secretary at the Foreign Office, his strict formality in addressing officials broke with the Office's easy-going familiarity. His grasp of the issues was unimpressive. Barclay noted: 'He seemed to lack not only the background knowledge but also the ability to comprehend the essentials of the problems before him.' In addition, he seemed 'to be appalled by the amount of work he was expected to do'.[3] Morrison had developed a particular method of operating in his previous posts. A small team would meet and draft a major speech that he had to give. In discussion this would be amended, with Morrison adding his own ideas, until a final version was produced displaying a distinctive style. At the Foreign Office he never had the time or will to establish a team to perform these tasks. As a result the speeches he gave were based on the precise but lifeless drafts of officials. His biographers observe:

> Perhaps his brain had deteriorated, disguised till now by his earlier speech-writing team. More certainly he was hindered by not having himself properly mastered his subject and so not being clear in his own mind. The House of Commons and the press quickly sensed this uncertainty and were surprised as well as bored by the poor quality of his speeches.[4]

Attlee told Dalton in September: 'His ignorance was shocking. He had no background and knew no history.' He added that 'H.M. always reads off a sheet of paper in Cabinet; he hadn't got any of it in his head.'[5]

To be fair to Morrison he did have other preoccupations. Shortly after taking office his wife was diagnosed as having cancer. On 21 March, Attlee entered hospital for treatment of a duodenal ulcer, leaving Morrison as acting Prime Minister. This occurred when Gaitskell was presenting his scheme to apply charges on false teeth and spectacles under the National Health Service. At a time of growing defence expenditure, the Chancellor needed to rein in spending elsewhere and chose an area widely seen to be profligate. The political controversy this provoked lasted until late April when Bevan, Minister of Health, and Wilson, President of the Board of Trade, resigned.[6]

FRANKS IN LONDON, MARCH 1951

It was in such circumstances that Franks returned to Britain for consultations, at Bevin's request,[7] and arrived on 8 March. According to Hall, 'he came to see me immediately he arrived to get the latest gossip'. Interestingly, in view of Strang's minute of 6 November 1950, Hall's diary continued:

> He asked me how his stock was here. I told him it was high in Whitehall but that there was press gossip against him, to the effect that he was hardly known in the US. Several stories of that sort

> have been put out, and P[lowden] suspects that someone in the FO has been passing them to leading Opposition members.[8]

Hall recorded in June 1953 how Plowden 'took great pains to force the FO to say that they did not feel any criticism of Oliver'.[9] On his arrival Franks met Bevin and two days later he called formally on Morrison. On telling an American reporter of this, he drew attention to the fact that he had worked before as an official for Morrison at the Ministry of Supply.[10]

Before the Ambassador returned to the United States on 22 March he attended several meetings which raised interesting points about Anglo-American relations. On 9 March he joined the Atomic Energy (Official) Committee. Its minutes remain closed,[11] but Franks's contribution was referred to in September:

> It was felt that to go ahead on our own and show the Americans that we were not dependent on them, and indeed had something they hadn't got was perhaps the best way of getting them to co-operate (cf. Sir Oliver Franks' views as expressed to the AE(O) Committee on 9 March).[12]

Discussion of atomic energy was continued in his meeting with the Chiefs of Staff on 14 March. Their talks were recorded in a confidential annexe kept in a separate file and given a special circulation. They examined the British wish to use certain US facilities for testing a UK atomic weapon. Franks said that the Americans desired an agreement but that this was being delayed by domestic circumstances in the United States. He added that, in the absence of any assurance of assistance, there was much to be said for going ahead with British plans, provided that they knew that they could in fact do so without US assistance. In addition, he suggested that it might be a good idea if the question of US co-operation for the testing of the United Kingdom atomic weapon were raised in the Combined Policy Committee on Atomic Energy, which had not met for some time and of which both he and Acheson were members. There was general agreement that if the approach by Lord Tedder of BJSM to General Bradley were unsuccessful, there was much to be said for raising the matter in the Combined Policy Committee.[13] The Ministerial Committee on Atomic Energy decided on this approach in its meeting on 15 March.[14]

Franks also gave his views to the Chiefs of Staff on a number of other matters. He said that the Americans seemed taken aback by the strength of British feeling at the appointment of the US Admiral,

Fechteler, as the Supreme Allied Commander in the Atlantic. The Ambassador approved the idea of a simultaneous approach to the State Department by the Embassy and to General Marshall by Lord Tedder of the BJSM on the question of the appointment of a British Admiral as Supreme Commander in the Mediterranean. On Anglo-American liaison arrangements, Franks said that in the last 15 months he had noticed a change in Anglo-American relations as between governments. There was no doubt that the Americans regarded Britain as their one really dependable ally. They were prepared to make arrangements to give effect to any assistance the British might require, but if there were any question of such assistance being made known to a third country then the Americans would take steps to cover up such assistance. It would help him, as Ambassador, if he could be given a general line on this issue of the relationship. Should Britain continue to concentrate on covert arrangements; alternatively, should they try to cultivate an overt system? In discussion there was general agreement that, in view of the American sensitivity to publicity, they should concentrate on strengthening the current covert bilateral arrangements – for example, the relationship between Lord Tedder and the US Joint Chiefs of Staff, which was particularly close.

At his next meeting, held on 20 March, Franks developed these themes on the general Anglo-American relationship. Discussion revealed certain differences between London on the one hand, and Franks and the Embassy on the other. The Ambassador was joined, at his request, by Strang, Makins and Dixon to consider the broad question of the future relationship with the United States. Franks felt that the Americans had re-established the 'old partnership relationship at least on a covert basis'. He was not confident, though, that this could be made overt, for he thought that they might 'find difficulty in openly acknowledging the relationship'. Makins, however, doubted whether the United States was treating Britain on a partnership basis, even on a covert basis. He mentioned several cases of inconsiderate and unco-operative behaviour by the United States. He added that although Britain's capacity was growing, that of the United States was growing even faster, so that the disparity in strength between the two powers would become even greater. Dixon also expressed his doubts, wondering whether the Americans 'were not taking us into their confidence in regard to their long term plans ... American grand strategy might be based on a ... strategic air offensive launched from island and forward bases.' Strang also thought that the Americans might be concealing their long-term aims. But Franks doubted whether any long-term secret US policy existed. The meeting closed with agreement that Britain should continue to promote the partnership relationship on a covert basis. Morrison minuted on the record of the conversation:

> I am inclined to good fellowship, cordiality – combined with frankness, readiness to assert ourselves. At times we have perhaps been a bit too lame. But Anglo-American fundamental friendship is essential, but it can't be on the basis of being pushed around.[15]

Further indication of Franks's thinking at this time can be gained from two talks he had on his return to the United States. They also reveal the candid approach he was willing to adopt with Acheson; and indeed with John Foster Dulles, who, although a Republican, was appointed special consultant to Acheson in March 1950 and specifically responsible for negotiating the Japanese Peace Treaty. He saw Acheson on 2 April. He explained how the British government had been under increasing pressure and had had to cope with crises about once a week; everyone was tired, the Foreign Office 'had been practically leaderless' with Attlee, Bevin, Younger and Strang all contributing a little but with Dixon and Makins contributing most of the leadership. He felt that there would probably be no great change with the new Foreign Secretary. Morrison, he added, would have antennae out for political manoeuvring. The Foreign Secretary 'will be more flexible in both the good and bad sense. He will be easier to deal with, but he will tend to bend a principle without bending it to the cracking point.' Acheson asked whether the British had some policy they were not disclosing to the Americans. Franks replied that in a way this amused him, for he had been asked the same question in London. He reassured Acheson that US fears were groundless. The Ambassador added that inertia and exhaustion and lack of leadership constituted the problem in London. He thought that the United States 'definitely had to take the leadership in this period'.[16]

Three days later Franks spoke to Dulles, who asked, as had Acheson on the 2nd, about the delays on the part of the British in the talks over the Japanese Treaty. Franks offered a partial explanation:

> for several months the Foreign Office has been without real guidance and direction from the top and ... while it knew that a change was inevitable, it did not know when or in what form that change would come. It was, therefore, difficult for important decisions to be taken when guidance was being divided between several Ministers assisted from time to time by opinions received from Mr. Bevin's sick bed. However, this situation has now changed and Sir Oliver was confident that there would be more prompt action from now on.[17]

The conversations in London and Washington revealed the somewhat unsettled character to everyday relations, partly due to disagreement over China and partly because of the lack of leadership as Bevin's health declined. Thus Morrison inherited rather than created these defects in shared understanding, though his approach did not help ease the situation. Franks, as the most highly regarded British figure in American circles, was necessarily to the forefront of efforts to engender greater harmony and mutual respect.

Meanwhile, Anglo-American differences over Korea were lessening. General Ridgway saved the situation for the UN forces and, by March 1951, Seoul had been recaptured. The advance back to the 38th Parallel was underway. But this time the Americans shared the British aversion to 'rollback'. A more measured approach by the US government led to a dispute with General MacArthur, the main focus of British anxieties since November and what Franks characterised as 'MacArthuritis' when he talked to Dean Rusk.[18] On 11 April MacArthur was relieved of all his commands, after criticising the conduct of the war to a Republican Congressman. Ridgway succeeded him. Acheson gave Franks advance warning of the move on the 10 April. When he confirmed the decision, he urged on the Ambassador that 'the less said by all of us the better.'[19]

The matter did not end there, for the Republicans secured a congressional hearing into the General's dismissal. While this was proceeding, the British were anxious to do nothing that would create problems for Truman and Acheson. Paul Gore-Booth, head of British Information Services in the United States, reported that the removal of MacArthur 'has let loose a flood of nastiness in this country such as I have never seen before.'[20] The General raised the matter of British trade with the Soviet Union and China in his hearings.[21] In an attempt to assuage American criticism, Britain declared, in May, an embargo on the sale of rubber to China through Hong Kong, and voted at the United Nations for various sanctions. In addition, Franks gave a radio interview designed to reassure the American public. He emphasised British efforts to resist communism in the Far East and to minimise the differences that were alleged to exist between the British and Americans.[22] By June, with the military situation in Korea stabilised and the Americans, somewhat reluctantly, ready to pursue armistice negotiations, which began in July and dragged on for two more years, the tensions on this issue had gone.[23]

CRISIS IN IRAN

By this time a new crisis had arisen. The Anglo-Iranian Oil Company

(AIOC) was a vital British asset. At Abadan it possessed the largest refinery in the world, and was Britain's greatest single overseas investment, the plant alone being valued at £120 million in 1946. It provided valuable energy to the British economy and important dollar earnings.[24] In July 1949 a new 'supplemental' agreement was reached between AIOC and the Iranian government. Although it contained important concessions, it was voted down in the Iranian parliament, the Majlis, in December 1950. The Iranian Prime Minister, Razmara, tried to secure further concessions in an atmosphere of rising tension, but the company persistently refused to move. On 7 March he was assassinated. The Shah was reluctant to appoint as the new Prime Minister Dr Mossadeq, the leading nationalist and opponent of British influence. However, there appeared to be no alternative – while Mossadeq was in opposition, he and the forces supporting him made government impossible. On 27 April he was appointed Premier. On 2 May nationalisation of AIOC was proclaimed as Iranian law.

This developed from being a British crisis into a problem for Anglo-American relations because the two countries proposed different solutions to the matter. The British response was heavily influenced by the reporting of the Ambassador in Tehran, Sir Francis Shepherd, who said 'I think we should fight for [the] retention by the Anglo-Iranian Oil Company, as far as possible, of the control of the industry they have built up … The disappearance of the A.I.O.C. and its replacement by [an] international consortium would be a considerable blow to our prestige in this country.'[25] The Americans felt that Britain would have to accept equal profit-sharing. Acheson recognised that, since Saudi Arabia had secured a 50–50 split of profits with the US oil company, Aramco, nothing less would be accepted by other Middle Eastern countries. The leading American advocate of this stance was George McGhee, Assistant Secretary of State for the Near East, South Asia and Africa, who was a successful oil man. When he was a Rhodes Scholar at Oxford in the 1930s Franks had been his moral tutor.[26]

Franks therefore had the difficult task of ensuring American sympathy for the British position when Acheson and his leading officials were critical of British proposals for solving the problem. Moreover, much of the material sent from London was difficult to use. Gore-Booth wrote from Washington that assertions about the Iranians being incompetent to run an oil industry were not 'much good in a country which lets Mexicans take over US interests there'.[27] The situation was not helped by Morrison's poor performance. Younger noted: 'he has not yet got down to the job. His handling of it, though fairly adroit, has been thoroughly superficial, and even the House has begun to notice how ignorant he is every time he answers questions.'[28] The Ambassador was fortunate that both Acheson and McGhee respected him. He adopted an emollient approach to talks with US officials, trying to find a way of bridging the gap between the two powers while faithfully representing the opinions of each country to the other.

In a series of meetings with McGhee, Franks tried to achieve a common approach to the Iranians. But from the very beginning the Ambassador was concerned about his guidance from London: 'I must record that I see little chance, within my present instructions, of finding a solution, however it may be presented, which will induce the Americans to lend us their active support in any negotiations with the Persians.'[29] There would be no US commitment to co-operation until the British provided some definite proposals for a settlement which were reasonable in the light of the present situation in Iran.[30] His disquiet was such that he telephoned London and 'pleaded for as much imaginative latitude as possible in the instructions he was expecting to receive'. In particular, he shared the American belief that 'we should make a bow in the direction of nationalisation'.[31]

Franks and McGhee held the last in their series of meetings on 17 and 18 April to a background of mounting tension – on the 16th strikes had closed the Abadan refinery.[32] The Ambassador reported the Foreign Office's belief that the problem should be approached in two stages: first, diplomatic efforts to pave the way for negotiations between AIOC and the Iranian government; secondly, the negotiations themselves. In this first stage the British Ambassador in Tehran could explain his government's desire to establish a new relationship with respect to the oil industry. Since the negotiations in the second stage would be between the Iranian government and AIOC, the British Ambassador could do no more than suggest the broad lines of any agreement. These now included greater gestures to the Iranians, as Franks had urged. They comprised: Iranian representations on the Board of Governors; equal sharing of profits; and the creation of a separate Iranian-owned firm to handle internal distribution of petroleum products. While welcoming these suggestions, McGhee felt that they did not go far enough to placate Iranian political forces demanding nationalisation.[33] At their second meeting on the 18th McGhee returned to this theme. He 'strongly recommended including in the British plan at least some facade of nationalization'. He added that, should the British be prepared to offer more to the Iranians, it might be possible for the United States to extend more support. Franks reacted to this 'with some vigour' (as he told London), pointing out

British concessions. McGhee admitted this and said the British 'would have our benevolent neutrality, although we could not lend support in the face of strong reaction'.[34] By persuading the Foreign Office to ease its stance, Franks could note that 'the Americans have moved considerably from their original disapproval and are now anxious to help out'.[35] McGhee gave his assessment of the situation to Acheson on 20 April. He believed that the British did not feel the pressure for nationalisation was as great as the State Department considered, and, consequently, 'the British believe that they can get by with fewer concessions than we think possible'.[36]

Franks probably favoured more of a 'bow to nationalisation' than the current British position accepted. Witness his view that 'The real trouble with A.I.O.C. is they have not got far enough past the stage of Victorian paternalism.'[37] When he met Acheson on 27 April, to reflect on his talks with McGhee, he sought to balance his personal preferences with the need to press the British case. He confirmed that differences between them seemed to revolve around different interpretations of the nature of the Iranian nationalist movement. He also conveyed some of the feeling generated in Britain by US statements about the issue. He said that 'when his people feel that they do not have something sensible to say, they don't say anything; our [American] people tend to have something to say, and say it. This causes a degree of irritation in the UK.' Nevertheless, he accepted that the 'Kipling type of technique' was not appropriate to the current Middle East, and that he would indicate to his government the serious view taken of developments in Iran by the United States.[38]

Besides taking a more serious view of the clamour for nationalisation, the Americans also favoured economic and technical assistance to the Iranians. When asked to comment on such a proposal, London instructed Franks to say that the offer of aid might stiffen Iranian resistance to a reasonable settlement of the oil question.[39] The Ambassador, however, did not pass on this message. Again he sought to soften the British position. The Embassy were apprehensive that 'if we conveyed to the State Department the gist of your telegram ... they would feel we were trying to persuade them not to help Persia in order to put more pressure on the Persians to make a satisfactory settlement of the oil dispute with us'. Franks felt that this might have lost the British the ground which they seemed to have gained with the State Department over the affairs of AIOC. The Foreign Office appeared pleased by the Ambassador's decision, minuting that the 'Ambassador has happily avoided loss of ground with the State Department'.[40] But the issue was to arise again in July and August.

Meanwhile, on 2 May nationalisation was proclaimed as Iranian law. In the face of this development, the Cabinet, on the 10th, considered possible military intervention.[41] When Franks spoke to Acheson and McGhee again on the 11th, he was told the Americans 'have grave misgivings with respect to the use of force', unless there was danger to British citizens requiring their evacuation, or Soviet intervention or communist seizure of power. As regards the principle of nationalisation, the Ambassador once more conducted his delicate balancing act. He told the Americans that, although his government had not accepted this, the climate of thinking in London was along such lines. When he reported to London, he did not include this comment. Instead, he urged 'most serious consideration' be given to the possibility of negotiating with the Iranians on the basis of nationalisation. He felt that 'at last we have the real opportunity to get American and British attitudes to these problems harmonised in strong co-operation after they had been divergent in some measure for too long'. For their part, the Americans said they were willing to advise the Iranians that US companies would not be willing to operate AIOC properties. The State Department was sensitive to the suggestion that part of the reason for lack of US support for the British on this issue lay in the competition between British and US oil companies.[42] Franks's efforts resulted in the Foreign Office declaring that they were 'ready to negotiate a settlement involving some form of nationalisation'.[43]

If differences over nationalisation were belatedly settled, the question of the use of force remained. American worries about military action were renewed when British paratroops were put on alert. Their particular concern centred on reports from London about the alerting of the 16th Airborne Brigade and statements by government spokesmen talking of an identity of view between the British and Americans. Acheson made clear to Franks that the United States would not sanction armed conflict between British troops and the present Iranian administration. [44]

On 3 June Franks appeared on the NBC television programme, 'Battle Report – Washington' to reassure American opinion that Anglo-American relations remained good. He said that the two peoples stood together in the 'constant and accelerated struggle for the sanity of the world'. He praised the United States for 'its leadership and the great burden it has carried' against aggression in Korea. Finally, he stressed the great sacrifices Britain was making so as to contribute the maximum to 'our partnership in the cause of freedom'.[45]

RETURN TO LONDON

The Ambassador returned to Britain on 13 June partly for a holiday timed to coincide with the 500th anniversary of Glasgow University where he was to receive an honorary degree. This was the first time in his ambassadorship that he was to visit Britain twice in the same year for consultations. On his arrival he tried to reassure British opinion. He warned against magnifying US criticisms of Britain: 'I say that because on a great area of policy we are in broad agreement.'[46] During his visit in March he had been told of press rumours about his competence as Ambassador. This time they were printed by the *Daily Express* on 19 June in its opinion column. It began: 'Who is the man pictured here? Do you recognise him? Feel no shame if you cannot recall the name. Hardly anyone knows it. But everyone should.' Britain's unknown ambassador has been tried and found wanting, it continued, in interpreting Britain to the American people and, worse still, he has not interpreted Britain to the United States government. He should be replaced. It concluded: 'Antagonism and distrust, discord and misunderstanding – these are the fruits of Sir Oliver's years in Washington. The wasted years. The years of decline and dissipation – the dissipation of good will.'[47] It seems highly likely that this criticism was instigated by the newspaper's proprietor, Lord Beaverbrook. His private papers contain a memorandum to him from Arthur Christiansen, editor of the *Daily Express*, saying, 'We cannot sustain any criticisms of Oliver Franks's scholastic career. As you will see from the attached memo, he did very well indeed.' Presumably, Beaverbrook had asked his editor to discover whether they might also criticise Franks's academic credentials.[48] What motivated Beaverbrook is uncertain. Perhaps he was responding to what he saw as a personal sleight. Franks later recalled that both he and Beaverbrook had recently travelled to Britain on the Queen Mary and he had not spoken to him.[49]

Franks was defended the next day in the *News Chronicle* by Robert Waithman, who noted that

> He has worked tirelessly and successfully to improve the conditions with which he and all the rest of us are faced. In the opinion of pretty nearly everyone who knows the facts Sir Oliver Franks has been one of Britain's best ambassadors in America.

The intense strain in Anglo-American relations, Waithman said, was due to differences on important issues rather than to the role of individuals.[50] The *Washington Post* also came to the Ambassador's defence. In reporting the attack by the *Daily Express*, the London

Embassy told Washington that the more responsible newspapers had taken no notice of the subject.51

Further difficulties for Anglo-American relations confronted Franks on his arrival. Two British diplomats disappeared on 25 May; they had defected to the Soviet Union. Donald Maclean was head of the American Department of the Foreign Office and had served in the Washington Embassy for the first three months of Franks's ambassadorship. Guy Burgess had been Second Secretary at the Embassy, August 1950 to April 1951, when he was recalled to the Foreign Office because of his behaviour. The final straw came when he was stopped three times in the same day for reckless driving.[52] The Embassy had not wanted to accept Burgess but London had compelled them to take him. He came from the Far Eastern department but Hubert Graves, the Embassy's Counsellor who dealt with the Far East, refused to take him. So he worked with Denis Greenhill who was at the Middle East desk in the chancery. He soon found Burgess to be 'totally useless'.[53] Maclean had been under suspicion for some time. He was tipped off that the net was closing on him by Kim Philby, First Secretary at the Embassy from September 1949 to June 1951 and responsible for intelligence co-ordination between Britain and the United States, but not then known to be a Soviet spy. It was the *Daily Express* that broke the news on 7 June with its headline 'Yard Hunts Two Britons'.[54] American newspapers quickly picked up the story, and the Embassy reported that the disappearance had created a major sensation. The *Washington Post* observed: 'Mr. Attlee's government ought to be reminded that at this touchy point in Anglo-American relations lack of confidence in British security precautions merely feeds hysteria here.'[55] Sir Christopher Steel, Political Minister and Chargé d'Affaires in Franks's absence, reported that the American reaction was all the more severe because Maclean had been in charge of the Foreign Office American section and Burgess had had access to Far Eastern information.[56] American public unease at the case was reflected in an article in *US News & World Report* on 20 July. It spoke of British complacency and that 'secrets of the highest order – atomic and diplomatic went with Donald Maclean and … Burgess'.[57] The furore surrounding the case was such that the Permanent Under Secretary, Strang, later declared that he had had, for a time, to cover this matter to the exclusion of almost everything else.[58]

An assessment prepared for the US Joint Chiefs of Staff in 1955 concluded that all high-level plans and policy information were compromised, that all British and some US diplomatic codes and ciphers were known to the Soviet Union, and that they should 'enquire into who may be taking the place of these two men … [as] it is inconceivable that the pipeline dried up … on 25 May'.[59] In 1951 Acheson and Walter Bedell Smith were alarmed by the implications for internal security. The defections thus accelerated the onset of positive vetting by the British. But, as Richard J. Aldrich says, 'The long-term impact … was damaging not devastating. Compartmentalisation meant that many co-operative transatlantic activities continued undisturbed.' Acheson and Smith were also worried about the defections' encouragement of growing public paranoia.[60] As Christopher Andrew observes: 'The most enduring damage done by Philby and the other leading Cambridge moles … was to help lead a minority of intelligence officers on both sides of the Atlantic into a wilderness of mirrors, searching in vain for the chimera of a still vaster Soviet deception.'[61]

On the very day that Burgess and Maclean disappeared, Makins submitted a memorandum on his impressions of America after his visit of 7–22 May. His observations, he said, reflected conversations with Franks and 'I think he would be in substantial agreement with what I have set down.' 'Anglo-American relations', Makins reported, 'did not seem to be as bad as they looked from London.' MacArthur was virtually a spent force. American opinion, though, was alert and sensitive, particularly in relation to Britain – anti-British emotion could be set off at a touch. As regards Iran, he felt that this would need 'most careful handling from the political and public relations angle'. He added that Americans believed that AIOC had mismanaged things. As a result: 'After China, Iran is now the most delicate and difficult specific problem in the Anglo-American relationship.'[62] Such thoughts were brought to a number of talks that Franks had with Foreign Office officials in the last week of June and first week of July.[63]

He met the Chiefs of Staff on 27 June where he discussed the enquiry concerning General MacArthur, noting that it had been seized upon by all who had a grievance against the administration. US relations seemed to have emerged from proceedings in much the same state as before the hearings. Turning to the American response to the Soviet UN representative Malik's proposal for a ceasefire in Korea, the Ambassador thought that overtures should be taken seriously. He added that, providing their conditions were not completely unacceptable, there appeared to be some hope of a peaceful settlement. On the Iranian crisis, he observed that the Americans had come to regard the British attitude as very reasonable whilst that of the Iranians was utterly the reverse; they had at last realised their own strategic interests were affected as well as ours. Their attitude to a British resort to military action was more difficult. It seemed to him that unless there was a clear risk of communist action in Iran, then Britain could not count on US support for military action.[64]

A second meeting on 2 July saw Franks addressing the question of testing in the United States of the British atomic bomb. He emphasised that difficulties over Anglo-American co-operation in the nuclear field, resulting from the McMahon Act, remained serious. The meeting confirmed their decision taken in March (with Franks present and concurring) that, if action at the Chiefs of Staff level failed, then the Ambassador would raise the matter with Acheson in the Combined Policy Committee (CPC).[65] The talks between the military proved unsuccessful. On 27 August the CPC considered the issue. However, the British felt that to accept the terms proposed would mean 'we should suffer a tremendous loss of prestige'. Moreover, they would be denied valuable information which could be obtained by employing a full team of scientists. The Chiefs of Staff decided that they should proceed with a British operation at Montebello.[66] This decision confirmed the essential British stance as encapsulated by Franks's remark that the whole question of British relations with the United States on atomic energy concerned whether the United States treated Britain as a first-class power.[67]

The Middle East was covered in a meeting at the Foreign Office on 29 June. Franks pointed out that US agreement to the establishment of an Allied Command in the Middle East as part of NATO and the new US policy of grant aid to Middle Eastern countries would completely change the Anglo-American relationship in the region. So far, the effort deployed in the Middle East had been wholly British. It would not be the same in the future. So he believed 'it was important to decide what we considered it was essential we should do on our own and what we should do jointly with the Americans'.[68]

OPTIONS ON IRAN – NEGOTIATION VERSUS FORCE

During Franks's stay in London the tension over Iran mounted. Before his departure from Washington, he had suggested that every informal endeavour be made to get talking started. He wondered whether someone of high standing in AIOC might visit Tehran, for he had found that a 'trustworthy and responsible businessman not involved by previous experience in immediate local difficulties can be very valuable'.[69] A delegation from AIOC subsequently visited Iran but it encountered what the State Department called a 'position not only completely unreasonable but designed to remove all hope negots [*sic*] with Brit [*sic*] except on terms complete capitulation to Iran nationalization demands.'[70] Morrison asked the International Court of Justice for an injunction against Iran. In response, the Iranians denied the jurisdiction of the court and gave the AIOC manager at Abadan, A. E. C. Drake, and his British workers a week to choose whether to work for the new National Iranian Oil Company or leave. The Cabinet on 21 June considered military and naval action at Abadan, while AIOC threatened to close down its refinery because of a new Iranian anti-sabotage law. HMS *Mauritius* was moved to the waters near Abadan.[71]

Such was the situation when Franks arrived back in Washington on 4 July. That same day he met Acheson, Nitze, McGhee and H. Freeman Matthews, Deputy Under Secretary of State, at the house of Harriman, special assistant to Truman. They spoke for 2 hours and Franks, in Acheson's words, 'left no doubt how seriously and angrily both the British Government and public viewed what they regarded as the insolent defiance of decency, legality and reason by a group of wild men in Iran'. They all agreed that armed intervention would only produce great trouble. As a way forward, Acheson suggested that Harriman should go to Tehran to try and re-start negotiations. Franks felt the value of such a venture depended upon the constructiveness of the ideas he might bring. Was this just part of a process by which the AIOC would progressively give way until Mossadeq had secured what he wanted? Acheson maintained that this was not the case. Reflecting on the conversation, Franks believed there was merit in taking up the proposal. Acheson and the State Department wanted to help Britain over Iran but were limited by US public opinion which saw old-fashioned imperialism as the cause of the trouble. US involvement in the search for a solution would be beneficial. If Harriman failed due to Iranian intransigence, then popular opinion would support Britain. If the mission got negotiations going, then disaster would have been averted.[72]

Morrison, at first, was opposed to the mission.[73] He came to accept the proposal when Harriman's instructions shifted from mediation between the parties to an attempt to get Mossadeq in line with the recommendations of the International Court which had found in favour of Britain.[74] Acceptance of Harriman was urged on the Cabinet by Gaitskell, who was a personal friend of the American, whom he described as 'friendly and sympathetic to the United Kingdom Government'.[75] Franks observed of Harriman that 'He is responsive to personal attention and it is worth while cultivating the right approach to him. He much prefers informal conversations outside the office to formal and official meetings.'[76]

On 16 July Harriman arrived in Tehran and had talks with Iranian officials and members of the British Embassy. Failing to make progress, he went to London on 27 July and managed to persuade the British government to send a mission to Iran led by a Cabinet Minister. He had hoped that Gaitskell would be able to lead the mission, but, instead, he had to accept Richard Stokes, Lord Privy Seal.[77] Franks saw Acheson on 2 August and discussed developments, saying that he was without instructions and that his observations were purely personal. He described Harriman's visit to Iran as a 'God send'. However, Franks continued, he was sure 'we were a long way from any satisfactory solution of the Iranian oil problem'. Franks felt that there was a grave danger that the talks would break down if Harriman left Tehran, for Stokes was 'a bluff, genial, open and hearty man, not accustomed to dealing with the Iranian mentality'. Given Mossadeq's capacity, like Nehru, to rationalise his emotions, the Ambassador thought it would be 'difficult for Stokes and Mosadeq [*sic*] to find a common language'.[78]

Franks's reservations were well founded. The Stokes mission of 4–22 August submitted an eight-point proposal, which Harriman thought reasonable, but, contrary to guidance, Stokes made them known to the public. The Iranians rejected them. With this the mission returned to Britain, indicating that the negotiations were suspended. In September matters came to a head. On the 25th the Iranian government declared that British employees at Abadan would be given a week's warning to leave the country. Two days later the Cabinet met with the option of a military seizure of the refinery under consideration. Morrison maintained that the government should not allow the expulsion of the British workers. But Attlee pointed out the United States's consistent opposition to the use of force. The Cabinet agreed that they could not afford to break with the Americans over Iran. On 4 October the British staff left Abadan.[79]

The position reached by October was to remain the same in its essentials for the remainder of Franks's time as Ambassador. While Britain favoured a policy of mounting pressure on Mossadeq, believing that the nationalist support for him was superficial, the Americans felt that the nationalist feeling was real and substantial, that Mossadeq could not be easily deposed, and so some new initiative was needed.[80] The Americans wanted to safeguard British interests but they distinguished sharply between the interests of Britain and those of AIOC.[81] Franks summarised the outlook: 'the Americans are convinced that we ought to show ourselves ready to negotiate with Musaddiq [*sic*] as long as he is there, realising that on all grounds a settlement must be reached fairly soon and that this settlement must include the complete disappearance of A.I.O.C in any shape or form from Persia itself'.[82]

Franks was sympathetic to the US perspective. Yet his misgivings about Morrison's inflexible approach were restrained when compared to the private strictures of Younger who accepted US criticism of Britain's failure to recognise the strength of Iranian nationalism. If both believed that AIOC's behaviour was a hangover from British imperialism, Younger also thought that the government had been let down by the company which had been greedy and short sighted. Yet he did not believe the government could escape responsibility when they held 51 per cent of the shares. The conduct of his colleagues, he continued, did not appear in a good light. Several had approached the issue in an emotional way, wanting 'strong action'. Foremost in this group was the Foreign Secretary, whom he called 'ignorant, amateurish, cheap and reactionary'. Morrison was saved, on the whole, by the fact that he accepted the official view but the Foreign Office got it wrong too. Younger was shocked to see Roger Makins also advocating the use of force.[83] He found the Middle Eastern experts unconvincing.[84]

In his reflections on the oil crisis a decade later Strang was equally critical. Morrison did not seem to know his own mind, did not inspire and stimulate his officials and did not secure the primacy of the Foreign Office on the issue. He had no special authority with the Prime Minister. Attlee chaired the Ministerial Committee on Iran because Morrison could not be given the role, as he wrote strong minutes but did not press his view. So the Prime Minister, not the Foreign Secretary, determined policy. Strang also acknowledged his own shortcomings: he did not give his mind sufficiently to Iran; he ought to have controverted the views of the Treasury and the Board of Trade; and he should have organised better co-ordination of the matter in the Foreign Office.[85]

THE JAPANESE PEACE TREATY

The last weeks of the Labour government did achieve a qualified success on two issues – the Japanese Peace Treaty and the use of US bases in Britain. Franks was not involved in the detailed discussions on the peace with Japan but made important contributions at key moments in the negotiations – either on his own initiative or by invitation from both governments. He helped to ease misunderstandings and offered sage advice on how to proceed.

Progress on a treaty was slow until Dulles, given special responsibility for the peace settlement, visited Japan in January 1951. On his return he told Franks that he thought that there were only a few appreciable differences between the British and Americans and that they should aim to produce a draft treaty which could be signed by June.[86] When Franks visited London in March he recommended that Dulles be invited to London to concentrate on the difficult procedural points. The Foreign Office wanted this to be in mid-April and asked F. S. Tomlinson, the official at the Washington Embassy responsible for the treaty, if this would be too late to catch US policy in a formative stage. He answered that he thought they had not reached any firm conclusions; and that their position was likely to remain fluid for some time.[87] The Americans sent their draft treaty to the British on 23 March. The British draft was not despatched until 7 April, by which time relations on the issue had become tense.

On 6 April, Dulles told Franks that 'In recent weeks … he had come to feel we were drifting seriously apart.' Two British stances in particular troubled him: the desire to invite the communist Chinese to participate in the talks on a treaty; and the belief that Japan should renounce sovereignty over Taiwan (Formosa) and cede it to 'China', thereby leaving open the final decision on whether the communists or nationalists should assume control. Franks replied that Dulles should have no misgivings about British motives, for they also wanted a peace treaty favourable to Japan rapidly concluded. But Britain had an important role in the Pacific and wanted to set out its thinking on the matter. He felt sure that differences could be argued out. Commenting on the discussion, the Ambassador believed that Dulles was deliberately exaggerating his troubles with the British but that 'he was exaggerating something which really existed as a state of his mind'. Nevertheless, the meeting did produce worthwhile results. Dulles said he was ready to see a joint Anglo-American draft treaty – an idea which was swiftly endorsed by the Foreign Office. Moreover, Franks proposed on a purely personal basis that he thought the next stage should be talks in Washington or London between the specialists from each country – a suggestion which resulted in such discussion first in Washington and then in London. The Ambassador concluded that he thought Dulles 'felt better at the end of the talk possibly because he had got it all off his chest. It may be a bad thing to make someone specialise on one subject for too long.'[88]

When the Embassy received the British draft treaty, Franks decided that it should be sent to John M. Allison, the principal State Department official dealing with the topic. This was the wisest course, he thought, given Dulles's current suspicious mood. This decision was rewarded with a sympathetic response. Allison believed that the process of reconciling Anglo-American views should not present insuperable obstacles.[89]

There followed a series of nine Anglo-American meetings in Washington.[90] At Franks's suggestion (who did not participate in them), they began by seeking the maximum area of agreement on the text of the treaty before turning to thornier procedural questions such as the involvement of communist China.[91] Franks was able to report at the end of the talks that they had narrowed though not eliminated the area of disagreement.[92] Moreover, Dulles's attitude seemed more auspicious: 'His tone was calm and he showed understanding of our difficulties, though not disposed to minimise his own.'[93]

Dulles then held talks in London on 4–9 and 14 June.[94] In the Washington discussions the Americans had shown a disposition to understand the British stance on Chinese participation and Taiwan, but both these issues remained unresolved. There were also two major differences in the content of the treaty: security against potential Japanese military resurgence, and commercial worries about the re-emergence of Japan's exceptional competition before the Second World War, particularly in textiles. Once again Franks had wise counsel for London, recognising the 'human' side to diplomacy: 'I am sure that Dulles should be given the very best butter. He seems to me very responsive to treatment which obviously recognises his own statesmanship and importance.'[95]

Morrison opened discussions by telling Dulles on 4 June that 'the United States and Great Britain should publicly be known to march in step in their future policy toward Japan'.[96] This they achieved on 14 June when they produced a joint Anglo-American draft Peace Treaty.[97] It reflected the disparity in power between the two countries. Moreover, Morrison had in the back of his mind the prospect that the United States would make a separate peace with Japan, if an Anglo-American deal was not achieved: 'This would have most damaging effects on our future relations with the United States and our prestige in the Far East.'[98] Britain had to accept most American wishes. On the question of Japan's future attitude to Communist China Morrison conceded a compromise arrangement whereby Japan would be free, after signature of the treaty, to decide which Chinese regime to recognise. According to Buckley, the Foreign Office must have expected the Japanese would recognise the Peking government, but Dulles had the approximate agreement of the Japanese Prime Minister, Yoshida, that Tokyo would not recognise Peking.[99] Indeed, Franks had suggested as early as February that the 'Americans are almost certain to encourage … the making of an agreement between the Japanese and the Chinese Nationalists.'[100] Nevertheless, there were successes for the British. Dulles accepted that neither the communists nor the nationalists should be invited to the peace conference.

Moreover, the meetings seemed to remove his misgivings about working with the British on the issue. Steel, Minister at the Washington Embassy and Chargé d'Affaires in Franks's absence, reported:

> As you know, he [Dulles] is a rather dry individual, but there is no mistaking the genuineness of his personal satisfaction and also his feeling that the successful surmounting of our differences in this case is an important step on an altogether wider plane.[101]

A number of minor amendments were made before the Anglo-American draft was circulated, on 15 August, to all the allied governments and any difficulties were settled bilaterally between each government and the United States. In the meantime, Dulles had to persuade American opinion to accept it. He proved most successful in this task. As Franks told London, he was greatly helped in this by regular US press reports to the effect that the British were being reluctantly compelled to accept the United States' point of view. Given that such stories assisted him with the extremists in his own Republican Party, the Ambassador said that the Embassy had wondered whether he did not initiate them himself, for he was far from unhappy with them.[102]

The San Francisco Peace Conference of 4–8 September met merely to give international approval to what had already been settled in advance. Given this character and its duration, the original idea was that neither Morrison nor the Minister of State, Younger, needed to be present. But during a dinner the Ambassador was told by Acheson, with Dulles concurring, that they hoped that Morrison would be able to attend. Acheson added that this would be the perfect cover for discussion on general topics. Franks felt that this deserved the Foreign Secretary's serious consideration, especially since he knew Morrison had wanted for some time to have an early opportunity for talks with the Secretary of State. Morrison somewhat reluctantly agreed to attend part of the conference. He had planned a holiday in Norway for late August and hoped the conference could be delayed to allow him to arrive for the final proceedings and signature if the latter could be held on 10 September. Franks replied that he had consulted Acheson and Dulles who were most anxious to help but could not delay until the 10th. The Ambassador managed to get Morrison and the Americans to accept shifting signature by a day to the 8th.[103] The Foreign Secretary would arrive on the evening of 7 September and Franks would lead the British delegation up to that stage. But while Morrison was on holiday the Prime Minister decided that, in view of the decision of the Soviet Union to attend the conference, British public opinion would expect a minister to be present. So Younger would lead the British party until the arrival of Morrison.[104]

The conference proved to be a great success, despite the presence of the Soviet Union. This no doubt owed a good deal to the rather half-hearted tactics of the Soviets, the refusal of the other delegates to tolerate Soviet obstructive tactics and Acheson's firm chairmanship of the meeting. Indeed, his handling of the conference gave him a personal triumph with the American public and, in particular, with the west coast public.[105] Franks also enjoyed a considerable success in the eyes of at least one member of the British government. Younger observed:

> Oliver Franks is a tower of strength. Although I saw him last autumn, I had never really worked with him until this week. Intellectually he is most formidable and has an astonishing grasp of the basic factors in all the problems with which he is concerned, i.e. at the moment all the problems which we discuss with the Americans. He is reputed to be Olympian and alarming. There is an element of this, but I think it is quite unintentional. So far as I am concerned, any feeling of alarm is merely due to the sense that if one says anything wild, or based on superficial judgements it will be promptly punctured! I felt somewhat awkward at first, because he had originally been named to lead the delegation until Herbert Morrison arrived at the end of the week, and then I came in over his head. I am however quite satisfied that there was no petty ill-feeling on his side. I gather he holds the view that on all big occasions the people with the political responsibility ought to lead.[106]

After the conference Morrison attended meetings in Washington with Acheson on 10–11 September and with Acheson and Schuman on 12–14 September.[107] Acheson later observed of his talks with the Foreign Secretary: 'he wasn't a disagreeable person, but he sometimes gave the impression of being sort of petty and irritable and he said things in the most irritating way'.[108] Interestingly, Morrison seems to have formed a more favourable opinion of Acheson. He approved a note describing Acheson's helpfulness and understanding of the British position and inserted 'outstanding' to characterise the American.[109]

AGREEMENT ON US BASES

Taking place at the same time were Anglo-American Political–Military talks, a continuation of the intermittent conversations to which Franks and Slessor had secured American agreement in late January. The British continued to be worried about the lack of information about the US Strategic Air Plan and how it would affect US bases in Britain. Morrison met Acheson on 11 September and urged progress on the issues of consultation before use of the atomic bomb, and the need for an agreement on the use of the American bases in Britain. Acheson said that, as regards these bases, 'he saw no difficulty in the question of prior consultation with the UK before those bases were used'.[110] Two days later there was an Anglo-American Political–Military meeting, attended by Franks, F. W. Marten of the Foreign Office, and Sir William Elliot, head of BJSM since July, for Britain, and General Bradley, Matthews and Nitze for the United States.[111] The Americans now accepted that 'prior consultation and agreement with the UK would obviously be required' over the matter of operations from the bases. On the question of prior consultation of the British on use of the atomic bomb, Nitze suggested this be 'left open for consideration in the light of the circumstances existing at the time'. The Americans showed Franks a memorandum outlining the kind of statement they could accept. He read it and told Nitze, 'I see you are a behaviourist.'[112] Franks now wanted to check and think about the matter further. However, with the general election due on 25 October, time was against the British. Attlee was anxious to achieve an agreement, for this might become an election issue requiring a government statement. The Americans deduced as much from the 13 September meeting: they noted that Franks 'was clearly under instructions to find as broad an area as possible, and as easy language for us to take as possible'.[113] A British draft was submitted on 15 October. Its key passage ran: 'The question of their use in an emergency naturally remains a matter for joint decision in the light of the circumstances at the time.'[114] This was slightly amended in a meeting between Franks and Matthews which Truman then endorsed on the 17th. It read:

> The use of these bases in an emergency would be a matter for joint decision by His Majesty's Government and the United States Government in the light of the circumstances prevailing at the time.[115]

Franks had helped achieve an agreement. Although it was not entirely satisfactory to him, he recognised that it represented the furthest the Americans were prepared to go on the issue.[116] Yet the Americans regarded it as 'thin'. They wanted its prompt acceptance, noting 'If Churchill is returned to head the government he will doubtless want to get a greater commitment from us. We would be in a better position to withstand his onslaught if this statement had already been agreed upon.'[117] Moreover, a report by the Office of Intelligence and Research warned of pushing both the British and the French too far – for this might cause the fall of the respective governments and their replacement by administrations unwilling to accept the bases.[118]

NOTES

1. Younger Diary, 28 March 1951.
2. Bodleian Library, Oxford, Gore-Booth Papers, Ms.Eng.c.4518, M. A. Hamilton to P. H. Gore-Booth, 13 March 1951.
3. Barclay, *Ernest Bevin*, pp. 95–6.
4. B. Donoughue and G.W. Jones, *Herbert Morrison: Portrait of a Politician* (London: Weidenfeld & Nicolson, 1973), pp. 512–13.
5. Quoted in Morgan, *Labour in Power*, p. 465.
6. See Donoughue and Jones, *Morrison*, pp. 485–91; Morgan, *Labour in Power*, pp. 444–55.
7. PRO, FO 800/517, US/51/10, Franks to Bevin, 21 February 1951. In November 1950 it had been remarked that Franks needed to visit London soon, since his planned trip that summer had been cancelled. See FO 800/517, US/50/51.
8. Cairncross (ed.), *Hall Diaries 1947–1953*, p. 150 (21 March 1951 entry).
9. Ibid., p. 275 (25 June 1953 entry).
10. *New York Herald Tribune*, 28 March 1951.
11. They are at PRO, CAB 134/32.
12. PRO, FO 371/93203, GE5/105G, minute by W. Harpham, 25 September 1951.
13. PRO, DEFE 4/41, COS (51) 48th Meeting, 14 March 1951; DEFE 32/2, Secretary's Standard File, SSF/950/B, Confidential Annexe to COS (51) 48th Meeting.
14. Its records, like those of the Official Committee on Atomic Energy, remain closed. They are in CAB 134/32. But the decision of AE(M)(51) 1st Meeting is noted in DEFE 32/2, Secretary's Standard File, COS (51) 109th Meeting, 2 July 1951.
15. PRO, FO 371/90931, AU1054/11, record of a talk by Sir P. Dixon, 20 March 1951.
16. HSTL, Acheson Papers, Box 66, Memorandum of Meeting, 2 April 1951.
17. FRUS, 1951, VI, Part 1, p. 966, Memorandum of Conversation, 5 April 1951.
18. FRUS, 1951 VII p. 296, Memorandum of Conversation, 5 April 1951.
19. PRO, FO 800/639, FE/51/4, Franks to FO, Tel. No. 1082, 11 April 1951; also at *DBPO*, 2nd Series, IV, No. 143, which contains, at note 1, reference to Franks's advance hint about the move.
20. Bodleian Library, Oxford, Gore-Booth Papers, Ms.Eng.c.4518, P. Gore-Booth to M. A. Hamilton, 17 April 1951.
21. PRO, FO 371/90903, AU1013/20, Washington to FO, No. 405(S), 5 May 1951.
22. King's College, London, Liddell Hart Centre for Military Archives, Elliot Papers, 3/3/2, broadcast by the British Ambassador on 18 May 1951, British Information Services text, 17 May 1951. BIS managed to ensure the broadcast received nationwide coverage. See Gore-Booth Papers,

Ms.Eng.c.4518, P. H. Gore Booth to M. A. Hamilton, 17 May and 3 June 1951.

23. On developments March–July 1951 see C. MacDonald, *Britain and the Korean War* (Oxford: Blackwell, 1990), pp. 47–8, 54–5; MacDonald, *Korea*, pp. 91–115; and Acheson, *Present at the Creation*, pp. 512–38.
24. W. R. Louis, 'Musaddiq and the Dilemma of British Imperialism', in J. A. Bill and W. R. Louis (eds), *Iranian Nationalism and Oil* (London: I. B. Taurus, 1988), p. 229.
25. Quoted in Louis, *The British Empire in the Middle East*, p. 654.
26. George McGhee, *Envoy to the Middle World: Adventures in Diplomacy* (New York: Harper & Row, 1983), p. 334; for Acheson's views see Acheson, *Present at the Creation*, pp. 505–7.
27. Bodleian Library, Oxford, Gore-Booth Papers, Ms.Eng.c.4518, P. Gore-Booth to M. A. Hamilton, 2 May 1951.
28. Younger Diary, 13 May 1951.
29. PRO, FO 371/91470, EP1023/18, Franks to FO, Tel. No. 1081, 10 April 1951.
30. PRO, FO 371/91471, EP1023/6, Franks to FO, Tel. No. 900, 27 March 1951.
31. PRO, FO 371/91471, EP1023/32, minute by R. Makins of telephone call, 12 April 1951.
32. PRO, FO 953/1152, PG13437/3, minute by D. A. Logan, 24 April 1951.
33. FRUS, 1952–54, X (Iran 1951–54), No. 12, pp. 30–5, memorandum of conversation, 17 April 1951.
34. Ibid., No. 13, pp. 37–42, memorandum of conversation, 18 April 1950.
35. PRO, FO 371/91471, EP1023/39, Franks to FO, Tel. No. 1194, 18 April 1951.
36. FRUS, 1952–54, X, p. 42n.
37. PRO, FO 371/91529, EP1531/241, Franks to Strang, 21 April 1951.
38. HSTL, Acheson Papers, Box 66, memorandum of conversation, 27 April 1951. Gaddis Smith wrongly attributes the Kipling remark to Acheson in his *Dean Acheson*, p. 339.
39. PRO, FO 371/91493, EP11345/7, FO to Washington, Tel. No. 1765, 28 April 1951. The US proposal is included in an undated paper shown to Franks on 17 April, FRUS, 1952–54, X, pp. 35–7.
40. PRO, FO 371/91493, EP11345/10, Franks to FO, Tel. No. 414(S), 8 May 1951. The Embassy also avoided tension with the Americans over Morrison's request that they complain to Acheson about the tone of McGhee's remarks in recent talks. Franks said he did not want to see Acheson again so soon on such a matter. Instead, a member of the Embassy staff saw McGhee who was more reasonable. Neither Steel nor Burrows of the Embassy was keen to complain to Acheson thinking it might sour their good relations with McGhee. FO 371/91528, EP1531/223, 235, FO to Washington, Tel. No. 1755 and Washington to FO, Tel. No. 1304, both 28 April 1951; FO 371/91531, EP1531/291, Steel to Bowker, 30 April 1951.
41. See Morgan, *Labour in Power*, p. 467.
42. FRUS, 1952–54, X, No. 21, pp. 51–4, Acheson to Embassy in Iran, 11 May 1951; PRO, FO 371/91533, EP1531/308, Franks to FO, Tel. No. 1488, 12 May 1951.
43. PRO, FO 371/91533, EP1531/308, FO to Franks, Tel. No. 2022, 14 May 1951.
44. FRUS, 1952–54, X, No. 22, p. 54, Gifford to State Department, 16 May 1951; PRO, FO 371/91535, EP1531/354, Franks to FO, Tel. No. 1547, 17 May 1951.
45. *New York Herald Tribune*, 4 June 1951; see also HSTL, Truman Papers, Official File 48, Box 215.
46. *Daily Herald*, 14 June 1951.
47. *Daily Express*, 19 June 1951. Interestingly, the *Daily Express* of 10 January had attacked the head of BIS in the United States, calling its activities a waste of money. Its opening line was 'Who is Mr Paul Gore-Booth?', Gore-Booth

Papers, Ms.Eng.c.4550.

48. House of Lords Record Office, Beaverbrook Papers, Bbk/H/148, A. Christiansen to Beaverbrook, 25 June 1951. I am grateful to Annie Pinder of the HLRO for discovering and sending me a copy of this document.
49. Interview with Lord Franks, 24 May 1990.
50. *News Chronicle*, 20 June 1951.
51. NA, Wash. DC, State Department Decimal Files 1950–54, Box 2594, 601.4111/6–2151, London Embassy to State Department, 21 June 1951, enclosing the *Daily Express*, 21 June 1951 report of *Washington Post* defence of Franks. See also: PRO, FO 371/90932, AU1054/9.
52. NA, Wash. DC, RG 59, State Department Decimal Files 1950–54, Box 2594, 601.4111/3–1451, Governor J.S. Battle of Virginia to State Department, 14 March 1951; ibid., 601.4111/4–1851, Sir C. Steel (Minister at British Embassy) to J. Simmons (Head of Protocol, State Department), 18 April 1951.
53. Denis Greenhill, *More by Accident* (York: Wilton 65, 1992), pp. 72–3.
54. On these developments see R. Cecil, *A Divided Life: A Biography of Donald Maclean* (London: The Bodley Head, 1988), pp. 126–49.
55. PRO, FO 371/90931, AU1054/25.
56. Ibid., AU1054/23, Steel to FO, Tel. No. 1803, 8 June 1951.
57. PRO, FO 371/90932, AU1054/34, Burrows (Counsellor at the British Embassy) to American Department, 17 July 1951, enclosing *US News & World Report*, 20 July 1951, pp. 13–16.
58. Churchill College, Cambridge, Strang Papers, STRN 2/10, 'Comment on Mr Rohan Butler's Study of British Policy in the Relinquishment of Abadan in 1951', 4 February 1963.
59. Colonel R. Totten, 'National Security Implications Resulting from the Defection of British Diplomats, Donald Duart McLean [*sic*] and Guy DeMoncy Burgess', 18 October 1955 in Richard J. Aldrich (ed.), *Espionage, Security and Intelligence in Britain, 1945–1970* (Manchester: Manchester University Press, 1998), pp. 139–40.
60. Richard J. Aldrich, *The Hidden Hand: Britain, America and Cold War Intelligence* (London: John Murray, 2001), pp. 424–8.
61. C. Andrew, *For the President's Eyes Only: Secret Intelligence and the American Presidency from Washington to Bush* (London: HarperCollins, 1996), pp. 195–6.
62. PRO, FO 371/90931, AU1054/21, Makins, 'Impressions of America', 25 May 1951.
63. PRO, FO 371/91011, AU1891/3, various minutes on the arrangements for Franks's visit.
64. PRO, DEFE 4/44, COS(51) 105th Meeting, 27 June 1951.
65. Ibid., COS(51) 109th Meeting, 2 July 1951; DEFE 32/2, Secretary's Standard File, SSF/950/B, Confidential Annexe to COS(51) 109th Meeting.
66. PRO, DEFE 32/2, Secretary's Standard File, SSF/950/B, Confidential Annexe to COS(51) 140th Meeting, 5 September 1951.
67. Gowing, *Independence and Deterrence*, I, p. 265.
68. PRO, FO 371/91185, E1024/36, Record of a Meeting at the Foreign Office, 29 June 1951.
69. PRO, FO 371/91537, EP1531/421, Franks to FO, Tel. No. 1654, 26 May 1951.
70. FRUS, 1952–54, X, No. 29, p. 66, editorial note.
71. Morgan, *Labour in Power*, pp. 468–9; Acheson, *Present at the Creation*, pp. 506–7.
72. PRO, FO 371/91555, EP1531/864, Franks to FO, Tel. No. 2060, 4 July 1951 and Tel. No. 2068, 5 July 1951.
73. Ibid., EP1531/864, FO to Franks, Tel. Nos. 2897–2898, 7 July 1951.
74. PRO, FO 371/91559, EP1531/913, Franks to FO, Tel. No. 2097, 7 July 1951;

FRUS, 1952–54, X, No. 36, pp. 81–4, memorandum of conversation, 7 July 1951; ibid., No. 40, pp. 89–91, memorandum of conversation, 12 July 1950; Acheson, *Present at the Creation*, pp. 507–8.

75. Louis, *The British Empire in the Middle East*, p. 676.
76. PRO, FO 371/91563, EP1531/1007, Franks to FO, Tel. No. 2173, 13 July 1951.
77. FRUS, 1952–54, X, No. 41, p. 92, editorial note; Acheson, *Present at the Creation*, pp. 508–9.
78. HSTL, Acheson Papers, Box 66, memorandum of conversation, 2 August 1951. Strang also demurred: 'we should be gambling', if we sent Stokes who 'has never been really tested in international negotiation' and who 'is impulsive and at times indiscreet'. FO 800/653, Pe/51/22, Strang minute for Morrison, 25 July 1951.
79. FRUS, 1952–54, X, No. 65, p. 130; Acheson, *Present at the Creation*, pp. 509–10; Louis, *The British Empire in the Middle East*, pp. 686–9; PRO, CAB 128/20, CM 60(51), 27 September 1951.
80. PRO, FO 371/91591, EP1531/1630, Franks to FO, Tel. No. 3116, 26 September 1951.
81. PRO, FO 371/91592, EP1531/1661, Franks to FO, Tel. No. 3147, 28 September 1951.
82. PRO, FO 371/91596, EP1531/1770, Franks to FO, Tel. No. 3223, 5 October 1951.
83. Younger Diary, 3 October 1951.
84. Younger Diary, 3 September 1951.
85. Churchill College, Cambridge, Strang Papers, STRN 2/10, 'Comment on Mr Rohan Butler's Study of British Policy in the Relinquishment of Abadan in 1951', 4 February 1963.
86. PRO, FO 371/92532, FJ1022/100, Franks to FO, Tel. No. 606, 28 February 1951.
87. PRO, FO 371/92533, FJ1022/121, C. H. Johnston to F. S. Tomlinson, 13 March 1951; FO 371/92536, FJ1022/185, F. S. Tomlinson to C. H. Johnston, 20 March 1951.
88. PRO, FO 371/92539, FJ1022/227, Franks to FO, Tel. No. 1030, 6 April 1951. See also R. Buckley, 'Joining the Club: The Japanese Question and Anglo-American Peace Diplomacy, 1950–1951', *Modern Asian Studies*, Vol. 19, No. 2, 1985, p. 308.
89. PRO, FO 371/92540, FJ1022/262, Tomlinson to Johnston, 9 April 1951; ibid., FJ1022/264, Tomlinson to Johnston, 10 April 1951.
90. PRO, FO 371/92545, FJ1022/336 and 342, FO 371/92546, FJ1022/357, and FO 371/92547, FJ1022/366 for minutes of the meetings, 25 April to 4 May.
91. PRO, FO 371/92540, FJ1022/265, Franks to FO, Tel. No. 1163, 16 April 1951.
92. PRO, FO 371/92547, FJ1022/366, Franks to FO, Tel. No. 1381, 4 May 1951.
93. PRO, FO 371/92546, FJ1022/361, Franks to FO, Tel. No. 1362, 3 May 1951.
94. PRO, FO 371/92553, FJ1022/498, FO 371/92554, FJ1022/513–516, 518, FO 371/92556, FJ1022/546–549, 562–563 for the minutes of the meetings.
95. PRO, FO 371/90916, AU10113/5, Franks to R.H. Scott, 21 May 1951. On the 'human' side to diplomacy see Sir Nicholas Henderson, 'Lord Franks: An Appreciation', *The Times*, 5 November 1992, p. 19.
96. PRO, FO 800/639, FE/51/20, Records of a Meeting between the Secretary of State and Mr. John Foster Dulles on 4 June 1951.
97. See text in FRUS, 1951, VI, Part 1, pp. 1119–33.
98. Morrison to Cabinet, CAB 128/19, CM 41(51), 7 June 1951; cited in Lowe, *Containing the Cold War*, p. 54.
99. R. Buckley, *Occupation Diplomacy: Britain, the United States and Japan 1945–1952* (Cambridge: Cambridge University Press, 1982), pp. 176–7. This

agreed communiqué was, at Dulles' request, never published: PRO, FO 371/99402, FJ1026/3.

100. PRO, FO 371/92531, FJ1022/75, Franks to FO, Tel. No. 449, 13 February 1951.
101. PRO, FO 371/92560, FJ1022/630, C. E. Steel to W. Strang (FO), 18 June 1951.
102. PRO, FO 371/92586, FJ1022/1168, Franks to FO, Tel. No. 842(S), 20 August 1951. Dulles's tendency to leak to the press was hinted at by Allison in a talk with Tomlinson of the Embassy in April. See FO 371/92540, FJ1022/247, Tomlinson to Johnston, 9 April 1951.
103. PRO, FO 371/92568, FJ1022/781, Franks to FO, Tel. No. 2221, 18 July 1951 and FO to Franks, Tel. No. 3153, 19 July 1951; FJ1022/810, Franks to FO, Tel. No. 2265, 20 July 1951. Morrison's conduct did not please Gore-Booth, who observed that Bevin would never have appeared four days late for a conference. Gore-Booth Papers, Ms.Eng.c.4517, Gore-Booth to M. A. Hamilton, 23 September 1951.
104. PRO, FO 371/92587, FJ1022/1195, FO to Franks, Tel. No. 3787, 22 August 1951.
105. PRO, FO 371/92598, FJ1022/1404, R. H. Scott to Strang, 10 September 1951. See FO 371/92594, FJ1022/1343, 1354 and FO 371/92595, FJ1022/1361, 1366 for records and summaries of the conference sessions.
106. Younger Diary, 9 September 1951.
107. See PREM 8/1432 for records of the talks; see L of C, Harriman Papers, container 312, for US Briefing Book, Vols I–II.
108. *Princeton Seminars*, microfilm, roll 3, frame 1042, 12 December 1953.
109. PRO, FO 371/124966, ZP23/26G, P. Dixon, 'Impressions of San Francisco, Washington and Ottawa, September 1951', 25 September 1951.
110. HSTL, Acheson Papers, Box 66, memorandum of conversation, 11 September 1951.
111. Ibid., memorandum of conversation, 13 September 1951.
112. Perhaps, this appropriately philosophical remark by Franks meant that he thought the Americans were offering the prospect of a particular type of response acceptable to the British – a 'conditioned' response rather than one emerging from a legal formula. On behaviourism, see Alan Bullock and Oliver Stallybrass (eds), *Fontana Dictionary of Modern Thought* (London: Fontana, 1977), p. 57.
113. FRUS, 1951, I, p. 890, summary of a discussion, 13 September 1951.
114. PRO, FO 115/4525, 44/5/51, minute by F. W. Martin, 15 October 1951.
115. Quoted in J. Baylis, 'American Bases in Britain: The Truman-Attlee Understandings', *The World Today*, Vol. 42, Nos. 8–9, August/September 1986, p. 157.
116. The general lines of this paragraph are based on: ibid., pp. 155–9; Duke, *US Defence Bases*, pp. 70–1, Gowing, *Independence and Deterrence*, I, pp. 315–8.
117. FRUS, 1951, I, p. 893.
118. Declassified Documents Retrieval System [DDRS], fiche 78, 292B, Department of State, Office of Intelligence and Research, 'Reactions of UK and France to Assumed Proposed Use Atomic Weapons by US', 17 September 1951.

PART V:

THE RETURN OF THE CONSERVATIVES

'[M]uch work will have to be done if we are to keep Anglo-American relations running smoothly.'

Anthony Eden to Oliver Franks, 10 September 1951, in Dutton, *Anthony Eden*

'Eden feels the Prime Minister gives in too easily to the Americans.'

Newsweek, 14 April 1952

—12—

Working with Churchill and Eden

ON 25 OCTOBER the Conservatives won the general election securing a majority of 26 over Labour and 16 overall. Winston Churchill became Prime Minister and appointed Anthony Eden as Foreign Secretary. In his memoirs Eden suggested that he and the Prime Minister rarely disagreed on foreign policy, repeating Winston Churchill's remark that 'you could put each of us in a separate room, put any questions of foreign policy to us and nine times out of ten we would give the same answer'.[1] Close observers of the relationship did not share this view. Lord Moran, Churchill's personal doctor, recorded in his diary:

> The PM always claims that Anthony and he agree on most things in the field of foreign affairs, though it is not very noticeable; they don't seem, for instance, to have much in common … in their approach to Americans … Winston has appointed Anthony as his heir … but he still regards him as a young man, and is not much influenced by his views.[2]

Evelyn Shuckburgh, Eden's Principal Private Secretary, noted in his diary a conversation with David Pitblado and Jock Colville, Churchill's Joint Principal Private Secretaries: 'We are agreed about the need to smooth from time to time the relations between our two masters.'[3] The condition of their relationship has been aptly described as a 'situation of affection tempered with tension'.[4] The apprehension was not eased by Eden's expectation that he would succeed Churchill as Prime Minister in a matter of months, nor by the Foreign Secretary's constant ill-health.[5]

Eden was vastly experienced on the international scene and possessed a detailed knowledge of foreign affairs. The Foreign Office welcomed him. Molly Hamilton of the American Department declared: 'The Office heaved a (perfectly silent) sigh of relief when Eden replaced H. M[orrison].'[6] But he did not prove to be an easy master and was less popular than Bevin. No doubt the intermittent bouts of nerves did not help.[7] Under him there would be continuity in foreign policy. In his memoirs, he wrote about Bevin: 'I was in agreement with the aims of his foreign policy and with most that he did.' He noted that they met frequently and discussed events informally.[8] There was not the same close relationship with Acheson that Bevin had enjoyed, but the spirit of Anglo-American co-operation was maintained. Acheson remarked in his memoirs: 'Eden and I worked easily together, agreed on basic matters, where he was a resourceful and strong ally.'[9] Eden noted that Acheson 'never forgot what was due to an ally and worked in the spirit of equal partnership, even though the United States carried so much the heavier load'.[10] But he added:

> Despite a natural courtesy, his gifts can edge him to intolerance. He does not suffer fools gladly, which suffering is a large part of diplomacy. Yet Mr Acheson is above all a loyal colleague. I would never hesitate to go tiger-hunting with him. If there were occasional squalls in our dealings, our relations usually gained from them.[11]

Within days of the Conservatives' return there was press speculation about Franks remaining as Ambassador. On 30 October, the *Daily Herald* suggested that he might return to London soon after Princess Elizabeth's impending visit. It speculated that he might be replaced by a member of Churchill's party, such as Earl Mountbatten or Lord Halifax. The report concluded that the Ambassador was understood recently to have expressed a desire to return to Britain and resume as Provost of Queens College, Oxford.[12] The next day, the *Manchester Guardian* scotched such rumours, maintaining that there was no foundation for reports that Franks was to be replaced. It said that he had been appointed, at his own request, for a period of not more than four years; and that, since that period would expire in May, he would probably insist then on retiring from public life.[13] This turned out to be close to what Franks actually did. Whatever the reasons for these rumours, they were not based on any misgivings of the Ambassador about the new government. He observed much later that he was not bothered about the change of government, since he was neither a socialist nor a conservative but 'an extinct Gladstonian liberal'.[14]

Now that he was Prime Minister once more, Churchill was keen to re-establish the Anglo-American ties he had enjoyed during the Second World War – after all, he virtually personified the political and emotional commitment to the special relationship. Eden, however, did not feel the same unqualified affection for the United States. As Holland has said, 'Of all the major British statesmen of the Second World War Eden had been least integrated into the machinery of the

Anglo-American alliance.' Eden did not dislike Americans but he was committed to the ideal of independent British power. 'Where Churchill was prepared to trade-in a large measure of autonomy if it meant an accretion of real power, for Eden the only power worth having was that which was authentically national in its derivation.'[15] Moreover, Eden shared the Foreign Office's twin, but contradictory, fears that 'the US might either revert to isolationism or be "overzealous" in pursuing the Cold war'.[16] Yet there were also indications that he might have succumbed to the 'illusion of British greatness' and his speeches on an American tour in summer 1951 'suggest that, like Churchill, he hoped to re-establish the Special Relationship on that basis of equality which the diplomacy of the later war years should have convinced him was unrealistic'.[17]

On 5 November Churchill sent a message to Truman, through Franks, proposing that they meet sometime in December. Truman's reply of the 6th said that the earliest possible date would be 27 December. In a further exchange of notes it was settled that the Prime Minister and Foreign Secretary should visit Washington at the beginning of January.[18] Churchill described his hopes for the visit in a message to Truman on 10 December: 'My wish and object is that we should reach a good understanding of each other's point of view over the whole field, so that we can work together easily and intimately at the different levels as we used to do.'[19] Throughout December both sides were busy with preparations. It was decided that, as regards public speeches, Churchill should address Congress, and that Eden should speak at Columbia University, where he was due to receive an honorary degree. The Foreign Secretary agreed, on the advice of the Washington Embassy, to lunch with the whole of the Senate Foreign Relations Committee, and to meet informally and off-the-record a number of selected journalists.[20] Churchill was warned by Makins not to expect a return to the working habits of the wartime alliance. He told the Prime Minister that 'Truman is not FDR and his method of working is different.' Since the President took advice, Makins added, the procedure for the talks was likely to be formal with morning and afternoon meetings with a fixed agenda, Truman being accompanied by his principal ministers and advisers and specific questions being remitted for discussion and report by groups of advisers.[21]

CHURCHILL IN WASHINGTON: PREPARATIONS

Among the welter of papers prepared for the talks two stand out as indicative of the British outlook at that time. Makins submitted on 29

November a memorandum entitled 'Objectives in the Washington Talks'. He suggested that the primary objective should be to improve the tone of the Anglo-American relationship. After listing the main issues that needed addressing, he concluded:

> The Anglo-American partnership is difficult to manage owing to the increasing disparity of power within it. We are on a difficult wicket at the moment because, however we try to disguise it, we are back in the breadline for the third time in six years. The Prime Minister's arrival in the USA will coincide with another disquieting disclosure about the run on reserves. This will add to the impression already created in the USA by Persia and Egypt that the British Empire is in liquidation.[22]

Robert Cecil, head of the American Department, presented a paper on 'The Present State of Anglo-American Relations' on 8 December. He said that Britain was 'anxious to maintain our special relationship with the United States Government by demonstrating that Britain is America's most reliable ally'. But, he added, the level of the British rearmament programme and our greater dependence upon imported raw materials aggravated our economic difficulties and threw us 'even more into the arms of the United States'. This 'vicious circle', he continued, caused anti-American feeling in Britain and American impatience with our weakness, especially in Congress. Cecil maintained that the 'Americans are anxious we should be strong and even that we should show our strength, but they are not agreed what should be the price in terms of dollars and United Kingdom economic controls'. He concluded that Britain had reached a period when an attitude of sweet reasonableness would not necessarily yield results. He proposed that a firm attitude be adopted in the conversations.[23]

What both of these assessments brought home was the recurrence of economic difficulties for Britain. The balance of payments on current account went into deficit again in 1951 as a result of a swift increase in import prices, in particular raw materials, the growth of government stockpiling achieved through increased imports, and industry's inability to expand export production. The nationalisation of AIOC greatly worsened the situation by reducing dollar revenue from the oil and increasing dollar expenditure to purchase alternative supplies. By the second half of 1951 the total deficits of Britain and the sterling area were £750 million, causing reserves to fall from £1,381 million at the end of June 1951 to £834 million by December 1951.[24] Such a situation brought Cecil to observe that the Americans were increasingly asking whether there was a cure to continued British economic crises.[25] Indeed, this caused the Americans to contemplate 'whether and to what extent the United States should provide the United Kingdom with economic assistance'.[26]

These economic worries led the new Chancellor of the Exchequer, R. A. Butler, to consider the possibility of a waiver of the December payment of the interest on the US loan. He telegraphed Franks for his advice, saying he would prefer not to do this 'unless the Americans themselves would welcome it'.[27] Franks, in his reply, recognised that the political aspect of this was the most important. He believed that if Butler felt Britain faced a long-term prospect of great dollar difficulties and repeated requests for aid, then the government should claim the waiver. But, he added, if there was a real chance of overcoming these difficulties with only a temporary injection of aid, then he hoped the Chancellor would be able to take the risk of not claiming the waiver. Franks seemed to favour the second option, for he warned about the difficulty of securing a broad sensible treatment of the issues by the US Secretary of the Treasury, Snyder; and he thought it possible that economic conditions might improve.[28] Butler heeded this advice and did not claim the waiver.

When Churchill sent Truman the general list of topics that he had in mind for the talks, they included the economic position and problems of the United Kingdom, and the raw materials issue, in particular steel. Other topics included: organisation for Western defence; the Atlantic and other Commands; the Strategic Air Plan and use of the atomic bomb; technical co-operation in atomic energy; and co-operation in the Far East, SE Asia and the Middle East.[29]

In their preparations for the Truman–Churchill conversations, US officials gave their views of relations with Britain and of what constituted the key issues. A Policy Planning Staff paper declared that the United States had 'a special relationship with the UK which involves consultation between us on a wide range of matters of joint concern'. It assumed that Churchill aimed to use the visit to develop what he regarded as an Anglo-American partnership.[30] Paul Nitze, director of the Policy Planning Staff, told a meeting of State Department officials and representatives of the Joint Chiefs of Staff that the special relationship had not worked well since Bevin became ill, that it 'has not worked at all well with Mr Morrison'. He added that American public opinion was more favourable to Britain now that Churchill had returned to office. He felt that 'we can hope for a sounder relationship with the Churchill government than we have had with Mr Morrison'. But he warned that they did not want 'to reconstruct the Roosevelt–Churchill relationship of the last war'.[31]

US officials drew up a list of issues that they felt that Churchill might raise in the talks. On the general relationship it was pointed out that the British, and especially Churchill, advocated from time to time a more overt type of relationship. The Prime Minister was thought to favour something approaching the wartime Combined Chiefs of Staff, which US Chiefs opposed. The brief for Truman advised against conceding this, because of the probable effect on other allies and the possible limitation of American freedom of action. On atomic energy it was expected that the British would raise the questions of consultation on the use of atomic weapons and use of bases in Britain, and closer technical collaboration in the entire atomic field. Truman was advised that the United States must retain freedom of action regarding a decision to use atomic weapons. In addition, the brief maintained that there appeared no solid basis for further expansion of collaboration, despite the recent British atomic weapon test.[32]

On 29 December, Churchill and Eden and the British delegation set sail for the United States on board the *Queen Mary,* arriving on 5 January.[33] Hall, head of the Cabinet Economic Section, who joined the delegation, recorded in his diary: 'I think we have all been too concerned about an agenda and not ready enough to accept the truth that W[inston] just wants to re-open relations.'[34] Hall also noted that Franks had received a GCMG in the New Year's honours, observing 'presumably this is a pay off and he won't be renewed in May'.[35] The Embassy reported to London that the general tone of the press and radio was of great personal warmth and friendliness for Churchill. But it also reported the comments of the *New York Daily News*:

> old Winnie is coming cap in hand. Eventually, the grand old man will have to cough apologetically, lay his last card down, and plead as eloquently as he can for still more US help to staple together what is left of the British Commonwealth.[36]

CHURCHILL IN WASHINGTON: DISCUSSIONS

Churchill held talks in Washington 5–9 January, spent 9–11 January in New York, and then visited Ottawa for discussions on the 12th to 15th, returning to Washington for the 16th to the 18th. He gave his address to Congress on the 17th. Eden stayed in Washington 5-10 January and then went to New York, where he delivered a speech at Columbia University. He spent the 13th to the 15th in Ottawa. The main issues covered in the conversations were co-operation in the Middle East, over Iran, in particular; the British economic position and the question of raw materials; the reorganisation of Western defence and the

European Army or European Defence Community (EDC); the Atlantic Command; and Japan's relations with China.[37]

Franks accompanied Churchill and Eden on their first meeting of the visit with Truman and Acheson for dinner on 5 January aboard the presidential yacht *SS Williamsburg*. General Bradley, Lovett, Secretary of Defence, Snyder, Harriman and Gifford, Ambassador in London, also attended on the American side. The British were joined by Lord Ismay, Secretary of State for Commonwealth Relations, and Lord Cherwell, Paymaster General and Churchill's adviser on atomic energy. Acheson recorded that the 'meeting was most successful. The atmosphere was excellent'. He added that Churchill had said that he had never attended a meeting where 'the atmosphere was so conducive to close and cordial relations between the two countries'.[38] The questions of a European army, Egypt and Iran were outlined, as well as the general situation in the Middle East and Far East. Acheson raised the matter of Japan's relations with China, saying that Yoshida's government wanted to establish peaceful political and trade relations with Nationalist China. Churchill said he had supported the Labour government's recognition of China, but he thought its later policy on China had been wrong. Eden spoke, 'rather strongly' in Acheson's view, against the American view that Japan should enter relations with Taiwan, feeling it violated the understanding with Morrison. But Acheson felt that the Japanese were free to reach an accommodation with the Nationalists if they wished.[39]

Churchill left the meeting in good spirits. He told Moran: 'Oh I enjoyed it so much; we talked as equals.' Franks believed that it 'was a good beginning'. Eden was more cautious. Churchill was pleased with the atmosphere of friendliness and remarked: 'I do hope that Anthony will meet the Americans over China, which really does not matter to us. Then they in turn might meet us about Egypt or Persia, which matter a lot.'[40]

Discussions did not run as easily when Franks hosted a dinner at the British Embassy on 6 January. They exposed tense relations between Eden and Acheson which the Ambassador worked hard to alleviate. After the meal, there were conversations from nine o'clock until shortly after one. The main topics were the Far East and the Middle East. Acheson in his memoirs observed that his visitors were drawn to 'courses high in debating appeal whose impracticalities are revealed only through considerable factual knowledge'. He added that he pressed his points about Iran to Eden 'with such asperity and impatience as to require subsequent amends'.[41] Eden was told that the difficulties had arisen, not because of the failure of the US government to support strong measures, but because of foot-dragging – a reluctance to make reasonable concessions – by AIOC when Razmara was Prime Minister.[42] Acheson told the Foreign Secretary that 'the business of Foreign Minister today was very different from what it was when Lord Palmerston was handling things like this'.[43] Franks helped to assuage the difficulties. The next day he told Acheson that Eden was wounded by the incident. Thereafter, the US Secretary of State was more careful about Eden's feelings.

In the course of raising this matter, Franks spoke candidly to try to elicit an American response which would be conducive to greater harmony. The Ambassador made some observations about Eden's mind. He said that the Foreign Secretary had one great asset and that was political instinct. He was not trained in any kind of rational processes. He knew that he was now at point A, which he did not like, and he saw point B, where he would prefer to be. If he was asked as to how he could move from point A to point B, then you were pursuing the impossible, for this was something he was incapable of doing. Nor could he explain why he preferred point B to point C. He just had a strong 'feel' that he wanted to be at another place. Acheson recorded Franks as saying:

> you've got to work around and if you have differences and you think you ought to be somewhere else, you have to do it other than as though you were arguing a case ... all you do is baffle and confuse him and rather humiliate him because you show him that he ought'nt to want to do what he wants and that upsets him.[44]

The first formal meeting was held at 11 a.m. on 7 January.[45] It covered, first of all, the economic position of Britain. Churchill gave the United Kingdom's gold and dollar deficit figures – $940 million. He also reported that the British rearmament programme would now cost £5,200 million rather than the projected £4,700 million and that this was due entirely to price rises. But the British, he continued, would make the maximum contribution they could in the face of these difficulties. This led to a discussion on raw materials. The British need for steel and US requirements for tin, copper, nickel and aluminium were mentioned. Discussion then turned to reorganisation of NATO. Eden favoured a permanent NATO Council to replace the meetings of the Deputies. The main work of the Organisation should be in the hands of a Secretary-General (or Director General if that title was preferred) and based at a permanent headquarters. Acheson responded by saying that these proposals appeared very similar to those favoured by the United States. This matter was subsequently considered at the Lisbon meeting of the North Atlantic Council of

20–25 February and was to involve Franks in a way he would not have predicted. Hall described Churchill at this first formal meeting as 'very bad indeed on the economic side and I thought on other things too'. He thought Eden 'a bit better' but that altogether it was 'a poor show on our side'.[46]

During lunch for the British delegation, Churchill launched an attack on the decision, taken by the Labour government shortly before leaving office, that command of the Atlantic should be given to an US Admiral. The Chief of the Imperial General Staff, Field-Marshall Slim, the First Sea Lord, Sir Rhoderick McGrigor, and Lord Ismay all pressed him to accept the scheme, for the British had secured all that really mattered – in a war the First Sea Lord would be in control. In recording this, Moran said that 'Franks interjected in his cool way that it was an issue which only counted on paper'.[47] But Churchill would not accept this. Leslie Rowan, head of the Overseas Finance Department of the Treasury and former Economic Minister at the Washington Embassy, was moved by this to observe:

> Winston could no longer see things in perspective ... One day he was ready to fight to the last ditch to get his way about the Atlantic Command – it seemed to him that national prestige was at stake – the next day he did not appear to care what four hundred million Chinese thought of England.[48]

This issue resurfaced in the second formal meeting at 5 p.m. on the 7th. The Prime Minister said he was not convinced of the necessity of a Supreme Command in the Atlantic. He preferred to see matters settled between the United States Chief of Naval Operations and the First Sea Lord with differences being referred to a NATO standing group. The Americans could not accept this, feeling the issue had already been decided. In what the American record called a 'heated discussion', Churchill asked that the British side be allowed to consider the issue further. It was agreed to defer the question for further consideration.[49] The meeting also covered atomic energy. Truman said that the political–military discussions had already considered situations that might or might not lead to general war and the consequent use of atomic weapons. But he explained that there were limits under existing law as to how far the military talks could go. In response to Churchill's desire for the fullest possible co-operation, it was agreed that Makins and Cherwell should discuss matters with the Atomic Energy Commission and others.[50] They obtained little further technical data from the Americans, but Churchill was told, on the 18th, about the US war plan and this was followed up by a series of briefings for the British military later in the year.[51]

There were two further formal meetings on the 8th. At 11 a.m. the co-ordination of policies in the Middle East was examined and the current military position in Korea was outlined. At 5.30 p.m. the raw materials problems were scrutinised, progress on a European army was considered, and it was agreed that the British and American deputies should pursue the agreed proposals for NATO reform with the other deputies.[52] The next day a communiqué was issued jointly by Truman and Churchill. It suggested a harmony of outlook on EDC, the Middle East and Far East, and on the future organisation of NATO. Moreover, it repeated the formula agreed by Franks in October 1951 on the use of US bases in Britain: it would be 'a matter for joint decision by His Majesty's Government and the United States Government in the light of the circumstances prevailing at the time'.[53] The American calculation of October had proved accurate: Churchill had sought, but the Attlee agreement had thwarted, a more expansive formula.

It seems probable that Churchill's departure on 9 January, not returning until the 16th, and Eden's move to New York on the 10th were both influenced by Franks. The Ambassador told Moran:

> He does not want the PM to outstay his welcome in Washington; while he is here Truman and Dean Acheson would have him on their minds. The Ambassador had seen signs that he might stop on. He ought to get away by the 19th. If he wants to stay longer it must be in New York – not Washington.[54]

This astute advice led Moran to record his assessment of Franks:

> Franks is unlike anyone here. For one thing he does not seem tired. The clarity of his pronouncements reminds one that he is a scholar … He is too, an exile, only waiting for his release to return to Oxford, so that no man is his master – and he thinks for himself. As the PM's host, he is at once firm and polite.[55]

If the main subject of difficulty for the Prime Minister involved the Atlantic Command, the main concern for Eden, after the exchanges over Iran, was the question of Japan's relations with China. This was discussed by the Foreign Secretary and Franks with Acheson and Dulles on 10 January. Dulles explained that the Americans had received a communication from the Japanese Prime Minister, Yoshida, stating the intentions of the Japanese government and that it would probably be necessary to use the communication during the Senate's consideration of the Peace Treaty with Japan. Eden felt that the course of action the Americans proposed was not wise. He believed it would have been better if nothing had been done or said until after the coming into effect of the multilateral treaty.[56] Acheson said that Yoshida would ask about the result of the conversation. He hoped that Sir Esler Dening, Ambassador-designate to Japan, would be instructed to say that the British did not disagree if the Japanese wanted to open talks with Taiwan on the lines recently discussed by Dulles in Tokyo. Eden outlined the likely instructions to Dening: the British government would have preferred no commitments until Japan regained full sovereignty; there was agreement to disagree between Britain and the US.[57] Acheson might legitimately have thought, therefore, that Eden was saying we still disagree but go ahead.

Eden returned to London on 15 January and the Yoshida letter was published on the 16th, declaring the intention of the Japanese to pursue an agreement with Taiwan.[58] The Foreign Secretary was distressed by this, believing that Acheson should have given a copy of the letter to Franks so that they could have discussed it at the 10 January meeting. He was surprised that no advance notice of the intention to publish was given by the Americans.[59] According to Acheson's memoirs, Franks was shown the Yoshida letter.[60] Perhaps the Ambassador was, therefore, at fault in not drawing this fully to Eden's attention. However, the record of the meeting of the 10th makes clear that the purpose of the letter and its intended use by the Americans were revealed to the Foreign Secretary. Further investigation of the issue by officials and Eden in late January showed that American behaviour had not been as devious as the Foreign Secretary claimed. The British record revealed that the United States had hinted at what was to happen, had referred to the letter and confirmed that Franks had seen a copy. Eden honestly admitted: 'I don't remember this; my fault no doubt.' But he retained his view of Dulles, minuting (on another matter) on 6 February: 'Dulles is so tricky that I wonder whether he may not try to use this, like he did showing the Yoshida letter to H. M. Ambassador + [sic] taking it away again.'[61] What he did have grounds for complaint about was the failure to tell him of the intent to publish and the manner in which it would be done. When Franks saw Acheson on 16 January he was asked to convey his strong regret at what had happened. Acheson was apologetic about the manner in which matters had been handled.[62]

Churchill addressed Congress on 17 January. Although it 'was received with respect, admiration and affection',[63] the speech did not secure an immediately favourable impact. Denis Rickett, head of the British Treasury and Supply Delegation in Washington, felt it 'seemed to lack spontaneity and inspiration'.[64] Yet Franks believed that the address 'built up a fund of trust and goodwill which should stand us in good stead for some time to come'.[65] The visit ended on 18 January with the issue of two joint documents, which Franks helped to draft. A statement on the Atlantic Command extended the British home command to the 100 fathom line. Churchill accepted the appointment of a Supreme Commander, but observed that this did not meet his objections. In a communiqué the United States undertook to supply Britain with a million long tons of steel in 1952, and in return the United Kingdom would provide the Americans with supplies of aluminium and tin.[66]

CONSEQUENCES

Franks summed up the talks in a letter to Eden on 27 January. He began by saying that they left the impression that Britain again had a Foreign Secretary who 'could create and state effectively a policy for Britain which was also a positive contribution to the general policies of the West'. As regards Churchill, he noted that US officials were struck by the 'vigour and mastery with which the Prime Minister put forward the British case'. He thought there had been real progress in the Far East. It was on the Middle East that he was least happy. On Egypt there was mutual understanding but on Iran they had not achieved a reasonable degree of common understanding. His main impression was that the visit would 'ripen into a closer partnership and renewed mutual trust in proportion as in the near future we show ourselves masters of our own economic destiny'. Eden replied that these views coincided closely with his own.[67] Despite certain differences, the talks had realised their principal objective of 'increased understanding and a better atmosphere for the transaction of future business'.[68]

Franks may have been instrumental in the success of the American visit by Churchill and Eden, but his days as Ambassador were numbered. When Eden and Acheson met at the North Atlantic Council in Lisbon in February, designed to settle questions of NATO reorganisation, they agreed that Franks was the best man for the job of Secretary General.[69] After it was realised that the Ambassador had not been consulted, it was decided that Lester Pearson, Canadian Secretary of State for External Relations, should telephone him. Acheson recalled later that Franks was angry about how this was done and said he would not consider the appointment, but, when pressed to do so, the Ambassador said he would think about it. Acheson was told by the Canadian Ambassador, Hume Wrong, that Franks would not accept the post. Although he felt it 'was pretty dangerous' to do so, the US Secretary of State telephoned the British Ambassador hoping to persuade him. Acheson afterwards recalled a conversation in 'Oliver's iciest tones'. When the American said he hesitated to raise the matter again, Franks replied 'Dean, I wholly commend your hesitation.'[70] Acheson told Eden of his deep disappointment that Franks did not accept the offer.[71] The Americans felt that the issue had been bungled. David Bruce, US ambassador in Paris, told the veteran reporter for the *New York Times*, C. L. Sulzberger, that Eden had done a 'sloppy job' – Franks had been offered the post without any official inquiry ahead of time.[72] The Lisbon meeting did at least succeed in its main task. As Shuckburgh, Eden's Private Secretary, attested: 'agreement was reached over the German contribution to Western defence and the relationship of the EDC with NATO'.[73]

The offer of the position of Secretary General to NATO was a clear indication that the ambassadorship of Franks was drawing to a close. The *Observer*, on 2 March noted that Eden had invited him to serve for another term but he had declined for personal reasons.[74] On 27 April, *The Sunday Times* reported that he had agreed to remain until after the Presidential election in November.[75] Franks was wise to decide this, for there were clear signs of difficulties in relations between him and the Foreign Secretary. The furore over the Yoshida letter had not caused Eden to respect the Ambassador, while the handling of the NATO Secretary-Generalship had not endeared the Foreign Secretary to Franks. Moreover, there were everyday irritations in their contacts. On 17 June, the Ambassador reported a meeting with Dulles who said Eisenhower (a candidate in the November presidential election) and he wanted to move to a less restrictive policy on trade with Eastern bloc, particularly in the Far East. It occasioned Eden's waspish minute: 'It is extraordinary + [*sic*] rather unhelpful that Sir Oliver Franks should report this without any explanation or comment.' Franks's reticence had been due to uncertainty about Dulles's relation to Eisenhower and therefore the importance of his utterances, for his anxiety to become Secretary of State had seen Dulles perform a tightrope walk between the rival Republicans, Taft and Eisenhower.[76] This might have been part of a wider pattern of intermittent testiness by Eden. Witness his Private Secretary's remark that he found himself justifying the Foreign Office to the Foreign Secretary, defending startled officials from his all too experienced and well-documented strictures.[77] But knowing that others encountered the same treatment was small comfort and little encouragement to continue as Ambassador.

A further sign of difficulty came on the same day. On the afternoon of 17 June, Franks telephoned Acheson, saying he had received a message from Eden proposing political–military talks on South-East Asia to try and reach bilateral agreement prior to the trilateral meetings in London. Franks acknowledged that the Embassy had raised this on the 16th only to be told that there was not sufficient time. But the Ambassador said that he was directed by Eden to speak personally to Acheson about it and felt compelled to do so. The tenor of his comments in the US record suggests that Franks was unconvinced by his instructions, that he accepted the US position and considered Eden's request as unrealistic.[78]

The Ambassador visited Britain on 22–29 June, a trip which overlapped with Acheson's bilateral and trilateral conversations in London with Eden and Schuman, of 24–28 June.[79] On 25 June, both men received the degree of DCL (Doctor of Civil Law) from Oxford University. Franks came to Britain again on 6 September. When he returned he sent a message to Truman indicating that he was retiring as Ambassador and was planning to leave the United States about the end of November. In addition, he requested that Sir Roger Makins be considered as his successor. On 2 October, Franks received the President's approval of his successor and was told that the Americans would like to release a statement expressing regret at the Ambassador's departure.[80] This was published on 4 October along with the announcement of the end of Franks's mission.[81] He saw Truman to say farewell on 26 November.

On the same day he gave a valedictory address to the National Press Club. He urged his listeners not to be misled about Britain. Three times it had been said it was finished – in 1947, 1949 and 1951 – but each time it had recovered and continued on. He accepted, though, that the British economy was not sufficiently strong to allow his country to play its full part. He then said that the Anglo-American relationship was complementary to the other relationships that each power enjoyed. If the British did not agree with the Americans, he suggested that they not say they were 'false friends'. Britain may have good reasons for its views. He proposed, instead, that they should come and argue with the British.[82] The next day, which was Thanksgiving Day, he gave a radio talk. To the delight of the technicians, it was within about 10 seconds of the time wanted. It was carried twice over the CBS network and its entire text was published in the *San Francisco Chronicle*. Paul Gore-Booth was especially pleased, describing the Press Club speech as 'exactly right, a mixture of reminiscence and political wisdom' and the radio address as 'extremely effective and moving'. The *New York Times* spoke of the Ambassador's 'beautiful and moving farewell'. The *Washington Post* declared that this envoy with a first-rate mind and most agreeable and persuasive personality had left a host of friends. As the Embassy reported, comment on Franks's remarks was very favourable – even in normally unfriendly papers. So Franks's departure passed in what Gore-Booth called a 'blaze of admirable speeches and warm and friendly editorials'.[83]

If he made his farewells amid a glow of high regard, his mission ended with an episode of rather sharp personal animosity. It occurred in New York away from his (possibly soothing) influence. Franks characteristically hit the right note in seeking to lessen any consequent tension. Difficulties arose from British support for an Indian resolution on repatriation of Chinese and North Korean prisoners of war. Acheson felt it did not sufficiently stress that the repatriation would be voluntary, even though President-elect Eisenhower agreed with the British position. On 19 November Eden and Selwyn Lloyd, Minister of State, were subjected for over an hour to a harangue by Acheson, suggesting that they had not dealt honourably with the United States. Franks wisely commented: 'Dean Acheson's state of mind was largely occasioned by the intolerable situation of being and having to act as Secretary of State when he has no real power and position.'[84]

Perhaps this incident explains why the British journalist, Henry Brandon, has suggested that Franks left on an 'angry, disappointed note'. His diary recorded the Ambassador as saying, shortly before leaving:

> The American mistake is that they are trying all the time to impose their way of doing things on the Europeans … They have acquired a habit of putting on all the pressures whenever the Europeans do not follow … Americans behave in Europe as if it belonged to them.[85]

On reading these words much later, Franks commented that he did not leave the United States in such a mood – one had to keep talking.[86] It seems probable that Brandon did not capture the Ambassador's state of mind quite correctly. The identification of American pressure appears to be accurate, for Franks had spoken of the United States' imperialist tendencies in a letter of December 1949.[87] However, the sense of disappointment, anger and demoralisation were not characteristic of the man. This was at odds with the theme running through his time in Washington – a belief that problems, however difficult, could be solved.

NOTES

1. A. Eden, *The Memoirs of Sir Anthony Eden: Full Circle* (London: Cassell, 1960), p. 247.
2. Lord Moran, *Winston Churchill: The Struggle for Survival 1940–1965*, p. 559 (24 June 1954 entry).
3. E. Shuckburgh, *Descent to Suez: Diaries, 1951–56* (London: Weidenfeld & Nicolson, 1986), p. 28 (16 December 1951 entry).
4. Gore-Booth, *With Great Truth and Respect*, p. 187.
5. Shuckburgh, *Descent to Suez*, p. 14: 'We used to carry with us a black tin box containing various forms of analgesic supplied by his doctor.'
6. Bodleian Library, Oxford, Gore-Booth Papers, Ms.Eng.c.4518, M. Hamilton to P. Gore-Booth, 7 November 1951.
7. Victor Rothwell, *Anthony Eden: A Political Biography, 1931–1957* (Manchester: Manchester University Press, 1992), p. 107; Shuckburgh, *Descent to Suez*, pp. 35, 56 and 73 for examples of irritability.
8. Eden, *Full Circle*, p. 21.
9. Acheson, *Present at the Creation*, p. 578.
10. Eden, *Full Circle*, p. 21.
11. Ibid., p. 200.
12. *Daily Herald*, 30 October 1951.
13. *Manchester Guardian*, 31 October 1951.
14. Interview with Lord Franks, 24 May 1990.
15. Robert Holland, *The Pursuit of Greatness: Britain and the World Role, 1900–1970* (London: HarperCollins, 1991), pp. 268–9.
16. Rothwell, *Eden*, p. 116.
17. David Dutton, *Anthony Eden: a Life and a Reputation* (London: Arnold, 1997), pp. 322–3. The State Department's Psychological Strategy Board noted that the election of the Conservatives 'has strengthened the nostalgia for the time when Britain was a global power, and hypersensitivity to playing the role of junior partner manifests itself in reflections on American inexperience'. See FRUS, 1952–54, I, p. 1486; quoted in Peter Boyle, 'The "Special Relationship" with Washington', in John W. Young (ed.), *The Foreign Policy of Churchill's Peacetime Administration, 1951–1955* (Leicester: Leicester University Press, 1988), p. 37.
18. PRO, FO 371/90937, AU1059/lG and 2G, Franks to FO, Tel No's 3517 and 3524, 5 and 6 November 1951; ibid., AU1059/3G, FO to Washington, Tel. No. 5551, 9 November 1951, and Franks to FO, Tel. No. 3567, 10 November 1951; see also FRUS, 1952–54, VI, Part 1, No's 311–13, pp. 693–5.
19. PRO, FO 800/835, US/51/33, FO to Washington, Tel. No. 5984, 10 December 1951.
20. PRO, FO 371/90937, AU1059/9G contains seven telegrams, 4–17 December 1951, on these topics.
21. PRO, FO 371/90938, AU1059/41G, minute by Makins, 29 November 1951.
22. Ibid., Makins, 'Objectives in the Washington Talks', 29 November 1951.
23. PRO, FO 371/90932, AU1054/52, Cecil, 'The Present State of Anglo-American Relations', 8 December 1951.

24. Plowden, *An Industrialist*, pp. 138–9.
25. PRO, FO 371/90920, AU1021/22, Minute by R Cecil, 13 December 1951.
26. L of C, Harriman Papers, container 342, memorandum for the President, 3rd Draft 12/27 (presumably 27 December 1951).
27. PRO, FO 800/835, US/51/19, FO to Washington, Tel. No. 5721, 21 November 1951.
28. Ibid., US/51/25, Franks to FO, Tel. No. 3687, 23 November 1951.
29. PRO, FO 371/90938, AU1059/43G, FO to Washington, Tel. No. 6247, 23 December 1951.
30. FRUS, 1951, IV, Part 1, No. 453, pp. 980–1, Policy Planning Staff Paper, 20 November 1951.
31. Ibid., No. 454, p. 986, record of a State–Joint Chiefs of Staff Meeting, 21 November 1951.
32. HSTL, Truman Papers, PSF, General File, Box 115, Churchill 1951–53 folder, 'Brief Notes on Questions Prime Minister Churchill Might Raise', no date, no author identified. See also Ibid., Box 116, Churchill–Truman meetings–papers prepared for US–UK relations. Britain had successfully exploded an atomic device in September.
33. On the voyage and arrival see Shuckburgh, *Descent to Suez*, pp. 30–2 (29 December 1951 and 5 January 1952 entries).
34. Cairncross (ed.), *Hall Diaries 1947–1953*, p. 192 (5 January 1952).
35. Ibid., p. 190 (3 January 1952 entry).
36. PRO, FO 371/97588, AU1021/1, Franks to FO, Tel. No. 15(S), 4 January 1952; ibid., AU1021/3, Reports Division, Washington Embassy to FO, 5 January 1952.
37. On these meetings see Alan P. Dobson, 'Informally Special? The Churchill-Truman talks of January 1952 and the state of Anglo–American Relations', *Review of International Studies*, Vol. 23, No. 1, January 1997, pp. 27–47; and John W. Young, *Winston Churchill's Last Campaign: Britain and the Cold War, 1951–1955* (Oxford: Clarendon Press, 1996), pp. 67–87.
38. FRUS, 1952–54, VI, Part 1, No 329, p. 731, memorandum of a dinner meeting by Acheson, 5 January 1952.
39. Ibid., pp. 730–39 for record of meeting; see also ibid., No. 330, pp. 740–3 for Bradley's record, 5 January 1952.
40. Moran, *Churchill*, p. 355 (5 January 1952 entry).
41. Acheson, *Present at the Creation*, p. 600.
42. FRUS, 1952–54, VI, Part 1, No. 332, pp. 745–6, memorandum of a dinner meeting by Acheson, 6 January 1952.
43. *Princeton Seminars*, roll 3, frame 1133, 13 December 1953.
44. Ibid., frame 1134, 13 December 1953.
45. PRO, FO 800/836, US/52/4 for British record; FRUS, 1952–54, VI, Part 1, No. 333, pp. 746–55 for US record.
46. Cairncross (ed.), *Hall Diaries* 1947–1953, pp. 193–95 (8 January 1952 entry).
47. Moran, *Churchill*, p. 356 (7 January 1952 entry).
48. Ibid., p. 357.
49. FRUS, 1952–54, VI, Part 1, No. 338, pp. 770–773, US Minutes of 2nd Formal Meeting, 7 January 1952, 5–7 p.m.; see PRO, FO 800/836, US/52/7 for British records.
50. FRUS, 1952–54, VI, Part 1, No. 337, pp. 763–6, US minutes of 2nd Formal Meeting, 7 January 1952, 5–5.45 p.m.
51. Young, *Churchill's Last Campaign*, p. 80.
52. FRUS, 1952–54, VI, Part 1, No. 340, pp. 774–86 (11 a.m.) and No. 344, pp. 794–802 (5.30 p.m.); PRO, FO 800/836, US/52/9 (11 a.m.) and US/52/10 (marked as 5 p.m. in the record).

53. FRUS, 1952–54, VI, Part 1, No. 353, pp. 837–9.
54. Moran, *Churchill*, p. 358 (8 January 1952 entry).
55. Ibid.
56. PRO, FO 800/781, FE/52/5, conversation between Eden and Acheson, 10 January 1952.
57. PRO, FO 371/99403, FJ10310/4, Franks to FO, Tel. No. 107, 10 January 1952.
58. See Acheson, *Present at the Creation*, p. 759 for text of letter.
59. PRO, FO 371/99403, FJ10310/8, FO to Washington, Tel. No. 313, 16 January 1952.
60. Acheson, *Present at the Creation*, p. 604.
61. PRO, FO 371/99404, FJ10310/42 and 43.
62. PRO, FO 371/99403, FJ10310/10, Franks to FO, Tel. No. 186, 16 January 1952; HSTL, Acheson Papers, Box 67, memorandum of conversation, 16 January 1952.
63. PRO, FO 371/97580, AU1013/4, Washington to FO, Tel. No. 74(S), 19 January 1952.
64. Martin Gilbert, *'Never Despair': Winston S. Churchill, 1945–1965* (London: Heinemann, 1988), p. 691.
65. PRO, FO 371/97593, AU1051/31, Franks to Eden, 27 January 1952.
66. FRUS, 1952–54, VI, Part 1, Nos 359 and 360, pp. 857–9.
67. PRO, FO 371/97593, AU1051/31, Franks to Eden, 27 January 1952, and Eden to Franks, 6 February 1952.
68. PRO, FO 371/97588, AU1021/6, minute by Robert Cecil, 23 January 1952.
69. FRUS, 1952–54, V, Part 1, p. 155, Acheson–Eden Dinner Meeting, 24 February 1952.
70. *Princeton Seminars*, roll 4, frames 1366–1369, 14 February 1954; HSTL, Acheson Papers, Box 67, memorandum of telephone conversation with Ambassador Wrong and Ambassador Franks, 27 February 1952. In recalling this many years later he conveyed the same irritation. Interview with Lord Franks, 24 May 1990. In a letter of 4 March Franks offered sympathy to Eden over his bout of 'flu, saying he had suffered similarly about two weeks earlier. Given the rarity of letters from the Ambassador, Franks was perhaps sending a message about the handling of this matter. See Birmingham University Library, Avon Papers, AP 20/44/33.
71. FRUS, 1952–54, V, Part 1, p. 294, Acheson to Eden, 7 March 1952.
72. C.L. Sulzberger, A *Long Row of Candles: Memoirs and Diaries, 1934–1954*, (New York: Macmillan, 1969), p. 730.
73. Shuckburgh, *Descent to Suez*, p. 35.
74. *Observer*, 2 March 1952; cited in A. Seldon, *Churchill's Indian Summer, 1951–55* (London: Hodder, 1981), p. 387.
75. *The Sunday Times*, 27 April 1952.
76. PRO, FO 371/97590, AU1023/21, Franks to FO, 17 June 1952 and miscellaneous minutes; ibid., AU1023/23, Franks to R. Makins, 9 July 1952.
77. Shuckburgh, *Descent to Suez*, p. 12.
78. NA, Wash. DC, RG 59, State Department Central Decimal Files, 1950–54, 790.00/6–1752, Memorandum by Secretary of State, 17 June 1952.
79. FRUS 1952–54, VI, Part 1, p. 870, editorial note. There were also seven meetings with British officials.
80. NA, Wash. DC, RG 59, State Department Decimal Files 1950–54, Box 2594, 601.4111/9–3052 and 601.4111/10–252.
81. *New York Times*, 4 October 1952.
82. Library of Congress, audio-tape No. 5552, Franks's speech to National Press Club, 26 November 1952; printed copy in Gore-Booth Papers, Ms.Eng.c.4551.

83. Bodleian Library, Oxford, Gore-Booth Papers, Ms.Eng.c.4518, P. Gore-Booth to J. Boyd, 3 December 1052; PRO, FO 371/97581, AU1013/54, Washington to FO, Tel. No. 2041(S), 6 December 1952; FO 371/97646, AU1892/2, Washington to FO, No. 2060, 10 December 1952.
84. Churchill College, Cambridge, Selwyn Lloyd Papers, SELO 4/28, Diary, 13 and 19 November 1952; Shuckburgh, *Descent to Suez*, pp. 53–4; Henry Pelling, *Churchill's Peacetime Ministry, 1951–55* (London: Macmillan, 1997), pp. 49–50; D. R. Thorpe, *Selwyn Lloyd* (London: Jonathan Cape, 1989), p. 167.
85. H. Brandon, *The Retreat of American Power*, (London: Bodley Head, 1973), pp. 159–60.
86. Interview with Lord Franks, 24 May 1990.
87. See p. 143.

Epilogue: End of a Mission

FRANKS'S ADMINISTRATION of the British Embassy in Washington was characterised by exacting standards but no sharp tone in the Eden manner. The Ambassador's presence and intellect were daunting for many diplomats. For Adam Watson he was 'an inspiring role model: wonderfully lucid and perceptive, clear in his instructions to me and to others, but lacking in personal warmth'.[1] Nicholas Henderson recalls one of the frequent visits the Ambassador made to talk to members of different branches of the mission:

> He would often in the afternoon in the embassy, leave his office and stroll along the corridor to mine, where he would sit, stretching out his legs, and, puffing at his pipe, tell me that he was relaxing. It was essential, he explained, to set aside periods of rest during the day.

Henderson noted that such was the tension within himself that he could say nothing.[2]

The Ambassador was very accessible when needed. Normal correspondence on publicity was with Mrs Hamilton, on high policy with Christopher Warner. There were no routine meetings of Embassy staff, but there were fortnightly meetings where each of the senior staff gave a talk on their activities.[3] The Embassy was an efficient machine that operated largely without Franks's direct intervention. He later observed:

> I did not need to alter it much. I might have words about, say, the telegrams the counsellor for Far Eastern affairs was sending up. I was more like a political minister of a department while the PUS ran the machine ... I concentrated on what really involved the basic Anglo-American relationship.[4]

It was the normal practice, as a matter of courtesy, for any new appointments to the Embassy to be sent to the Ambassador for formal approval. In Washington this was handled by successive Ministers – Jock Balfour, Derick Hoyer Millar and Christopher Steel – and senior Counsellors – Denis Allen and Bernard Burrows.[5] Franks was happy to allow the regular, everyday activities of the mission to be conducted by the various area and subject specialists. The more senior figures – Minister and Counsellor – became involved as the issues became more important and when protocol required that an official of comparable rank met his American counterpart. The Ambassador concentrated on certain topics which touched the fundamental relationship, such as NATO, devaluation, Korea, burden-sharing, the Japanese Treaty; when an important decision was needed; and when there were talks at the highest level. On the most important features of such matters Franks would draft letters, despatches and telegrams; on others he would let his staff prepare drafts. But, when he did not draft a despatch, he always gave careful instructions over its drafting.[6]

So the success of the Embassy owed a great deal to the work of its staff at all levels and to the trust placed in them by Franks. Different parts of the mission became prominent as issues demanded. So the financial experts made significant contributions during the negotiation of the ERP bilaterals and during the devaluation, while the military were involved over the Korean War. The military were a special case, since there existed a separate mission, the BJSM, which was theoretically subordinate to the Embassy but largely autonomous in practice. Most military matters were channelled through this agency. Much like the various sections of the Embassy, it operated independently until a major issue arose. Then the Ambassador and the head of the BJSM would work together – as they did in the political–military talks initiated by the outbreak of the Korean War. There was also the traditional military attaché at the Embassy. One attaché described his job as being partly the Ambassador's military representative, meeting people and seeing manoeuvres and partly a public relations officer. The most important function, he maintained, was executed outside Washington when, as the Ambassador's representative, he visited areas which had never seen a British officer and knew little of Britain and the British.[7]

Sometimes someone could provide valuable insights outside his normal area of competence. Thus, the agricultural attaché was praised for his report on the American people. Franks sent it to London, saying that he found its comments of real interest. London agreed, feeling that its point about the American desire for conformity was rather better made than Franks's own reflections on fascism, which had been forwarded two months earlier.[8]

A great deal of his time as Ambassador was just reacting to one thing after another. From time to time he went away to think in his house and tried to devise a new line. He would lock the door and take the telephone off the hook. It was, he noted, difficult to get time to think. He locked himself away for two hours so as to be able to write the letter to Attlee on sending ground troops to Korea.[9]

The Ambassador benefited also from links with the Commonwealth Embassies, with whose Ambassadors he held fortnightly meetings. Franks described these as being between formal and informal: 'It was friendly talk with common purposes. No minutes were kept; it was not institutionalised. I reported back to the Foreign Office any clear conclusions we reached.'[10] The Canadians were easily the most important among the Commonwealth colleagues. Hume Wrong was the Canadian Ambassador throughout Franks's time and he regarded him as 'by a head and shoulders the most interesting of the ambassadors', while the 'Canadian Foreign Service was the best there was at the time'. In two different ways the Canadians were particularly useful to Franks and the Washington Embassy. In the first place, 'they could talk back to the Americans in a way others could not. They could say of an American stance, "that's silly". It was not diplomatic language, it was [that] of first cousins who were arguing.'[11] Secondly, they were valuable sources of information. For example, George Ignatieff told them about his Embassy's conversations with the Americans about the possible use of nuclear weapons against the Soviet Union. They mainly covered Korea and whether the Soviet Union would become involved, if there was an extension of action against communist China. In essence, the Americans thought they could bomb airfields in Manchuria so long as their action was not seen as a real threat to Mao's China. British diplomats were reassured about this. They did not disclose their knowledge of this in subsequent talks with the Americans.[12]

Embassy ties went beyond the administration and other missions. The aim was to keep in touch with opinion and feelings in politics generally and among the American public. For six nights a week from September to May there were dinners in or out. Embassy gatherings were of two main types: the large-scale reception and the smaller dinner party. Invitations to the former were regarded as bestowing on their recipients considerable social cachet. Witness the account of the impending visit of Princess Elizabeth in October 1951. 'If you were tapped for the party, it showed you had passed the final exam. If you weren't, you were just a social bum.' The 'dickering for invitations was earnest to the point of frenzy'. This time the Ambassador showed more common sense than did Sir Ronald Lindsay for the previous royal visit in 1939. Lindsay was spirited away, lest he be set upon by the wives of Congressmen who did not receive invitations. But Franks 'is a mighty sage character': he invited the wives.[13]

In addition, there were endless talks with journalists and others. Since the first law of a journalist, if he gets a scoop, is to publish come what may, there was trust of them up to a point. James Reston and Arthur Krock, both of the *New York Times,* came to talk to the Ambassador. He would give a general impression to Reston who would then tell Franks what he had garnered from other ambassadors. Franks often dined with Joseph Alsop and Assistant Secretaries of State and the odd Senator. There would be a party of perhaps 16. After dinner there would be a free-for-all discussion. Franks accepted this as part of the Ambassador's job in the United States. His predecessor, Lord Inverchapel, did not take to these conversations. As they only happened in the United States, traditional diplomats did not care for them. Aubrey Morgan advised Franks on how to cope with them.[14]

Franks sought to meet people outside Washington too. He toured the country, so that by the end of his term he had visited all 48 states (as there were at that time). This was partly to carry out what he had been enjoined to do at the time of his departure in 1948. Franks recalled, that 'I was to be Ambassador to the United States and not just to the US state was impressed on me. I think it was by Lord Halifax.'[15] This could involve quite a heavy schedule. In a letter to his parents in 1949 he noted of a trip to Princeton: 'It was very pleasant, except that yesterday we were not alone from 9.30 to 8.30 for a moment but always talking to, or being talked to, by people.'[16] In one week in May 1950 he visited five cities, delivered nine speeches, toured various municipal buildings and gave two press conferences.[17] There was a general programme of visits which sought to re-enforce Anglo-American harmony and assuage any doubts. Often, a pre-arranged trip would be used to press home a British message. In addition, there were talks that were specially arranged to deal with particular periods of difficulty, such as over China in 1951. At times of deepest concern articles were written under Franks's name – such as in *Look* in May 1951 and in *Saturday Review of Literature* in October 1951. Sometimes the British inspired articles. Paul Bareau, the respected financial journalist, was persuaded by the Foreign Office, on prompting from Paul Gore-Booth of BIS, to write a column in the *New York World Telegraph* defending British trade with China and the Soviet Union.[18]

The purpose of all this was to ensure a healthy and vibrant and close association between the two powers. Franks encapsulated the position at the ceremony commemorating the statue of Field Marshal Dill, chairman of the BJSM 1940–44. The relationship could not be taken for granted. It had to be continually made afresh; they had to argue their sides.[19] This was a recurrent theme throughout his embassy: recognition of differences was allied to optimism about the prospects of solving them, if approached with sincerity.

NOTES

1. Adam Watson, *Times Literary Supplement*, 24 December 1993, p. 22.
2. Sir Nicholas Henderson, 'Lord Franks: An Appreciation', *The Times*, 5 November 1992, p. 19.
3. Bodleian Library, Oxford, Gore-Booth Papers, Ms.Eng.c.4517, 'Note of a Talk with Mr Edwards', n.d. [probably August–October 1949].
4. Interview with Lord Franks, 24 May 1990.
5. Greenhill, *More by Accident*, p. 72.
6. Interview with Lord Greenhill, 24 February 1994, cited in Antonia Balazs, 'Oliver Franks' Washington Embassy: A Study in Anglo-American Relations' (University of Oxford M. Litt., 1994), p. 9.
7. PRO, FO 371/81718, AU1201/1, Franks to Bevin, enclosing Report of Military Attaché (J. C. Windsor Lewis), 23 March 1950.
8. PRO, FO 371/81616, AU1016/36, Franks to Wright, enclosing Report by Agricultural Attaché (Duckham), 21 September 1950.
9. Interview with Lord Franks, 24 May 1990.
10. Ibid.
11. Ibid.
12. PRO, FO 371/ 99218, F10345/9, minute by C. W. Harrison, 7 April 1952 on US–Canada meeting of 29 February.
13. Jack Wilson, 'The British are Coming – Grab your Pearls, Girls and Hike to the Embassy', *Look*, 23 October 1951, p. 156.
14. Interview with Lord Franks, 24 May 1990.
15. Ibid.
16. Franks to parents, 7 May 1949 (Franks Papers, Worcester College, Oxford); quoted in Danchev, *Franks*, p. 112.
17. Franks to parents, 6 May 1950 (Franks Papers, Worcester College, Oxford); cited in Balazs, *Franks' Embassy*, p. 49.
18. PRO, FO 371/90955, AU1122/1, Washington (Gore-Booth) to M. A. Hamilton, 21 February 1950; *New York World Telegraph*, 6 March 1950.
19. HSTL, Truman Papers, OF 48, Box 215, Franks's remarks, 1 November 1950.

Conclusion

'The process of putting a general idea, or set of ideas, to the Americans is a lengthy one and success depends often on reiteration and very largely on the respect felt for the person putting the ideas across.'

Sir Oliver Franks to Sir William Strang, April 1952

IN DIPLOMATIC theory ambassadors are essentially channels of communication, and only occasionally do they manage to achieve influence. In practice, however, they can have a considerable impact. Sir Oliver Franks had the responsibility of representing the policies and interests of Britain to the Americans, and reporting the policies and opinions of the United States in circumstances that were particularly propitious for the Anglo-American relationship, for the institutional contribution of the Embassy and for his personal role.

The special relationship had emerged from the pursuit of the common goals of defeating Nazi Germany, Mussolini's Italy and Imperial Japan. It was revived by the emergence of another common enemy in Soviet Russia. The consequent cold war alliance was a product not only of a shared geopolitical and ideological concern for the expansion of communism, but also of the individual interests of the two powers. Britain was the United States' only possible major ally with the required world-wide territories, garrisons and armed forces; with global trading and financial interests; and with the reliability as a political and military partner. Britain's support was needed if Truman's foreign policy was to enjoy the domestic backing that was essential to its success. British backing for the United States in the United Nations was also important, because they could influence certain members. For the British a close association with the United States was vital to the task of remaining a great power. As a partner Britain would have access to the top table in international politics. Yet, just as during the Second World War, there were differences between the two countries on issues not immediately concerned with the common enemy. The British government was therefore keen to stress the cold war to help secure American assistance. When, in 1951, there appeared some prospect of a lessening of Soviet-US tension, Sir Roger Makins explained how this would be to the disadvantage of the British who might now lose the American help against the threat from the Soviet Union.[1] But British policy contained the paradox of wanting to downplay the cold war on other issues: it discounted the communist threat in Iran and suggested that the cold war should not deter them from recognising communist China.

If for much of the Second World War London had competed in a losing battle with Washington as the major centre of the alliance, by the onset of the cold war the main hub of activity had unquestionably moved to the US capital. The British Embassy in Washington thus had the potential to be at the heart of a vital relationship. Whether that was realised depended upon the quality of the Ambassador and his relations with the senior figures in the British and US governments. The wartime Embassy had played an enormous role. But the Ambassador, Lord Halifax, had been little more than a supervisor and figurehead. Contacts between Churchill and Roosevelt and between British and US agencies enjoyed a life autonomous of the Embassy. When Lord Inverchapel succeeded Halifax as Ambassador in 1946 most normal diplomatic practices were restored. Both Attlee and Bevin for Britain and Truman for the United States were willing to allow a greater role for the Embassy. But Inverchapel was not able to take advantage of the opportunity, due to limitations of talent and temperament and to his unimpressive personal relations with senior politicians and officials on both sides of the Atlantic. Given his low opinion of Truman, it is hardly surprising that he failed to establish any real rapport with the US administration.

It was only with the arrival of Franks in May 1948 that the British Ambassador to the United States utilised the renewed relationship in the cold war and the centrality of Washington in world affairs to seize the opportunity to make a pivotal contribution. Alastair Buchan has pointed out that the US Ambassadors in London John Winant (1941–46), Averell Harriman (1946), and Lewis Douglas (1947–50) were nearly as important links in the chain of diplomatic interchange as Lothian (1939–41), Halifax and Inverchapel, their counterparts in Washington. It was only with Franks that Washington became unambiguously 'the place where serious business must be transacted'.[2] Franks possessed the intellect and temperament to do well and he enjoyed very good ties with the most important individuals in Britain and the United States.

Diplomats who are trusted can have influence in shaping aspects of policy. The giving of such trust depends upon the relations between envoy and minister. In this Franks was most fortunate. He enjoyed very good relations with Attlee and Bevin, both of whom greatly valued his judgement, as did Cripps and Gaitskell. They shared a common outlook and view about tactics. Even when they disagreed, they never abandoned complete confidence in one another. But with Bevin's departure in March 1951 there ended his most effective relationship with London. With Morrison relations were less intimate and less effective. Mutual respect was established between the Ambassador and Eden, but they were never close. The new Foreign Secretary seemed, at times, somewhat taut in his dealings with Franks. The debacle over the NATO Secretary-Generalship was, in some ways, an epitome of their relations. Churchill was too much of an individual to be swayed by the Ambassador, too confident of his own ability to read American opinion and feelings and too sure of his own schemes to give particular weight to Franks's advice. So the last year of the ambassadorship saw Franks reporting to the Americans on the basis of a less intimate appreciation of the thinking of his government.

With the Americans he enjoyed excellent relations. He and Truman had considerable mutual respect, if at a distance, since it was only really at the Attlee and Churchill visits that they had a period of regular close contact. The President regarded him as 'a fine diplomat' who had 'a keen mind and a friendly approach to the questions before us'.[3] With Marshall relations were reserved and correct. But with Acheson he had an extraordinary relationship. A great deal of his success was due to their understanding. Their candid, confidential conversations allowed each man to understand the other nation's point of view. With such a bridge it was easier to overcome difficulties. At times they recognised the short-comings of their own government's viewpoint and they devised means of altering each of them to achieve a solution. Close examination of their discussions reveals that they were serious exchanges of view. Each accepted the integrity of the other and the legitimacy of his country's position. They then proceeded to pursue the issues in a vigorous manner. As Franks later noted, they argued to an agreement. He also referred approvingly to Attlee's praise for Bevin, that the Foreign Secretary's greatest asset was standing up to the Americans.

It was not only on policy that Franks made himself valuable to Acheson. The latter described the envoy as a 'great help and comfort to me'.[4] This was particularly important from 1950 onwards when the Secretary of State was subjected to considerable pressure from Congress and the media on his administration of the State Department and in his response to communism. There can be no doubt that Acheson had enormous regard for Franks. When he tried to secure his appointment as Secretary-General of NATO in 1952 he did so, he later explained, because Franks was someone of power and prestige who could talk to governments and not just a civil servant who would always be seeking his instructions.[5] Yet, despite the talk of intimacy of relations which contributed to the efficacy of their collaboration, theirs was essentially a highly productive functional relationship. They shared mutual respect, indeed admiration, and clearly liked one another. But after they left office there was little regular contact. Such correspondence as there was did not show them opening up to each other. Acheson, for all his abundant self-confidence and acerbic wit, was, like so many others, somewhat in awe of Franks. The tentative nature of the telephone call from Lisbon in February 1952 reveals as much.

This personal special relationship between Franks and Acheson gave the Ambassador added opportunity for influence because Acheson enjoyed the President's confidence and because the State Department in these years was pre-eminent in shaping US foreign policy. The Foreign Office recognised at the time that Acheson wielded more influence than his predecessors.[6] Its uniqueness only became clear much later. As James Chace has observed, 'No secretary of state in this century possessed the power Truman granted to Acheson.'[7] Franks had a voice at the very centre of US policy-making.

Given such astonishing access to the inner counsels of the Truman administration, it is hardly surprising that throughout his mission there was no sign from American officials or the press that he was failing in his tasks. In Britain, however, rumours circulated in late 1950 and early 1951, finally appearing in the *Daily Express* in June, suggesting that the Ambassador was not giving British interests sufficient emphasis. Eden has observed that there is an inevitable tendency to be drawn to the viewpoint of one's host nation, if one spends too much time in their company, isolated from the outlook of the home government.[8] Franks recognised this danger. That is why he favoured regular visits to London – not only to gain an appreciation of the substance and tone of opinion in Britain but also because American officials realised that comments made after such visits were more valuable because they were likely to reflect the latest thinking by the British government. Between 1948 and 1950, however, pressure of events made them less frequent than he would have liked.

Franks took maximum advantage of the importance of Anglo-American relations and the potential prominence of the Embassy. He cultivated the opportunity of confidential contact with Acheson. However, such circumstances would only produce valuable results if his performance was properly attuned to the situation. He proved exceptionally adept in accomplishing this. In both raucous and more friendly exchanges he was the interlocutor *par excellence* in the eyes of both governments for most of his term. This was achieved through a shrewd combination: he adopted a general approach which appealed to the politicians and officials and he showed extraordinary ingenuity in steering a path through difficulties.

His general approach was encapsulated in a message to London at a time of friction in December 1949. He recommended that

> an absolutely consistent endeavour should be made to raise questions between us to the level of reasonable discussion. I do not think this will be easy, but we shall have all the assistance here that our friends like Acheson can give.[9]

But being reasonable alone was insufficient. A positive approach would help. He maintained: 'I feel sure that a constructive approach consistently and patiently advocated would yield dividends.'[10] His way of operating took account of American as well as British concerns. As Adam Watson, a junior member of the Embassy, observed:

> Part of his success lay in his ability to serve the 'other side'. He steered discussion and found a formula that met the needs of all parties. He seemed to sherp for the American administration. He was mindful that a successful Anglo-American partnership required that the Americans should get what they wanted.[11]

His success in this endeavour was confirmed by Paul Nitze: 'Everybody valued Oliver. He was much more influential than ... he wasn't representing his country; he was, in effect, doing that but he did it in a way in which he became a US leader.'[12]

Such procedures made the task of handling major issues much easier. But without Franks's organisational skills many matters would not have been dealt with so smoothly. In the negotiations for a North Atlantic Pact, in the talks on devaluation, and during the visits of Attlee and Churchill, Franks ensured that the participants had a sense of purpose. He usually summarised the discussions to help clarify the progress thus far. He also sought to have the British case prepared in advance and to delegate difficult issues to sub-committees, where they were usually tackled in a spirit of co-operation. He preferred to keep meetings small, so that they did not sprawl and, as each individual gave an opinion, the central problems were lost from view. It was not just in their organisation that Franks helped in the conduct of meetings. He seems to have had a quite remarkable talent for creating harmony and a spirit of co-operation. This was recognised by a wide range of observers – from

Douglas Jay in 1949 in the difficult talks on devaluation to General Slim at the Truman–Attlee meetings in December 1950. Various figures during his public life identified him as the best chairman that they had encountered – from Ernst van der Beugel in the1940s to Bryan Gould at Worcester College, Oxford in the 1960s.[13]

If the deployment of these talents ensured that Anglo-American relations were predominantly harmonious, Franks's ambassadorship was, nevertheless, punctuated by numerous instances of difficulty, irritation and downright disagreement. Tensions surfaced over the devaluation of the pound and over Iran. Obstacles emerged in the talks on the Japanese Peace Treaty. Perhaps the period of most acute problems came over the Korean War from November 1950 to January 1951 and the British fear that there might be an escalation to war with China. His last year as Ambassador also saw a squabble over the Yoshida letter and sharp words by Acheson on Korean POWs. In all of these cases Franks helped to ameliorate differences.

Doing justice to his impact on specific issues requires placing his contribution in the context of other influences. It is often difficult to separate various inter-related activities. In the two most important issues to arise during his embassy he played a central role. He was instrumental in promoting a sense of despatch in the talks on a North Atlantic Treaty. His deft pressure led the negotiators to produce a draft pact by December 1948, and he assumed a crucial role in finding an acceptable formula for the contentious article 5. His robust support for US action in Korea echoed his government's viewpoint. He also stressed their concern to detach Taiwan from the conflict and the need to remove any reference to 'centrally directed communist action' from the US-sponsored resolution at the United Nations. He accomplished both these goals. The British commitment of ground forces in Korea owed a great deal to his forceful representation of American thinking.

On devaluation, his reporting of American opinion helped sway the decision to devalue. It was largely on his advice that it was agreed to reveal this to the Americans at the start of talks, an action which pleased the United States and thereby made the devaluation less troublesome. He successfully steered a path through the difficulties in co-ordinating an Anglo-American approach on the Iranian oil crisis. The negotiations on the Japanese Peace Treaty were conducted without his daily involvement. However, he made important interventions and eased misunderstandings at key moments. In particular, he was effective in working with Dulles and in advising London on how to handle talks with him. His talent for finding the appropriate language was utilised in both the October 1951 bases deal and in the January 1952 communiqué on the same issue.

There were two areas where his influence was less effective. He offered wise advice on the Schuman Plan, recognising its likely significance for Franco-German relations, but his opinion was ignored. On rearmament he was too sanguine and he helped persuade ministers against appealing for direct US aid. His reasoning on this issue points to the nature of his general influence. He argued throughout his ambassadorship for close Anglo-American relations and regularly assessed the extent to which Britain was regarded as special or merely part of the European queue in American eyes. He maintained that this could only be achieved if Britain was economically strong and not dependent upon US aid. This was why he favoured British development of the atomic bomb: it would show the scale of British power. This outlook – that Britain could retain great power status – was consonant with the thinking of the senior politicians and officials of the time. This, perhaps, best explains his effectiveness. He presented thoughtful and astute advice on how to secure what ministers wanted. He gave a lecture in 1948 called 'The Quest for Strength'.[14] In a way this was the central theme of British policy in the early postwar years. It could serve as a motto for his ambassadorship.

NOTES

1. PRO, FO 371/90903, AU1013/8, minute by Roger Makins, 14 February 1951.
2. A. Buchan, 'Mothers and Daughters (or Greeks and Romans)', *Foreign Affairs*, Vol. 54, 1976, p. 659; cited in Danchev, *Franks*, p. 116.
3. Harry S. Truman, *Memoirs. Volume II: Years of Trial and Hope, 1946–1952* (New York: New American Library, 1965), pp. 460, 467.
4. Acheson, *Present at the Creation*, p. 324.
5. *Princeton Seminars*, roll 4, frame 1366, 14 February 1954.
6. PRO, FO 371/81615, AU1016/5, minute by J. R. Mackenzie, 16 February 1950.
7. James Chace, *Acheson: The Secretary of State who Created the American World* (New York: Simon & Schuster, 1998), p. 441.
8. Eden, *Full Circle*, p. 249.
9. PRO, FO 371/82937, UEE59/lG, Franks to Strang, 31 December 1949.
10. PRO, FO 371/84120, FK1023/207, Franks to FO, Tel. No. 3232, 30 November 1950.
11. Adam Watson in *Times Literary Supplement*, 24 December 1993, p. 22.
12. Quoted in Peter Hennessy and Caroline Anstey, *Moneybags and Brains* (Glasgow: University of Strathclyde, 1990), p. 34.
13. For van der Beugel see p. 34; Bryan Gould obituary of Franks, the *Guardian*, 17 October 1992, p. 28.
14. Oliver Franks, 'The Quest for Strength', *Proceedings of the Academy of Political Science*, Vol. 23, No. 2, 1948–50, pp. 205–18.

Bibliography

MANUSCRIPT SOURCES

GOVERNMENT PAPERS

Public Record Office, Kew, London

CAB 21	Cabinet Registered Files
CAB 128	Cabinet Minutes
CAB 129	Cabinet Memoranda
CAB130	Cabinet Committees
CAB131	Cabinet Committees
CAB 134	Cabinet Committees
DEFE 4	Chiefs of Staff (COS) Papers
DEFE 31	COS: Secretary's Standard Files
FO 115	Washington Embassy Papers
FO 370	Chief Clerk's Papers
FO 371	General Correspondence
FO 800	Private Office Papers:
	Ernest Bevin
	Herbert Morrison
	Anthony Eden
FO 953	Foreign Publicity Files
PREM 8	Prime Minister's Papers
PREM 11	Prime Minister's Papers
T 236	Treasury: Overseas Finance Division
T 237	Treasury: Overseas Finance Division
T 269	Treasury: Devaluation of the Pound Historical Papers
T 273	Bridges Papers

National Archives, Washington DC

Record Group 56, Treasury, Records of the National Advisory Council on Monetary and Financial Policies:

Briefing Books 1946–1953
Memorandums 1946–1953

Record Group 59, State Department Decimal Files, 1945–49
Record Group 59, State Department Decimal Files, 1950–54
Record Group 59, State Department Decimal Files, State Department Lot Files:
Lot 54 D 224
Lot 54 D 379
Lot 64 D 563
Lot 74 D 170

Brotherton Library, Leeds University

CIA Research Reports Europe 1946–1976 (Frederick, MD: University Publications of America, 1983)

Confidential US State Department Central Files. Great Britain: Foreign Affairs 1945–49 (Frederick, MD: Microfilm Project of University Publications of America, 1985), 10 reels.

Documents of the National Security Council 1947–77 (Washington, DC : Microfilm Project of University Publications of America, 1980), 5 reels.

Official Conversations and Meetings of Dean Acheson 1945–1953 (Frederick, MD: Microfilm Project of University Publications of America, 1980), 5 reels.

The Princeton Seminars, Microfilm made by Truman Library of discussion by Acheson and US government officials on Acheson's time as Secretary of State 1953–54, 4 reels.

Public Archives of Canada, Department of External Affairs, File 283 (s), North Atlantic Security Pact, 69 microfiches.

Records of the Joint Chiefs of Staff, Part 2: 1946–1953. Europe and Nato (Frederick, MD: Microfilm Project of University Publications of America, 1980), 9 reels.

Harry S. Truman Office Files (Frederick, MD: Microfilm Project of University Publications of America, 1989), 84 reels.

British Library of Political and Economic Sciences (London School of Economics and Political Science)

Declassified Documents Reference System (DDRS) (bi-monthly volumes, 1975 onwards)

Private Papers

Britain

Birmingham University Library
Avon Papers

Churchill College, Cambridge
- Cadogan Papers
- Colville Papers
- Selwyn Lloyd Papers
- Strang Papers

Trinity College, Cambridge
- Butler Papers

Liddell Hart Centre for Military Archives, King's College, London
- Ismay Papers
- Elliot Papers

British Library of Political and Economic Sciences, London
- Dalton Diary
- Davies Papers

Bodleian Library, Oxford
- Attlee Papers
- Gore-Booth Papers
- Inverchapel Papers

Lady Younger (courtesy of Professor Geoffrey Warner)
- Kenneth Younger Diary

United States

Seeley G. Mudd Library, Princeton University, Princeton, NJ
- J. F. Dulles Papers
- J. F. Dulles Oral Collection :
  - Lord Franks
  - J. C. Holmes
  - Lord Sherfield
- G. F. Kennan Papers

Harry S. Truman Library [HSTL], Independence, MO
- Acheson Papers
- Elsey Papers
- Springarn Papers
- John W. Snyder Papers
- Truman Papers
  - Official File
  - President's Secretary's File
  - Post Presidential File
- James Webb Papers
- Oral History Interviews:
  - E. Berthoud
  - C. Bohlen
  - D. Marris
  - Lord Franks

H. M. Hirschfeld
P. Hoffman
Sterling Memorial Library, Yale University
Acheson Private Papers
Lippmann Papers
Manuscripts Division, Library of Congress, Washington, DC
W. Averell Harriman Papers
Paul H. Nitze Papers

Printed Original Sources

British Documents on the End of Empire, Series A, Volume 2, Part II, ed. Ronald Hyam (London: HMSO, 1992).

British Documents on the End of Empire, Series A, Volume 3, Part I, ed. David Goldsworthy (London: HMSO, 1994).

Command Papers (Cmd Series) (Selected papers).

Documents on British Policy Overseas, 1st Series, Vols I and III, ed. R. Butler *et al.* (London: HMSO, 1984, 1986).

Documents on British Policy Overseas, 2nd Series, Vols I–IV, ed. R. Bullen *et al.* (London: HMSO, 1986–91).

Documents on Germany Under Occupation, ed. B. R. Von Oppen (London: Oxford University Press for RIIA, 1955).

Documents on International Affairs 1947–1952, 5 vols, various editors (London: Oxford University Press for RIIA, 1952–55).

Foreign Office List and Yearbook, various years.

Foreign Relations of the United States, 1945 to 1952–54, various editors (Washington, DC: US Government Printing Office, 1955–89).

House of Common Debates, 1945–52 (selected columns.).

New York Times 1948–1952.

Royal Institute of International Affairs Newspaper Cuttings Collection, 1948–52.

The Times 1948–52.

Washington Despatches 1941–1946, ed. H. G. Nicholas (London: Weidenfeld & Nicolson, 1981).

Publications by Franks.

The Experience of a University Teacher in the Civil Service (London: Oxford University Press, 1947).

Central Planning and Control in War and Peace (London: London School of Economics and Political Science/Longmans, Green and Co., 1947).

'The Quest for Strength', *Proceedings of the Academy of Political Science*,

Vol. 23, No. 2, 1948–50, pp. 205–18.
'A Declaration of Interdependence', *Saturday Review of Literature*, 13 October 1951.
American Impressions (London: London School of Economics and Political Science, 1954).
The American Outlook in Foreign Affairs (Leeds: University of Leeds, 1954).
Britain and the Tide of World Affairs (London: Oxford University Press, 1955).
'Mr. Truman as President', *The Listener*, Vol. LV, 14 June, 1956, pp. 787–8.
'Britain and Europe' in Stephen R. Graubard (ed.), *A New Europe?* (London: Oldbourne Press, 1964), pp. 89–104.
'Lessons of the Marshall Plan Experience', in OECD, *From Marshall Plan to Global Interdependence* (Paris: OECD, 1978).
'The Anglo–American "Special Relationship", 1948–1952', in W. R. Louis (ed.), *Adventures with Britannia: Personalities, Politics and Culture in Britain* (London: I. B. Taurus, 1995), pp. 51–75.

Books

Abramson, Rudy *Spanning the Century: The Life of Averell Harriman, 1891–1986* (New York: William Morrow & Co, 1992).
Acheson, Dean *Sketches from Life of Men I Have Known* (London: Hamish Hamilton, 1961).
—— *Present at the Creation: My Years in the State Department* (New York: W.W. Norton, 1969).
Aldrich, Richard J. *The Hidden Hand: Britain, America and Cold War Intelligence* (London: John Murray, 2001).
Anderson, Terry H. *The United States, Great Britain and the Cold War* 1944–1947 (Colombia, MO: University of Missouri Press, 1981).
Balfour, John *Not Too Correct an Aureole: The Recollections of a Diplomat* (Salisbury: Michael Russell, 1983).
Barclay, Sir Roderick *Ernest Bevin and the Foreign Office 1932–1969* (London: Privately printed, 1975).
Barker, Elisabeth *The British Between the Superpowers, 1945–1950* (London: Macmillan, 1983).
Bartlett, C. J. *'The Special Relationship': A Political History of Anglo–American Relations since 1945* (London: Longman, 1992).
Baylis, John *Anglo–American Defence Relations 1939–1984: The Special Relationship* (London: Macmillan, 2nd edn, 1984).
Becker, Josef and Franz Knipping (eds) *Power in Europe? Great Britain. France, Italy and Germany in a Postwar World, 1945–1950* (Berlin &

New York: Walter de Gruyter, 1986).

Bell, Coral *The Debatable Alliance: An Essay in Anglo–American Relations* (London: Oxford University Press for RIIA, 1964).

Beloff, Max *New Dimensions in Foreign Policy* (London: Allen & Unwin, 1961).

Best, Richard A., Jr *'Co-operation with Like-Minded People': British Influences on American Security Policy, 1945–1949* (New York: Greenwood Press, 1986).

Bohlen, Charles E. *Witness to History 1929–1969* (New York: W. W. Norton & Co. 1973).

—— *The Retreat of American Power* (London: The Bodley Head, 1973).

Brandon, Henry *Special Relationships: A Foreign Correspondent's Memoirs From Roosevelt to Reagan* (London: Macmillan, 1989).

Brinkley, Douglas (ed.), *Dean Acheson and the Making of US Foreign Policy* (London: Macmillan, 1993).

Bullock, Alan *Ernest Bevin: Foreign Secretary 1945–51* (New York: W. W. Norton & Co., 1983).

Bundy, McGeorge *Danger and Survival: Choices About the Bomb in the First Fifty Years* (New York: Random House, 1988).

—— (ed.) *The Pattern of Responsibility* (Boston, MA: Houghton, Mifflin, 1952).

Byrnes, James *Speaking Frankly* (London: Heinemann, 1947).

Cairncross, Alec *Years of Recovery: British Economic Policy 1945–51* (London: Methuen, 1985).

—— *The British Economy since 1945: Economic Policy and Performance, 1945–1990* (Oxford: Blackwell, 1992).

—— (ed.) *The Robert Hall Diaries 1947–1953* (London: Unwin Hyman, 1989).

Calvocoressi, Peter *Survey of International Affairs 1947–1948* (London: Oxford University Press/RIIA, 1952).

—— *Survey of International Affairs 1949–1950* (London: Oxford University Press/RIIA, 1953).

Campbell, Duncan *The Unsinkable Aircraft Carrier: American Military Power in Britain* (London: Paladin, new edn 1986).

Cecil, Robert *A Divided Life: A Biography of Donald Maclean* (London: The Bodley Head, 1988).

Charlton, Michael *The Price of Victory* (London: BBC, 1983).

Charmley, J. *Churchill's Grand Alliance: The Anglo-American Special Relationship, 1940–1957* (London: Hodder and Stoughton, 1995).

Clarke, Sir Richard *Anglo-American Economic Collaboration in War and Peace 1942–1949*. ed. Alec Cairncross (Oxford: Clarendon Press, 1982).

Clay, Lucius D. *Decision in Germany* (London: Heinemann, 1950).

Cohen, Michael J. *Truman and Israel* (Berkeley, CA: University of California Press, 1990).

Conant, James B. *Anglo-American Relations in the Atomic Age* (London: Oxford University Press, 1962).

Danchev, Alex *Oliver Franks: Founding Father* (Oxford: Clarendon Press, 1993).

Deighton, Anne (ed.) *Britain and the First Cold War* (London: Macmillan, 1990).

Dickie, James *'Special' No More. Anglo-American Relations: Rhetoric and Reality* (London: Weidenfeld & Nicolson, 1994).

Dilks, David (ed.), *The Diaries of Sir Alexander Cadogan, 1938–1945* (London: Cassell, 1971).

Dimbleby, David and David Reynolds *An Ocean Apart: The Relationship between Britain and America in the Twentieth Century* (London: BBC Books/Hodder & Stoughton, 1988).

Dobson, Alan P. *Anglo-American Relations in the Twentieth Century* (London: Routledge, 1995).

Dockrill, Michael *British Defence Since 1945* (Oxford: Blackwell, 1988).

Dockrill, Michael and John W. Young (eds), *British Foreign Policy, 1945–1956* (London: Macmillan, 1989).

Dockrill, Saki *Britain's Policy for West German Rearmament 1950–1955* (Cambridge: Cambridge University Press, 1991).

Donoughue, Bernard and G. W. Jones *Herbert Morrison: Portrait of a Politician* (London: Weidenfeld & Nicolson, 1973).

Duke, Simon *US Defence Bases in the United Kingdom: A Matter for Joint Decision* (London: Macmillan/St Antony's College, Oxford, 1987).

Dutton, David *Anthony Eden: A Life and Reputation* (London: Arnold, 1997).

Eden, Sir Anthony *The Memoirs of Sir Anthony Eden: Full Circle* (London: Cassell, 1960).

Edmonds, Robin *Setting the Mould: The United States and Britain 1945–1950* (Oxford: Clarendon Press, 1986).

Farrar-Hockley, A. *The British Part in the Korean War*. Vol. I, *A Distant Obligation*, Vol. II, *An Honourable Discharge* (London: HMSO, 1990, 1995).

Feis, Herbert *Between War and Peace: The Potsdam Conference* (Princeton, NJ: Princeton University Press, 1960; Oxford: Oxford University Press, 1960).

—— *From Trust to Terror: The Onset of the Cold War 1945–1950* (New York: W. W. Norton & Co., 1970).

Foot, Rosemary *A Substitute for Victory* (Ithaca, NY: Cornell University Press, 1990).

Gaddis, John Lewis *The United States and the Origins of the Cold War 1941–1947* (New York: Columbia University Press, 1972).

—— *Strategies of Containment: A Critical Appraisal of Postwar American National Security Policy* (New York: Oxford University Press, 1982).

—— *The Long Peace: Inquiries into the History of the Cold War* (New York and Oxford: Oxford University Press, 1987).

Gardner, Richard N. *Sterling–Dollar Diplomacy: Anglo-American Collaboration in the Reconstruction of Multilateral Trade* (London: Clarendon Press, 1956).

Gerson, Louis L. *John Foster Dulles* (New York: Cooper Square Publishers, 1967).

Gilbert, Martin *'Never Despair': Winston S. Churchill 1945–1965* (London: Heinemann, 1988).

Gladwyn, Lord *The Memoirs of Lord Gladwyn* (London: Weidenfeld & Nicolson, 1972).

Gore-Booth, P. H. *With Great Truth and Respect* (London: Constable, 1974).

Gowing, Margaret (assisted by Lorna Arnold) *Independence and Deterrence,* Vol. I: *Policy Making;* Vol. II: *Policy* (London: Macmillan, 1974).

Greenhill, Denis *More By Accident* (York: Wilton 65, 1992).

Hamby, Alonzo *Man of the People: A Life of Harry Truman* (New York: Oxford University Press, 1995).

Harriman, W. Averell and Elie Abel *Special Envoy to Churchill and Stalin 1941–1946* (London: Hutchinson, 1976).

Hathaway, Robert, M. *Ambiguous Partnership: Britain and America, 1944–1947* (New York: Columbia University Press, 1981).

—— *Great Britain and the United States Relations Since World War II* (Boston, MA: Twayne, 1990).

Healey, Denis *The Time of My Life* (London: Michael Joseph, 1989).

Henderson, Sir Nicholas *The Birth of Nato* (London: Weidenfeld & Nicolson, 1982).

Hennessy, Peter *Whitehall* (London: Secker & Warburg, 1989).

—— *Never Again: Britain 1945–1951* (London: Vintage, 1993).

—— *The Hidden Wiring: Unearthing the British Constitution* (London: Indigo, 1996).

—— *Muddling Through: Power, Politics and the Quality of Government in Postwar Britain* (London: Gollancz, 1996).

Hewlett, Richard G. and Francis Duncan *History of the United States Atomic Energy Commission, Volume 2: Atomic Shield, 1947–1952* (University Park, PA: Pennsylvania University State Press, 1969).

Hogan, Michael J. *The Marshall Plan: America, Britain and the Reconstruction of Western Europe, 1947–1952* (Cambridge:

Cambridge University Press, 1987).

Immerman, Richard H. *John Foster Dulles and the Diplomacy of the Cold War* (Princeton, NJ: Princeton University Press, 1990).

Isaacson, Walter and Evan Thomas *The Wise Men: Six Friends and the World They Made: Acheson, Bohlen, Harriman, Kennan, Lovett, McCloy* (London & Boston, MA: Faber and Faber, 1986).

James, Robert Rhodes *Anthony Eden* (London: Weidenfeld & Nicolson, 1986).

Kaplan, Lawrence, S. *A Community of Interests: NATO and the Military Assistance Program, 1948–1951* (Washington DC: USGPO, 1980).

—— *The United States and NATO: The Formative Years* (Lexington, KY: University of Virginia Press, 1984).

—— *NATO and the United States: The Enduring Alliance* (Boston, MA: Twayne, 1988).

Kaplan, Lawrence, S. *et al. NATO After Forty Years* (Wilmington, DE: Scholarly Resources, 1990).

Kaplan, Lawrence, S. (ed.) *American Historians and the Atlantic Alliance* (Kent, OH: Kent State University Press, 1991).

Kennan, George F. *Memoirs 1950–1963* (New York: Pantheon Books, 1972).

Lacey, Michael J. (ed.) *The Truman Presidency* (Cambridge: Woodrow Wilson International Center for Scholars and Cambridge University Press, 1989).

Lane, Ann and Howard Temperley (eds) *The Rise and Fall of the Grand Alliance, 1941–1945* (London: Macmillan, 1995).

Lee, Steven *Outposts of Empire: Korea, Vietnam, and the Origins of the Cold War in Asia, 1949–1954* (Toronto: McGill-Queens University Press, 1995).

Leffler, Melvin P. *A Preponderance of Power: National Security, the Truman Administration and the Cold War* (Stanford, CA: University of Stanford Press, 1992).

Leigh-Pippard, Helen *Congress and the US Military Aid to Britain: Interdependence and Dependence, 1945–1956* (London: Macmillan, 1995).

Levantrosser, William F. *Harry S. Truman: The Man from Independence* (New York: Greenwood, 1986).

Louis, William Roger *The British Empire in the Middle East, 1945–1951: Arab Nationalism, the United States and Postwar Imperialism* (Oxford: Clarendon Press, 1984).

Louis, William Roger and Hedley Bull (eds), *The 'Special Relationship': Anglo-American Relations Since 1945* (Oxford: Clarendon Press, 1986).

Lowe, Peter *The Origins of the Korean War* (London: Longman, 1986).

—— *Containing the Cold War in East Asia: British Policies Towards Japan, China and Korea, 1948–1953* (Manchester: Manchester University Press, 1997).

MacColl, Rene *Deadline and Dateline* (London: Oldbourne Press, 1956).

MacDonald, Callum A. *Korea: The War before Vietnam* (London: Macmillan, 1986).

—— *Britain and the Korean War* (Oxford: Blackwell, 1990).

Macdonald, Ian S. *Anglo–American Relations Since the Second World War* (New York: St Martin's, 1974).

McGhee, George *Envoy to the Middle World: Adventures in Diplomacy* (New York: Harper & Row, 1983).

McLellan, David S. *Dean Acheson: The State Department Years* (New York: Dodd, Mead & Co., 1976).

McNeill, W. H. *America, Britain and Russia: Their Cooperation and Conflict, 1941–1946* (Oxford: Oxford University Press/RIIA, 1953).

Mallaby, George *From My Level: Unwritten Minutes* (London: Hutchinson, 1965).

Manderson-Jones, R. B. *The Special Relationship: Anglo-American Relations and Western European Unity 1947–1956* (London: Weidenfeld & Nicolson/LSE, 1972).

Marrett, R. *Through the Back Door* (Oxford and London: Pergamon Press, 1968).

May, Ernest, R. *'Lessons' of the Past: The Use and Misuse of History in American Foreign Policy* (New York: Oxford University Press, 1978).

Millis, Walter (ed.) (with the collaboration of E. S. Duffield) *The Forrestal Diaries* (New York: The Viking Press, 1951).

Milward, Alan S. *The Reconstruction of Western Europe 1945–51* (London: Methuen, 1984).

Miscamble, W. S. *George F. Kennan and the Making of American Foreign Policy, 1947–1950* (Princeton, NJ: Princeton University Press, 1992).

Morgan, Kenneth O. *Labour in Power 1945–1951* (Oxford: Clarendon Press, 1984).

Neustadt, Richard E. *Alliance Politics* (New York: Columbia University Press, 1970).

Nicholas, H. G. *Britain and the United States* (London: Chatto and Windus, 1963).

Nitze, Paul H. (with Ann M. Smith and Steven N. Rearden) *From Hiroshima to Glasnost. At the Centre of Decision: A Memoir* (London: Weidenfeld & Nicolson, 1990).

Northedge, F. S. *Descent from Power: British Foreign Policy 1945–1973* (London: George Allen & Unwin, 1974).

Organisation for Economic Co-operation and Development *From Marshall Plan to Global Interdependence: New Challenges for the*

Industrialized Nations (Paris: OECD, 1978).
Ovendale, Ritchie (ed.) *The Foreign Policy of the British Labour Governments, 1945–1951* (Leicester: Leicester University Press, 1984).
—— *The English-Speaking Alliance: Britain, the United States, the Dominions and the Cold War 1945–1951* (London: George Allen & Unwin, 1985).
Pach, Chester P. *Arming the Free World* (Chapel Hill, NC: University of North Carolina Press, 1991).
Pearson, Lester B. *Memoirs. Volume II 1948–1957. The International Years* (London: Victor Gollancz, 1974).
Pelling, Henry *The Labour Governments 1945–51* (London: Macmillan, 1984).
—— *Britain and the Marshall Plan* (London: Macmillan, 1988).
Pimlott, Ben *The Political Diary of Hugh Dalton, 1918–40, 1945–60* (London: Jonathan Cape/LSE, 1986).
Pimlott, Ben (ed.), *The Second World War Diary of Hugh Dalton, 1940–45* (London: Jonathan Cape/LSE, 1986).
Plowden, Edwin *An Industrialist in the Treasury: The Post-War Years* (London: André Deutsch, 1989).
Pogue, Forrest C. *George C. Marshall: Statesman, 1945–1959* (New York: Penguin, 1989).
Porter, Brian *Britain and the Rise of Communist China: A Study of British Attitudes, 1945–1954* (London: Oxford University Press, 1967).
Reid, Escott *Time of Fear and Hope: The Making of the North Atlantic Treaty 1947–1949* (Toronto: McClelland & Stewart, 1977).
Reid, Escott *Radical Mandarin: The Memoirs of Escott Reid* (Toronto: University of Toronto Press, 1989).
Reston, James *Deadline: A Memoir* (New York: Random House, 1991).
Reynolds, David *The Creation of the Anglo-American Alliance, 1937–1941* (London: Europa, 1981).
—— *Britannia Overruled: British Policy and World Power in the Twentieth Century* (London & New York: Longman, 1991).
Reynolds, David, Warren F. Kimball and A. O. Chubarian (eds) *Allies at War: The Soviet, American, and British Experience, 1939–1945* (New York: St Martin's Press, 1994).
Riste, Olav (ed.), *Western Security: The Formative Years: European and Atlantic Defence, 1947–1953* (Oslo: Norwegian University Press, 1985).
Roberts, Frank *Dealing with Dictators: The Destruction and Revival of Europe, 1930–1970* (London: Weidenfeld & Nicolson, 1991).
Roosevelt, Kermit *Countercoup: The Struggle for the Control of Iran* (New York: McGraw-Hill Book Co., 1979).
Rusk, Dean *As I Saw It* (New York: Penguin, 1991).

Schaller, Michael *The American Occupation of Japan: The Origins of the Cold War in Asia* (New York & Oxford: Oxford University Press, 1985).

Seitz, Raymond, *Over Here* (London: Weidenfeld and Nicolson, 1998).

Seldon, Anthony *Churchill's Indian Summer: The Conservative Government 1951–1955* (London: Hodder & Stoughton, 1981).

Shlaim, Avi *The United States and the Berlin Blockade, 1948–1949: A Study in Crisis Decision-Making* (Berkeley and Los Angeles, CA: University of California Press, 1983).

Shuckburgh, Evelyn *Descent to Suez: Diaries 1951–56* ed. John Charmley (London: Weidenfeld & Nicolson, 1986).

Shulman, Milton *How to Be a Celebrity* (London: Reinhardt & Evans, 1950).

Smith, Bradley F. *The Ultra-Magic Deals and the Most Secret Special Relationship, 1940–1946* (Shrewsbury: Airlife, 1993).

Smith, Gaddis *Dean Acheson* (New York: Cooper Square Publishers, 1972).

Smith, Joseph (ed.) *The Origins of NATO* (Exeter: Exeter University Press, 1990).

Smith, Walter Bedell *Moscow Mission 1946–1949* (London: William Heinemann, 1950).

De Staercke, André (ed. Nicholas Sherwin) *NATO's Anxious Birth: The Prophetic Vision of the 1940s* (New York: St Martin's Press, 1985).

Steiner, Zara (ed.) *The Times Survey of the Foreign Ministries of the World* (London: Times Books, 1982).

Strang, Lord *The Foreign Office* (London: George Allen & Unwin, 1955).

—— *Home and Abroad* (London: André Deutsch, 1956).

—— *The Diplomatic Career* (London: André Deutsch, 1962).

Stueck, William *The Korean War: An International History* (Princeton, NJ: Princeton University Press, 1995).

Sulzberger, C. L. *A Long Row of Candles: Memoirs and Diaries, 1934–1954* (New York: Macmillan, 1969).

Tang, James Tuck-Hong *Britain's Encounter with Revolutionary China, 1948–54* (London and New York: Macmillan/St Martin's Press, 1992).

Thorpe, D. R. *Selwyn Lloyd* (London: Jonathan Cape, 1989).

Truman, Harry S. *Memoirs. Volume I: Year of Decisions, 1945, Volume II: Years of Trial and Hope, 1946–1952* (New York: New American Library, 1965).

Vandenberg, Arthur H. Jr (ed.) *The Private Papers of Senator Vandenberg* (Boston, MA: Houghton Mifflin Co., 1952).

Varsori, Antonio *Europe 1945–1990s: The End of an Era?* (Basingstoke: Macmillan, 1995).

Watt, Donald Cameron *Britain Looks to Germany: British Opinion and Policy Towards Germany Since 1945* (London: Oswald Wolff, 1965).

—— *Succeeding John Bull. America in Britain's Place 1900–1975: A Study of the Anglo-American Relationship and World Politics in the Context of British and American Foreign-policymaking in the Twentieth Century* (Cambridge: Cambridge University Press, 1984).

Wheeler-Bennett, John *Friends, Enemies and Sovereigns* (London: Macmillan, 1976).

Williams, Francis *A Prime Minister Remembers* (London: Heinemann, 1961).

Williams, Philip M. *Hugh Gaitskell* (Oxford: Oxford University Press Paperback, 1982).

Williams, Philip M. (ed.) *The Diary of Hugh Gaitskell 1945–1956* (London: Jonathan Cape, 1983).

Woods, Randall B. and Howard Jones *Dawning of the Cold War: The United States' Quest for Order* (Athens, GA: University of Georgia Press, 1991).

Yergin, Daniel *Shattered Peace. The Origins of the Cold War* (New York: Penguin, new edn, 1990).

Young, John W. *Britain, France and the Unity of Europe 1945–1951* (Leicester: Leicester University Press, 1984).

—— *Winston Churchill's Last Campaign: Britain and the Cold War 1951–1955* (Oxford: Clarendon Press, 1996).

Young, John W. (ed.) *The Foreign Policy of Churchill's Peacetime Administration 1951–1955* (Leicester: Leicester University Press, 1988).

Zametica, John (ed.) *British Officials and British Foreign Policy, 1945–50* (Leicester: Leicester University Press, 1990).

Articles and chapters

Academicus (pseud.), 'Britain Sends a New Kind of Ambassador', *New York Times Magazine*, 2 May 1948.

Acheson, Dean. 'No Yearning To Be Loved – Dean Acheson talks to Kenneth Harris', *Listener*, Vol. 85, No. 2193, 8 April 1971, pp. 442–4.

Adamthwaite, Anthony 'Britain and the World, 1945–9: The View from the Foreign Office', *International Affairs*, Vol. 61, No. 2, Spring 1985, pp. 221–35.

—— 'Overstretched and Overstrung: Eden, the Foreign Office and the Making of Policy, 1951–55', *International Affairs*, Vol. 64, No. 2, Spring 1988, pp. 241–59.

Anon. 'Some Person of Wisdom', *Time*, Vol. 54, No. 13, 26 September 1949, pp. 17–20.

Anstey, Caroline 'The Projection of British Socialism: Foreign Office Publicity and American Opinion, 1945–1950', *Journal of Contemporary History*, Vol. 19, No. 3, April 1984, pp. 417–51.

Anstey, Caroline 'Foreign Office Publicity, American Aid and European Unity Mobilizing Public Opinion 1947–1949', in J. Becker and F. Knipping (eds), *Power in Europe?* (Berlin and New York: Walter de Gruyter, 1986).

Baylis, John 'American Bases in Britain: The "Truman-Attlee Understandings"', *The World Today*, Vol. 42, Nos. 8–9, August/September 1986. pp. 155–9.

Boyle, Peter, 'America's Hesitant Road to NATO', in Joseph Smith (ed.), *The Origins of NATO* (Exeter: Exeter University Press, 1990).

—— 'The British Foreign Office View of Soviet–American Relations, 1945–46', *Diplomatic History*, Vol. 3, No. 3, Summer 1979, pp. 307–20.

—— 'The British Foreign Office and American Foreign Policy, 1947–1948', *Journal of American Studies*, Vol. 16, No. 3, 1982, pp. 373–89.

—— 'Britain, America and the Transition from Economic to Military Assistance, 1948–1951', *Journal of Contemporary History*, Vol. 22, No. 3, July 1987, pp. 521–37.

Buckley, Roger 'Joining the Club: The Japanese Question and Anglo–American Peace Diplomacy, 1950–1951', *Modern Asian Studies*, Vol. 19, No. 2, 1985, pp. 299–319.

—— 'Working with MacArthur: Sir Alvary Gascoigne, UKLIM and British Policy towards Occupied Japan', in Ian Nish (ed.), *Aspects of the Allied Occupation of Japan* (London: LSE/International Studies, 1986), pp. 1–14.

Burk, Kathleen 'Britain and the Marshall Plan', in Chris Wrigley (ed.), *Warfare, Diplomacy and Policies: Essays in Honour of A. J. P. Taylor* (London: Hamish Hamilton, 1986), pp. 210–30.

Clark, William 'Scholar, Ambassador, Banker', *Radio Times*, 12 November, 1954, p. 5.

Danchev, Alex 'Taking the Pledge: Oliver Franks and the Negotiation of the North Atlantic Treaty', *Diplomatic History*, Vol. 15, No. 2, Spring 1991, pp. 199–219.

Dilks, David 'Britain and Europe, 1948–1950: The Prime Minister, the Foreign Secretary and the Cabinet', in Raymond Poidevin (ed.), *Origins of the European Integration (March 1948–May 1950)*, Actes du Colloque de Strasbourg, 28–30 November 1984 (Brussels: Bruylant, 1986), pp. 391–418.

—— '"The Great Dominion": Churchill's Farewell Visits to Canada, 1952 and 1954', *Canadian Journal of History*, Vol. 23, No. 1, April

1988, pp. 49–72.

Dingman, Roger 'Truman, Attlee and the Korean War Crisis', in Ian Nish (ed.), *The East Asian Crisis 1945–1951: The Problem of China, Korea and Japan* (London: LSE International Studies, 1982), pp. 1–42.

Dockrill, M. L. 'The Foreign Office, Anglo-American Relations and the Korean War, June 1950 – June 1951', *International Affairs,* Vol. 62, No. 3, Summer 1986, pp. 459–76.

—— 'The Foreign Office, Anglo–American Relations and the Korean Truce, Negotiations July 1951–July 1953', in James Cotton and Ian Neary (eds), *The Korean War in History* (Manchester: Manchester University Press, 1989), pp. 100–19.

Farrar, Peter N. 'Britain's Proposal for a Buffer Zone South of the Yalu in November 1950: Was it a Neglected Opportunity to End the Fighting in Korea?' *Journal of Contemporary History,* Vol. 18, No. 2, April 1983, pp. 327–51.

Folly, Martin H. 'Breaking the Vicious Circle: Britain, the United States, and the Genesis of the North Atlantic Treaty', *Diplomatic History,* Vol. 12, No. 2, Winter 1988, pp. 59–77.

Foot, Rosemary 'Anglo-American Relations in the Korean Crisis: The British Effort to Avert an Expanded War, December 1950 January 1951', *Diplomatic History,* Vol. 10, No. 1, Winter 1986, pp. 43–57.

Frazier, Robert 'Did Britain Start the Cold War?: Bevin and the Truman Doctrine', *Historical Journal,* Vol. 27, No. 3, September 1984.

Gormley, James 'The Washington Declaration and the "Poor Relation": Anglo-American Atomic Diplomacy, 1945–1946', *Diplomatic History,* Vol. 8 No. 2, Spring 1984.

Harrod, Roy 'Hands and Fists Across the Atlantic', *Foreign Affairs,* Vol. 29, 1951.

Henrikson, Alan K. 'The creation of the North Atlantic Alliance, 1948–1952', *US Naval War College Review,* 32, May–June 1980, pp. 4–39.

Hosoya, Chihiro 'Japan, China, the United States and the United Kingdom, 1951–2: The Case of the "Yoshida Letter"', *International Affairs,* Vol. 60, No. 2, Spring 1984, pp. 247–59.

Jervis, Robert 'The Impact of the Korean War on the Cold War', *Journal of Conflict Resolution,* 24, No. 4, December 1980, pp. 563–92.

Jong-yil, Ra 'Special Relationship at War: The Anglo–American Relationship during the Korean War', *Journal of Strategic Studies* Vol. 7, No. 3, September 1984, pp. 301–17.

Kent, John 'The Egyptian Base and the Defence of the Middle East, 1945–1954', *Journal of Imperial and Commonwealth History,* Vol. 21, No. 3, September 1993, pp. 45–65.

Kent, John and John W. Young 'The "Western Union" Concept and

British Defence Policy, 1947–48' in Richard Aldrich (ed.), *British Intelligence, Strategy and the Cold War* (London: Routledge, 1992), pp. 166–92.

Lawford, Valentine 'Three Ministers', *Cornhill Magazine*, Vol. 169, No. 1010, Winter 1956–57, pp. 73–99.

Lowe, David 'Mr Spender Goes to Washington: An Ambassador's Vision of Australian–American Relations, 1951–1958', *Journal of Imperial and Commonwealth History*, Vol. 24, No. 2, pp. 278–95.

Newton, Scott 'The 1949 Sterling Crisis and British Policy Towards European Integration', *Review of International Studies*, Vol. 11, No. 3, July 1985, pp. 169–82.

Ovendale, R. 'Britain, the USA and the European Cold War, 1945–8', *History*, Vol. 67, No. 220, June 1982, pp. 217–35.

—— 'Britain, the United States and the Recognition of Communist China', *Historical Journal*, Vol. 26, No. 1, March 1983, pp. 139–58.

Petersen, Nikolaj. 'Who Pulled Whom and How Much? Britain, the United States and the Making of the North Atlantic Treaty', *Millennium: Journal of International Studies*, Vol. 22, No. 2, Summer 1982, pp. 93–114.

Reynolds, David. 'The Origins of the Cold War: The European Dimension, 1944–1951', *Historical Journal*, Vol. 28, No. 2, June 1985, pp. 497–515.

—— 'A "Special Relationship"? America, Britain and the International Order Since the Second World War', *International Affairs*, Vol. 62, No. 1, Winter 1985–86, pp. 1–20.

—— 'Roosevelt, Churchill and the Wartime Anglo-American Alliance, 1939–1945: Towards a New Synthesis', in H. Bull and W. R. Louis (eds), *The 'Special Relationship': Anglo-American Relations Since 1945* (Oxford: Clarendon Press, 1986).

—— 'Britain and the New Europe: The Search for Identity Since 1940', *Historical Journal*, Vol. 31, No. 1, March 1988, pp. 223–39.

—— 'The "Big Three" and the Division of Europe, 1945–48: An Overview', *Diplomacy & Statecraft*, Vol. 1, No. 2, July 1990, pp. 111–36.

Schwartz, Thomas, A. 'The "Skeleton Key" – American Foreign Policy, European Unity, and German Rearmament, 1949–54', *Central European History*, Vol. XIX, No. 4, December 1986, pp. 369–85.

Sherfield, Lord 'On the Diplomatic Trail with LBP: Some Episodes 1930–1972', *International Journal*, Vol. 29, No. 1, 1973–74, pp. 71–89.

—— 'Britain's Nuclear Story 1945–52: Politics and Technology', *Round Table*, Vol. 65, No. 258, April 1975, pp. 193–204.

Shlaim, Avi 'Britain, the Berlin Blockade and the Cold War', *International Affairs*, Vol. 60, No. 1, Winter 1983–84, pp. 1–14.

Smith, Beverly 'Britain Tries a New One on Us', *Saturday Evening Post,* 13 November, 1948, pp. 30, 180, 182.

Smith, Raymond and John Zametica 'The Cold Warrior: Clement Attlee Reconsidered, 1945–7', *International Affairs,* Vol. 61, No. 2, Spring 1985, pp. 237–52.

Tomlinson, J. 'The Attlee Government and the Balance of Payments, 1945–1951', *Twentieth Century British History,* Vol. 2, No. 1 (1991), pp. 47–66.

Waithman, Robert 'A Notable Ambassador', *Spectator,* December 5 1952, pp. 755–6.

Warner, Geoffrey 'The United States and the Origins of the Cold War, *International Affairs,* Vol. 46, No. 3, July 1970, pp. 529–44.

—— 'The Truman Doctrine and the Marshall Plan', *International Affairs,* Vol. 50, No. 1, January 1974, pp. 82–92.

—— 'The United States and the Rearmament of West Germany 1950–54', *International Affairs,* Vol. 61, No. 2, Spring 1985, pp. 279–86.

—— 'The Anglo–American Special Relationship', *Diplomatic History,* Vol. 13, No. 4, Fall 1989, pp. 479–99.

Wiebes, Cees and Zeeman, Bert 'The Pentagon Negotiations March 1948: The Launching of the North Atlantic Treaty', *International* Affairs, Vol. 59, No. 3, Summer 1983, pp. 351–63.

Wolf, David, C. '"To Secure a Convenience": Britain Recognizes China – 1950', *Journal of Contemporary History,* Vol. 18, No. 2, April 1983, pp. 199–326.

Young, J. W. 'Churchill's "No" to Europe: The Rejection of European Union by Churchill's Post–war Government, 1951–1952', *Historical Journal,* Vol. 28, No. 4, December 1985, pp. 923–37.

Theses

Alcock, Christian Peter 'Britain and the Korean War 1950–1953.' PhD. Thesis, Manchester University, 1986.

Anstey, Caroline 'Foreign Office Efforts to Influence American Opinion, 1945–1949' PhD. Thesis, London School of Economics and Political Science, 1984.

Wright, Newman Parley Jr 'The Origins of the North Atlantic Treaty: A Study in Organization and Politics' PhD. thesis, Columbia University, New York, 1977.

Index

Abbott, Douglas C. 126, 133
Acheson, Dean 8, 14, 19, 21, 32, 33, 60, 189, 210, 219;
Anglo-Iranian Oil crisis, 204–7, 211–13;
bipartisanship in foreign policy 147–8;
character 105–6;
and devaluation of the pound 125–34 *passim;*
and Eden 228, 233–4, 236–237, 240;
and Franks 106–7, 116, 132, 141–2, 143, 144, 148–9, 150, 161–2, 170, 202, 203, 211, 213, 217, 238–9, 240, 253, 254, 256;
Korean War 158–71 *passim*, 177–9, 186, 187, 190, 191–4;
May 1950 London conferences 150–3;
and North Atlantic Treaty 108–14;
recognition of Communist China 145–7;
repatriation of Chinese and North Korean prisoners of war 241, 256.
and Truman 105, 194n;
Truman–Attlee talks (1950) 185–91 *passim;*
Truman–Churchill talks (1952) 232–8 *passim;*
UN resolution on China 191–4;
and Yoshida letter 236–7, 256;
Achilles, Theodore 93
Algeria 96, 108
Allen, Denis 15, 42, 97, 140, 247
Allison, John M. 215
Anglo-Iranian Oil Company (AIOC), *see* Iran
Atomic energy 12, 19, 20, 56;
Declaration of Trust (1944) 5;
Franks in London (March 1951) 200;
Franks in London (July 1951) 212;
Hyde Park aide memoire 5;
McMahon Act (1946) 28, 29, 181, 212;
towards the *modus vivendi* (1945–48) 27–9;
Quebec Agreement (1943) 5, 28, 29;
Truman–Attlee talks 188;
Truman–Churchill talks (1952) 232, 235–6
US bases agreement 218–20;
Attlee, Clement 27, 28, 35, 36, 39, 45, 50, 51, 52, 76, 86, 125, 126, 127, 128, 132–3, 147, 164, 165, 168, 169–70, 170–1, 180, 184, 185, 186, 202, 214, 219, 247, 252, 253, 255
Washington talks (1950) 181–2, 185–91 *passim*

B.29 bombers 84–6, 180–1
Balfour, Sir John 15, 17, 56, 60, 66, 247
Bareau, Paul 249
Battle, Lucius D. 114
Beaverbrook, Lord 208
Berlin blockade 8, 81–6, 96, 114, 115–16
Beugel, van der, Ernst 34, 256
Bevan, Aneuran 185, 199
Bevin, Ernest 28, 33, 35, 37, 38, 39, 43, 51, 55, 60, 66, 67, 68, 72, 81, 82, 83, 84, 142, 145, 147, 148, 149, 185, 189, 200, 202, 227, 228, 231, 252, 253; Attlee in Washington (1950) 181–2, 189; devaluation 122, 124, 125, 127, 128, 130, 131, 133–4; German rearmament 182–3; Korean war 161–2, 165, 170–1, 179; May 1950 London conferences 150–3; NATO 87, 88, 89, 90, 109, 110, 115; rearmament 169–70, 182–3, 184; retirement 198.
Bidault, Georges 33, 82, 87
Bohlen, Charles 16, 65–6, 86, 90, 93, 112, 114
Bonnet, Henri 92, 93–4
Bradley, General Omar 161, 164, 165, 166–7, 186, 190, 200, 219, 233
Brandon, Henry 106–7, 241
Bretton Woods Agreements 31
Bridges, Sir Edward 185, 195n
Britain, *see* Attlee, Bevin, Chiefs of Staff, Churchill, Cripps, Eden, Foreign Office, Franks, Makins, Morrison
British Embassy, Washington, *see* Washington Embassy
British Information Services (BIS) 10, 13, 53, 58, 65, 249
British Joint Staff Mission (BJSM) 10, 11, 40, 43, 87, 160, 200, 201, 219, 247, 249
Broad, Philip 58
Brook, Sir Norman 88
Bruce, David 239
BRUSA Agreement (1943) 44
Burgess, Guy 198, 209–10
Burrows, B. A. B. 15, 175, 221n, 247
Butler, R. A. 231
Byrnes, James F. 89

Cadogan, Sir Alexander 10, 115
Caine, Sir Sydney 120, 121, 122, 143
Canada 27, 30, 41, 119, 148, 190, 193, 232, 248; and North Atlantic Treaty 90–6 *passim*, 108–14 *passim*, 125; and devaluation of the pound 126–7, 131–4 *passim*
Cecil, Robert 230
Central Intelligence Agency (CIA) 8, 44
Cherwell, Lord 233, 235
Chiang Kai-shek 145, 147, 158, 187
Chiefs of Staff (COS) 36, 37, 39, 40, 88, 160, 161, 200, 210–11
China 144–5, 158, 161, 171, 177–9, 181, 187, 191–4, 203, 216, 233, 236–7, 249; recognition of the communist regime 145–7, 252
China lobby 145, 146, 155–6n
Churchill, Winston 3, 6, 36, 59, 86, 219, 252, 255; and Eden 227–9; as Prime Minister 227–38
Truman–Churchill talks (1952) 229, 231, 232–8
Clark Kerr, Archibald, Lord Inverchapel 17, 25n, 50, 51, 57, 58, 60n, 70, 87, 249, 252
Clay, Lucius D. 83, 90
Cockcroft, Professor John 5
Cold War 68–9, 81, 125, 229, 251–2
Colville, Jock 227
Combined Boards 5, 27
Combined Chiefs of Staff 4, 5, 10, 40, 43, 87, 232
Committee of European Economic Co-operation (CEEC) 34–5, 54–5, 70
Connally, Senator Thomas 109–13 *passim*
Councils of Foreign Ministers (CFMs) 45, 82, 83, 87, 115–16, 125
Cripps, Sir Stafford 76, 120, 122, 123 124, 125, 127, 128, 133–4, 147, 184, 253
Czechoslovakia 81, 85, 90, 114

Daily Express 208–9, 221, 254
Dalton, Hugh 31, 32
Dening, Sir Esler 237
Dill, Field Marshal Sir John 4, 249
Dixon, Sir Pierson 38, 192, 201, 202
Douglas, Lewis A. 58, 62n, 67, 75–7, 83, 84, 96, 97, 125, 130, 131, 148, 149, 151, 161, 165, 168, 252

Dudley, Alan 58
Dulles, John Foster 163–4, 202, 214–17, 236–7, 239, 256

Economic Co-operation Administration (ECA) 54, 69, 120, 122, 124, 126, 184
Eden, Sir Anthony 225, 232; and Acheson 228, 233–4, 236–7, 240; and Churchill 227–9; and Truman–Churchill talks (1952) 229, 232–8 *passim*; and Yoshida letter 236–7
Edwards, E. P. N. 13, 58
Egypt 36, 37, 198, 230, 238
Eisenhower, Dwight D. 40, 41, 189, 239
Elliot, Sir William 219
European Defence Community (EDC) 182–3, 188, 233, 236
European integration xv, 35, 58, 140–2
European Recovery Program (ERP), *see* Marshall Plan

Far Eastern Commission (FEC) 144
Finletter, Thomas A. 69, 74, 79n, 122
Foreign Office xvi, 11, 39, 41, 57, 59, 139–40
Formosa, *see* Taiwan
Forrestal, James 85
France 81, 181, 257; and German rearmament 182–3, 188; and May 1950 London conferences 150–3; and North Atlantic Treaty 87, 90, 91–6 *passim*, 108–14 *passim*; and Schuman Plan 141, 153–4
Franks, Sir Oliver xv, xvi, xvii, 13, 14, 15, 17, 45, 63, 82, 103, 175, 251; Acheson 106–7, 116, 132, 141–2, 143, 144, 148–9, 150, 161–2, 170, 202, 203, 211, 213, 217, 238–9, 240, 253, 254, 256; agreement on US bases 86, 218–19, 224n, 256; Anglo-Iranian Oil crisis 203–7, 211–14, 256; appointment as Ambassador 50–3; arrival in USA 65–7; atomic bomb 188, 200, 211, 219–20; Attlee 51–2, 85, 253; Attlee in Washington (1950) 182, 185–91; Berlin blockade 83–4, 86; Bevin 51, 52, 85, 253; Bilateral Agreements on ERP 69–77; briefing for ambassadorship 55–60; Burgess and Maclean 198, 209–10; character and talents 20–1, 52, 115–16, 127, 134, 235, 236; Churchill 228, 235, 236, 238, 253; devaluation of the pound 119–35, 256; Dulles 202, 215, 216, 217, 236–7, 239, 256; Eden 233–4, 236–7, 238–40, 244n, 253; embassy activities 246–9; end of his mission 240–2; Japanese Peace Treaty 214–18, 256; Korean War 158–71, 173n, 177–81, 186, 187, 190, 191–4, 256; life up to 1946 18–20; May 1950 London conferences 150; London visit (February 1950) 144–7; London visit (March 1951) 199–202, 215, 220n; London visit (June–July 1951) 208, 210–11; Marshall 99n, 253; Marshall Plan 34–5, 54–5; Morrison 204, 206, 214, 217, 221n, 253; National Press Club speech 67–8, 81; post of NATO Secretary-General 238–9, 253; rearmament 183–4, 257; recognition of Communist China 145–7; repatriation of Chinese and North Korean prisoners of war 241, 256; Schuman Plan 153–4, 257; standing as Ambassador 185, 198, 199–200, 208–9, 228; talks on North Atlantic Treaty 86–96, 108–14, 256; Truman 253; Truman–Churchill talks (1952) 231–8; Yoshida letter 236–7, 256
Fuchs, Klaus 148

Gaitskell, Hugh 127, 184, 199, 212–13, 253
Gascoigne, Sir Alvary 144
German rearmament, *see* European Defence Community (EDC)
Germany xv, 31, 32, 71, 73, 75, 81–6, 115–16, 182–3, 185, 188, 251, 257
Gifford, Walter 233
Gore-Booth, Paul 203, 204, 221n, 224n, 240–1, 249
Government Communications Headquarters (GCHQ) 44
Graves, Hubert A. 145, 209
Greece 32, 82, 96, 108, 109, 114
Greenhill, Denis 209
Gromyko, Andrei 161

Halifax, Lord 16, 53, 228, 249, 252
Hall, Robert 50, 60, 123, 124, 128, 131, 134, 144, 199–200, 232, 234
Hall-Patch, Sir Edmund 55, 57
Hamilton, M. A. 58, 198, 227, 246
Harriman, W. Averell 4, 54, 58, 65, 66, 69, 122, 184, 212, 233, 252
Harrod, Roy 175
Henderson, Loy W. 38
Henderson, Nicholas 17, 114, 118n, 246
Hickerson, John D. 56, 88–9, 89–90, 90, 93, 97–8, 109, 110, 114
Hiss, Alger 148
Hoffman, Paul G. 54, 69, 76, 126, 133, 140, 143
Holmes, John C. 143, 182
Hong Kong 160, 185, 198
Hopkins, Harry 3
Hoyer Millar, F. R. 16, 71, 93, 94, 97, 110, 129, 148, 247
Hull, Cordell 7

Ignatieff, George 248
India 32, 35
Indo-China 154
Intelligence co-operation 5–6, 43–5
International Monetary Fund (IMF) 31, 120–2, 128, 131
Inverchapel, *see* Clark Kerr, Archibald
Iran 96, 108, 109, 114, 198, 230; Anglo-Iranian Oil Company crisis, 203–7, 210, 211–14, 232, 238, 256
Ismay, Lord 233, 235
Israel 8, 67
Italy 81, 90, 96, 108, 113, 251

Japan xv, 71, 73, 75, 144, 145, 186, 233, 236–7, 251
Japanese Peace Treaty 144, 198, 202, 214–18, 256
Jay, Douglas 127, 256
Jebb, Gladwyn 10, 36, 90, 92, 94, 166, 192, 194
Jessup, Philip C. 105, 115–16, 161, 164, 171, 190
Johnson, Louis 144

Kelly, Sir David 161
Kennan, George F. 32, 65–6, 91, 92, 93, 107, 129, 133, 141
Kennedy, John F. 3, 15
Keynes, John Maynard xv, 8, 30
Kirkpatrick, Sir Ivone 90
Korea 71, 158–9
Korean War xv, 8, 86, 139, 154, 158–71, 177–80, 181, 182, 185, 186, 187, 190, 191–4, 203, 207, 236, 247, 248

Lend-Lease 6, 7, 27, 30, 31
Lippmann, Walter 129, 145
Lloyd, Selwyn 240
Lovett, Robert A. 55, 72, 84, 88, 91, 92, 94, 107, 108, 110, 233

MacArthur, General Douglas 144, 163–4, 166, 171, 177, 178, 179, 190, 203, 210
McCarthy, Senator Joseph 148
McGhee, George 204, 205–7, 212
McGrigor, Sir Rhoderick 235
Maclean, Donald 12, 198, 209–10
McMahon Act (1946), *see* Atomic energy
Macmillan, Harold 3
McNeil, Hector 75
Makins, Roger Mellor 28, 29, 51, 56, 58, 73, 76, 87, 99n, 120, 134, 135, 154, 193, 201, 202, 210, 214, 229–30, 235, 240, 251
Malaya 160, 185, 186
Malik, Yakov A. 115–16, 210
Marjolin, Robert 55

Marshall, George C. 4, 8, 20, 33, 38, 65–6, 72, 73, 82, 84, 87, 88, 89, 90, 91, 92, 99n, 105, 107, 114, 201, 253
Marshall Plan xv, 32, 33–5, 50, 52, 54, 55, 57, 58, 65, 67, 69–77, 119, 120, 126, 131, 147, 150, 183, 184
Marten, F. W. 219
Martin, William McChesney 120, 124, 128, 137n
Masaryk, Jan 56
Matthews, H. Freeman 169, 212, 219
Middle East 35–9, 56, 67, 87, 88, 185, 211, 232, 233, 236, 238
Molotov, Vyacheslav 33, 38, 65, 86
Moran, Lord 227, 233, 235, 236
Morgan, Aubrey 53, 54, 63, 249
Morrison, Herbert 126, 227, 231, 253; Acheson, Dean 218; Anglo-American relations 202; Anglo-Iranian Oil Company crisis 204–5, 212, 213, 214, 221n; appointment as Foreign Secretary 198; Japanese Peace Treaty 216–18; traits as Foreign Secretary 198–9, 203, 204–5, 214, 221n, 224n
Mossadeq, Dr Mohammed 204, 212, 213
Most Favoured Nation status 71, 79n, 75
Mutual Defence Assistance Programme 142

National Advisory Council on Monetary and Financial Policy (NAC) 120, 128
National Security Agency (NSA) 44
News Chronicle 208
Nitze, Paul H. 97, 184, 190, 212, 219, 231, 255
North Atlantic Treaty, *see* North Atlantic Treaty Organisation (NATO)
North Atlantic Treaty Organisation (NATO) xv, 69, 86–96, 97–8, 108–14, 140, 184, 189, 234, 238–9, 255
NSC–68 167–8

Organisation of European Economic Co-operation (OEEC) 55, 59, 69, 70, 141

Palestine 8, 32, 36, 37–8, 45, 66–7, 68
Pearson, Lester 133, 238
Perkins, George W. 144, 150, 166
Permanent Under-Secretary's Committee 140, 147, 152, 156n
Philby, H. A. R. 'Kim' 209–10
Pitblado, David 227
Pleven Plan, *see* European Defence Community (EDC)
Pleven, Rene 181, 182–3
Plowden, Edwin 34, 50, 76, 168, 185, 200
Potsdam Conference (1945) 81

Reagan, Ronald 3
Reid, Escott 110
Rhee, Syngman 158
Rickett, Denis 238
Ridgway, General Matthew B. 194, 203
Roosevelt, Franklin D. 3, 6, 7, 8, 89, 231, 252
Rowan, Sir Leslie 70, 134, 173n, 184, 235
Rusk, Dean 146, 171, 191, 203

Sargeant, Sir Orme 35, 53, 59
Schuman Plan 153–4, 257
Schuman, Robert 94, 115, 181, 218
Second World War xv, xvi, 3–7
Seitz, Raymond 1
Shuckburgh, Evelyn 152–3, 227, 239
Slessor, Air Marshall Sir John 160, 181, 190, 219
Slim, Field Marshal Sir William 165, 186, 188, 235, 256
Smith, Walter Bedell 65, 115, 210
Snyder, John W. 120, 124, 125, 126–7, 128–129, 133, 134, 231, 233
Sokolovsky, General Vasily 83
Southard, Frank A. 120
Soviet Union, *see* USSR
Spaak, Paul-Henri 55, 141
Spaatz, General Carl 40, 42
Spofford, Charles 168–9, 183, 184
Stalin, Josef 86, 115
State Department, *see* United States, State Department
Steel, Sir Christopher 16, 209, 217, 221n, 247
Stephenson, Colonel William 5
Sterling 31, 119; devaluation 119–35
Sterling area 35, 58, 59, 183, 184
Stokes, Sir Richard 213, 223n
Strang, Sir William 142, 143, 150, 185, 199, 201, 202, 209, 214, 223n, 251
Strachey, John 175, 192
Supreme Commander Allied Powers (SCAP), *see* MacArthur, General Douglas

Taiwan 145, 158, 161–3, 215, 256
Tedder, Air Marshal Sir Arthur 42, 160, 161, 164, 165, 188, 200, 201
Thorp, Willard L. 72, 73, 74, 75
Tizard, Sir Henry 5
Tomlinson, F. S. 215
Truman, Harry 7, 8, 17, 27, 32, 37, 41, 56, 67, 76, 89, 90, 91, 95, 97, 111, 113, 114, 130, 132, 142, 160, 161, 171, 178, 180, 181, 203, 212, 219, 229, 240, 251, 252, 253, 254
Truman Doctrine 32
Truman–Attlee meetings (1950) 186–91 *passim*
Truman–Churchill meetings (1952) 231, 232–8
Turkey 32, 67, 82, 96, 108, 109, 114

UKUSA Agreement (1948) 44
Union of Soviet Socialist Republics (USSR) 36, 45, 56, 57, 65, 67, 77, 87, 114, 145, 147, 203, 211, 218, 249, 251, 252; Berlin blockade 81–6, 115–16, 151, 209–10; Korean War 158–9, 161–2, 163, 179
United Nations (UN) 10, 86, 158, 159–60, 163, 170–1, 178, 191–4, 203
United Nations Relief and Rehabilitation Agency (UNRRA) 19
United States:
  US Embassy, London 4, 16, 55, 57, 69, 77, 130–1, 143, 160
  US Joint Chiefs of Staff 90, 161, 201, 210, 231, 232
  US political system 7–9
  US State Department 7–8, 9, 89, 105, 106, 107, 124, 128, 129–30, 148, 150–1, 167–8, 207, 254
  US Treasury 119–35 *passim*

Vandenberg, Senator Arthur 91, 109–13 *passim*
Vandenberg, General Hoyt 40, 42

Washington Embassy xvi, xvii, 3, 9–15, 41–2, 56–7, 82, 83, 86, 87, 91–6, 129, 160, 206, 221n, 246–9, 252
Warner, Christopher 246
Washington Post 208, 209, 241
Watson, Adam 246, 255
Webb, James E. 105, 124, 130, 150
Welles, Sumner 7
'Western Union' 82, 87, 90, 125
Wheeler-Bennett, John 53, 54
Wilson, James Harold 127, 128, 199
Wilson Smith, Henry 122, 123, 124, 134
Winant, John 252
Wright, Michael R. 38, 39, 56, 58, 66
Wrong Hume 92, 111, 133, 146–7, 239, 248

Yalta Conference (1945) 81
Yoshida Shigeru 216, 236–7
Younger, Kenneth 153, 154, 160, 178, 185, 192, 202, 204–5, 214, 217, 218

Zelikow, Philip 1